Libraries
to the People

Libraries to the People

Histories of Outreach

Edited by
ROBERT S. FREEMAN *and* DAVID M. HOVDE

with a foreword by
Kathleen de la Peña McCook

McFarland & Company, Inc., Publishers
Jefferson, North Carolina, and London

Library of Congress Cataloguing-in-Publication Data

Libraries to the people : histories of outreach /
edited by Robert S. Freeman and David M. Hovde ;
with a foreword by Kathleen de la Peña McCook.
p.   cm.
Includes bibliographical references and index.

ISBN 0-7864-1359-X (softcover : 50# alkaline paper)

1. Library outreach programs—United States—History—19th century.
2. Library outreach programs—United States—History—20th century.
I. Freeman, Robert S.   II. Hovde, David M.

Z711.7.L53   2003   021.2'0973—dc21   2002153802

British Library cataloguing data are available

On the cover: Hand model, Angie Sexton; photograph of library, ©2002 Eyewire.

Manufactured in the United States of America

*McFarland & Company, Inc., Publishers
Box 611, Jefferson, North Carolina 28640
www.mcfarlandpub.com*

Contents

III. INNOVATIVE OUTREACH SERVICES

Acknowledgments

Special thanks go to Pam De Bonte, Mark Jaeger, Dot Lanzalotto, Pat Whalen, and Leonard Farnsworth, all of Purdue University Libraries, for their invaluable assistance in the production of this work. The president and trustees of Purdue University provided a sabbatical leave for David Hovde that facilitated the early gathering of materials. We are both grateful for the support of Emily R. Mobley, the Dean of Libaries at Purdue University, and the Purdue Libraries Research Grant Selection Committee for financial assistance in our research.—R.S.F. and D.M.H.

Foreword

The essays in *Libraries to the People: Histories of Outreach* reflect on the extension of library services to populations without access to books or collections and demonstrate the connection of librarians to the broader social framework over the last two hundred years. United States library history, as it has often been transmitted, largely recounts the growth of the public library movement as institutional growth. This growth has been measured in service outlets, collection size, circulation figures, and registered borrowers. By contrast, *Libraries to the People* provides a series of tightly focused studies of innovation and experimentation that taken together show the sustained effort librarians have made to extend their services to isolated communities and those with less means.

This contrast is most apparent when library outreach is viewed in the context of the common school movement. In the mid–1800s, as the case for public support of education was made by Horace Mann, family and school district libraries published by Harper & Brothers were among the first resources developed to support universal education. Similar efforts were made in Indiana as part of a progressive educational system. This ideal was also carried out by benevolent societies as evidenced in the collections rotated for the American Navy and Merchant Marine.

Support for adult education in the United States was fostered by educational philosophers like John Dewey (*Democracy and Education*, 1916) and Eduard Lindeman (*The Meaning of Adult Education*, 1926), who argued that the participation of citizens in informed social action was the hallmark of a democratic society. This general mood of growing confidence and faith in adult education and lifelong learning helped support library outreach efforts such as Essae Martha Culver's demonstration libraries in Louisiana, public library collections for African Americans, the work of women's clubs to organize over 4,600 traveling libraries, and library programs for the foreign born.

In 1932 Myles Horton established the Highlander School as an adult education center for social change, to provide educational experiences that would enable people to engage in democratic leadership. Such a spirit imbued the librarians who participated in the open-air school movement or encouraged citizens in radio broadcasts to learn about government through access to municipal library materials. Through-out the years of the Great Depression, libraries provided people with the means to continue their education and to develop an understanding of social issues in light of cultural and economic factors.

The histories of outreach in this volume take up new challenges following the publication of Michael Harrington's *The Other America* (1962), which delineated the unequal distribution of wealth in the United States. Paulo Freire's *Pedagogy of the Oppressed* (1970) was influential for providing a model allowing oppressed citizens to gain more control of their lives. Both of these works help us to understand the development of tribal libraries, services to prisoners, and the backwoods library as services to people for whom the resources of the broader society have been denied. The fact that traditional library responses neglected current issues was emphasized by the publication of *Synergy* at the Bay Area Reference Center in San Francisco. The outreach movement during the War on Poverty has been addressed by Kathleen Weibel's *Evolution of Library Outreach 1960–1975* (1982) and is now enhanced by the addition of the essays in this volume.

Through analysis of the essays brought together here by Robert S. Freeman and David M. Hovde, it is possible to view librarians in the United States as people who have used multiple approaches toward contributing to the sweep of progressive change through broad access to culture and information—contributions that continue today. It is the kind of intense experimental outreach service presented in *Bringing Libraries to the People* that has moved U.S. librarianship to the expansive philosophy of equal access that defines it.

In these brave examples of outreach in isolated and poor communities in the United States are examples that may be extended to the ideals of the development of human capabilities described in the writing of Nobel Prize winner Amartya Sen, who has identified poverty as life deprived of individual development. Through examples of library outreach to those serving in ships at sea for long periods, to those incarcerated, to those seeking more than the basic necessities on tribal lands, there can be gained a sense of hopefulness in education as the treasure within. Through the riches made available in libraries, people will gain the knowledge to struggle against oppression, develop their innate abilities, and live in a state of awareness that they can effect change. In a dozen ways the authors in *Libraries to the People* explore the possibilities that librarians have tapped to reach out to those overlooked by traditional modes of service.

Kathleen de la Peña McCook
University of South Florida

Introduction

New conditions bring forth new problems and demand new
solutions. Libraries in some form are almost as old as the race.
It was steam when the bobbing cover of the teakettle suggested
confinement of the vapor, but how different from what the
word steam means today. The lightening [*sic*] on Franklin's kite
hardly gave promise of the telephone, phonograph, cable,
wireless telegraphy and other modern miracles. The chief factor
in our new conditions is quick and cheap transportation.
Railways, trolleys, express, mail, rural free delivery, telegraphs,
cables, telephones, compel us to readjust our ideas in the light
of new conditions and possibilities.[1]

— *Melvil Dewey, 1901*

But not until very recent years did the library begin to conceive
of its duties as extending into the entire community, instead of
being limited to those who voluntarily entered its doors. The
modern public library believes that it should find a reader for
every book on its shelves and provide a book for every reader in
its community, and that it should in all cases bring book and
reader together.[2]

— *Arthur E. Bostwick, 1929*

This collection of essays began with two programs at the 51st meeting of the
American Library Association's Library History Round Table (LHRT), held at the
1999 Annual Conference of the American Library Association in New Orleans. As
program planners, we sought and received co-sponsorship with the Library Research
Round Table, the Social Responsibilities Round Table, and the Office for Literacy and
Outreach Services. We deeply appreciate their participation. We were also honored
that Carla Stoffle of the University of Arizona and Kathleen de la Peña McCook of

the University of South Florida served as moderators. We were delighted with the number and the diversity of submissions for the programs. Regrettably, some participants were unable to contribute to this volume; we have, however, included other papers that enhance the thematic strength of the collection.

In this volume we examine the contributions of librarians and educators in the United States who have endeavored to extend services to populations that previously did not have access to a library. Many individuals, active before the public library movement or working outside it, introduced the joys of reading to people beyond the walls of established libraries. Others, within the public library movement (regarded by many as beginning in 1876), integrated outreach efforts into existing structures. Publishers and booksellers, driven by economic motives, also supported these efforts. All explored innovative ways to bring books and library services to underserved populations. Our contributors analyze the motives inspiring such efforts, along with the intellectual content offered, the services provided, and methods of organization. Some motives, particularly those moralistic and religious, may not resonate widely today, yet are among essential, formative influences in the history of American libraries.

"Outreach" and the earlier term "extension" express the concept that lends this collection thematic strength. According to the *International Encyclopedia of Information and Library Science* (1997), outreach refers to the services provided by a library outside its usual location, particularly those intended to attract new users or to appeal to groups in the community who do not make full use of conventional services. Target groups are typically the housebound, ethnic minorities and people in districts of socio-economic deprivation.[3]

In the *Encyclopedia of Library History*, William J. Wilson states: "In the broadest sense, library extension service can be defined as any activity extending library service to otherwise unserved individuals or geographic areas."[4] Families in rural Indiana, Arkansas, and Louisiana, African Americans in Tennessee, Native Americans on reservations, immigrants in large cities, sailors at sea, and inmates in prisons are among the "target groups" our contributors have described.

These essays go beyond the historic public library movement and its discussions of outreach. One may adopt William F. Poole's (1876) narrow definition of a public library as an institution that is "established by state laws, is supported by local taxation and voluntary gifts, is managed as a public trust, and every citizen of the city or town which maintains it has an equal share in its privileges of reference and circulation."[5] Alternatively, one may prefer the more liberal definition of Carleton Bruns Joeckel (1935), who hesitated to specify that funding derive exclusively from taxation or other government sources: "The only really essential requirement in the definition of a public library is that its use should be free to all residents of the community on equal terms."[6] Some of the outreach programs mentioned by our contributors did not fit the Poole definition, either because they antedated the public library movement or because they received little support from local taxation. Such programs, nevertheless, helped define the modern public library which, according to Arthur E. Bostwick (1929), had only recently begun "to conceive of its duties as extending to the entire community, instead of being limited to those who voluntarily entered its door."[7]

Libraries to the People constitutes a collection of historical sketches rather than a comprehensive or systematic account. It offers readers a variety of examples from two hundred years of outreach by private individuals and groups, benevolent societies, professional associations, government agencies, and libraries in the United States. The essays appear in three sections: (I.) Benevolent and Commercial Organizations; (II.) Government Supported Programs; and (III.) Innovative Outreach Services. Our categories are not mutually exclusive; nearly all of the outreach programs in one category have characteristics of those in another. Indeed, historically, most outreach has involved collaboration between organizations of different types. For instance, the traveling library programs discussed by Paula D. Watson in the first section were organized by women's clubs in cooperation with state library commissions and then subsumed by state or public libraries. However, since these programs originated in large measure in women's clubs, we placed the chapter under benevolent and commercial organizations. Similarly, Barry W. Seaver describes radio broadcasts produced by a government agency, the New York Municipal Reference Library. However, since the broadcasts employed new technology, we placed the chapter under innovative outreach services. Within each section, our arrangement approximates chronology.

Florence M. Jumonville begins her survey "Books Along the Bayous: Reading Materials for Two Centuries of Rural Louisianians" with the late eighteenth century, when the region had only a few social and rental libraries, and concludes with the 1960s when public libraries were finally established in all of Louisiana's parishes. In describing the growth of public libraries in the state, she highlights the contribution of Essae Martha Culver, who directed a cooperative project with the Louisiana Library Commission that demonstrated how a library could be organized so that books would be available throughout a rural parish. With support from the ALA, the Carnegie Corporation, and the League of Library Commissioners, Culver overcame the obstacles presented by Louisiana's bayous and its languages and cultures—Francophone and Anglophone. By 1969 the entire state was "Culver-ized."

Some library historians regard the traveling libraries organized by Melvil Dewey in the 1890s as the beginning of public library extension.[8] A traveling library, or itinerating library, is by definition a portable collection of books or other materials sent to a location for a limited period and then forwarded to another location. Yet as early as the 1830s, several states had begun similar programs, distributing portable libraries to school districts. Although school district libraries did not travel from one location to another, they served as precedents for traveling libraries and were clearly an example of publicly supported library outreach. In "Harper & Brothers' Family and School District Libraries, 1830–1846," Robert S. Freeman discusses the publishing, marketing, distribution, and reception of two of the best-selling collections or "libraries" in the mid-nineteenth century. As a leading publisher and, thus, a major force in the broad religious and social reform movements of the period, the Harpers helped to shape education in American homes and schools. Their marketing of inexpensive, portable libraries that offered moral and practical instruction to the masses resonated with families as well as with superintendents of education, including John A. Dix and John C. Spencer of New York, and Horace Mann and

Barnas Sears of Massachusetts. New York and Massachusetts were among the first states to order hundreds of Harper libraries for their school districts.

Traveling libraries brought an improvement over school district libraries by addressing the problem of stagnant collections. Participants rotated or exchanged volumes among several localities, keeping collections fresh and stimulating reader interest. In "Benevolence at Sea: Shipboard Libraries for the American Navy and Merchant Marine," David M. Hovde describes how the American Seamen's Friend Society (ASFS) introduced rotation as a principal feature of the traveling libraries it loaned to ships' crews, beginning in 1858. The ASFS is one of several benevolent societies that placed libraries on sailing vessels. Hovde considers the relationship of these societies to the ALA and the public library movement.

The traveling library programs of the 1890s and early 1900s represent a second attempt by states (again beginning in New York and Massachusetts) to deliver library services to isolated communities. When Melvil Dewey, State Librarian of New York, sent out his first traveling library in 1893, women's clubs around the country took up the task of organizing traveling libraries. In "Valleys Without Sunsets: Women's Clubs and Traveling Libraries," Paula D. Watson focuses on the importance of club work to state and public library programs and underscores the growing sense of empowerment felt by women involved in the club movement. Many club women participated in traveling library work in order to relieve the loneliness of people, especially women, in isolated rural districts and to facilitate the expansion of personal networks.[9]

Five of our papers discuss outreach activities to specific groups: seamen (discussed above), immigrants, prisoners, African Americans, and Native Americans. In "The ALA Committee on Work with the Foreign Born and the Movement to Americanize the Immigrant," Plummer Alston Jones, Jr., recounts the history of the ALA's Committee on Work with the Foreign Born (CWFB). The CWFB came into being during the heady days following the success of the ALA's programs during World War I. While nativists and their representatives in Congress clamored for immigration restrictions and passed the National Origins Act of 1924, the CWFB viewed immigrants as Americans-in-the-making and encouraged instruction in English and preparation for naturalization. Jones portrays public librarians and CWFB leaders, such as John Foster Carr and Eleanor Edwards Ledbettter, as activists devoted to the social and economic advancement of immigrant communities.

In "Reachin' Behind Bars: Library Outreach to Prisoners, 1798–2000," Larry E. Sullivan and Brenda Vogel discuss library services for convicted criminals. In the early nineteenth century the few prison libraries in operation attempted to inculcate prisoners with the moral and religious ideals of the dominant, white middle-class culture. In the 1870s penologists made rehabilitation a higher priority than retribution, and prisons began creating educational opportunities, including well-stocked libraries. Describing prominent examples, important studies, state and federal legislation, and ALA involvement, this chapter surveys the progress made by prison libraries from the 1890s to the 1980s. Much of this progress has been reversed, however, in the past ten years with the implementation of "get tough" policies emphasizing punishment over rehabilitation.

New York and Massachusetts established the first school district libraries in the

1830s. More than a dozen states followed their example and established school district and township libraries of their own. In our study of "The Indiana Township Library Program, 1852–1872," we examine the values and motives of the program's creators. We discuss the problems encountered, identifying factors such as a lack of local commitment and the decline of readers' interest in collections that seldom grew or changed. Despite the failure of the township and school district libraries to become a sustaining force in education, these libraries, the first in many communities, successfully demonstrated both the benefits of reading and the desirability of publicly supported libraries.

With "The Adult Collection at Nashville's Negro Public Library, 1915–1916" Cheryl Knott Malone adds a new chapter to the story of the struggle to provide library services to African Americans during the years of state sponsored segregation. Malone has written extensively on the history of separate black libraries, including those in Louisville and Houston.[10] Her research complements other recent work on African American library history included in collections such as *Handbook of Black Librarianship* edited by E. J. Josey and Marva L. DeLoach and *Untold Stories: Civil Rights, Libraries, and Black Librarianship* edited by John Mark Tucker.[11] Malone focuses here on the opening-day collection a white librarian developed for Nashville's Negro Public Library. She examines the collection both as an example of the collection development strategies of a large public library and as a lost opportunity to reconsider, examine, and meet the differing needs of a minority audience. Despite the fact that some of the collection supported the mythology of the Old South and the status quo, records show many African Americans used and appreciated the library.

Lotsee F. Patterson discusses the still brief history of Native American tribal libraries in her "Historical Overview of Tribal Libraries in the Lower Forty Eight States." Prior to the influx of federal monies in the early 1970s, few tribes had the resources available to establish library services. Since then, federal support and tribal leadership have combined to create limited services among approximately half of the three hundred plus tribes in the lower forty-eight states. Patterson, a long-time chronicler and participant in this story, describes the successes and reviews funding, training, and related problems that challenge the libraries emerging in these communities.

Some quite innovative forms of outreach involved much more than providing books. In "Electronic Outreach in America: From Telegraph to Television," John W. Fritch discusses American librarians' use of electronic technology as a means of outreach prior to the advent of networked computers. Beginning with the limited use of the telegraph for reference service, Fritch details the adoption of the telephone in the 1870s and radio in the 1920s. He reviews several pioneering efforts to use radio to promote library services, including the activities of the ALA's Library Radio Broadcasting Committee, in a time when some feared that radio would exacerbate the decline of reading. He also gives examples of libraries providing films, phonograph recordings, and talking books, and reviews early attempts to develop television programs.

In "On the Roof of the Library Nearest You: America's Open-Air Libraries, 1905–1944," Gerald S. Greenberg demonstrates that when librarians brought book collections to parks, roofs, lawns, and beaches in the early 20th century, they, like the promoters of the open-air school movement, were responding to concerns about the high risk of communicable diseases when people crowded together in public areas. Here Greenberg goes beyond his earlier work, "Books as Disease Carriers: 1880–1920."[12] Whatever the risk of infection indoors, open-air libraries proved especially attractive to readers during summers before the wide use of air-conditioning. In describing the methods and designs of these libraries in Boston, New York City, Los Angeles, Honolulu, Mexico City, and Seville, Spain, Greenberg proves sensitive to the aesthetic aspects of reading outdoors. Open-air libraries proved especially attractive during the Great Depression, but after World War II, as modern medicine began eradicating communicable diseases and air-conditioning cooled public buildings, the collections moved back indoors.

Barry W. Seaver, in "The Use of Radio to Promote the Municipal Reference Library of the City of New York," describes how a library used radio to enhance the civic education of the listening audience and advertise the programs and collections of the library. The mission of the Municipal Reference Library was to collect and disseminate information in order to increase the efficiency of local government agencies, improve decision-making, and create a politically educated electorate. In 1928, in order to better accomplish this, the librarian, Rebecca Browning Rankin, turned to radio station WNYC and created a series of weekly broadcasts. During the next ten years she produced over 300 programs dealing with topics such as the operations of city government, government programs in other cities, and city elections.

In "*Synergy*, Social Responsibility, and the Sixties: Pivotal Points in the Evolution of American Outreach Library Service," Toni Samek discusses *Synergy*, the alternative library journal published by San Francisco Public Library's experimental Bay Area Reference Center (BARC) in the 1960s. A typical issue of *Synergy* listed outstanding additions to the SFPL's reference collection and a bibliography on a topic not covered in the usual publishing channels. Recognizing San Francisco as a "trend-mecca" with everything from campus riots to gay liberation, *Synergy*'s first editor, Celeste West, argued that the city's diversity could not be reflected in library collections unless someone assembled fugitive materials from the alternative press. Describing traditional catalogs, indexes, and selection tools as "rear-view mirrors" that did little to meet the public's current information needs, *Synergy*'s staff members trained themselves to discover and create access to many diverse forms of information. They called upon librarians not only to conserve and organize information, but to generate and promote new information, especially when it related to neglected topics and current issues.

In "For the Love of Books: Eddie Lovett and His Backwoods Library," Emily J. Branson and John Mark Tucker recount the personal saga of one man with a deep passion for reading who established a library both as a teaching instrument for his children and as a resource to share with his neighbors in and around the rural hamlet of Banks, Arkansas. The son of a black sharecropper, he was allowed to complete only eight grades of school in the segregated, depression-era South. In "bringing libraries to the people" of his family and community, Lovett had defied exceedingly high odds and won the admiration and appreciation of readers and library supporters nationwide. He gained national visibility when Charles Kuralt profiled him and his library on CBS television. When he lost the library to fire in 1975, concerned citizens from all over the USA donated books, allowing him to rebuild and to continue his quest for knowledge.

This collection presents several significant innovations in outreach by a variety of individuals and groups both inside and outside the sphere of the American public library movement. Early outreach efforts such as the Indiana Township Library Program, the ASFS libraries, and the traveling libraries organized by women's clubs contributed to the foundation of what has come to be expected of a modern public library. These expectations include outreach to underserved ethnic and social groups and the use of new technologies to bring library services into the home. In 1971 Eleanor Frances Brown painted this picture of a modern library: "Here is a library—and a staff—reaching out into the community in every conceivable manner, no longer waiting only for those who would come of their own accord, finding the real needs of the people, and satisfying those needs—with something for everyone!"[13] Regardless of their origins or organizational structures, the common purpose of outreach programs has been to uplift underserved populations by bringing them library services that the majority culture has taken for granted. Of course, the goal has also been to enable the individual reader or listener to expand his or her own vision and to reach out in turn to family and community.—R.S.F. and D.M.H.

NOTES

1. Melvil Dewey, *Traveling Libraries*, University of the State of New York Home Education Department, Bulletin 40 (Albany: U of the State of New York, 1901): 1.

2. Arthur E. Bostwick, *The American Public Library* (New York: D. Appleton, 1929): 1.

3. John Feather and Paul Sturges, eds., *International Encyclopedia of Information and Library Science* (New York: Routledge, 1997): 354.

4. William J. Wilson, "Extension Services," *Encyclopedia of Library History*, ed. Wayne A. Wiegand and Donald G. Davis (New York: Garland, 1994) 190–92.

5. U.S. Bureau of Education, *Public Libraries in the United States of America: Special Report*, vol. 1 (Washington, D.C.: Government Printing Office, 1876) 477. See also Jesse H. Shera, *Foundations of the Public Library: The Origins of the Public Library Movement in New England, 1629–1855* (Shoe String Press, 1965) 156–57.

6. Carleton Bruns Joeckel, introduction, *The Government of the American Public Library* (Chicago: U of Chicago Press, 1935) x.

7. Bostwick 1.

8. Donald C. Potter, "Extension Work, Public Library," *Encyclopedia of Library and Information Science*, ed. Allen Kent and Harold Lancour, vol. 8 (New York: Marcel Dekker, 1972) 335.

9. Watson's paper complements Christine Pawley's recent study, "Advocate for Access: Lutie Stearns and the Traveling Libraries of the Wisconsin Free Library Commission, 1895–1914," *Libraries & Culture* 35 (Summer 2000): 434–58. This won the LHRT's Justin Winsor Prize in 1999.

10. See her "Books for Black Children: Public Library Collections in Louisville and Nashville, 1915–1925," *Library Quarterly* 70 (April 2000): 179–200; and "Autonomy and Accommodations: Houston's Colored Carnegie Library: 1907–1922," *Libraries & Culture* 34 (Spring 1999): 95–112. This won the LHRT's Justin Winsor Prize in 1997.

11. E. J. Josey and Marva L. DeLoach, eds., *Handbook of Black Librarianship* (Lanham, MD: Scarecrow Press, 2000); John Mark Tucker, ed., *Untold Stories: Civil Rights, Libraries, and Black Librarianship* (Champaign: Publications Office, Graduate school of Library and Information Science, University of Illinois, 1998). *Untold Stories*, like the present volume, resulted from programs of the LHRT.

12. Gerald S. Greenberg, "Books as Disease Carriers, 1880–1920," *Libraries and Culture* 23 (1988): 281–294.

13. Eleanor Frances Brown, *Library Service to the Disadvantaged* (Metuchen, NJ: Scarecrow Press, 1971) 1.

I. Benevolent and Commercial Organizations

1. Books Along the Bayous: Reading Materials for Two Centuries of Rural Louisianians

Florence M. Jumonville

Professional library service to the people of Louisiana began to unfold on a hot July night in 1925 when Essae Martha Culver stepped off the train in Baton Rouge. With what she later described as "the valor of ignorance," she had come from California to assume the post of executive secretary of the newly established Louisiana Library Commission, which was funded by the Carnegie Corporation of New York to demonstrate the value of libraries to rural populations. Intending to remain just long enough to launch the Carnegie project, Miss Essae, as she would be called with the utmost fondness and respect, had purchased a round-trip ticket, but she never used the second half. Instead, she stayed for the rest of her life and witnessed the establishment of public libraries throughout Louisiana.[1]

From a bibliophile's viewpoint, the situation in Louisiana in 1925 was bleak. Only four free public libraries, underfunded and poorly equipped, existed beyond the metropolis of New Orleans. Isolated efforts to fill the void by providing rudimentary library services usually involved paying a fee. Bookstores were fewer yet. As one writer put it, "While, in certain sections, Louisiana could rightfully claim an unusual degree of culture, unfortunately ... she stood in the basement in regard to illiteracy. Libraries, except for the private libraries of the plantation home and the limited libraries of the public school, were entirely outside the experience of the two-thirds of the population which was rural." Before she arrived, Miss Essae had little realized that the task before her would involve organizing the entire state.[2]

Apart from its "bookless" condition, Louisiana would present unique challenges. One of them involved topography. European explorers first reached the present State of Louisiana by sea in the early sixteenth century. From that time to this,

11

water has played a major role in shaping Louisiana's destiny, largely because there is so *much* of it. Of the state's 48,000 square miles, 3,500 are occupied by rivers, bayous, creeks, and lakes; the Gulf of Mexico constitutes Louisiana's 400-mile southern boundary; and rivers form her borders on the east and west. The proximity of water has influenced many aspects of local experience, ranging from the strategic site chosen for the port city of New Orleans to the land deal which made it part of the United States, from viable crops to available types of recreation.[3] It also has influenced, both for better and for worse, efforts to make books available throughout Louisiana.

Another important factor was the people and their varied cultures. As an observer would write in 1959, "Louisiana is different. Every place is different, but Louisiana is more so. Retaining much of the flavor of the old world, its [sixty-four] counties are parishes, its laws are based on the Napoleonic Code, and its French inheritance is—well, French."[4] Claimed by France in 1682 and colonized in the early 1700s, the province also was settled by Acadian refugees from Nova Scotia who found a congenial home in French-speaking Louisiana and whose descendants clung to the language of their forebears well into the twentieth century. In 1762 France ceded Louisiana to Spain, which governed the province until 1803. After a three-week return to French rule, the Louisiana Purchase made the region part of the United States. Despite nearly four decades in power, Spain never succeeded in supplanting the French language. As Governor Esteban Rodriguez Miró reported to his government in 1788, "The introduction of the Spanish language in this colony is an object of difficult attainment, which it will require much time to accomplish." Efforts to establish a government-supported school in 1771 had failed because parents refused to enroll their children.[5] The endeavor is noteworthy in library history, however, because a free library was to accompany the school, "open to the clergy and honest persons who may wish to go at convenient hours to study there without interfering with the hours devoted to public education." No mention was made of lending the books, but the matter was moot because the library apparently never materialized. By 1780 the publications intended for its shelves could no longer be found.[6]

The inhabitants of colonial Louisiana reportedly had just as little interest in adult education. A visitor from France wrote in 1802, "There is neither a college, nor a library here, whether public or private. The cause of the last defect is obvious. A librarian would starve in the midst of his books, unless he could teach his readers the art of doubling his capital at the end of the year."[7] In 1926, State Superintendent of Education T. H. Harris wrote:

> I think it is unquestionably true that we, of the South, read but little, and there is not much constructive effort on the part of the educated portions of the population to change conditions in this respect, and yet, this question of reading is perhaps the most important of all questions that we face, for it is by reading that people are enabled to spend their leisure time profitably and enjoyably, and to secure information required to do their work efficiently.[8]

During the century and a quarter that separated those statements, books could be obtained in Louisiana—but usually for a price. From the earliest settlement, affluent planters and city-dwellers provided books for the enjoyment and edification of their families. Most of the books were brought or ordered from France, for during the colonial period, business opportunity was all but nonexistent in the province. That a bookstore may have existed can only be inferred from the fact that the local printer sold some of the materials he printed. With the Louisiana Purchase came the establishment of American government and the abolition of colonial restrictions. Newcomers, mostly French or American opportunists, swelled the population of New Orleans from approximately 7,000 in 1803 to 12,000 by 1806. Within another four years it had more than doubled, and by 1820 had reached 41,000.[9] The first to arrive found that no public library had yet been organized in Louisiana, although in 1805 the territorial legislature enacted comprehensive legislation designed to establish schools at all levels, from the university on down, and, further to spread knowledge, to incorporate libraries in the hinterlands and in New Orleans.[10] Prospective readers soon found an alternative: the social library, a collection of books gathered and owned cooperatively for the communal use of persons who organized themselves specifically for that purpose. Also in 1805, the legislature incorporated the New-Orleans Library Society, a stock company which served its shareholders from 1806 until it failed in 1830.[11]

The Touro Free Library Society was incorporated in 1824 "for the purpose of extending knowledge and promoting virtue among the inhabitants" of New Orleans. Housed in the Presbyterian Church, its collection initially contained more than one thousand volumes and soon exceeded seven thousand. Although the act of incorporation required subscribers to pay fees of five dollars and annual contributions of three dollars, city directories announced that "any person may have the use of books, gratis." Named in honor of philanthropist Judah Touro, who may have been a benefactor, the library probably represented the first attempt in Louisiana to make books available without charge. It ceased operation in 1832 or 1833.[12]

To supplement these government-authorized activities, businesspersons—usually booksellers or other merchants—operated reading rooms and rental libraries in conjunction with businesses such as coffee-houses. Two of the earliest opened in 1811. One was maintained at the office of the *Moniteur de la Louisiane*, the city's oldest newspaper; the Widow Roche, a seller of books, stationery, and sundries, administered the other. From the late 1820s until her death from cholera in 1833, an Irish milliner and bookseller named Mary Carroll operated "New-Orleans Reading Rooms" above her book and stationery store. In 1831 a single facility served as Mr. Frémaux's circulating library, "where books may be had by the month or by the single volume," and as headquarters for Madame Frémaux's business; she was a midwife. In an era when few libraries admitted women, circulating libraries were the first to serve them, even to seek their patronage. It was no coincidence that some of these libraries were associated with places women would frequent, such as millinery and stationery stores and the offices of a midwife. Not surprisingly, therefore, the first female librarians in Louisiana were those who, like the Widow Roche and Mary Carroll, oversaw circulating libraries.[13]

One of the New Orleans booksellers who operated a circulating library deserves further mention because he served customers in rural Louisiana. Antoine Louis Boimare arrived in New Orleans from France in the early 1820s and soon established a bookstore. By 1825 he had added a reading room, and within three years more he was operating a circulating library. Local readers paid $1.50 per month, $8.00 for six months, or $15.00 per year. They were permitted to take home four or five volumes at a time and to exchange them between the hours of 9:00 A.M. and 5:00 P.M., excluding Sunday. Borrowers residing on the plantations could check out as many as twenty books at once, upon payment of $2.00, $10.00, or $18.00. Boimare furnished locked boxes in which he shipped publications from his shop to distant patrons via steamboat; they returned the books in the same containers. Each box was equipped with two identical keys, of which Boimare kept one and his customer the other.[14]

The bookstore and circulating library prospered. In 1832 Boimare purchased property on Royal Street, where he constructed a fine building with a shop on the ground floor, a reading room on the second level, and space where local artists could display their work. The circulating library now contained more than ten thousand volumes, and Boimare anticipated increasing its inventory. During the night of March 4–5, 1833, fire broke out in the upper part of the structure and completely engulfed it. Passersby attempted with some success to rescue part of the stock, but despite the fire brigade's valiant efforts, the building was lost. Unable to recover financially, Boimare declared bankruptcy in November 1834. The fire spelled the demise of the first library on record that served patrons in a portion of rural Louisiana.[15]

Circulating libraries soon spread beyond New Orleans. One of the earliest operated in the South Louisiana town of Franklin, in the heart of plantation country. Robert Wilson, editor of the *Planters' Banner*, established a reading room in association with his newspaper, and on February 18, 1847, he added a library. Planters living in the vicinity contributed many of the books, facilitating the collection's growth from about 150 works to nearly 300 in less than two months. The annual fee was $5.00, or fifty cents per month for "transients," but there were many exceptions. Subscribers to the *Banner* who resided at least twelve miles from Franklin received free admission, as did "strangers" for one week and apprentices at all times. "Mechanics working in the country" were not charged on Sundays, and schoolboys had free access daily from 1:00 to 2:00. Wilson operated the library until late 1848, when he sold the *Banner* to Daniel Dennett and joined the California gold rush. It is likely that the collection then contained approximately 1,000 volumes. Sometime in 1849 Dennett closed the library for repairs and evidently never reopened it. The fate of its holdings is unknown.[16]

During the next decade, transitory attempts would be made to establish libraries in other areas. In Baton Rouge, for example, the Young Men's Library Association opened a public reading room in the Athenaeum. A Bossier Parish Library was set up in the courthouse at Bellevue when John M. Sandidge, a planter and a Congressman, donated his private collection for that purpose in 1857. The idea of a public library in Bossier was promoted at that time, but to no avail.[17] Near the end of the nineteenth century, however, meaningful effort began to burgeon, not coincidentally at about the same time that the women's club movement headed South.

Women's clubs had their beginning in New York and Boston in 1868 and spread across the country in the 1880s. The first in the South was the Women's Club, initiated in New Orleans by writer Elizabeth Bisland in 1884. Founded to provide women with opportunities to discuss literature, the groups soon began to take a more active interest in community life. In the Jefferson Davis Parish town of Jennings a women's club, formed in 1885 for the mutual aid and the social and intellectual improvement of its members, followed this pattern. The surrounding area consisted largely of prairie land which was being populated by large numbers of young men setting up homesteads. It was a treat for the men to spend weekends in town, staying at the hotel and enjoying its newspapers, magazines, and books. Concerned about the young men's cultural betterment as well as their own, the club women concluded that Jennings needed a library and reading room. Within a year they renamed their organization the Library Society, located appropriate quarters, and acquired books by donation and by purchase.[18]

In Baton Rouge the library movement began around 1900 when a local chapter of the United Daughters of the Confederacy set up a facility in the old Washington Fire Company No. 1 Hall. New Iberia's first library was established in 1918 by the women of the First Methodist Church for use by church members, but soon they opened it to neighborhood children and then to the public. The Methodist Church housed the collection until 1940, when the Iberia Community Library was constructed on a lot donated by the parish school board. Another women's club targeted a younger segment of the population. In 1932 Les Vingt-Quatre Club, a women's service organization in Lafayette, opened a lending library for children with a collection of fifty books. Open on Saturdays, it issued forty books, nearly its entire holdings, each week. When the Great Depression necessitated ending the school year after seven months, the demand for books increased so greatly that the library could not meet it, although its collection then numbered four hundred titles. In 1942 the juvenile library evolved into the Lafayette Municipal Library.[19]

Nationwide, organizing a community library proved to be an ideal project for club women, for it entwined with the original purpose of literary discussion, and it extended their traditional roles beyond the thresholds of their homes while avoiding competition in male spheres. A drawback in most communities was the absence of a permanent location, but the early donation of a suitable building enabled the Library Society of Jennings to avoid this obstacle. In 1901 a fire destroyed most of the collection, but the society succeeded in selling its property and buying a more desirable lot, with more than two thousand dollars left in the treasury. Wanting to construct as large and as fine a library as possible, the women of Jennings, like their library-minded counterparts in towns across the country, approached the Carnegie Corporation for funding.[20]

Andrew Carnegie's success in the steel business had brought him great wealth, and he held the widespread nineteenth-century belief that the affluent had a moral responsibility to provide cultural institutions for the less fortunate. Early experiences with books may have contributed to his choice of public libraries as the major outlet for his benevolence: his father, a weaver, had helped to found a circulating library in his small hometown in Scotland, and as a youth Andrew had limited access to a private library. Carnegie funding for libraries began in the United States on a limited basis in 1886 and took an important turn in 1891 with the first grant to a town with which Carnegie had no personal connection. Through the Carnegie Corporation, it continued long after Andrew's death in 1919.[21]

The philanthropist believed that a community could receive no better gift than a library, provided that the community accepted it as public property, on the same basis as a schoolhouse, and maintained it for the citizens' use. Carnegie offered construction funds only, and his gifts were not without restrictions. A community usually had to have a population of one thousand to ten thousand, it was expected to own the site of the prospective library, and it was required to pledge ten percent of the gift amount annually for maintenance. If these conditions were met, Carnegie would consider donating an amount based on the town's population. Jennings, which in 1907 was granted the sum of ten thousand dollars, was one of five Louisiana localities which received Carnegie funds. The others were New Orleans (1902), which received $350,000 for a main library and five branches (Napoleon Avenue, Royal Street, Algiers Point, Canal Street, and Dryades Street); Lake Charles (1902) and Alexandria (1907), each of which obtained $10,000; and Shreveport (1923), which built the Shreve Memorial Library at a cost of over $260,000.[22]

None of these institutions had been organized under the provisions of state law; indeed, no such legislation existed until 1910. The library law passed in that year enabled the establishment of public libraries, the creation of library boards, and financing from public funds, but it failed to provide for adequate funding, for the employment of a trained administrator, or for cooperation among city and parish libraries or among multi-parish libraries. Unaware of those flaws, library advocates considered the next logical step to be the formation of a state library commission which would lead in setting up libraries throughout the state. World War I interrupted the effort, and not until 1920 was appropriate legislation enacted. Meanwhile, in 1915, the members of the Louisiana Federation of Women's Clubs undertook to bring traveling libraries to Louisiana. Already functioning elsewhere in the nation, this program aspired "to put good literature within the reach of every Louisianian." Soon books stood ready for shipment in "strong-hinged cases" to communities that requested them, and more requests arrived than could be filled.[23]

After the war ended, the Louisiana Federation of Women's Clubs had the chance to secure the American Library Asssociation War Collection of three thousand volumes, books bought for the troops overseas, on the condition that a state-sanctioned organization would administer them. That opportunity gave impetus to the creation of the Louisiana Library Commission. The existing library law made no provision for such an agency, but, at the federation's urging, in 1920 the state legislature enacted a law which authorized the governor to appoint a commission consisting of five members, two of them women, which would employ a trained and experienced executive secretary. Although the governor promptly appointed qualified commissioners, not until 1922 was funding appropriated—one thousand dollars for the next biennium. The money was quickly spent on organizing and cataloging the books acquired from the American Library Association (ALA) and from the traveling library collection. Prospects for additional funding, and for the future of libraries in rural Louisiana, were discouraging.[24]

At the national level, the dearth of rural libraries concerned the membership of the ALA and the League of Library Commissions. The latter group, as an organization of states which were striving to improve library services to their citizens, "had little power or contact with those that were unconvinced, and above all it had no funds for promotional, educational or demonstrative purposes." With ALA support, league president Milton J. Ferguson presented a plan of action to the Carnegie Corporation and obtained a three-year grant of fifty thousand dollars to promote library development in one state, which, it was hoped, would serve as an exemplar to others. Louisiana met many of the requirements: "it had a fairly workable state library commission law, which, however, was not operating because of lack of funds; it was assuredly well toward the bottom of the class in library development, but, at the same time it had a few influential citizens who were interested in the project."[25] Of the thirteen states which applied for the funds, some not only touted their own merits, but also pointed out Louisiana's disadvantages. Nevertheless, Louisiana prevailed.

The most critical decision awaiting the newly reconstituted library commission was the appointment of an executive secretary to direct the project. Milton Ferguson, acting as an advisor to the commission in this matter, "promised to send a southern woman," but instead recommended the employment of Essae Culver, whose experience in library service included organizing the Salem (Oregon) Public Library and directing county libraries in California. In the latter "she learned how to fit the library's service to the needs of the community and the interests of the people."[26]

> Miss Culver entered county library service in the romantic days when "a librarian on horseback with a pack mule and Indian guide might go over steep trails, through unfrequented country, taking with her mental food to the remotest dwellers" and where counties are larger than many states.... In the county service she experienced "the joy of work which comes from the satisfaction of being able to meet the great need of the rural people."[27]

Ferguson quickly became convinced that this appointment was "one of the most influential elements in the program of library development the State has experienced."[28]

Miss Essae lost little time in getting to work, although she conceded twenty-five years later that "she was more than slightly dismayed" by the task before her. Within a week of her arrival, she had secured quarters on the main floor of the State Capitol. Delayed by late delivery of the furnishings, the office opened to the public on November 1 with reference service to legislators and the loan of books to the citizenry.[29] Meanwhile, Miss Essae surveyed the existing libraries of the state and, based on her findings, made six recommendations:

1. That the Commission members and the Executive Secretary give publicity and encouragement to the organization of parish libraries throughout the State, since the parish seems the logical unit for organization in Louisiana, as the county is in other states, and that as much supervision be given after organization as possible by the Executive Secretary in order to help make them successful. This supervision is especially important since there are no trained workers available to administer them, and upon the success of the first organized library depends, to a large extent, the future development in the State.

2. That, since the book resources of the Commission are very limited, large loans be made only to those libraries organized under the law and provided with location and custodian.

3. That, as far as resources allow, an informal service be given to individuals living in districts without library facilities of any kind; that package library service be given for club and class use; that supplementary book service be given to other libraries in addition to any advice and help in administrative problems requested; and that reading lists be supplied to libraries and individuals in furtherance of the adult education program.[30]

4. That an adequate library law be formulated for presentation at the next session of the State Legislature. [It was, and it passed.]

5. That the resources of the Commission be placed at the service of all state officials and the state legislators at all times, and especially during the next session of the Legislature.

6. That the Commission give all possible cooperation and encouragement to the establishment of a training course for librarians in the State.[31]

This last recommendation was the genesis of Louisiana State University's Graduate School of Library and Information Science.

Miss Essae explained the reasoning behind the first three recommendations as follows:

> The parish library was chosen as a primary project rather than the traveling library, because it has been found in other states that while the traveling library spreads books quickly over a wider territory, it does not tend to bring about the establishment of libraries adequately supported. The traveling library at best gives a superficial service and cannot meet the needs of any community. The secretaries of two state library commissions [California and Wisconsin] reported that better results in bringing about permanent library establishment were obtained from a county library demonstration than from years of traveling library service. It was felt that a book club service, where an effort would be made to fit the collection to the interests of the group, would more adequately serve those districts where a parish library service was not immediately possible, than a fixed collection such as is usually sent in a traveling library. Bringing about the establishment of permanent, adequately supported libraries was the goal of the Commission.[32]

Essae Culver is credited with having "conceived, developed and perfected the library demonstration method of library extension which [would be] used as a pattern by other states and countries."[33] "The plan was to show the people of the state how a library could be organized so that books would go into every part of the parish and serve the young and old, and the dweller in remote rural districts as well as town." Typically, the Louisiana Library Commission provided cataloged books, the salary of a trained librarian, and direction and supervision; the parish contributed housing, utilities, furnishings, and the salaries of the non-professional staff. At the end of the demonstration period, usually one year, the responsibility to fund the program passed to the parish.[34]

Because Louisiana had just nineteen towns of at least five thousand people and because assessments were low, a large unit—the parish—was advocated for libraries, just as it was the unit for government and schools. The library law of 1925 left open the possibility of multi-parish libraries, a concept then untried but which would succeed in Louisiana.

In the effort to develop an interest throughout the State in the parish as the logical unit for library organization the members of the Louisiana Library Commission decided upon arranging for two parish demonstrations as the very best way to spread the idea. If possible, the Commission agreed, one was to be in north Louisiana and the other in the southern part of the State. Many parishes were considered, but it was finally decided that Richland, in the north, and Jefferson Davis, in the south, would be the best for the purpose.[35]

Richland's population of twenty-one thousand was spread over some five hundred square miles, mostly farmland and swamps which were considered worthless until the then-recent discovery that they harbored natural gas. The Police Jury had already adopted its budget for the year, and the Richland Library Association's treasury of fourteen hundred dollars was insufficient for a trained librarian's salary. A member of the community, Mrs. Pendleton Morris, enrolled in library courses at her own expense and accepted the position at a minimal salary. The school board offered rent-free facilities, and Louisiana's first demonstration library was opened in April 1926 with headquarters at Rayville. Soon there were eighteen branches, one of them in a settlement seven miles past the nearest gravel road, which was often inaccessible for weeks at a time.[36]

During the early years, Miss Essae addressed meetings of community groups, parent-teacher organizations, service clubs, women's clubs, and agencies of local government across the state to inform them of the commission's services and to muster support.[37] In 1932, for example, she spoke in the Vermilion Parish town of Abbeville, where, she had been told, the women had "sweated blood" to raise three hundred dollars for a library. The audience, which included the president of the police jury, the head of the Chamber of Commerce, and the superintendent of schools, was presumed not to be sympathetic with the library cause. At the conclusion of her talk, Miss Essae noticed for the first time a white-haired woman, attired in the style of four decades earlier, at the rear of the room. Lenora Vaughan told the group,

> I have lived on Pecan Island for 40 years. When I got married I realized that I would be an ignoramus if I did not learn to read. Gentlemen, the only reason I'm able to talk to you now, is because of the scraps of papers and magazines I found lying around that I picked up and read. Today, I'm writing the story of my life so that my grandchildren will have something to read.

She had come by boat and on foot to appeal on behalf of her four hundred island neighbors for funding for the library. One of the politicians, who had been elected on an economy platform and was expected to voice the strongest opposition, jumped to his feet and promised to appropriate as much money as necessary for the library. The episode convinced Miss Essae that "books mean just as much to the uneducated as they do to the most scholarly."[38]

Conditions in Vermilion Parish exemplified some of the obstacles presented by Louisiana's culture and topography. Of its 34,000 inhabitants, ninety percent spoke French but probably little English, which contributed to the parish's ranking as one of the three with the highest rates of illiteracy. This had obvious implications for

book selection and staffing. Also, Vermilion is a parish of much water. Pecan Island, where the self-taught reader resided, was literally a swamp-surrounded island to which the boat came once per week. Similar circumstances prevailed in Terrebonne Parish, where in 1939 library headquarters and four branches opened, including one in an ice cream parlor which was "favorably located in being near both the picture show and the postoffice." Terrebonne residents of French ancestry, who read English with difficulty, if at all, turned to reading children's books to improve their skills. A French-speaking staff member rode on bookmobile trips to isolated areas, which often included stops along the bayous. Many citizens routinely arrived at the bookmobile by boat.[39]

For part of April and all of May 1927, Miss Essae's diary reads simply, in large, underlined letters, "Flood," for the raging Mississippi River was necessitating travel by boat where it had never occurred before. The fledgling Vermilion Parish library remained open, along with a pharmacy and a grocery. With most of the parish under water, prospective borrowers—and the librarian—paddled and waded to the library.

> As the water came up to the floor of the porch, the steps were removed in order that the boats could more easily unload their passengers, and each boat took away books to supply not only all the members of the family, but usually the neighbors as well. Sixty books per day in a community of 1,499 population would be a fair circulation under the best of conditions, but under the difficult traveling conditions it is a record that is eloquent.[40]

A farmer pointed out, "It's an ill wind that blows no good, and the flood brought us the reading habit…. With everything a lake outside, people just naturally took to reading. Mrs. Morris kept the library open, and I've seen boys carrying books away in flour sacks."[41]

The flood paralyzed the work of the Louisiana Library Commission. Although little damage to library materials occurred, there was a loss of momentum in parishes where the library movement was underway. "Even the parishes far removed from Flood waters reacted to the general depression and all activity toward establishment of new libraries stopped." As Milton Ferguson noted, "It is hard to talk libraries to a man whose farm is under water, whose stock is drowned or scattered, and whose crops are destroyed." Because the progress made in Louisiana to date was jeopardized by the state's dire economic situation, the Carnegie Corporation extended its grant funding for two more years to enable the library commission's work to continue.[42]

Another complication involved service to African Americans. These were the days of segregation and prejudice, as Miss Essae had discovered shortly after she arrived in Louisiana. During a speech in Lafayette, she complimented the state's progress against illiteracy and attributed what remained to the French-speaking Cajuns and the African American population in parishes where tax support was inadequate to fund the dual school system. Following the talk, she was reprimanded for using the pejorative term "Cajun" and for her assessment of the cause of illiter-

Opposite: Bookmobile stop at Bayou du Large, Terrebonne Parish, Louisiana.

acy. Assailing her as an "outsider" who "did not understand," Henry Gill from the New Orleans Public Library claimed that African Americans "were not capable of education and did not want it." He advocated collecting scholarly materials but denigrated extension service. After that session, Miss Essae "[r]eturned home more weary than I have ever been."[43]

With such attitudes to be overcome, the achievement of parish-wide service to African Americans in Webster Parish was even greater. African Americans comprised about half of the parish's population of 24,700, scattered over five hundred square miles. Special funding was available to establish libraries for African Americans in a qualified parish, and Webster, where an excellent school system was accessible to every child, met the criteria. The demonstration library opened in 1929 and within two years offered ten branches or distribution points for white readers and the same number for black ones. Service to the latter group developed rapidly, despite predictions to the contrary. The parish library also served as a model for cooperation between public and school libraries.[44]

Not every parish demonstration succeeded. Jefferson Davis Parish, in the heart of rice country in southwestern Louisiana, opened its library in 1927. Somewhere around thirty percent of its twenty thousand residents were African Americans. The white population was divided almost equally between educated northerners and westerners who had arrived within recent decades, and descendants of the Acadians who had sought refuge in Louisiana in the eighteenth century. Many of the latter could neither read nor write, and some did not speak English. The town of Jennings boasted a Carnegie library, and a library run by club women served another community. Circulation at the demonstration library was good, notably among the French school children. "In some of these French homes where the parents were not able to read[,] they were eager for the children to bring home the books and read to them, especially when the books contained pictures, as the parents were interested in studying the pictures with the children."[45]

When the proposal to levy a one-mill tax to fund the library went before the electorate, there was every reason for optimism, but the proposal failed. Supporters attributed the defeat to the effects of the flood and to the unwillingness of Jennings residents to support the parish library as well as the one in their town. Although it was not continued, the demonstration was considered a success because it proved to the people and to the commission "that the people were hungry for something to read and would read good books if they were made accessible to them."[46] Another failure occurred in Vermilion Parish, where the demonstration period ended in 1932, during the depths of the Great Depression, and continued financing was impossible. The parish tried again nine years later and passed the necessary tax.[47]

Jefferson Davis Parish, however, remained without a parish library until 1968. The intervening years were eventful ones for the library movement in Louisiana. A statewide Citizens' Library Movement was organized in 1937 to support library development, in 1940 Miss Essae became the first woman from the South elected to the presidency of the American Library Association, the Louisiana Library Commission changed its name to the Louisiana State Library in 1946, federal funding to libraries became available in 1956, Sallie Farrell became state librarian in 1962 upon Miss Essae's retirement at the age of eighty, and the last of the other sixty-three parishes established libraries. Eventually, the Louisiana Library Commission's first failure became the Louisiana State Library's last success when the Jefferson Davis Parish Library finally was dedicated. Miss Essae lived to see the entire state "Culverized."[48] Still, it was not enough for the zealous librarian. When library service reached every corner of every parish, she said, "the [next] goal must be to make the good better and the better best."[49] Toward that end, under the able leadership of Thomas Jaques, the State Library of Louisiana—it changed its name again—continues to strive. Louisiana libraries have come far since the Louisiana Library Commission received "the best [investment] the Carnegie Corporation made in an experiment of [this] kind."[50]

NOTES

1. Quoted by Linda June Gifford, "Into 'Bookless' Louisiana: Essae Martha Culver and the Louisiana State Library," M.Ed. thesis, Louisiana State University in Shreveport, 1993, 6; "National Publication Lauds State Librarian," Baton Rouge (LA) *State Times*, 15 Jan. 1959; Sarah Irwin Jones, "A Goal Is Realized: Parish-wide Library Service Throughout Louisiana," *LLA Bulletin* 31 (Fall 1968): 93.

2. Louisiana Library Commission, *Report on the Louisiana Library Demonstration, 1925–1930* (New York: League of Library Commissions, 1931) 16–20 (quotation); Gifford, "Into 'Bookless' Louisiana" 6.

3. Louisiana was described as "bookless" by Margaret Dixon and Nantelle Gittinger, *The First Twenty-Five Years of the Louisiana State Library, 1925–1950* (Baton Rouge, LA: Louisiana State Library, 1950) 3; Walter Pritchard, *Walter Pritchard's Outline of Louisiana Studies.* ed. Sue Eakin (Gretna, LA: Pelican Publishing Co., 1972) 3–10; Charles Dufour, *Ten Flags in the Wind: The Story of Louisiana* (New York: Harper & Row, 1967) 3.

4. "National Publication Lauds State Librarian."

5. Quoted by Charles Gayarré, *History of Louisiana: The Spanish Domination* (New York: William J. Widdleton, 1866) 204–205.

6. David K. Bjork, trans. and ed., "Documents Relating to the Establishment of Schools in Louisiana, 1771," *Mississippi Valley Historical Review* 11 (Mar. 1925): 565 (quotation); Roger Philip McCutcheon, "Libraries in New Orleans, 1771–1833," *Louisiana Historical Quarterly* 20 (Jan. 1937): 152.

7. Berquin-Duvallon, *Travels in Louisiana and the Floridas, in the Year, 1802, Giving a Correct Picture of Those Countries*, trans. John Davis (New-York: I. Riley & Co., 1806) 52. The situation persisted well into the nineteenth century. See Joseph G. Tregle, Jr., *Louisiana in the Age of Jackson: A Clash of Cultures and Personalities* (Baton Rouge, LA: Louisiana State UP, 1999) 27–29.

8. Louisiana Library Commission, *Report on the Louisiana Library Demonstration* 20.

9. Florence M. Jumonville, "Frenchmen at Heart: New Orleans Printers and Their Imprints, 1764–1803," *Louisiana History* 32 (1991): 279–310; Robert Clemens Reinders, "A Social History of New Orleans, 1850–1860," diss., U of Texas at Austin, 1957, 6–9. Estimates of the population in 1803 and 1806 vary.

10. *Acts Passed at the First Session of the Legislative Council of the Territory of Orleans* (New Orleans: Printed by James M. Bradford, 1805) 304–335. This legislation seems the more remarkable when one considers that a New York law enacted in 1835, which established school district libraries open to the general public, is considered the earliest recognition of the state's duty to provide books to its citizens. George S. Bobinski, *Carnegie Libraries: Their History and Impact on American Public Library Development* (Chicago: American Library Association, 1969) 4. That a public library was indeed anticipated is substantiated by a letter written on 3 Aug. 1805 by Gov. William C. C. Claiborne to Secretary of State James Madison, seeking permission to use a federal building "as a Library Hall for the Public Library about to be established in this City." *Official Letter Books of W. C. C. Claiborne, 1801–1816.* ed. Dunbar Rowland, vol. 3 (Jackson, MS: Printed for the State Department of Archives and History, 1917) 148–149.

11. The first social library in America was the Library Company of Philadelphia, founded in 1731 by Benjamin Franklin. It still flourishes today, supported largely by subscription fees paid by its members. Such fees were less costly than buying books, and many English colonists supported social libraries. David Kaser, *A Book for a Sixpence: The Circulating Library in America* (Pittsburgh, PA: Beta Phi Mu, 1980) 13; Orleans Territory, *Acts*, 1st sess., 1805, 322–335; New Orleans (LA) *Louisiana Gazette*, 11 Nov. 1806: 3; New Orleans (LA) *Courrier de la Louisiane*, 11 Jan. 1830: 3.

12. *Acts Passed at the Second Session of the Sixth Legislature of the State of Louisiana* (New Orleans:

Printed by Peter K. Wagner, 1824) 158–165 (first quotation). Information about the Touro Free Library appears in New Orleans city directories from 1824 through 1832 but is absent from the 1834 edition, which was issued in December 1833. John Adems Paxton, *Supplement to the New-Orleans Directory of the Last Year* (New-Orleans: J. A. Paxton, 1824) 18 (second quotation); John Adems Paxton, *The New-Orleans Directory and Register* (New-Orleans: Printed for the Author, 1827), n. pag.; John Adems Paxton, *The New-Orleans Directory and Register* (New-Orleans: Printed for the Author, 1830), n. pag.; S. E. Percy & Co., *The New-Orleans Directory* (New-Orleans: Printed for the Authors, 1832) 209; *Michel's New Orleans Annual and Commercial Register* (New Orleans: Gaux & Sollée, Printers, 1833).

13. Roger Philip McCutcheon, "Books and Booksellers in New Orleans, 1730–1830," *Louisiana Historical Quarterly* 20 (Jul. 1937): 616; New Orleans (LA) *Courrier de la Louisiane*, 19 Aug. 1811: 3; Paxton, *New-Orleans Directory* (1830); James Stuart, *Three Years in North America*, 3d ed., rev., vol. 2 (Edinburgh: Printed for Robert Cadell, 1833) 212–213; New Orleans (LA) *Courrier de la Louisiane*, 27 Dec. 1831: 2 (quotation); Kaser 116–120.

14. One A. L. Boimare, a merchant from France, arrived in New Orleans from Le Havre on board the *Helvetia* on 4 Dec. 1820, and is probably the future bookseller. His age, cited as 34, is an error; he actually was 24. Carl A. Brasseaux, *The "Foreign French": Nineteenth-Century French Immigration into Louisiana*, Vol. I: *1820–1839* (Lafayette, LA: Center for Louisiana Studies, U of Southwestern Louisiana, 1990) 59; New Orleans city directories, 1823–1838, especially John Adems Paxton, *The New-Orleans Directory and Register* (New Orleans: Printed for the Author, 1823), n. pag.; Edward Larocque Tinker, "Boimare: First and Still Foremost Bibliographer of Louisiana," *Papers of the Bibliographical Society of America* 24 (1931): 34; New Orleans (LA) *Passe-Tems*, 5 Mar. 1828: 488. See Florence M. Jumonville, "Books, Libraries, and Undersides for the Skies of Beds: The Extraordinary Career of A. L. Boimare," *Louisiana History* 34 (Fall 1993): 237–259.

15. *New-Orleans Directory*; *L'Abeille de la Nouvelle-Orléans* (LA), 12 Dec. 1832: 3; New Orleans (LA) *Courrier de la Louisiane*, 5 Mar. 1833: 3; 7 Mar. 1833: 3.

16. Walton R. Patrick, "A Circulating Library of Ante-bellum Louisiana," *Louisiana Historical Quarterly* 23 (Jan. 1940): 131–133.

17. Mark T. Carleton, *River Capital: An Illustrated History of Baton Rouge* (Woodland Hills, CA: Windsor, 1981) 201; Clifton D. Cardin, *Bossier Parish History, 1843–1993: The First 150 Years* (Princeton, LA: C. D. Cardin, 1993) 181.

18. Abigail A. Van Slyck, *Free to All: Carnegie Libraries & American Culture, 1890–1920* (Chicago: U of Chicago Press, 1995) 125–127; Patricia Brady, "Literary Ladies of New Orleans in the Gilded Age," *Louisiana History* 33 (Spring 1992): 153–154; Walter D. Morse, *The Birth of Jennings and Jennings Firsts* ([n.p., 1959?]) 38–40.

19. Carleton 201; Ruth Lefkovits and Carla Klapper, "A History of the New Iberia Library," in *New Iberia: Essays on the Town and Its People*. ed. Glenn R. Conrad, 2d ed. (Lafayette, LA: Center for Louisiana Studies, U of Southwestern Louisiana, 1986) 454–455; *Lafayette, Its Past, People and Progress* (Baton Rouge: Moran, 1980), 56–57.

20. Van Slyck 132–135; Morse 38–40.

21. Bobinski 3–13, 40–45; Van Slyck 1, 8–9; Theodore Jones, *Carnegie Libraries Across America: A Public Legacy* (New York: John Wiley & Sons, 1997) 3–13.

22. Bobinski 3–13, 40–45; Jones 3–13, 145; Work Projects Administration, *Louisiana: A Guide to the State* (New York: Hastings, 1941) 370.

23. Louisiana Library Commission, *Report on the Louisiana Library Demonstration* 16, 21, 25; Shirley Knowles Stephenson, "History of the Louisiana State Library, Formerly Louisiana Library Commission," diss., Louisiana State U, 1957, 6–10 (text of Act 149 of 1910, 437–439); "Rural 'Travelling Libraries' Want of Federated Women," New Orleans *Item*, 24 Apr. 1921 (quotations), in Louisiana Library Commission [Scrapbook], 1925–1928, State Library of Louisiana.

24. Stephenson 10–15; "The News with Orene Muse," transcript of broadcast over WJBO radio, July 9, 1945, in Essae M. Culver files, State Library of Louisiana.

25. Louisiana Library Commission, *Report on the Louisiana Library Demonstration* 7–9.

26. Stephenson 20–21; Essae Martha Culver, "Diary 1925" (first quotation from July 24); Velma Taylor, "The Life of Essae M. Culver Is the Story of LA. Libraries," Baton Rouge: *State-Times*, 16 May 1962, in Essae M. Culver files, State Library of Louisiana (second quotation).

27. *Current Biography: Who's News and Why, 1940*. ed. Maxine Block (New York: H. W. Wilson, 1940) 214.

28. Louisiana Library Commission, *Report on the Louisiana Library Demonstration* 10.

29. Dixon and Gittinger, *First Twenty-Five Years*, 6 (quotation); Culver, "Diary 1925," 28 Jul., 14 Aug.; Louisiana Library Commission, *Report on the Louisiana Library Demonstration* 15–16, 26–27.

30. Louisiana Library Commission, *Report on the Louisiana Library Demonstration Libraries* 24.

31. Louisiana Library Commission, *Report on the Louisiana Library Demonstration* 25.

32. Louisiana Library Commission, *Report on the Louisiana Library Demonstration* 25 (quotation); Stephenson 26.

33. Taylor, "The Life of Essae M. Culver."

34. "Even Floods Fail to Stop Drawing of Library Books," New Orleans (LA) *Times-Picayune*, 12 June 1927, in Louisiana Library Commission [Scrapbook], 1925–1928; Stephenson 37; Julia King Avant, "Extending Library Service to Rural Areas in Louisiana, 1956–1969," diss. Indiana, 1972, 48–56.

35. Stephenson 25–26; Louisiana Library Commission, *Report on the Louisiana Library Demonstration* 32 (quotation).

36. Renee B. Stern, "Carrying Opportunity into the Parishes: Libraries Afford Striking Examples of What Extension Work Means to the Farming Communities," New Orleans (LA) *Times-Picayune*, 6 May 1928, in Essae M. Culver files, State Library of Louisiana; Louisiana Library Commission, *Report on the Louisiana Library Demonstration* 27–28.

37. A partial list of speaking engagements noted in Essae Culver's diary during the first two months of 1926 illustrates her rigorous schedule: the American Library Association mid-year conference, Chicago, Jan. 1; Jennings Library Board, Jan. 27; Monroe Library Board, Feb. 8; some seventy-five citizens of Richland Parish, Rayville, Feb. 9; Home Department meeting, Tallulah, Feb. 10; Government Club of LSU, Baton Rouge, Feb. 11; Minden Police Jury, Feb. 23, and PTA, Feb. 24; PTA, Shreveport, Feb. 25; and Shreve Memorial Library Commission, Feb. 26. Among her early modes of transportation were "by machine" (10 Oct. 1925) and "milk train" (9 Dec. 1925).

38. Annabelle Armstrong, "If You Have Library Problems, Just Ask Miss Essae M. Culver," Baton Rouge (LA) *State Times*, [22 Dec. 1945?], in Essae M. Culver files, State Library of Louisiana; Stephenson 82.

39. Armstrong, "If You Have Library Problems"; Louisiana Library Commission, *Ninth Biennial Report of the Louisiana Library Commission, 1940–1941* (Baton Rouge: The Commission, 1941) 32; Louisiana Library Commission, *Eighth Biennial Report of the Louisiana Library Commission, 1938–1939* (Baton Rouge: The Commission, 1940) 18–19; "Establishment of Branches" (mimeographed page), "Terrebonne Parish Library Demonstration [Scrapbook], 5 Nov. 1939–31 Dec. 1940," in State Library of Louisiana.

40. Essae M. Culver, Diary 1927, following 15 Apr.; "Even Floods Fail to Stop Drawing"; Louisiana Library Commission, *Report on the Louisiana Library Demonstration* 34 (quotation).

41. Stern, "Carrying Opportunity."

42. Louisiana Library Commission, *Report on the Louisiana Library Demonstration* 39 (first quotation), 11 (second quotation).

43. Essae M. Culver, Diary 1926, 9 Jan.

44. Louisiana Library Commission, *Report on the Louisiana Library Demonstration* 43–48; Louisiana Library Commission, *Fourth Biennial Report of the Louisiana Library Commission, 1930–1931* (Baton Rouge: The Commission, 1932) 12.

45. Louisiana Library Commission, *Report on the Louisiana Library Demonstration*, 35–37 (quotation, 37).

46. Lousiana Library Commission, *Report on the Louisiana Library Demonstration* 38 (quotation); miscellaneous clippings, Louisiana Library Commission [Scrapbook], 1925– 1928.

47. Stephenson 85, 135–140.

48. Sarah Irwin Jones, "Goal Is Realized" 93; Essae M. Culver and Nantelle M. Gittinger, "A History of the Citizens' Library Movement," *LLA Bulletin* 17 (Winter 1954): 18–23; Louisiana State Library, *Twelfth Biennial Report of the Louisiana State Library, Formerly Louisiana Library Commission, 1946–1947* (Baton Rouge: The Library, 1948) 9; Robert Charles Smith, "A Historical Study of Selected Effects of Federal Funding upon Public Libraries in Louisiana, 1956–1973," diss., Louisiana State U, 1975, 1; Taylor, "Essae M. Culver"; "National Publication Lauds State Librarian" (quotation). Essae Culver died on 3 Jan. 1973, at the age of 90. Dick Wright, "Librarian Emeritus Dies at 90," Baton Rouge (LA) *Advocate*, 4 Jan. 1973, in Essae M. Culver files, State Library of Louisiana.

49. Taylor, "Essae M. Culver."

50. Letter, Milton James Ferguson to Miss Essae M. Culver, 3 Jul. 1945, in Essae M. Culver files, State Library of Louisiana.

2. Harper & Brothers' Family and School District Libraries, 1830–1846

Robert S. Freeman

Every where throughout America, on the wings of every wind are their publications disseminated. Who shall estimate the influence thus exerted for good or for evil? The refined lady of the world of fashion languidly peruses the last new novel from Cliff Street, in the retirement of her *boudoir*, and you shall find it in the hands of the passenger in the down steamer on the great Mississippi. The lawyer and the divine, the client and the parishioner, the physician and patient alike bend over the pages of their volumes. In the silence of the backwoods, you may see the pioneer with a well-thumbed number of the Family Library, and the volunteer in the interior of Mexico, beguiles the interim of camp duty with the feats and fortunes of James' heroes. How important is it, in view of this powerful influence over the public mind, that the energies of the *Harperian* press should be directed to proper ends? How vitally momentous to the morals of a great continent that good books alone should be sent forth under the sanction of their approval!

> — *"A Day Among Bookmen and Bibliopoles,"* Southern Literary Messenger *(Jan 1848)*[1]

Why should we leave it to Harper & Brothers and Redding &
Co. to select our reading?

Henry D. Thoreau, Walden[2]

Histories of library outreach usually concentrate on the ideas and actions of
public librarians, teachers, religious and philanthropic societies, professional associations, or government agencies that have endeavored to bring library services to
people who would otherwise not have them. In this essay, however, I focus on a
commercial publishing enterprise that not only sold and distributed millions of
books to a variety of people and institutions, including libraries, but also selected,
published, printed, and marketed its own "libraries."

In the early 1830s, at the dawn of mass-market publishing, J. & J. Harper of New
York began publishing collections with names like Harper's Library of Select Novels, Harper's Classical Library, and The Boy's and Girl's Library.[3] A "library" in this
sense is a series or set of uniformly bound and uniformly priced books issued by the
same publisher. Two of the most popular and successful libraries produced by any
publisher in this period were Harper's Family Library and Harper's School District
Library.

Published from 1830 to 1842, the Family Library grew to 127 titles in 187 volumes. The School District Library, published from 1838 to 1846, grew to 210 titles
in 295 volumes, but more than half of these were duplicates of titles in the Family
Library (see Appendix A). Printed from stereotype plates, the libraries remained in
print for more than twenty years after their completion.[4] Over eighty percent of the
titles were reprints of well-received British works. As the Family Library expanded
and became profitable, an increasing number of untested American works such as
Benjamin Thatcher's *Indian Biography* and Richard Henry Dana, Jr.'s, *Two Years
Before the Mast* were introduced.[5] The School District Library continued this trend
toward a higher proportion of works by Americans. It also featured several works
by women (see Appendix B). The books were pocketsize (18mo, 10cm × 16cm or 4"
× 6¼"), a quality often highlighted in advertisements by Dr. Johnson's comment:
"Books that you may carry to the fire, and hold readily in your hand, are the most
useful after all."[6] The books were also relatively cheap, selling for about forty-five
cents each. In 1830 this was about one fourth of day's wage for an artisan, half of a
day's wage for a manual laborer, and a full day's wage for an agricultural worker.[7]
Volumes could be purchased separately or in sets. Each set had about fifty volumes
and came in a hardwood box with built-in shelves and a hinged-door. Attached to
the inside of the door was a catalog of the books and an introduction to the reading program.[8] The program encompassed the principal branches of "useful knowledge:" history, voyages and travel, biography, natural history, physical sciences,
agriculture, and the history of philosophy and religion. It was suggested that the
intellectual value of any one book was enhanced by its being part of an approved
system or "circle" of knowledge. The works in the Family Library were all non-
fiction. The School District Library, however, contained a few moralistic novels and
tales.

Before I describe and compare the contents of these two Harper libraries, I will
discuss: (1) the role of reading for moral improvement in early nineteenth-century

America and the perceived need for the sort of works featured in the libraries; (2) the Methodist background and connections of the Harpers; (3) advances in transportation and printing technologies that facilitated mass-market publishing; and (4) the economic and cultural advantages of mass-produced libraries as evidenced by several libraries, including some that appeared before the Harpers'.

READING FOR MORAL IMPROVEMENT

Since colonial times, American printers and publishers have worked closely with society's cultural authorities and reformers. In the early republic, after the Second Great Awakening had inspired a new zeal for social and moral reform, many printers and publishers became advocates and effective propagandists for an ideology of literacy that equated reading with the development of public and private virtue.[9] Their moral cause was to promote a reading habit among the people and to prescribe or select what the people read. In the new democracy with increasingly diverse suffrage and expanding boundaries, they thought it was crucial that as many citizens and families as possible be educated and have the means of improving themselves, their communities, and their nation. In the 1830s the white population of the United States reached twelve million and had an adult literacy rate of over eighty percent, among the highest in the world.[10] Although literacy rates were lower in some areas (especially the South and West), ministers commented that there was no shortage of people who could read. The problem was that these men and women were not reading the kinds of works that would improve them. Amidst an abundance of newspapers, lives of bandits, and novels of "a Gothic taste and overstrained morality," social reformers and some publishers recognized a need for more books of useful knowledge and moral wisdom.[11]

In the early nineteenth century, newspaper offices, general stores, book shops, circulating libraries, subscription libraries, and Sunday schools were sources of reading material, but most education and reading still took place in the family home, "the moral mainstay of the social order"—hence the appeal of a "Family Library."[12] As the century advanced, common schools played an increasingly important role in education. By the 1840s several states, including New York and Massachusetts, had established free, tax-supported libraries in their school districts—hence the appeal of a "School District Library." Selling in the tens of thousands to individuals, families, schools, school districts, libraries, and even ships, the Family and School District Libraries represent an early, mass-market effort to influence and make a profit on the education of middle-class Americans.

METHODIST BACKGROUND AND CONNECTIONS OF THE HARPERS

The Methodist environment in which the Harper brothers grew up had a positive influence on their individual decisions to become printers and on the success of their printing and publishing endeavors. Their father, a Long Island carpenter and farmer, was the son of a Methodist from Suffolk, England. Their mother, the daughter of a Lutheran Dutch family, became a Methodist soon after she was married. Methodist preachers with their saddlebags full of books were often guests at the Harper home. "The best room was reserved for them, and it was called 'the Preacher's bed-room'."[13]

In his dissertation on *The Availability of Books and the Nature of Book Ownership on the Southern Indiana Frontier, 1800–1850*, Michael Harris shows that the act of distributing books was very important to the followers of John Wesley. Wesley believed that people would not "grow in grace unless they give themselves to reading."[14] He exhorted his brethren to "take care that every society be duly supplied with books."[15] The dissemination of good books, whether through giving, lending, or selling, was a glorious duty. Good books included the Bible, other religious works, and morally improving secular works. Wesley wrote to an Oxfordshire circuit rider in 1782:

> You should take particular care that your circuit be never without an assortment of all the valuable books, especially the *Appeals*, the *Sermons*, Kempis, and the *Primitive Physick*, which no family should be without.... You are found to be remarkably diligent in spreading the books: let none rob you of this glory.[16]

In order to coordinate the publishing and selling of books and to share any profits, the Methodist Church in America established the Methodist Book Concern in 1789.[17] The Concern hired a variety of printers to prepare the cheap books the ministers sold. Ministers were allowed to sell these books on the condition that they send the cash from the sale back to their presiding elders for redistribution. This system changed in 1800 when the preachers were simply allowed to keep between fifteen and twenty-five percent upon the wholesale price for all the books they sold.[18]

In their 1814 *Report of a Missionary Tour Through that part of the United States which lies West of the Allegany Mountains*, Samuel J. Mills and Daniel Smith wrote that the Concern

> sends out an immense quantity of these books. We found them almost everywhere. In the possession of the obscurest families, we often found a number of volumes.... It puts to the blush all the other charitable institutions in the United States.[19]

It should be noted that Mills and Smith were not Methodists.

Based on their background, class, and education, the Harper boys might well have decided to become preachers like the men who visited their parents' home. Instead, they became printers and publishers, and yet, as such, they were able to make substantial, far-reaching contributions to the cause of reading for moral and social reform.

James Harper (1795–1869), the eldest of the four brothers, was inspired to become a printer while reading Benjamin Franklin's *Autobiography*. In 1811 he was apprenticed to a master printer in New York City, a Methodist friend of his father. Two years later John Harper (1797–1875) became an apprentice in another print shop in the city. In 1817 James and John acquired two old presses, rented a space, and started the firm of J. & J. Harper. Their younger brothers, Joseph Wesley

(1801–1870) and Fletcher (1806–1877) soon joined them. The name of the firm, however, did not change to Harper & Brothers until 1833.

The brothers seemed to function as parts of a single, highly effective organism. James supervised mechanical operations, John handled financing and purchasing, Joseph Wesley read proof and conducted correspondence, and Fletcher set type and managed the literary department. All were known as devout Methodists. Years later, in 1844, when James ran for mayor of New York City on the Reform Party ticket, he was identified not only with the American Republican Party's nativist anti–Catholicism, but also with the Bible—*Harper's Illuminated Bible.* As mayor he became famous for closing saloons on Sunday and requiring the police to wear uniforms.[20]

In the early years of their printing business, the Harpers benefited greatly from their Methodist connections. These included the Rev. Dr. Nathan Bangs, the principal manager of the Methodist Book Concern, and his son, Lemuel, who would become one of the most important auctioneers at the New York book trade sales.[21] Among the brothers' earliest printing jobs were two books, one for the Methodist Book Concern and one for friends of their "Methodist connexions": Caroline Matilda Thayer's *Religion Recommended to Youth* (1818) and an edition of the *Prayer Book of the Protestant Episcopal Church,* for which they manufactured their first stereotypes.[22] Eight years later they printed and published the *Works* of John Wesley in ten volumes.

In 1826 they also began publishing the *National Preacher,* a monthly journal featuring one or two sermons written by ministers of various Protestant denominations. Fortunately, when faced with the challenge of selling and distributing the magazine around country, the Harpers already knew about agents and where to find them. "Some agents were established book sellers but the majority were clergymen and students who took to the road during their vacations."[23] By 1831 the Harpers had two hundred agents selling advance subscriptions "in all twenty-five states, The District of Columbia, Arkansaw [*sic*] Territory, Choctow (Indian) Nation, Canada, and South America."[24] Furthermore, the *National Preacher* was collected and sold as an annual volume. Eugene Exman remarks that this magazine "was important for two reasons: it helped the brothers build up a list of agents and it demonstrated the value of a series, or library, of books."[25] Many of the agents, additional wholesalers, and retailers in places like Richmond, Cincinnati, and St. Louis were ready and willing to sell the Harpers' other publications as well.

IMPROVEMENTS IN TRANSPORTATION AND PRINTING TECHNOLOGY

For many years agents traveled mostly on horseback or in horse-drawn wagons, and shipped their books by wagon. In the mid-nineteenth century, however, there was a transportation revolution. Ronald J. Zboray describes the two stages of this revolution and their effects on the distribution of books in his *A Fictive People: Antebellum Economic Development and the American Reading Public.*[26] During the first stage, agents and books could travel by stagecoach on improved roads (such as the National Pike), by canal boat on the Erie Canal (which had just opened in 1825), and by steamboat on the Ohio River (the Age of Steam had just begun). Or they would travel by ship if going along the Atlantic seaboard to Charleston, Savannah, and around to New Orleans.[27] During the second stage of the transportation revolution, it was the railroad that finally "opened a national mass market for books and assured easy distribution of literature from publishers in New York, Philadelphia, and Boston."[28] Zboray remarks:

> Railroad development transformed the nature of community life for readers and oriented them outward to the national culture and away from local exigencies. Local institutions had to be ever more aware of the national context of their existence and had to make peace with the emerging national mass culture.[29]

The Harpers' success depended not only on Methodist connections, a network of agents, and improvements in transportation, but also on their ability to take advantage of the latest innovations in printing technology. New machines and techniques removed the physical barriers to mass production that had existed before. Foudrinier (1799) and Gilpin (1816) papermaking machines could produce paper on large continuous rolls instead of sheet by sheet. New cylindrical presses revolutionized the printing of newspapers. New steam-driven, flat bed presses proved much faster than the horse-powered and human-powered presses they replaced, and required no great strength to operate. The Harpers retired the horse that had powered the presses to the their Long Island farm and replaced many of their journeymen pressmen with "girls" and managers.[30]

The innovation in printing technology that contributed most directly to the Harpers' ability to produce a great quantity of books year after year was stereotyping. This is the process by which a mold is made of a type set and then used to cast a permanent metal plate that could be stored away and used for subsequent printings. The "advantages of stereotyping are confined to works in very large demand and for which the demand is continued long after the first publication. This allows the printer to always ensure that the market shall be supplied, while the stock is kept low."[31] Stereotyping also "encouraged publishers to engage in in-depth, long-term advertising campaigns" to boost not only the sales of a particular work but of related works by the same author or in the same series.[32] This technology was introduced to New York in 1813.[33] The Harpers made their first stereotypes in 1818 for the *Prayer Book of the Protestant Episcopal Church*, and were thus among the first publishers to do their own stereotyping.[34] By 1830 it had become a fairly regular procedure for them. Stereotyped series such as the Family Library and the School District Library were especially profitable and kept the firm alive through boom and bust cycles.[35] This technology also changed the character of the printing labor force by diminishing the work available for typographers and compositors.[36] The initial cost of making stereotypes was high, but publishers anticipated useful savings and progress for all:

> The capital which is thus saved by the process of stereotyping, involving as it does all the savings of interest, of insurance, of warehouse-room, and all those other manifold charges which attach to a large stock, of necessity goes to the encouragement of other literary enterprises, and of various labour which they involve.[37]

Improvements in printing technology have been given credit for the rapid development of the book trade, the lowering of prices, and the democratization of literature. However, they did not cause "such a drop in the price of books as to make them widely available."[38] While newspapers and religious tracts became affordable to the average worker earning $1.00 a day, most books continued to cost between $0.75 and $1.25. Clearly, for those "who had neither access to nor means for the purchase of books, libraries were of major importance."[39]

THE ECONOMIC AND CULTURAL ADVANTAGES OF PUBLISHERS' LIBRARIES

There were several economic advantages to publishing a library. Because of their physical uniformity, the books were cheaper to print, bind, and transport. Each book acquired additional value and appeal by virtue of its relation to other, often more desirable works in the series. Each book could be advertised at almost no extra cost wherever and whenever the series was mentioned. Demand for a book would continue as long as there was any desire for the series. With stereotyping it became simpler to print additional copies and maintain a constant supply of any title. It was also easier to offer customers more options, such as special groupings and different bindings. The Harpers repackaged the same title in several different libraries. They printed the name of the library and volume number only on the cover, not in the book or on its title page. Turning Family Library no. 11, Scott's *Letters on Demonology*, into School District Library no. 179 was simply a matter of changing covers.

There were also intellectual and cultural advantages to publishing and marketing a library, especially if it was supposed to be educational and morally instructive. Education required a course of reading, and a person seeking education was in the market for not one but several works, preferably works that were authoritative and part of an established system of knowledge. A person seeking moral improvement also found a library useful. If a man or woman knew that one work in the library had a certain general quality, such as moral authority, then he or she might think the other works possessed the same quality.

When advertising their libraries, publishers emphasized the uniform quality not only of the binding but also of the contents. The Harpers stressed that each work in the Family Library would be selected by a learned committee:

> Several gentlemen of high literary acquirements and correct taste, having been engaged to examine all new works as they emanate from the English press ... the public may rest assured that no works will be published by J. & J. H. but such as are interesting, instructive, and moral.[40]

Even after the Family Library had gained a good reputation, they continued to reassure the public: "Great pains have been taken that all the works selected to compose this series should be of the highest order as to literary merit, of the most instructive and pleasing character and entirely unexceptionable in their moral tendency and design."[41] Such assurance was undoubtedly attractive to those Americans in the East or on the Western frontier who felt insecure about their level of cultural sophistication or worried about their moral fitness.

When were the first "libraries" published? *The Oxford English Dictionary* (2nd ed.) gives early examples in its definition of "library" 2.b:

> Often used in the titles given by publishers to a series or set of books uniform or similar in external appearance, and ostensibly suited for some particular class of readers or for students of a particular subject, as in "The Library of Useful Knowledge" (1826–1856), "The Parlour Library" (consisting of novels, 1847–1863), "Bohn's Standard Library," etc. Formerly also in the titles of bibliographical works, and of periodicals.

The earliest usage, from 1692, refers to the title of a monthly journal. Despite a few other examples of pre–nineteenth-century usage, it seems that one of the earliest publisher's libraries in the English speaking world was Constable's Miscellany of Original and Selected Publications in the Various Departments of Literature, Science, & the Arts. Archibald Constable began publishing his Miscellany in Edinburgh sometime in the period of 1825 to 1827.[42] It cost 3s.6d (75 cents) per volume and reached eighty-two volumes before ceasing in 1835.[43] The London publisher Charles Knight, in cooperation with the Society for the Diffusion of Useful Knowledge, started the Library of Useful Knowledge in 1827 and the Library of Entertaining Knowledge in 1829, both at 4s.6d ($1.00) per volume. Knight and the Society, a Whig organization founded by Lord Brougham, intended these libraries for the education of the laboring classes. Their effort at social reform was soon matched in April 1829 when London's "most distinguished publisher," John Murray, created the Family Library, "the first Tory series of cheap books."[44] This Family Library consisted entirely of original copyrighted works intended for the common reader, selling at 5s ($1.25) per volume. By 1834, the year in which he discontinued this "remarkable effort to publish across class lines," Murray had issued twenty-two titles.[45] Nearly all of the works in these useful libraries were non-fiction.

The Harpers took the name for their own Family Library from Murray. They also took several of his titles without permission. Such "piracy" was both common and legal before the recognition of international copyright.[46] Thirteen works in Harper's Family Library were originally Murray's (see Appendix A). Borrowing from other British publishers as well, the Harpers acknowledged the works in the "various Libraries and Miscellanies now preparing in Europe, particularly the 'National' and the 'Edinburgh Cabinet' Libraries," and announced their intention to submit these works to their "committee of literary gentlemen" for possible inclusion in Harper's Family Library.[47] The Edinburgh Cabinet Library (Edinburgh, London: Oliver & Boyd, 1832–1852?) proved to be an especially rich source of titles.

In America several libraries appeared at about the same time as Harper's. The American Society for the Diffusion of Useful Knowledge, with headquarters in Boston, began publishing the American Library of Useful Knowledge in 1831. By reprinting British works from the original Library of Useful Knowledge and by introducing a few American works, the Society hoped to educate the masses and compete with the brash upstarts in New York.[48] They explained the need for the American Library of Useful Knowledge as follows:

> Notwithstanding the apparent abundance of books, and the constant outcry about their rapid multiplication and wide circulation, it is a literal fact, that

the best which appear are not accessible to the reading public, who, for want of them are compelled to the great detriment of their taste and morals, to take up with such as they can get. The effect of the present undertaking will be to apply a partial remedy to this evil; to place at the disposal of the community, in a cheap though at the same time very handsome form, a series of really valuable works on the several branches of learning, which, taken together will constitute of themselves a tolerably complete family library.[49]

There is only one significant difference between this plan and the Harper plan: the absence of the idea that the works should be interesting. The American Library of Useful Knowledge did not succeed, in part, because the British works it reprinted were too scientific and dry to appeal to a mass audience.[50] The Harpers reprinted British works too, but made sure that the works had already proved entertaining and popular. The Harper editions were also "carefully prepared from the last English edition with the omission of such parts as were deemed to be the least interesting, and some few verbal alterations in order to render it more useful and acceptable to the American reader."[51] Another reason for the failure of The American Library of Useful Knowledge was its cost of 62½ cents per volume. This was too expensive for the intended audience.

Also in the 1830s and 1840s, The American Sunday School Union, "the first national organization committed to universal basic literacy," issued at least four cheap libraries.[52] These included, by 1851, The Juvenile Library, A Child's Cabinet Library, the Village and Family Library, and the popular Sunday School and Family Library, which had one hundred books and sold for only ten dollars.[53] Most of these were children's books. There were also several publishers interested in promoting contemporary American authors. Wiley and Putnam's Library of American Books (1845–47), edited by Evert Duyckinck, was noteworthy in this regard. It featured fiction, poetry, literary criticism, and travelogues by authors such as Hawthorne, Melville, Poe, Fuller, and Simms.[54]

The Development and Contents of Harper's Family Library

If we assume that a successful publishing firm like Harper & Brothers often managed to understand and cater to the interests of its customers, then a list of its publications ought to reflect the topics and genres that were particularly important to or popular among its customer population. The growth of the Harper's Family Library and School District Library collections from 1830 to 1846 reflects several trends in American publishing, education, and literature. The increase, for example, in the number of fictional works in the School District Library indicates the increased willingness of reformers and educators to acknowledge the usefulness and morality of some fiction.

During this period, Harper & Brothers was fast becoming the largest publisher in America and the world.[55] While high volume sales of fiction accounted for some of its success, sales of non-fiction and educational works from the Family and School District libraries were steady and profitable.[56] After discussing the extraordinary success of John Abercrombie's *Inquiries Concerning the Intellectual Powers* (1834), which had sold over twenty thousand volumes, an article in the September 1839 *Southern Literary Messenger* reported that the other volumes in the Family Library sold "excellent well," from seven to twelve thousand each.[57] It would be helpful to know the exact sales of each title and of whole libraries, but this information was lost in the fire that destroyed the Harper plant in 1853.[58] Nevertheless, it is possible using advertisements and reviewers' comments to identify especially popular or well-received titles. This survey encompasses titles in both libraries, beginning with the Family Library.

The Family Library was designed to appeal to individual readers and educational institutions such as churches, schools, libraries, and the family. In 1830 the family home was still "the moral mainstay of the society" and the principal setting for basic education. In their advertisements the Harpers portrayed the *paterfamilias* and his wife reading books by the fireplace or at the family-table, surrounded by their sons and daughters:

> ...the publishers flatter themselves that they shall be able to present to their fellow-citizens a work of unparalleled merit and cheapness, embracing subjects adapted to all classes of readers and forming a body of literature deserving the praise of having instructed many, and amused all; and above every other species of eulogy, of being fit to be introduced, without reserve or exception, by the father of the family to the domestic circle.[59]

The Family Library offered a "collection of works in several departments of literature, forming a complete circle of useful, instructive and entertaining knowledge."[60] Although the Harpers and their literary advisers chose to exclude several genres and subjects (fiction, drama, children's stories, mathematics, and music), they succeeded in developing a collection that covered the world. More than half of the library consisted of history, voyages and travel, and biography.

The histories ranged from accounts of ancient cultures, such as J. Baillie Fraser's *History of Mesopotamia* and Henry Hart Milman's *History of the Jews*, to narratives of recent world events such as Philip de Segur's *History of Napoleon's Expedition to Russia*. Two or three works focused on Europe's Middle Ages, and one, William Robertson's *History of the Reign of the Emperor Charles V*, delved into the sixteenth century. Readers could learn more about these and other eras in the library's national histories of Italy, Spain, Ireland, England, Poland, and Russia. Studies of exotic lands, such as Sir John Francis Davis's *History of China* and Michael Russell's *History of Polynesia*, were balanced by Theodore Dwight's *History of Connecticut* and Charles Lanman's *History of Michigan*. Universal history was represented by Alexander Fraser Tytler's *Universal History* in five volumes, Sharon Turner's *The Sacred History of the World* in three volumes, and Jules Michelet's *Elements of Modern History*.

Voyages and travels were very popular in the early nineteenth century.[61] Europeans and Americans were still exploring many areas of the world: Africa, the Polar Regions, the Pacific, and the American West. Works on Africa included *The Life and Travels of Mungo Park*, Richard Lander's *Travels in Africa*, and Robert Jameson's *Narrative of Discovery and Adventure in Africa*. Sir John Leslie's *Narrative of Discovery in the Polar Seas* and William Parry's *Three Voyages for Discovery of a Northwest*

Passage represented Arctic exploration. Works on the Pacific were John Barrow's *A Description of Pitcairn's Island and Its Inhabitants*, the first book to inform Americans of the mutiny on the ship *Bounty*, and Philipp Franz Siebold's *Manners and Customs of the Japanese in the Nineteenth Century*, a book that piqued readers' curiosity about a country that was still closed to foreigners. American readers were also pleased to have Dana's *Two Years Before the Mast*, and cheap editions of Lewis and Clark's *History of the Expedition* and Alexander von Humboldt's *Travels and Researches*, all of which provided descriptions of North America's Pacific coast.

Biographies of political and military leaders enhanced the Family Library's coverage of history. John Williams's *Life and Actions of Alexander the Great* told of events in the ancient world. J. G. Lockhart' s *Life of Napoleon* and Robert Southey's *Life of Nelson* covered several decades of French and British military history. Biographies of important and exemplary Americans were especially recommended by reformers wanting to strengthen public virtue and national identity. James Paulding's *Life of Washington*, Jeremy Belknap's *American Biography*, and James Renwick's works on Jay, Hamilton, and De Witt Clinton contained much of the Library's information on American politics and government. Thatcher's *Indian Biography*, according to its subtitle, presented a "Historical account of those Individuals who have been distinguished among the North American Indians as Orators, Warriors, Statesmen, and other remarkable characters." Several biographies of explorers and travelers further strengthened the Library's already extensive coverage of the world.

Women were the subjects of only three biographical works: Henry Glassford Bell's *Life of Mary Queen of Scots*, Mrs. Anna Jameson's *Memoirs of Celebrated Female Sovereigns*, and John Memes's *Memoirs of the Empress Josephine*. Although not a biography, Mrs. A. J. Grave's *Woman in America: Being an Examination into the Moral and Intellectual Condition of American Female Society* was notable for expressing diverse opinions on the roles and identities of women.

Much of the science, natural history, religion, philosophy, and art in the Family Library was also found in biographies. David Brewster's *The Martyrs of Science; Or the Lives of Galileo, Tycho Brahe and Kepler* is representative of these. Science was itself the subject of Brewster's *Letters on Natural Magic Addressed to Sir Walter Scott* and Lord Brougham's *A Discourse on the Objects, Advantages, and Pleasures of Science*. Geology and natural history were represented by Charles A. Lee's *Elements of Geology*, W. Mullinger Higgins's *The Earth: Its Physical Condition*, James Rennie's *Natural History of Quadrupeds*, and Gilbert White's classic, *The Natural History of Selborne*. Andrew Combe's *Principles of Physiology* and John H. Griscom's *Animal Mechanism and Physiology* covered human anatomy. Mechanics and technology were represented only by Henry Moseley's *Illustrations of Mechanics* and Edward Hazen's *Popular Technology, or, Professions and Trades*, a work recommended for youth. Agriculture was represented by only one book, Edwin Lankester's *Vegetable Substances Used for the Food of Man*. This coverage of agriculture seems woefully inadequate when one considers that the country's economy and population were still predominantly agrarian.

There were several works in religion and philosophy. G. R. Gleig's *The History of the Bible* and William Paley's *Natural Theology* represented Judeo-Christian religion specifically, while several other works already mentioned, such as Turner's

Sacred History, treated their subjects within a religious framework. *The Life of Mohammed* by George Bush, a professor of Hebrew at New York University, was the first original American work in the Family Library. In philosophy there were Bacon's *Essays*, Locke's *The Conduct of Understanding*, Fenelon's *Lives of the Ancient Philosophers*, and the popular works of John Abercrombie, as much psychology as they were philosophy. C. S. Henry's *An Epitome of the History of Philosophy* was a translation of a French work by Louis Bautain "adapted by the University of France for instruction in the colleges and high schools." A reviewer for the *Southern Literary Messenger* wrote that it was "too much epitomised to be of any practicable utility...."[62] A reviewer for *The Ladies Repository*, however, urged that this *Epitome* "be introduced immediately as a text-book in all our schools, academies, and colleges."[63] Selected and edited for the common reader, such works inevitably received negative reviews from some scholars.

There were two works on economics: Francis Lieber's *Essays on Property and Labor* and Alonzo Potter's *Political Economy*. One book each was devoted to education and law, Henry I. Smith's *Education* and William A. Duer's *A Course of Lectures on the Constitutional Jurisprudence of the United States*.

The arts of painting and sculpture were treated in the biographical perspective of Allan Cunningham's *Lives of Eminent Painters and Sculptors*. Poetry was represented by two anthologies, both compiled by Americans: William Cullen Bryant's *Selections from American Poets* and Fitz-Greene Halleck's *Selections from the British Poets*. Finally, literature, especially poetry, was the subject of James Montgomery's *Lectures on General Literature, Poetry, &c.*

THE DEVELOPMENT AND CONTENTS OF HARPER'S SCHOOL DISTRICT LIBRARY

Thus far we have dealt with Harper's Family Library, a collection developed for individuals, families, and the private institutions responsible for most of the educational activity in the United States prior to the rise of common schools. With the "major upsurge in common schooling after 1830" and the increased involvement of state governments in education, a number of social reformers and educators proposed the establishment of free, tax-supported libraries attached to school districts, "but intended for both adults and children."[64] In 1835 the New York legislature, acting on the proposals of James S. Wadsworth, "the father of the school-district libraries of New York," passed a law that permitted voters in any school district to tax themselves up to twenty dollars in the first year and ten dollars in any succeeding years for the purpose of purchasing a library for the district. For Wadsworth and other civic-minded reformers whose ideology of literacy emphasized nation-building as well as character-building, free tax-supported libraries were, in part, a means to help stabilize frontier communities and safeguard democracy: "The stability of government and the security of property in all republics, depend, in great measure, upon the information of the common people."[65] Using political arguments, the advocates of school district libraries emphasized that the collections would contain "the history of nations, and especially that of our own country, the progress and triumph of the democratic principle in the governments on this continent."[66] Using economic arguments, they emphasized practical, scientific knowledge and recommended "instructive treatises upon political economy and agriculture, which cannot be without their just influence."[67]

Education reformers in other states also persuaded their legislatures of the need for tax-supported libraries. Massachusetts and Michigan passed school district library legislation in 1837, Connecticut in 1839, Rhode Island and the Iowa Territory in 1840, and Indiana in 1841.[68] By 1876 at least nineteen states had authorized some form of tax-supported library in their school districts.

After passage of the 1835 legislation, it became clear that very few New Yorkers would vote to tax themselves for the full cost of a library. Therefore the legislature passed a more generous law in April 1838 that distributed $55,000 annually for three years to the school districts on the condition that each district match its portion of the subsidy and spend the combined amount on a library.[69] The power over book selection, although vested in the districts' elected trustees, was now exercised by the superintendent of common schools. To guide the trustees, Superintendent John C. Spencer distributed a list of titles acceptable for purchase. He also urged consideration of the cheap libraries published by Harper & Brothers.[70] Despite complaints about the state's interference in what many thought a local responsibility, the new library program proved to be remarkably successful. In 1841 Governor William H. Seward reported:

> Of these school districts, there are very few which have not complied with the act providing for the establishment of School District Libraries, and there are at this time in these various district libraries about one million of volumes. Within the five years limited by the law, there will have been expended in the purchase of books, more than half a million of dollars.[71]

By 1846 there would be approximately 1,145,250 volumes in 10,812 New York school districts, an average of 106 volumes per district.[72] Other states, too, would revise their permissive library laws and subsidize district libraries.

The Harpers had been planning a school district library of their own since 1836.[73] In 1839, when Governor Seward announced the state's plan to invest over half-a-million dollars over five years on school district libraries, Fletcher Harper saw a great opportunity and traveled to Albany to meet Superintendent Spencer, the official in charge of recommending books to the districts. Fletcher was introduced to him by Thurlow Weed, the influential editor of the *Albany Journal*, a leading Whig, and an old friend of James Harper. The superintendent was impressed by Fletcher and realized that the Harpers could help his office overcome many of the difficulties in supplying ten thousand districts with cheap editions of approved works. According to Exman, Fletcher "left Albany with a commission in his pocket," the first known "state adoption."[74]

The Commonwealth of Massachusetts also turned to the Harpers at about the same time. In 1837 the Massachusetts School Commission under the leadership of Horace Mann appointed a committee to select titles for their own school district library, the Massachusetts School Library. They appointed the Boston publisher Marsh, Capen, Lyon & Webb to produce and package the libraries.[75] The publisher completed thirty-eight volumes by 1840 but then went out of business. Harper &

Brothers immediately bought the rights and the plates and began publishing the Massachusetts School Library for the Commonwealth. They also sold many of their own Harper's School District Libraries to Massachusetts.[76]

The Harpers' opportunism, although conspicuous, was not unique. Indeed, the sudden rise of tax-supported libraries in several states provided a "rich harvest" for publishers and booksellers.[77] In his *Foundations of the Public Library*, Jesse H. Shera reports:

> Soon publisher participation in local politics became so prevalent and subject to so many abuses that the state of New York found it necessary to pass, in 1856, a law forbidding school commissioners to act as the agents of publishers in the awarding of contracts for book purchase.[78]

Despite abuses and many shortcomings, the school district library system marked a significant advance in the development of American public libraries. Carleton Bruns Joeckel summarizes its contribution:

> Of the three essentials for an efficient library—books, staff, and building—the school-district system provided only books, and those inadequately. Nevertheless, it did much to establish certain principles which form the basis of our present public library system. For one thing, it provided for taxation for free library service and also for state aid to libraries, both important milestones in library history. Even more significant, perhaps, it recognized the library as an educational agency, an extension of the system of public education beyond the formal instruction offered by the schools; in other words, it was a movement toward what we now call "adult education."[79]

What were the differences between the Family and School District Libraries' collections? Although the School District Library shared 110 of its 210 titles with the Family Library, it differed from its precursor in several ways. It featured a higher proportion of agricultural and scientific works, juvenile literature, works by women, and "safe" fiction (see Appendix B). Its collection expanded in this way to meet the expectations of a broader audience and to address the needs of public instruction. In addition to the individuals, families, Sunday schools, and private institutions that had been purchasing the Family Library, the Harpers' audience now included more farmers, artisans, and trustees in the school districts, as well as legislators, superintendents of common schools, and governors in state capitals.

To meet the practical economic, technological, and scientific concerns of their new customers, the Harpers expanded their small selection of works on agriculture and science. They introduced editions of John Armstrong's *A Treatise on Agriculture*, Jesse Buel's *The Farmer's Instructor*, Jean-Antoine-Claude Chaptal's *Chemistry Applied to Agriculture*, and Micajah R. Cock's *American Poultry Book*. To those interested in mechanics and physics, they offered *Applications of the Science of Mechanics to Practical Purposes* by James Renwick and a theoretical overview of physics, *On the Connection of the Physical Sciences*, by Mary Somerville.

At least twelve women, seven of them American, contributed over twenty titles. Most of their works were moralistic, didactic fiction intended for young readers. Several had previously appeared in Harper's Boy's and Girl's Library. Maria J. McIntosh, an American who sometimes wrote under the name of Aunt Kitty, provided four works, including *Praise and Principles: Or, For What Shall I Live?* Another American, the popular Catherine M. Sedgwick, had five works, among them *The Poor Rich Man and the Rich Poor Man*. Other Americans with juvenile fiction were E. J. Cate, Mrs. Mary S. B. Dana (no relation to Richard Henry Dana, Jr.), Madeline Leslie, and Harriet Beecher Stowe, whose *Mayflower: or, Sketches of Scenes and Characters among the Descendants of the Pilgrims* was praised as a "series of beautiful and deeply-interesting tales, remarkable for a vigorous yet disciplined imagination."[80]

American women contributed a few works of non-fiction as well: *Life in Prairie Land* by Mrs. Eliza Farnham, *Tales from American History* by Eliza Robbins, and a work about women, *Sketches of the Lives of Distinguished Females ... Written for Girls, with a View to their Mental and Moral Improvement*, by an American Lady (Ann Hasseltine Judson).

The Rev. Francis L. Hawks, a popular preacher in the City of New York, wrote seven of the children's books in the library. His series "Uncle Philip's Conversations with the Children" ranged over a variety of topics from whaling to forestry, but history was Hawks's forte. The School District Library also included *Flowers of Fable*. Ever wary of their educational customers being shocked by fiction, the Harpers' advertisement for *Flowers of Fable* stated: "We think the reader will be pleased to find no vulgarity, no low scurrilous expressions or allusions. The purest taste and the most delicate modesty will meet with nothing to offend on the pages of this elegant little volume."[81] The most famous children's book in the library, a moralistic blend of fiction and natural history, was *The Swiss Family Robinson* by Johann David Wyss, translated from the German. "The purpose of this pleasing story is to convey instruction in the arts and Natural History, and, at the same time, to inculcate by example principles which tend to the promotion of social happiness."[82]

Although religious and educational reformers had come to acknowledge and appreciate the usefulness of some fiction in conveying moral lessons to children, many were still reluctant to recommend fiction to adults. The Harpers decided, nevertheless, to include one safe work of adult fiction in the library, Oliver Goldsmith's *The Vicar of Wakefield*.

Except for the fiction, children's literature, works by women, and the agricultural and scientific works, the collection profile of the School District Library remained similar to that of the Family Library. Works in history, voyages and travel, and biography continued to appear. Remarkably, the reader found two historical works by Friedrich Schiller covering "wars of religion" in the sixteenth and seventeenth centuries, *History of the Revolt of the Netherlands* and *History of the Thirty Years' War*. *The Orations of Demosthenes*, *Plutarch's Lives*, Xenophon's *The Cyropædia, or, Institution of Cyrus*, and Joseph Salkeld's *Classical Antiquities* demonstrated a stronger interest in ancient Greece and Rome. There was also a notable combination of voyages: Andrew Kippis's *Voyages Round the World from the Death of Captain Cook to the Present Time* and Charles Darwin's *Journal of Researches into the Natural History & Geology of the Countries Visited during the Voyage of H.M.S. Beagle*. The largest addition to biography and to the library as a whole was the nine-volume *American Biography*, "conducted by" Jared Sparks. Finally, the art of music was represented by Edward Holmes's *The Life of Mozart*.

CONCLUSION

From the 1830s through the 1850s the Harpers sold millions of books from the Family Library and School District Library to individuals, families, libraries, and private and public institutions, including thousands of school districts from Massachusetts and New York to Michigan and Indiana. The dissemination of so many good cheap books over so wide an area would have amazed and delighted the Methodist circuit riders who had visited the Harper home. In contrast to Thoreau, who found the ubiquitous influence of the Harpers and their "entirely unexceptionable" books disturbing, the unidentified author of "A Day Among Bookmen and Bibliopoles," the article excerpted at the beginning of this paper, expressed his approval of their influence:

> How important is it, in view of this powerful influence over the public mind, that the energies of the *Harperian* press should be directed to proper ends? How vitally momentous to the morals of a great continent that good books alone should be sent forth under the sanction of their approval!

It was certainly important to many of their customers that the books had been approved and recommended as "interesting, instructive and moral." The Harpers and their "gentlemen of high literary acquirements and correct taste," in consultation with educators and state officials, spent more than sixteen years developing these collections. They also closely monitored the sales and reviews of each work after its release, which enabled them to reconsider subsequent selections. In an otherwise excellent commentary on the district libraries, Jesse H. Shera refers to Harper's School District Library as an example of a "hastily assembled set of standard authors."[83] My research supports instead David Kaser's assertion that these libraries consisted of "carefully pre-selected titles" and made it possible for many communities lacking selection expertise to acquire "rather well-balanced regimens of reading."[84]

Although Harper's Family and School District Libraries represent an effort to influence and make a profit on the education of the American masses, it was an effort welcomed by many, especially the social and educational reformers who agreed with the Harpers about the people's need for cheap books that provided useful information and moral instruction. The accord that reigned between the publisher and leaders in education contributed to their mutual success. In their advertisements the Harpers used quotations from leading educators, who in their own speeches seemed to echo the rhetoric of the advertisements. Caleb Mills, the superintendent of public instruction for Indiana in 1854, and one of Harper's biggest customers, summarized the purposes and advantages of their libraries. He concluded that such well-selected libraries would improve the moral, intellectual, and economic condition of the people and the state:

> [The books] should also be of the choicest character, both in sentiment, diction and design, for their perusal will modify, control and characterize, in no slight degree, the style, language and opinions of the rising generation; nor will they be without their influence on maturer years.... In this way impor-

tant assistance could be rendered the parent, the teacher, the mechanic, the farmer, the merchant and the devotee of science. Each might receive valuable hints and suggestions that would give new impulse to effort, fresh inspiration to hope, and materially modify all their subsequent course.... A library based on such principles of selection could not fail to prove an inestimable blessing, both to the rising and risen generation, an honor to the State, and a rich source of moral and intellectual elevation to the people of every township.[85]

APPENDIX A
HARPER'S FAMILY LIBRARY (FL). WORKS LISTED WITH VOLUME NUMBERS IN BOTH THE FAMILY LIBRARY AND HARPER'S SCHOOL DISTRICT LIBRARY (SDL).

Harper's Family Library (1830–1842) had a total of 127 works in 187 volumes. One hundred and ten of these works were reissued in the SDL. The form of each title is based on its entry in *Harper's Illustrated Catalogue of Valuable Standard Works* (New York: Harper & Brothers, 1847).

* = work previously published in Murray's *Family Library* (London: John Murray, 1829–1834).

Titles	FL no.	SDL no.
Abercrombie's Essay on the Intellectual Powers	37	22
Abercrombie's Philosophy of the Moral feelings	58	40
Bacon's Essays, and Locke on the Understanding	171	170
Barrow's Life of Peter the Great*	65	35
Barrow's Pitcairn's Island and the Mutiny	31	86
Belknap's American Biography	161–163	146–148
Bell's Life of Mary Queen of Scots	21–22	285–286
Brewster's Letters on Natural Magic*	50	98
Brewster's Life of Sir Isaac Newton*	26	27
Brewster's Lives of Galileo, Tycho Brahe, and Kepler	130	152
Brougham's Pleasures and Advantages of Science	179	126
Bryant's Selections from American Poets	111	114
Bucke's Beauties, Harmonies and Sublimities of Nature	145	163
Bucke's Ruins of Ancient Cities	134–135	160–161
Bunner's History of Louisiana	176	180
Bush's Life of Mohammed	10	
Camp on Democracy	138	
Circumnavigation of the Globe	82	31
Combe's (Andrew) Principles of Physiology	71	15
Court and Camp of Napoleon	29	181
Crichton's History of Arabia	68–69	
Croly's Life of George IV	15	
Cunningham's Lives of Celebrated Painters	17–19, 66–67	229–231
Dana's Two Years Before the Mast	106	127
Davenport's Perilous Adventures	159	158
Davis's China and the Chinese	80–81	29–30
Dick's Celestial Scenery	83	24
Dick's Improvement of Society	59	
Dick's Sidereal Heavens	99	135
Dover's Life of Frederick the Great	41–42	
Duer's Constitutional Jurisprudence of the U.S.	160	232

Titles	FL no.	SDL no.
Dwight's History of Connecticut	133	139
Euler's Natural Philosophy	55–56	33–34
Fenelon's Lives of the Ancient Philosophers	140	156
Ferguson's History of the Roman Republics Abridged	187	214
Fletcher's History of Poland	24	182
Florian's Moors in Spain	177	117
Franklin, Life and Writings of Franklin	92–93	51–52
Fraser's Historical and Descriptive Account of Persia	70	187
Fraser's History of Mesopotamia	157 .	201
Galt's Life of Lord Byron	9	
Gleig's History of the Bible	12–13	
Graves's (Mrs.) Woman in America	166	184
Griscom's Animal Mechanism	85	57
Hale's United States	119–120	96–97
Halleck's Selections from British Poets	112–113	115–116
Hazen's Popular Technology	149–150	177–178
Head's Life of Bruce, The African Traveler*	128	121
Henry's Epitome of the History of Philosophy	143–144	174–175
Higgins's Physical Condition of the Earth	78	39
History of Iceland, Greenland, and the Faroe Islands	131	155
History of Denmark, Sweden and Norway	136–137	164–165
Humboldt's Travels and Researches	54	80
Irving's Life and Writings of Oliver Goldsmith	121–122	109–110
James's History of Chivalry and the Crusades	20	26
James's History of Charlemagne	60	176
Jameson's (Mrs.) Discovery and Adventure in Africa	16	18
Jameson's (Mrs.) Lives of Celebrated Female Sovereigns	33–34	41–42
Keightley's History of England	114–118	102–106
Lander's Travels in Africa*	35–36	171–172
Lanman's History of Michigan	139	159
Lee's Elements of Geology	178	86
Leslie's Discovery in the Polar	14	67
Lewis and Clarke's Travels	154–155	198–199
Lieber's Essays on Property and Labor	146	162
Life of Dr. Johnson	109–110	122–123
Lives and Voyages of Drake, Cavendish, Dampier	30	48
Lives of Distinguished Men of Modern Times	123–124	118–119
Lockhart's Life of Napoleon*	4–5	13–14
Lossing's History of the Fine Arts	103	157
Mackenzie's Life of O. H. Perry	126–127	107–108
Maury's Principles of Eloquence	184	183
Memes's Memoirs of the Empress Josephine	28	173
Michelet's Elements of Modern History	170	241
Milman's History of the Jews*	1–3	
Montgomery's Lectures on Literature	64	23
Moseley's Illustrations of Mechanics	180	66
Mudie's Guide to the Observation of Nature	57	20
Murray's British India	47–49	
Murray's Historical Account of British America	101–102	111–112
Murray's Travels of Marco Polo	173	275
Natural History of Insects*	8, 74	67
Natural History of the Elephant	164	58
Paley's Natural Theology	96–97	68–69
Park, Life and Travels of Mungo Park	105	125
Parry's Three Voyages to the North Pole	107–108	100–101

Titles	FL no.	SDL no.
Paulding's Life of Washington	75–76	1–2
Potter's Hand–book for Readers and Students	165	242
Potter's Political Economy	183	124
Pursuit of Knowledge Under Difficulties	94–95	55–56
Rennie's Natural History of Birds	98	82
Rennie's Natural History of Quadrupeds	104	89
Renwick's Life of John Jay and Alexander Hamilton	129	
Renwick's life of De Witt Clinton	125	
Robertson's History of America Abridged	185	213
Robertson's History of Charles V Abridged	186	219
Russell's View of Ancient and Modern Egypt	23	
Russell's History of Palestine	27	25
Russell's History of Polynesia	158	224
Russell's History of the Barbary States	73	137
Russell's Life of Oliver Cromwell	62–63	36–37
Russell's Nubia and Abyssinia	61	185
Sargent's American Adventure by Land and Sea	174–175	153–154
Scott's Letters on Demonology*	11	179
Segur's History of Napoleon's Expedition to Russia	141–142	150–151
Selections from the Spectator	181–182	84–85
Sforzosi's History of Italy	79	
Siebold's Japan and the Japanese	132	149
Smedley's Sketches from Venetian History*	43–44	233–234
Smith's Festivals, Games	25	277
Smith's History of Education	156	209
Southey's Life of Lord Nelson*	6	295
Spalding's History of Italy	151–153	203–205
St. John's Lives of Celebrated Travelers	38–40	
Stone's Border Wars of the Revolution	167–168	
Taylor's History of Ireland	51–52	
Thatcher's Indian Biography	45–46	168–169
Ticknor's Philosophy of Living	77	
Turner's Sacred History of the World	32, 72, 84	238–240
Tytler's Discovery in North America	53	207
Tytler's Universal History*	86–89	60–65
Upham on Imperfect and Disordered Mental Action	100	113
Vegetable Substances Used for the Food of Man	169	59
Voyages Around the World	172	294
White's Natural History of Selborne	147	166
William's Life of Alexander*	7	32
Wrangell's Expedition to Siberia	148	167

Appendix B
Harper's School District Library (SDL) continued.
Works listed are those not found in Harper's Family Library

The School District Library (1838–1846) had a total of 210 works in 295 volumes. The 100 works listed below did not duplicate works in the Family Library. The 110 works duplicated in the Family Library are indicated in Appendix A.

Titles	SDL no.
Alden's Elizabeth Benton	288
Armstrong's Treatise on Agriculture	88

Titles	SDL no.
Barrow's Three Voyages within the Arctic Regions	258
Bell's Life of Rt. Hon. George Canning	261
Biblical Legends of the Mussulmans	260
Blake's Juvenile Companion	283
Buel's Farmer's Instructor	53–54
Butler's Analogy of Religion	222
Cate's (Miss E. J.) Year with the Franklins	276
Chaptal's Chemistry Applied to Agriculture	90
Cock's American Poultry-book	228
Combe's (George) The Constitution of Man	220
Cook's Voyages Around the World	211
Crowe's History of France	141–143
Dana's (Mrs.) Young Sailor	287
Darwin's Voyage of a Naturalist Round the World	255–256
Day's Sandford and Merton	218
Dendy's Philosophy of Mystery	248
Dick's Practical Astronomer	250
Dunham's History of Spain and Portugal	191–195
Dunlap's History of New York	49–50
Dwight's Signers of the Declaration of Independence	91
Edgeworth's (Miss) Moral Tales	244–245
Edgeworth's (Miss) Rosamond	243
Ellis's (Mrs.) Temper and Temperament	272
Familiar Illustrations of Natural Philosophy	83
Family Instructor. By a Parent	138
Farnham's (Mrs.) Life in Prairie Land	257
Feuerbach's Remarkable German Criminal Trials	254
Flowers of Fable	271
Francis's Orators of the Age	269
Frost's Beauties of English History	278
Frost's Beauties of French History	280
Gaylord and Tucker's American Husbandry	129–130
Goldsmith's History of Greece	81
Goldsmith's History of Rome, abridged	87
Goldsmith's Vicar of Wakefield	225
History of Switzerland	190
History of the American Revolution	282
Hofland's (Mrs.) The Son of a Genius	8
Hofland's (Mrs.) Young Crusoe	210
Holmes's Life of Mozart	249
Horne's New Spirit of the Age	273
Howitt's (Mary) Who shall be the Greatest?	235
Hughes's (Mrs.) The Ornaments Discovered	44
Hutton's Book of Nature Laid Open	289
Isabel, or, the Trials of the Heart	281
Johnson's Economy of Health	217
Keeping House and Housekeeping	293
Keppel's Expedition to Borneo	263
Leland's Demosthenes	236–237
M'Intosh's (Miss M. J.) Conquest and Self-Conquest	200
M'Intosh's (Miss M. J.) Woman of Enigma	221
M'Intosh's (Miss) Praise and Principle	274
M'Intosh's (Miss) The Cousins	279
Mackenzie's Life of Paul Jones	251–252
Moore's Power of the Soul Over the Body	270

Titles	SDL no.
Moore's Use of the Body in Relation to the Mind	265
Nott's Counsels to Young Men	120
Paley's Evidences of Christianity	216
Parental Instruction	284
Parrott's Ascent of Mount Ararat	253
Perils of the Sea	21
Plutarch's Lives	92–95
Renwick's First Principles of Chemistry	136
Renwick's Natural Philosophy	196
Renwick's Practical Mechanics	99
Robbin's (Miss) Tales from American History	9–11
Salkeld's Grecian and Roman Antiquities	290
Salverte's Philosophy of Magic	267–268
Schiller's History of the Revolt of the Netherlands	266
Schiller's Thirty Years' War	264
Scott's History of Scotland	144–145
Seaward's Narrative of His Shipwreck	206
Sedgwick's (Miss C. M.) Means and Ends	212
Sedgwick's (Miss) Live and Let Live	28
Sedgwick's (Miss) Love Token	215
Sedgwick's (Miss) Stories for Young Persons	140
Sedgwick's (Miss) The Poor Rich Man and the Rich Poor Man	3
Sismondi's Italian Republics	189
Sketches of the Lives of Distinguished Females	291
Somerville (Mary) on the Physical Sciences	259
Sparks's American Biography	70–79
Stowe's (Mrs. H. B.) Mayflower	197
Swiss Family Robinson	4–5
Taylor's Modern British Plutarch	262
Thatcher's Indian Traits	16–17
Thatcher's Tales of the American Revolution	12
Twin Brothers (by Madeline Leslie)	223
Uncle Philip's American Forest	19
Uncle Philip's Conversations about the History of Virginia	43
Uncle Philip's History of Massachusetts	131–132
Uncle Philip's History of New Hampshire	133–134
Uncle Philip's History of the Lost Colony of Greenland	128
Uncle Philip's Natural History	45
Uncle Philip's Whale Fishery and the Polar Seas	46–47
Wealth and Worth	208
What's to be Done?	202
Whewell's Elements of Morality and Polity	246–247
Xenophon's History of the Expedition of Cyrus	188

Notes

1. "A Day Among Bookmen and Bibliopoles," *Southern Literary Messenger* 14.1 (Jan 1848): 58.

2. Henry D. Thoreau, "Reading," *Walden*, ed. J. Lyndon Shanley (Princeton: Princeton UP, 1971) 109. Redding & Co. was a periodical depot in Boston.

3. Mass-market publishing in the U.S. began in the 1820s and 1830s. According to John Tebbel, "Authorities are generally agreed that the movement toward literature for the masses began in England in 1827 with the establishment by Lord Brougham of the Society for the Diffusion of Knowledge;" see Tebbel, *The Creation of an Industry*, 1630–1865, vol. 1 of *A History of Book Publishing in the United States* (New York: Bowker, 1972) 240–41.

4. The Family Library was still being advertised as late as 1874 in *Harper & Brothers' Descriptive List of Their Publications* (New York: 1874). The School District Library had been dropped from their inventory sometime in the late 1860s.

5. *Two Years Before the Mast* (1840) appeared in both Harper's Family Library and Harper's School District Library, and sold more than 175,000 copies (a number equal to one percent of the population) in the decade 1840–1850, thus becoming a "best seller." *Indian Biography* (1832) sold nearly 125,000 copies in the decade 1832–1842. It was runner-up to three best sellers of 1832: Jacob Abbott, *The Young Christian*; Jane Austen, *Pride and Prejudice*; and Johann David Wyss, *The Swiss Family Robinson*, which appeared as Harper's Boy's and Girl's Library no. 2-3. In 1839 *The Swiss Family Robinson* appeared again as School District Library no. 4-5. See Frank Luther Mott, *Golden Multitudes: The Story of Best Sellers in the United State* (New York: Macmillan, 1947) 306, 318.

6. This quotation appears on the back cover or advertising inserts of nearly every volume of the Family Library. The source is "Apophthegms, Sentiments, Opinions, and Occasional Reflections," in the *Collective Edition of the Works of Samuel Johnson*, ed. Sir John Hawkins, vol. 11 (London: 1787) 196; rpt. in *Johnsoniana: Anecdotes of the Late Samuel Johnson*, ed. Robina Napier (London: George Bell, 1884) 125.

7. "Average Daily Wage Rates of Artisans, Laborers and Agricultural Workers, in the Philadelphia Area: 1785 to 1830," in U.S. Bureau of the Census, *Historical Statistics of the United States: Colonial Times to 1970, Bicentennial Edition*, Part 1 (Washington: GPO, 1975) 163. Family Library volumes were originally priced at forty-five cents each and School District Library volumes at thirty-eight cents each.

8. For a full-page color photograph of a surviving Harper's School District Library in its original wooden case with a catalogue on its door, see Michael Olmert, *The Smithsonian Book of Books* (Washington: Smithsonian Books, 1992) 212. The catalogue pictured was issued by the American Society for the Diffusion of Useful Knowledge and refers to the set as The American School Library. All of the books appear to be in very good condition, except for copies of *The Swiss Family Robinson*, J. G. Lockhart's *Life of Napoleon*, Thatcher's *Indian Traits*, and Mrs. Hughs's *Ornaments Discovered*, a moralistic treatment of natural history for young people.

9. Lee Soltow and Edward Stevens discuss ideologies of literacy in *The Rise of Literacy and the Common School in the United States: A Socioeconomic Analysis to 1870* (Chicago: U of Chicago Press, 1981) 18–22, 58–88.

10. Soltow and Stevens 155. Their estimate is based on the 1840 U.S. Census.

11. Henry S. Randall, quoted in New York Superintendent of Common Schools, *Annual Report, 1842-43*, 208–9; quoted in Sidney Ditzion, "The District-School Library," *Library Quarterly* 10 (1940): 568.

12. Soltow and Stevens 65.

13. James C. Derby, *Fifty Years Among Authors, Books and Publishers* (New York: G. W. Carleton, 1884) 88. Another source that provides details of the Harper brothers' upbringing and early years in business is J. Henry Harper, *The House of Harper: A Century of Publishing in Franklin Square* (New York: Harper & Brothers, 1912) 1–36.

14. John Wesley, *The Letters of John Wesley*, 8 vols., ed. John Telford (London: Epworth Press, 1931) 8: 247; quoted in Michael H. Harris, *The Availability of Books and the Nature of Book Ownership on the Southern Indiana Frontier, 1800–1850*, diss. Indiana U., 1971 (Ann Arbor: UMI, 1971) 33.

15. John Wesley, quoted in James Penn Pilkington, *The Methodist Publishing House: A History* (Nashville: Abingdon House, 1968) 11; quoted in Harris 33.

16. Wesley, *Letters* 7: 138; quoted in Harris 33.

17. Tebbel 186–87, 190.

18. Harris 35.

19. Quoted in Harris 36.

20. Eugene Exman, *The Brothers Harper: A Unique Publishing Partnership and Its Impact Upon the Cultural Life of America from 1817 to 1853* (New York: Harper & Row, 1965) 187–90, 194–95. At the time of the mayoral campaign, some prominent Catholics had been fighting the Bible readings and the use of Protestant books in the city's public schools; see also Tebbel 277.

21. Exman 48; Tebbel 232–34.

22. Exman 5–6.

23. Exman 16.

24. Exman 16.

25. Exman 17.

26. Ronald J. Zboray, *A Fictive People: Antebellum Economic Development and the American Reading Public* (New York: Oxford UP, 1993) 55.

27. Among northeastern publishers, the Harpers had a reputation for extensive connections in the South and in the West; see Zboray 13, 60–65.

28. Zboray 69.

29. Zboray 13. Zboray explores "the deep cultural ramifications of the relationship of the book to the railroad" in his fifth chapter, "The Railroad, the Community and the Book," 69–82.

30. "By 1833, the firm had installed a steam press … and the horse who had walked for years in circles around Daniel Treadwell's horsepower press was retired to the Harpers' Long Island farm, where he gave a classic demonstration of the conditioning process by walking around a tree in the pasture from seven in the morning until six at night, his usual working hours. When the noon whistle blew at a neighboring factory, he took off his customary lunch hour"; Tebbel 275; see also Zboray 6; Harper 25–26.

31. "The Commercial History of a Penny Magazine,—No III," *Monthly Supplement of the Penny Magazine of the Society for the Diffusion of Useful Knowledge* 107 (Nov. 1833): 470. This work appeared in four monthly supplements, Sept.–Dec. 1833. It offers a detailed account of contemporary printing operations and of the publishing ideas of the Society for the Diffusion of Useful Knowledge.

32. Zboray 10.

33. Exman 6.

34. Exman 5–6.

35. Tebbel 276–77.

36. Zboray 10.

37. "The Commercial History of a Penny Magazine,—No III" 472.

38. Zboray 11.

39. Soltow and Stevens, 81.

40. Harper advertisement (1830) quoted in Exman 22. Examiners included George Bush, Dr. James E. DeKay, and Dr. Sidney Doane; see Eugene Exman, *The House of Harper: One Hundred and Fifty Years of Publishing* (New York: Harper & Row, 1967) 11.

41. "Publishers' Advertisement" inserted in front of Thomas Upham, *Outlines of Imperfect and Disordered Mental Action*, Harper's Family Library, 100 (New York: Harper & Brothers, 1841) 2.

42. Sources disagree on the year in which Constable's Miscellany first appeared. The year 1825 is given in "Literature for the People," *The Times* [London] 8 Feb 1854, rpt. in *Littell's Living Age* 543 (Oct. 1854): 119. The year 1826 is from OCLC catalog record 19880502. The year 1827 is from Scott Bennett, "John Murray's Family Library and the Cheapening of Books in Early Nineteenth Century Britain," *Studies in Bibliography* 29 (1976): 141.

43. Prices of British volumes are given in "Literature for the People" 119. The equivalent U.S. prices are based on conversions suggested by Jo McMurty, *Victorian Life and Victorian Fiction: A Companion for the American Reader* (Hamden, CT: Archon, 1979) 47.

44. Bennett 140; "The Family Library," *Blackwood's Edinburgh Magazine* 26.2 (1829): 416.

45. Bennett 141.

46. Tebbel 558–61.

47. Publisher's advertisement on back cover of James A. St. John's *Lives of Celebrated Travelers*, vol. 2, Harper's Family Library 39 (New York: J. & J. Harper, 1832).

48. Tebbel 241. When Tebbel wrote that the American Library of Useful Knowledge (1831) was "without much doubt, the first attempt in America to reach the mass market with low-priced books," he apparently forgot about Harper's Family Library (1830).

49. "Art. IX.—American Library of Useful Knowledge," *North American Review* 33 (1831): 519.

50. Tebbel 242.

51. "Advertisement by the American Publishers" inserted in front of [G. L. Craig], *The Pursuit of Knowledge Under Difficulties: Its Pleasures and Rewards*, rev. ed. the Rev. Dr. Wayland, vol. 1., Harper's School District Library 94 (New York: Harper & Brothers, 1843) i–ii. Craig's work was originally compiled for the London Society for the Diffusion of Useful Knowledge.

52. Zboray 90.

53. Alice B. Cushman, "A Nineteenth Century Plan for Reading: The American Sunday School Movement," *The Hornbook Magazine* 33 (1957): 64–65; see also Anne M. Boylan, *Sunday School: The Formation of an American Institution, 1790–1880* (New Haven: Yale UP, 1988) 49–51.

54. Ezra Greenspan, "Evert Duyckinck and the History of Wiley and Putnam's Library of American Books, 1845–1847," *American Literature* 64 (1992): 678–93.

55. Exman 348. Other publishers among the largest in the world at the time were Longmans of London, Chambers of Edinburgh, and Brockhaus of Leipzig.

56. In 1853, according to an estimate of Henry J. Raymond, of the 1,549 works the Harpers had in print, 690 were general literature, 329 history and biography, 156 educational, 130 travel and adventure, 120 theology and religion, 96 art-science-medicine, and 28 dictionaries and gazetteers; quoted in Exman 358.

57. Probus [Park Benjamin], Letters from New York, No. II," *Southern Literary Messenger* 5.9 (Sept. 1839): 630. According to Benjamin, sales of Abercrombie's *Inquiries* exceeded those of Harper's 50-cent edition of Edward Bulwer-Lytton's bestseller *Rienzi* (1834); see Mott 306.

58. The account books and sales records for the period 1817–1853 were all destroyed; see Christopher Feeney, comp., *Index to the Archives of Harper and Brothers, 1817–1914* (Cambridge: Chadwyck-Healey, 1982). For a detailed account of the fire and damage see Exman 353–62. J. Henry Harper reported that the stereotype plates "were stored in their vaults, and ... were saved. The destruction of these would have been an incalculable loss, not only to the authors and publishers, but to American literature as well;" see Harper, *House of Harper* 97.

59. Publisher's advertisement on back cover of St. John's *Lives of Celebrated Travelers.*

60. *Harper's Illustrated Catalogue of Valuable Standard Works* (New York: Harper & Brothers, 1847) 140.

61. According to J. Henry Harper, the Lyceum movement and lecture bureaus stimulated the growing interest in biographies and works of travel and exploration; see Harper 63.

62. *Southern Literary Messenger* 8.5 (May 1842): 362–63.

63. *The Ladies Repository* 2.4 (April 1842): 127.

64. Soltow and Stevens 3; Joeckel 8.

65. [Barnard's] *American Journal of Education* 5 (1858): 395; quoted in Ditzion 550.

66. [William H. Seward, 1841], State of New York, *Messages from the Governors*, ed. Charles Z. Lincoln, 11 vols. (Albany: J.B. Lyon, 1909) 3: 858.

67. [Seward, 1841], State of New York, *Messages* 3: 878.

68. For an overview of "school library" legislation in the seven states mentioned and fourteen other states, see "School and Asylum Libraries," chap. 2, U.S. Bureau of Education, *Public Libraries in the United States of America: Their History, Condition, and Management: Special Report*, vol. 1 (Washington: GPO, 1876) 38–58. For discussions of school district libraries in the context of American library history, see Carleton Bruns Joeckel, *The Government of the American Public Library* (Chicago: U of Chicago Press, 1935) 8–14; David Kaser, *A Book for a Sixpence: The Circulating Library in America*, Beta Phi Mu Chapbook 14 (Pittsburgh: Beta Phi Mu, 1980) 86–88; and Jesse H. Shera, *Foundations of the Public Library: The Origins of the Public Library Movement in New England, 1629–1855* (Chicago: U of Chicago Press, 1949) 181–84. For summaries of contemporary journal articles on school district libraries, see Haynes McMullen, ed., *Libraries in American Periodicals Before 1876: A Bibliography with Abstracts and an Index* (Jefferson, NC: McFarland, 1983) 54–59.

69. Ditzion 553.

70. Ditzion 565.

71. State of New York, *Messages* 3: 858.

72. [Silas Wright, 1846], State of New York, *Messages* 4: 264.

73. Exman 106.

74. Exman, *House of Harper* 23. The story of Fletcher Harper's meeting with Superintendent Spencer is related in Derby 101–04; Harper 55–57; and Exman 106–08.

75. "Art. IX.—1. The School Library," *North American Review* 50 (April 1840): 505–15.

76. Exman 231, 252.

77. Joeckel 11–12.

78. Shera 240–41.

79. Joeckel 12.

80. *Harper's Illustrated Catalogue* 133.

81. *Harper's Illustrated Catalogue* 128.

82. *Harper's Illustrated Catalogue* 133.

83. Shera 240.

84. Kaser 87.

85. Caleb Mills, *Third Annual Report of the Superintendent of Public Instruction, in Documents of the General Assembly of Indiana at the Thirty-Eighth Session*, Second Part (Indianapolis: Austin H. Brown, 1855) 841.

development of an "American Seamen's Friend Society and Bethel Union."[11] In September Truair published a petition of support for such a national organization signed by one-hundred-and-fourteen ships' masters and mates.[12] Then in October a meeting of New York citizenry convened to develop a nationwide Seamen's Friend Society. In January 1826 another meeting took place that resulted in the adoption of a constitution and the election of officers. The new organization, however, failed to gain sufficient financial support and ceased to exist.

The American Seamen's Friend Society (ASFS) was reorganized in May 1828 with Smith Thompson as president and the Reverend Joshua Leavitt as general agent. Its first action was to begin publishing the *Sailor's Magazine* in order to call attention to itself and to the plight of seamen. The ASFS modeled its journal after *Sailor's Magazine and Naval Miscellany*, a publication of the British and Foreign Seamen's Friend Society and Bethel Union. With this magazine the ASFS leadership hoped to link with "the various local institutions already in existence for the good of seamen." Without these links, "our society can do nothing, in those places where societies already exist, beyond the influence of the Magazine in bringing forward the claims of Seamen, and in reporting the progress and success of various measures for their benefit."[13]

The ASFS became far more comprehensive than the proselytizing organizations that merely distributed tracts. Its goal was to affect all aspects of seamen's lives and to reform what they saw as an unjust economic system where the seamen had no voice.[14] Through the next decade, the ASFS and its auxiliaries built seamen's churches in American ports, supported chaplaincies in foreign ports, and set up boarding houses which prohibited alcohol, obscenity, gaming, and dancing. They formed banks to safeguard wages, handled mail, and aided the shipwrecked.[15] However, due to the corrupting influences of taverns and brothels, the members of the ASFS saw the limitations of reform efforts while the seamen were in port. The ASFS did what it could during the few weeks the seamen were in port, but saw the time at sea, away from these influences, as the period when reforming could be done through reading, "with only the ridicule of shipmates, and the workings of their own sinful hearts" as barriers.[16]

Despite their view of the seaman's life and culture, the members of the ASFS were aware that seamen belonged to a literate class eager for reading material. Boredom was a pervasive complaint on long sea voyages. "One that never was on a long voyage may think this foolish," said one seaman, "but they know little how dull times are sometimes."[17] Reading played a special role during these times for many seamen. William Whitecar wrote of the paucity of fresh reading material on his whale ship:

> On the 23rd of May we spoke the barque Ann, of Sag Harbor, and from her received papers five and a half months old, they were treasures to us, and were read with intense interest, advertisements and all coming in for a share of attention.... Newspapers were also sent to me; and I read them completely through, advertisements and all, with a degree of attention I had never before bestowed on a printed sheet.[18]

In 1837 the ASFS began placing libraries on vessels leaving the port of New York.[19] By 1839 the crews of eighty vessels, out of New York, Boston, Philadelphia, and New

Orleans had received libraries.[20] This experiment then ceased and for two decades no new libraries were loaned to ships.

In 1858 the ASFS renewed its interest in lending traveling libraries to ships. The Reverend H. Loomis, on 23 December 1858, wrote of the ASFS's plans to the Reverend Titus Coan:

> What thinks you of a sea colportage. Say put one or two pious sailors into the forecastle as part of the crew furnished with a library Hymn Books etc. for social meetings & Bible readings. He press gangs to the Chaplains in port, & report to us, all of course with the consent of Captains & owners?[21]

By February Loomis, in search of materials for the ship libraries, had developed the system by which the ships would be supplied with a list of instructions, Bibles, hymn books, tracts, and a small library for the forecastle.[22] By March of 1859 Loomis, in search of materials for the ship libraries, had contacted various private and commercial sources.[23] Before the year was out, ten libraries were sent from the port of Boston.[24]

In the 1860-61 fiscal year an additional 113 libraries were shipped out. By the end of the 1877-78 fiscal year 6,250 new libraries had been sent and 5,175 had been refitted and reshipped.[25] By 1940 the number of new libraries placed on ships reached 33,919.[26] This activity continued until 1967 with the last library leaving from the New York harbor.

DONORS

Although funding came from a variety of sources, including individual donors, ship crews, businesses, and the Women's Christian Temperance Union, nearly half of the libraries were funded by Sunday schools during the early years of the ASFS.[27] Through its publications the ASFS informed each donor about who received the library, the ship it was on, and the success it had in reforming the crew. Each library was given a number:

> The master of the ship *Imperial* writes of No. 9,566. The library you furnished my ship on her last voyage to Shanghai and return was very satisfactory. The books were appreciated by the crew, and I have always found interest in them in the different voyages I have made. I think whoever furnishes any of the books deserve all the thanks which they surely get from all seamen for their kind remembrance of those "who go down to the sea in ships."[28]

Donors kept in contact with the libraries through book plates that featured the name of the Sunday school, society, or individual that donated the library. The book plates asked readers to communicate with the donors personally. The ASFS regularly received letters from seamen with comments such as "the children of the Sabbath School cannot imagine the good which they do in raising funds to furnish the library...."[29] Many donors contributed only one library or less: "Mrs. Martha Richardson died suddenly leaving a little property. Her sister sent $12 for library."[30] Other donors paid for many libraries. The Countess of Aberdeen contributed funds for one hundred libraries in memory of her son, an American seaman lost at sea.[31]

The ASFS published three magazines. Each was aimed toward a different audience. The oldest publication, *The Sailor's Magazine*, which began in 1828, was designed specifically for seamen. It contained the proceedings of the organization, the activities of other societies working for the betterment of seamen, general literature on the sea and sailing, important news, and other features. *The Seamen's Friend* was similar in form and content, but was oriented towards donors, society members, pastors, and others who worked with or were concerned for seamen. *The Life Boat* was designed specifically for children of Sunday school classes.

Physical Description and Management of the Libraries

The "Little Red Box," as the ASFS called its libraries, was the symbol of the ASFS library program up to the 1940s. The boxes varied little in color and size over the years. The oldest of three libraries still in existence is number 449, which was refitted in 1865 and renumbered 1,391. It measures 13.5 inches wide, 26.875 inches tall, and 6.125 inches deep.[32] Later boxes were slightly larger. The earliest libraries contained up to fifty books, with an average of forty-three. The cost of the libraries to the donors was as little as $5.00 in the early years and as high as $25 from the First World War to 1940.[33]

The earliest concept of the library program involved loaning a library to a ship. A religious member of the crew was assigned the role of librarian. The ASFS felt that a crewman, rather than an officer, should serve as librarian because a crewman had a better understanding of the religious and educational needs of the men. The ASFS assumed that officers already had their own library.[34] Once the library was turned over to the crew a record was entered into the ASFS's Loan Library Register: "Library 668 shipped on Ship Celestial Empire of N. York for San Francisco. Capt. G. S. Taylor in care of the Mate Wm M. Baker (No. 1) 26 men June 2, 1863 Assigned to Orrin Thompson Esq., Enfield, CT Donation $10. Informed Oct 13…."[35] Library 668 served at least five other ships, and the last entry noted its reshipment in May 1879.

Each library included a page with instructions that stated the library was being loaned by the ASFS and asked that the books be used freely and not stolen or mutilated. It reminded the crew that care for the library would ensure another crew the opportunity to use it and that exchange of the library would enable them to receive a new one with a different set of books. The instructions concluded: "Knowledge is Power. Bear a hand and help us and yourselves, and you can have that power." The library also included a Librarian's Report form. The form asked for the library number, the name of the ship, the port of receipt and the year, number of the crew, number of readers, number of books read, names of the books that were most popular, number of signers of the "Ship Mate Temperance Pledge," number who knocked off swearing, number seemingly improved, number of religious services held, number of awakenings, number of hopeful conversions, number of professing Christians, and additional "facts and explanations." One librarian responded:

> …the books of this library have been read with much interest both by officers and crew. And I hope that lasting impressions have been upon many minds settled. I have taken good care of the books. And it gives me great pleasure to

The "Little Red Box," symbol of the American Seamen's Friend Society, 1859 to the 1940s. Reprinted from G. S. Webster, *The Seamen's Friend* (New York: ASFS, 1932).

circulate them containing as they do such precious truths and good instructions which seem to me must be productive of great good.[36]

The ASFS hoped to influence large numbers of seamen. This report from the *Sailor's Magazine and Seamen's Friend* in 1916 is typical:

> The whole number of new Loan Libraries sent to sea from the rooms of the American Seamen's Friend Society in New York and at Boston, Mass., from March, 1859 to April 1, 1916, was 12,034; and the reshipments of same for the same period were 15,379; the total shipments aggregating 27,413. The number of volumes in these libraries was 641,986, and they were accessible, by shipment and reshipment to 469,096 men.[37]

THE LIBRARIES AND THEIR CONTENTS

The early libraries lacked uniformity of content. Into the 1860s the ASFS still relied on tracts and "proper second-hand and shop-worn books."[38] Despite this, a systematic collection development began during the Civil War. This policy is explained in a handwritten document entitled "Analysis of a Ship's Library for Merchant Vessel." It is arranged in two columns: "Plan of Same" and "With a specimen library of 40 vols. as actually furnished." The former refers to types of books and the latter to titles. According to the author, two-thirds to three-fourths of the volumes should concern religion. Among the recommended books were a Bible, a Bible dictionary, and a volume of sermons.[39] Other religious books included religious biographies and histories, and works of fiction with a religious character, such as John Bunyan's *The Pilgrim's Progress*. This portion of the library should also have three to five volumes of foreign language material, in at least three languages. The secular portion was to include an almanac, a book on health and proper diet, one to two science books (preferably on natural philosophy and astronomy), history books (particularly dealing with the United States), travel literature (with two or three volumes on subjects of interest to seamen), and one or two volumes of biography and lighter reading.

In 1878 John S. Pierson published the ASFS's collection development policy in an expanded form.[40] It established four goals for each library. They were, in order of importance: religious instruction and impression, the culture and storing of mind, humanization, and recreation. Religious books were a means to the highest end, "though it is much to refresh, to form a taste for reading, to humanize, to educate, the noblest aim of the ship's library is the conversions of the soul. All other ends are made subordinate to, and intended to lead up to this."[41]

The secular goals of the library were represented by books in the second, third, and fourth categories of literature: "books of solid information;" "civilizing, softening, and humanizing books;" and "books of recreation and amusement." "Books of solid information" included an atlas, two or three volumes of voyages and travels, a history of the United States, a "stimulating bit of biography and topics concerning the ocean; such as shipwrecks, the sea and sailors, and oceanography." The ASFS, like other religious organizations of the period, distributed biographies of famous people to present their exemplary moral and religious traits.[42] Books on shipping and the sea were used to lure the seaman to the library. Once he became acquainted with the library, it was hoped that he would read the other works as well. "Civilizing, softening, and humanizing books" should

> healthily touch the imagination and the heart. The sailor, removed for so great a part of his life from the influences of society and the family, tends to become rough and coarse in his habits and tastes, and hard and material in his views of things. Whatever raises the head and heart to their proper practice of supremacy over the animal nature, or enlarges for him the domain of the ideal and the spiritual, is therefore specially beneficial to the sailor.[43]

To Pierson this broad class of literature required special attention. Several genres are part of this category. Pierson recommended poetry first, preferably lyrics of the "simple or narrative kind" by Cowper, Scott, and Longfellow. A second genre, fiction, was especially problematic. Pierson recognized the value of fictional prose stories, but insisted that the stories impart the values of the ASFS. Narratives such as *The Pilgrim's Progress, Ten Nights in a Bar Room, Uncle Tom's Cabin, Ben Hur, Little Lord Fauntleroy,* and *A Christmas Carol* met Pierson's criteria; dime novels, or "yellow-covered literature," did not.[44] While many seamen were accustomed to bringing a few such novels on board, the ASFS believed its library books would counter the effects of dime novels and ultimately win the hearts and minds of the seamen. An example of this is found in an 1862 report from the *Life Boat,* the ASFS publication aimed at the children of Sunday schools. "The first two months the crew seemed to be afraid of them, till all the novels and bad books were read, when they all found delight in reading the library books."[45]

Dime novels, "fiction of minimal literacy," attracted few proponents among reformers and professional librarians of the day.[46] A number of critics felt the stories of murder and larceny found in many of the books encouraged young readers into lives of crime.[47] Generally, however, the criticism was not that the books were inherently immoral, but that they were non-educational and, thus, a waste of valuable time.

Pierson urged great caution where fiction dealt mainly with social and domestic life. The novel, which he defined as the romance genre or "love story," would not be found in the ship's library. He stated that while the romance might not cause the seaman any moral harm, it would present an "unreal view of life," and whatever inspiration the seaman might receive from it would be only temporary. Pierson wrote that "a little bit of romance, which is so abundant a feature in actual life, is acceptable as long as it is in the context of religious teachings."[48]

One type of fiction Pierson did include in the libraries was the "pathetic" or sentimental story that dealt with "Mother, Home and Heaven." Among the authors of sentimental fiction were many ministers and women.[49] The theory behind the inclusion of this literature was

> that the nearest road for religious truth to the intellect and the will lies through the heart, and that, when the crust; which coarse surroundings and habits of stolid endurance have built up around the centre of feeling, is broken through by tears, spiritual influences may rush in at the gap.[50]

Sentimental fiction has received a great deal of criticism from period as well as modern day scholars who dismiss it for its "inferior literary merit."[51] Even Pierson stated it was "over-done." He nevertheless thought it was useful in the "religious teaching of simple minds."[52] Unlike the novel, it typically offered an explicit moral lesson.[53] Sentimental fiction was extremely popular with a broad spectrum of the American public. Harriet Beecher Stowe's *Uncle Tom's Cabin* and Timothy Shay Arthur's *Ten Nights in a Bar Room* are two classic examples.[54] Both were found in the ASFS libraries.

Pierson was not alone in his criticism of novels. When he warned that fiction presented an "unreal view of life," he was echoing the view of many librarians, including William Kite of Germantown, Pennsylvania, who, in 1876, excluded fiction from his library, because his patrons, factory girls, were of "the class most disposed to seek amusement in novels and peculiarly liable to be injured by their false pictures of life."[55] Nine years later, F. B. Perkins of the San Francisco Public Library also stated that his library had "no business" furnishing novels which he labeled as "licentious, immoral, or vulgar books."[56] In 1897 Helen E. Haines told a gathering of librarians that she, a reader of novels, was "not a proper person to present the subject of fiction to a gathering of librarians, who as a class sternly reprobate the reading of novels and yearn to see mankind ... following the straight and narrow path."[57]

Another category of literature included in the ASFS libraries was for "recreation and amusement." Such books were supposed to lighten the drudgery of onboard routine, were easy to comprehend, and were intended to increase reading skills and stimulate interest in reading higher forms of literature. Included in this body of literature were books classed as "juvenile fiction," such as *The Swiss Family Robinson*, "which were admirably adapted to the lower needs of the ship's library."[58]

Like many librarians of his day, such as Justin Winsor and William F. Poole, Pierson subscribed to the "taste-elevation" theory.[59] Fiction, although generally disapproved of, was thought to be a good vehicle to start the lower classes on the road to a higher literary culture. In 1876 William F. Poole made a typical comment about this use of fiction:

> Judged from a critical standpoint, such books are feeble, rudimentary, and perhaps sensational; but they are higher in the scale of literary merit than the tastes of the people who seek them; and like primers and first-readers in the public schools, they fortunately lead to something better.[60]

Occupational texts and guidebooks or success manuals, such as *The Young Man's Guide* and *The Young Man's Counsellor*, were also included in the libraries. These ubiquitous guidebooks were intended to render the reader "a worthy and useful and happy member of a great republic."[61] They taught rules of living and success in business, if the advice was followed.[62] They emphasized proper character formation, integrity, industry, economy, duties of a husband and various social skills. Ethical behavior in business and the proper relationship to family, society, country, and God were explained. Obtaining an education and reading of the right kind of books were discussed as the means toward culture building and advancement.[63]

The decades of ASFS publications are replete with comments from crews about the libraries. These include the positive responses to the program as well as letters of complaint. One seaman wrote that "the majority of the men pronounce the books to be too strictly orthodox."[64] One captain voiced a common complaint about the lack of foreign language books since most of his crew were non–English speakers.[65] A ship's librarian wrote: "Seamen complain of the dullness of many of the books, such as biographies and lengthy treatises on any subject which are beyond their comprehension."[66] One of the most dramatic complaints came from the U.S. gunboat *Huntress* of the Mississippi Squadron in 1865. Despite fifty readers among a crew of 115, the librarian wrote "none" in all the categories on the library questionnaire previously described.[67]

The ASFS library program is significant for two reasons. It was an early American library program that had a national, if not international, impact. Its longevity, 1858 to 1967, as a library outreach program to a specific group is unsurpassed. Second, although it falls outside of the main line of American public library history and the history of the American Library Association, it has had an influence on the ALA, as we will see.

THE UNITED STATES CHRISTIAN COMMISSION FOR THE ARMY AND NAVY

Another benevolent organization that provided libraries to seafarers was the United States Christian Commission of the Army and Navy (USCC). As its name indicates, unlike the ASFS, it only served the military. The USCC was one of three national level relief organizations formed by civilians to serve Union forces during the American Civil War. The other two were the United States Sanitary Commission and the Western Sanitary Commission. The main thrust of the Western Sanitary Commission and the U.S. Sanitary Commission was the support of the Hospital Corps and general health of the troops. The USCC's mission was the moral and spiritual well-being of the Union soldiers and sailors. The Western Sanitary Commission and the U.S. Sanitary Commission had minimal activity in the area of the provision of reading material, particularly to Naval forces, and will not be discussed here.[68]

LIBRARIES OF THE PRE–CIVIL WAR NAVY

Libraries did exist in U.S. Navy vessels prior to the USCC program. Beginning in 1828 the Navy authorized libraries on board its ships, however, these were strictly reference libraries for the day-to-day operations of a ship and its crew. The size and content of these libraries varied over time due the availability of funds.[69] Three prewar library lists for officers, officially sanctioned for Navy yards, and vessels, as well as fourteen titles for the crew, can be found in Harry Skallerup's *Books Afloat & Ashore.*[70]

The contents of one pre–Civil War era Navy ship's library is known. This is the library of the U.S. steam sloop *Narragansett.*[71] It was a subscription library and the membership included all ranks. The library catalog contains 328 entries, some with multiple titles such as *Marryat's Novels*. The material ranges from dime novels to standard works of fiction, biography, travel, history, and science. It also contained short ranges of magazines, such as the *New Monthly Magazine*, 1821–1825, and *Blackwood's Magazine*, 1833, 1837–1839. The fact that this was a subscription library, along with the dates of the magazines, indicates that the library was either compiled by donations or by private purchase and fell outside of naval supply.

The USCC Library Program

Formed in November 1861, the United States Christian Commission (USCC), an auxiliary of the Young Men's Christian Association (YMCA), was the first national level relationship with the military by the YMCA, and herein lies its significance to the story. From its headquarters in Philadelphia, the Commission directed several auxiliaries and field offices. These in turn served as distribution centers and organized the relief efforts of hundreds of local committees. The USCC established a system of agents and unpaid delegates, both clergy and laymen, who enlisted for a minimum of six weeks.[72] Depending on the need of a particular department, a delegate served a hospital, depot, division, or fleet as a field agent to facilitate the work of the chaplains and civilian volunteers. One New York delegate, for example, served eighty-five vessels of the West Gulf Blockading Squadron and a naval hospital.[73] As stated on the USCC commissioning form for delegates:

> His work will be that of distributing stores where needed, in hospitals and camps; circulating good reading matter amongst soldiers and sailors; visiting the sick and wounded, to instruct, comfort, and cheer them, and aid them in correspondence with their friends at home.[74]

One of the many needs of the soldiers and sailors not being met by the government was reading material. Long periods of inactivity and being away from home caused one man to write that he "longed more for something to read than for something to eat."[75]

The USCC began to provide reading material by distributing tracts from various tract societies, newspapers, and books. The hurried needs of the early days of the war made quality control a secondary issue. Because some of the material was less than satisfactory, "the feeling grew that the soldiers deserved the freshest and best that could be secured."[76] It was also understood that a library would be more desirable than just handing out individual volumes:

> There can hardly be a better or more effectual method of relieving the tedium of the camp or hospital, than that which appears in the supply of good books and other reading matter. This form of relief and instruction has been tested, and its value proved in a number of instances. When a book is presented to a soldier, it becomes his personal property, and perhaps it is highly esteemed on account of its being a present. It is natural for such cases, that the owner of the book should be desirous of preserving it from damage and disinclined to its frequent use by others. It is but a partial benefit, therefore, that is produced by the gift, while the books of a library, regarded as they are as common property, may perform an infinite extent of service.[77]

In August 1863 the Reverend Joseph C. Thomas, chaplain of the Eighty-eighth Illinois Volunteer Infantry Regiment, joined the USCC. He quickly directed that more secular books, magazines, and newspapers be provided to the Union forces:

> A great want of literature is felt, ... wholesome, broad, stirring, deep secular reading, as well as of earnest religious books. The point is to cater to every taste. The nearer you can bring home to the army, the more useful you are. Let the soldiers have the reading which will develop and enlighten, and such as they have been used to at home.[78]

The development of a traveling library system was his most important contribution. Thomas modeled his plan for a traveling library system on two other operations. One was that of the ASFS.[79] The other was developed by Chaplain William M. Haigh of the 36th Illinois Volunteer Infantry Regiment. This system included eleven libraries, each in a cubic-foot sized box. Haigh planned one each for the ten companies and one for the field grade officers, and designed the boxes to fit on regimental supply wagons.[80]

Extremely energetic, Thomas traveled to various cities and talked to high-ranking military officials and business leaders. To garner public support, he published his plans in handbills, booklets, and newspapers articles. In the summer of 1863 he attended the YMCA convention in Chicago and visited twenty-five publishers in New York, Philadelphia, and Cincinnati to gain support for his program.[81] Thomas finalized plans for his system in early 1864. Book selections were made from backlists of about one hundred publishers. The publishers sold the USCC the books at half price, and one publisher in each major publishing center acted as a clearing house for the collecting, packaging, and shipping of the books.

A total of 215 traveling library cases were built by the Army. Each contained 125 volumes and cost about fifty dollars.[82] Another seventy libraries contained seventy-five volumes each. The larger library cases were three feet square and eight inches deep and contained four shelves. The front hinged door panels, which opened at the center, were labeled "U.S. Christian Commission Loan Library," and numbered. Each library included a catalog arranged alphabetically by author, with additional space for thirty-five more titles. A separate card catalog was available for the convenience of bedridden hospital patients. The subject matter of the books included history, biography, poetry, fiction, science, and religion. The works were carefully chosen for the moral and spiritual improvement of their readers. Thomas refused all "yellow-covered literature" for the same reasons given by the ASFS.[83] He sought literature that was

> as comprehensive as the aims of life—a truth-filled literature whose golden light and genial warmth shall penetrate the individual, social, domestic, political, industrial, and pleasurable activities, and make them healthful and fruitful in all Heaven-approved usefulness and happiness. Such literature, our brave men have been accustomed to have.[84]

The Commission loaned these libraries for indefinite periods to hospitals, camps, depots, gunboats, and deep sea naval vessels. Chaplains or officers were given charge of the library and required to sign a statement whereby they pledged themselves to care for the library and to send a monthly report on its condition and use.

Ledgers were provided to record user statistics. These reports were sent to the USCC agent who monitored the location and status of each library:

> Library 224. U.S. Steamer Vanderbilt, Rio de Janerio, S.A. Monthly report for December 1865 and January 1866, by Lt. Comdr. C. S. Franklin: Volumes drawn 282, volumes lost 11. The library diffuses a vast amount of useful knowledge, and is a source of much pleasure to both officer and men.[85]

> Library 228. United States Flag Ship New Hampshire, Port Royal Harbor, S.C. Report for October, 1865, by Chas. Wiener, Librarian. Volumes drawn, two hundred and sixty-six; volumes lost, one. The library is having good effect. It is lessening profanity and intoxication.[86]

A delegate from the Naval Hospital in Norfolk, Virginia, reported:

> Our library succeeds admirably. The volumes were all taken, and many more would have been, could we have supplied them. We have them elegantly cataloged and numbered. It is carried through all the wards twice a week, and is very popular and useful. In fact, it promises more than any other instrumentality of the press we have employed.[87]

The USCC through its various state and local auxiliaries also created numerous libraries for hospitals and other facilities, but it was the traveling library program developed by Thomas that distinguished the USCC from other wartime benevolent societies and led to development of similar services in the second decade of the twentieth century.[88] The libraries were circulated until February 1867.[89] After ceasing its operations, the USCC donated the libraries to the government. Enough of the libraries survived to supply approximately fifty military posts and twenty-five naval vessels.

The parent organization of the USCC, the YMCA, continued to have a relationship with the American military. The USCC would be reactivated in 1898 during the brief war with Spain when once again it served the needs of American military personnel. Unfortunately, little of this effort can be found in relevant archives or published sources.[90] After that war, the War and Navy departments authorized the YMCA to build permanent facilities on various military bases. The first of these was a nine-story facility in the Brooklyn Navy Yard. By 1914 there were nine similar YMCA centers located on naval bases.[91] Two years later, responding again to a request from the military, the YMCA created recreational centers and a library program for the troops on the Mexican border. This library program, like the ASFS program, was a model for the American Library Association program during the First World War.[92]

POST–CIVIL WAR NAVAL LIBRARIES

By the 1880s larger libraries with a broad range of subjects existed on board some vessels. However, these collections were primarily intended for the officers. An example is the *Catalogue of Library Books Issued to Vessels of the U.S. Navy* printed in 1886. In the introduction it states: "Library books belonging to a ship are intended for the use of all officers attached to the vessel, also to be loaned to petty officers and men when the commanding officer may think expedient."[93] The primary function of the library was to support the ship's activities. Of the 394 titles, twenty-seven concerned legal and diplomatic topics. There were 103 military science, navigation, and naval engineering texts and sixteen reference titles. Only two religious books were present, a Bible and a prayer book. There were a number of titles for leisure reading including 146 titles of travel, history, and biography. No works of fiction were present.

By 1907 ships had both a ship's library and a crew library. Two thirds of the crew library on the battleship *Maryland* was comprised of fiction.[94] These libraries were the responsibility of the ship's navigator. They are described as containing naval and military history, mechanics, travel and adventure, biographies, and standard and modern fiction.[95] In 1902 the battleship *Olympia*'s combined libraries contained 1,100 titles with a crew complement of about 460. At the beginning of American involvement in World War I, and this may be due to the rapid mobilization, library materials only existed on capital ships, leaving the small escort and transport vessels and Naval air bases without such services.[96]

THE AMERICAN LIBRARY ASSOCIATION AND THE AMERICAN MERCHANT MARINE LIBRARY ASSOCIATION

World War I brought a new chapter to the story of shipboard library programs. The ASFS, at this time, still maintained its library program and the YMCA continued a relationship with the military that it had begun fifty-four years earlier. Further, as stated above, the Navy had its own limited library program. Yet, a new force came into the foreground with arrival of the American Library Association (ALA). It was the actions of the ALA during World War I and the post-war years that eventually led to the creation of the American Merchant Marine Library Association (AMMLA).

Although the AMMLA was founded in 1921, its history began soon after the United States declared war against the Central Powers on 6 April 1917. Following the declaration, the United States intensified a mobilization program that included the rapid increase and restructuring of the merchant marine, which lacked a sufficient number of ships and crews to ferry troops and supplies to Europe. This activity was the responsibility of the newly authorized United States Shipping Board (USSB).

Then in turn, in February of 1918, the Shipping Board established the Social Service Bureau. Alice S. Howard, wife of the director of the USSB's Recruiting Service, was appointed head of the Bureau and given a salary of one dollar a month plus office space, an assistant and a secretary. No operating budget was allocated.

Like the ASFS, the USCC, and the YMCA in previous wars and military expeditions, the Social Service Bureau engaged in a variety of activities to aid seamen. It facilitated communications between the men and their families, helped with legal issues, visited hospital patients, and created recreational facilities. Howard also enlisted the aid of the ALA. It was this cooperation between the two organizations that would lead to the founding of the AMMLA.

In April 1917, during a series of meetings between the War Department and the

Librarian of Congress, Herbert Putnam, the War Department asked the ALA to undertake the collection, distribution, and circulation of reading material in thirty-two army training camps in the United States.[97] The ALA Executive Board established the Committee on Mobilization and War Service Plans in the same month. The Committee recommended the appointment of a War Service Committee (WSC), which would be established in June of that year, to provide books for service personnel and solicit funds for its operations.

The American Library Association provided over seven million books to the Army and Navy during the war.[98] It placed libraries on American military installations throughout the world, as well as in troop ships, lighthouses, Coast Guard stations, war industrial plants, merchant vessels, and hospitals. Libraries were also sent to Siberia where Allied troops were involved in the Russian Civil War. The ALA also printed books in Braille for soldiers blinded in combat.

The work of the ALA and its WSC did not stop with the armistice in November 1918. The various library programs expanded to address other areas of concern, including merchant seamen.[99] On 1 July 1919 the WSC began library service to USSB vessels, and by mid–August it had supplied 320 ships with libraries of seventy volumes.[100] By July 1920, it had expanded its program to include all American merchant ships and placed over 239,490 books aboard 1,806 vessels.

The ALA was riding high from its war work and was not satisfied to return to its prewar library conditions. A new committee, the ALA's Committee on Enlarged Program, examined new programs to reach populations not previously served and began a "Books for Everybody" campaign. At the same time, the WSC was looking at disbanding its services. However, as it was in the process of jettisoning itself from the military, the WSC recommended continued service to the Merchant Marine.[101] Forrest B. Spaulding was put in charge of the service to the Merchant Marine, Coast Guard, light ships, and lighthouses.[102] Spaulding had been an ALA librarian at Fort Dodge, Iowa, an army training base, during World War I. Prior to this, while he served as the Superintendent of the Traveling Library Department of the New York Public Library, he was in charge of the selection of materials for the YMCA libraries on the Mexican border in 1916.[103]

At the 1920 ALA conference in Colorado Springs, the WSC noted that maritime organizations recognized that the ALA had demonstrated the need for library services to seamen.[104] Yet, the ALA quickly realized its postwar goals were beyond its abilities. The ALA approached various government agencies and maritime groups, but these turned down the responsibility due to lack of funds, limited facilities, or because they felt the program went beyond the scope of their work.[105] In March 1921 the USBB's Alice Howard, under the auspices of the ALA, met with members of the American Ship Owners Association in New York. At this meeting preliminary steps were taken for the incorporation of the AMMLA.[106] After some hesitation, the ALA appointed Howard chair of the committee to establish the AMMLA.[107] The AMMLA was subsequently incorporated and USSB's Social Service Bureau was disbanded.

ALA then turned over the remaining WSC funds and book stock to the new organization. There were more than 112,000 volumes in various cities throughout the United States and 5,000 overseas. The YMCA had 3,000 more in its port facilities.[108] Two years later, in 1923, the AMMLA was still collecting the books.

Fund Raising and Book Drives

Fund raising, collecting donated books, and expanding its services were the first activities of the AMMLA. In its eighty years of existence the Association has spent much of its time, energy, and resources reminding donors of the plight of seaman. It has relied almost entirely on used books donated by individuals, churches, clubs, public libraries, or remainders donated by publishers. The "used" nature of the material, however, has never been a damper to the enthusiasm of the AMMLA staff or the recipients of the service.

In 1923, once the initial ALA grant of $5,000 was in place, the AMMLA drew up lists of possible members and made appeals to shipping interests and corporations. The first large grants came from Standard Oil of New Jersey, the Lake Carrier's Association, and the Carnegie Corporation.[109] The total given for the year was just over $34,000. Funding sources have changed little since those first years. The AMMLA has regularly received donations from various maritime associations, shipping companies, unions, bequests, crews and individuals. In 2000 the donations, grants, and bequests amounted to $143,560.

The 1923 stock of War Service Committee books was quickly exhausted. Books exposed to the oceanic environments generally wore out quickly and a small number of libraries were also lost at sea along with the ships carrying them. Because of these conditions and limited financial resources, book drives became an important feature of the AMMLA's annual activities.

From the beginning the AMMLA placed book drop boxes in train depots and other strategic locations in various cities. In 1945 it began a spring book drive. Traditionally the drive has opened with a public ceremony attended by dignitaries from the maritime community, Navy, Coast Guard, and the U.S. government. In New York City, the AMMLA placed a lifeboat from a docked ship in front of a major office complex for one week. This boat served as a drop box for book donations. In recent years the Association has been unable to procure a lifeboat, but the book drive has continued. The 1952 book drive, for example, brought in 57,000 books and magazines. In 1999 the drive brought in over 165,000 books and magazines.

The Libraries

The libraries of the "Books for Everybody" program, created after World War I by the Committee on Enlarged Program, averaged eighty volumes. The contents included maritime related textbooks and technical manuals for career advancement, American history and citizenship, travel, and fiction. The early AMMLA libraries were of similar size and content, however, the libraries for the Great Lakes ships contained only twenty-five volumes. These early libraries were about sixty-five percent fiction, most of it recently published. One book published by the Social Service Bureau and later the AMMLA was the *Seamen's Handbook for Shore Leave* under the authorship of Alice Howard. The *Handbook*, published between 1919 and 1947, contained information about ports worldwide. Safe housing and banks, hospitals, union halls, points of interest, and police warnings were among the items covered.

Libraries then, as today, were delivered upon request to the vessel. The early libraries were packed in wooden cases with hinged covers. Each box was painted sea-green and A.M.M.L.A. was stenciled on the cover. A list of the contents was attached to the inside cover. The library was placed in custody of a crewman designated by the ship's captain and could be exchanged at any port AMMLA office.

By the late 1930s the libraries contained about forty books in a standup wooden bookcase with a two-door front. Nearly two-thirds of the books in these libraries were fiction, including "classics, mystery and adventure, literary novels and humor." Ten of the books were non-fiction, "stocked to follow the crew's interest."[110] Some ships received up to five libraries depending on the size of the crew and how compartmentalized the ship was.

By 1947 the AMMLA had created a specific formula for their libraries, developed through user surveys and other means over several years.[111] This formula includes at least twenty-six works of fiction and fourteen non-fiction titles. The fiction is described as consisting of two current best sellers, four former best sellers, eight perennials, two standards, one classic, one sea story, one adventure, one humorous fiction, two westerns, and four mysteries. Non-fiction works include two books on philosophy, psychology, or religion (generally that means a Bible and another work), one social science text, one popular science work, three works of general literature (poetry or essays), three works of biography, travel, or adventure, followed by two books on history and current affairs, one elementary study text, a dictionary, an atlas, and an almanac. A selection of paperbacks and magazines was also included. This formula was still followed into the 1990s, however, it is up to the discretion of each port representative to decide what each library contains. The AMMLA personnel often have a long-standing relationship with the crews which enables them to construct the libraries according to particular interests and requests of the crews.

Another service the AMMLA has undertaken since its inception is filling individual book requests. An individual can ask for a specific technical text to help in his career advancement. Since these texts are expensive and become dated quickly, the AMMLA cannot afford to provide each library with such material. It does however keep a number in stock and purchases others individually as the need arises.

Over the years, the AMMLA received numerous letters of thanks. In 1959, one seaman wrote: "I would ... like you to know how much merchant seamen afloat appreciate the books which you put aboard ships. For 39 years I have always found the A.M.M.L. boxes of books eagerly sought by crews when they had leisure time at sea."[112] Another wrote:

> To anyone who has never "gone down to the sea in ships" it would be difficult to imagine what a diversified, ample library of books means to a Seaman on a 35-day passage from New York to Karchi. Who can possibly envision the joy, the wide horizons, even possibly material advantages (not to mention the boredom relieved) that you have opened up to countless Seamen.[113]

The ALA, at its height, had twenty-nine distribution points operated by the WSC. At its start, the AMMLA operated out of only six ports. In 1922, however, it added the Coast Guard and Lighthouse Service, and by 1926 the number of port facilities had expanded to twelve.

The Association continued to expand until the end of Second World War. In 1925 nearly 4,684 libraries (containing 224,808 books) were loaned to 1,633 ships. Thirty-two Coast Guard stations and thirty-three lighthouses also received libraries. In 1930 the numbers increased to 5,967 libraries (containing 331,481 books and 200,000 magazines). These went to 1,515 ships, plus Coast Guard stations, lighthouses and lightships, hospitals, cable ships, and survey vessels. With the onset of World War II, the service skyrocketed, and by 1945 there were 3,874 ships with 12,001 libraries containing 758,800 books and 1,500,000 magazines. These figures do not include the numerous transport ships, Coast Guard vessels, and lightships served.

At the end of the war, the merchant marine began a steady decline. In 1959 the AMMLA presented 1,204 ships with 5,545 libraries, and filled 5,387 individual requests. By 1972 the AMMLA was in trouble. The traditional funding sources it had relied on since its inception could not sustain the organization.[114] The AMMLA began to consider merging with another organization in hopes of salvaging the library service. New York harbor organizations such as the South Street Seaport and the Seamen's Church Institute were considered. However, because their charters did not allow them to extend their services beyond that port, they were not able to consider merging with a national organization.[115] Inquiries were made toward merging with the United Seamen's Service, another national organization. Despite a vote against such a merger by the AMMLA trustees, the AMMLA Executive Committee voted in favor of the affiliation in June 1973.[116]

Since the merger, the AMMLA has continued in its traditional role. In 1990 the Association delivered only 2,046 libraries to 753 ships from six distribution centers. Of these libraries, 429 were sent by mail to ships in other ports. In 1992, 418 ships received 1,525 libraries. In 1999 AMMLA presented 2,633 ships with 3,892 libraries.[117]

CONCLUSION

The story of library outreach to seamen in the United States has it origins in Great Britain. In this country, as in Great Britain, religious organizations founded the programs. Their overall goal was socioeconomic and moral uplift through institutional and individual reform. Like their counterparts in the areas of abolition, education, workers' rights, women's rights, and temperance, the organizations had successes and failures on both local and national levels. The American Seamen's Friend Society was one of the many organizations in the early part of the nineteenth century that successfully entered into the national scene and became a national force in their area of concern. It took on issues of onboard abuse by officers and onshore abuse by those waiting to part the seamen from their wages. The ASFS lobbied for changes in legislation in regard for seamen's welfare and for multiple reforms in the United States Navy.

One method deemed successful by the ASFS for individual uplift and reform was through reading. From 1858 to 1967 the organization provided thousands of libraries to American merchant ships and United States Navy vessels. This library program became the principal model for the library program of the United States Christian Commission for the Army and Navy during the American Civil War. Both these organizations placed libraries on naval vessels during that conflict. A significant portion of the contents of these libraries consisted of religious material. Yet, other materials included those for general education and professional and personal advancement, literacy, reference, and recreational reading.

The work of the USCC in assisting the military became a model for future work by its parent organization, the YMCA. During the Spanish-American War and the 1916 Mexican border conflict the YMCA sent books directly to troops in the field. The YMCA also provided libraries to military bases in the early part of the twentieth century.

It was this work that became the most significant influence on the World War One library programs of the American Library Association for the American Army. The ALA gave little credit to the influence of either the ASFS or the YMCA for its success, yet both were foundational to the work that the ALA used to put itself on the map.[118] In 1920, Forrest B. Spaulding assessed the ASFS program by stating,

> The placing of books on board ships for the use of the crew is by no means a new thing. As early as 1859, the "Loan Libraries for Ships" was founded in New York and this institution, supported entirely by contributions from those interested in the welfare of seamen, can possibly lay claim not only to instituting one of the earliest systems of Traveling Libraries but to being one of the pioneers in the ranks of Special Libraries.[119]

From the war work of the ALA and the United States Shipping Board a new organization arose that began to serve the reading and educational needs of seamen. The American Merchant Marine Library Association, celebrating its eightieth year of service, still provides libraries to the American Merchant Marine.[120]

NOTES

1. Harry R. Skallerup, *Books Afloat & Ashore: A History of Books, Libraries, and Reading Among Seamen During the Age of Sail* (Hamden, CT: Archon Books, 1974) 18–19.

2. Mark S. Schantz, "Religious Tracts, Evangelical Reform, and the Market Revolution in Antebellum America," *Journal of the Early Republic* 17 (Fall 1997) 425–66. An example of this is a bound volume of tracts entitled *Illustrated Seamen's Narrative* (New York: American Tract Society, [18??]). In this volume examples include "Conversation in a Boat," "Letters to Seamen on First Coming Ashore," and "Help the Seamen." In at least one of these publications the intended audience is clearly known. On page 2 of *The Blue Flag* (New York: American Tract Society, 1861) it states, "The characters in the following story have been sketched in the hope of calling attention to the interests of our seamen, and of being useful to the sailors themselves."

3. Skallerup 20.

4. Ronald Hope, *Sea Pie: A Celebration of Fifty Years of "The Seafarer"* (London: Fairplay Publications, 1984) 145; and Grace M. Rose, "The British Library and Literature Service for Merchant Seafarers" thesis, Fellowship of the Library Association, 1980, 72.

5. Peter J. Wosh, *Spreading the Word: The Bible Business in Nineteenth-Century America* (Ithaca: Cornell UP 1994) 95.

6. Wosh 99.

7. *New York Evening Post* 5934 (29 June 1821): 2; Skallerup 43–45.

8. Roald Kverndal, *Seamen's Missions: Their Origin and Early Growth* (Pasadena, CA: William Carey Library, 1986) 45–50.

9. Eric Newby, *The Last Grain Race* (New York: Ballantine Books, 1971) 4–6.

10. Myra C. Glenn, "The Navel Reform Campaign Against Flogging: A Case Study in Changing Attitudes Toward Corporal Punishment," *American Quarterly* 35 (Fall 1983): 408–25. Comparing seamen and their working conditions with criminals and prisons continued into the twentieth century; see Robert D. Franklin, "The Public Library of the High Seas," *Library Journal* 63 (15 Mar. 1938): 227–31. In Eric W. Sage, *Seafaring Labour: The Merchant Marine of Atlantic Canada, 1820–1914* (Kingston: McGill-Queen's U Press, 1989), the reformist's image of the seaman is challenged. The image of an otherwise unemployable man or a criminal avoiding the law seems not to be accurate when he points out that the seamen were often children of fisherfolk, mariners, coastal farmers, and craftsmen, and grew up in pre-industrial coastal communities where class distinctions were blurred and the seaman's profession was respected. Craig J. Forsyth, *The American Merchant Seaman and His Industry: Struggle and Stigma* (New York: Taylor & Francis, 1989) 31–33, 38–39.

11. American Seamen's Friend Society, *Notes of Fifty Years' Efforts for the Welfare of Seamen* (New York: American Seamen's Friend Society, 1878) 15–16.

12. American Seamen's Friend Society, *American Seamen's Friend Society: First Annual Report* (New York: American Seamen's Friend Society, 1829) 6.

13. *American Seamen's Friend Society: First Annual Report* 19.

14. "The American Seamen's Friend Society," *The Life Boat* 1 (Jan. 1858) 4.

15. Hugh H. Davis, "The American Seamen's Friend Society and the American Sailor, 1828–1838," *The American Neptune* 39 (Jan. 1979): 50–51; American Seamen's Friend Society, *The Acts of the Apostles of the Sea* (New York: American Seamen's Friend Society, 1909) 42.

16. *American Seamen's Friend Society: First Annual Report*, 18.

17. Margaret S. Creighton, *Dog Watch and Liberty Days* (Salem: The Peabody Museum, 1982) 7.

18. William B. Whitecar, *Four Years Aboard the Whaleship* (Philadelphia: Lippincott, 1860) 127.

19. American Seamen's Friend Society, *American Seamen's Friend Society: The National Society Cooperating with All Who Aid Merchant Seamen* (New York: American Seamen's Friend Society, 1953) 11.

20. American Seamen's Friend Society, *Notes of Fifty Years* 33.

21. H. Loomis, Letter to the Rev. Titus Coan, 23 Dec. 1858, *American Seamen's Friend Society Letterbook 86*, American Seamen's Friend Society Collection, Manuscript Collection, G. W. Blunt White Library, Mystic Seaport Museum, Mystic, CT: 110–11. The forecastle or foc'sle is the raised deck at the front end of sailing vessels. For centuries the living quarters for the crew were in the decks below the forecastle.

22. H. Loomis, Letter to the Rev. G. Powell, 4 Feb. 1859, *American Seamen's Friend Society Letterbook 86*, 148.

23. H. Loomis, Letter to the Rev. G. A. Swamey, 16 Mar. 1859, *American Seamen's Friend Society Letterbook 86*, 207.

24. American Seamen's Friend Society, *Notes of Fifty Years* 57.

25. American Seamen's Friend Society, *Notes of Fifty Years* 106.

26. American Seamen's Friend Society, *Notes of Fifty Years* 12.

27. American Seamen's Friend Society, *Thirty-Sixth Annual Report of the American Seamen's Friend Society* (New York: ASFS, 1864) 8. An example of individual contributions is found in the account book of Mrs. L. M. Gardner of Ellsworth, CT, dated 16 Feb. 1859 to 31 Dec. 1867. In it she lists numerous donations to various organizations. On 1 January 1862 she lists a 50 cent donation to the ASFS along with Minnesota Sufferers and Sick & Wounded Soldiers; on 1 January 1865 she recorded a $1.00 donation to the ASFS along with donations to the U.S. Christian Commission and the Soldiers Aid Society. Private Collection of Mark D. Jaeger, Lafayette, IN.

28. "Editorial Paragraphes," *Sailor's Magazine and Seamen's Friend* 64 (Jan. 1892): 7.

29. A. S. Gowen, Letter to the Rev. S. H. Hall, 11 Apr. 1866, Box 2, Folder 5, American Seamen's Friend Society Collection, Manuscript Collection.

30. American Seamen's Friend Society, *Library Register 12*, American Seamen's Friend Society Collection, Manuscript Collection, 110–11.

31. "Loan Libraries," *Sailor's Magazine and Seamen's Friend* 62 (Jan. 1890): 5.

32. The three libraries are located in the G. W. Blunt White Library, Mystic Seaport Museum, Mystic, CT. See also, "Loan Libraries," *Sailor's Magazine and Seamen's Friend* 62 (Jan. 1890): 5 and "Loan Libraries," *Sailor's Magazine and Seamen's Friend* 68 (Jan. 1896): 3.

33. American Seamen's Friend Society, *Loan Library Register 80*, American Seamen's Friend Society Collection, Manuscript Collection; George Sidney Webster, *The Seamen's Friend* (New York: American Seamen's Friend Society, 1932) 90.

34. Loomis, Letter to the Rev. Titus Coan.

35. American Seamen's Friend Society, *Loan Library Register 2*, American Seamen's Friend Society Collection, Manuscript Collection.

36. Reuben Briggs, *ASFS Loan Library Report Library #1566*, Bark Montiqania, 1865, Box 2, Folder 5, American Seamen's Friend Society Collection, Manuscript Collection.

37. "Loan Libraries" *Sailor's Magazine and Seamen's Friend* 88 (June 1916): 94.

38. The Committee, "American Seamen's Friend Society-Loan Libraries," *Sailor's Magazine and Seamen's Friend* 39 (Dec. 1866): 114.

39. *Analysis of a Ship's Library for Merchant Vessel*, Box 2, Folder 6, American Seamen's Friend Society Collection, Manuscript Collection.

40. John S. Pierson, *Ships' Libraries: Their Need and Usefulness* (New York: American Seamen's Friend Society, 1878): 9–18; John S. Pierson, "Ships' Libraries and Ocean Colportage" *Sailors Magazine and Seamen's Friend* 50 (Nov. 1878) 323–340.

41. John S. Pierson, *Ships' Libraries*, 17.

42. Alice B. Cushman, "A Nineteenth Century Plan for Reading: The American Sunday School Movement" *Horn Book Magazine* 33 (Feb. 1957): 65.

43. Pierson, *Ships' Libraries* 10.

44. United States Christian Commission, *United States Christian Commission for the Army and Navy for the Year 1865, Fourth Annual Report* (Philadelphia: United States Christian Commission, 1866) 49.

45. C. W., "Novels Superseded," *The Life Boat* 4 (Oct. 1862): 62.

46. Bill Blackbeard, "Pulp and Dime Novels," in *Handbook of American Popular Literature*, ed. M. Thomas Inge (New York: Greenwood Press, 1988) 223.

47. Michael Denning, *Mechanic Accents: Dime Novels and Working-Class Culture* (New York: Verso, 1987) 49.

48. Pierson, *Ships' Libraries* 12.

49. Cushman, 159–166; Ann Douglas, *The Feminization of American Culture* (New York: Alfred A. Knopf, 1977), 96.

50. Pierson, "Ships' Libraries and Ocean Colportage" 327.

51. Frank Keller Walter, "A Poor But Respectable Relation: The Sunday School Library," *Library Quarterly*, 12 (July 1942): 737–38; Jane P. Tompkins, "Sentimental Power: Uncle Tom's Cabin and the Politics of Literary History," in *The New Feminist Criticism*, ed. Elaine Showalter (New York: Pantheon Books, 1985) 81–104.

52. Pierson, "*Ships' Libraries and Ocean Colportage*" 325.

53. This "pathetic" fiction was an attempt to translate Biblical morality and cultural values into settings nineteenth-century Americans could clearly comprehend; see R. Lawrence Moore, "Religion, Secularization, and the Shaping of the Culture Industry in Antebellum America," *American Quarterly* 41 (June 1989): 216–242.

54. Harriet Beecher Stowe's *Uncle Tom's Cabin* is considered by some critics to be the most influential novel written by an American. The power of her work was emphasized by Abraham Lincoln, who reportedly greeted Stowe by saying, "So you're the little woman who wrote the book that made this great war." Timothy Shay Arthur, one of the most successful authors of the genre, published over two hundred novels and collections of stories. His most famous work was *Ten Nights in a Bar Room*. His publishers frequently issued Arthur's first editions in printings of 25,000 copies. James M. McPherson, *Battle Cry of Freedom: The Civil War Era* (New York: Oxford UP, 1988) 90; Donald A. Koch; introduction, *Ten Nights in a Bar Room and What I Saw There*, by Timothy Shay Arthur (Cambridge: Harvard UP, 1964) xxvii–xxix.

55. Denning 48.

56. F. B. Perkins, "Free Libraries and Unclean Books," *Library Journal* 10 (Dec. 1885): 396.

57. "Books of 1896—II," *Library Journal* 22 (Mar. 1897): 140.

58. Pierson, *Ships' Libraries and Ocean Colportage* 325–326.

59. Patrick Williams, *The American Public Library and the Problem of Purpose* (New York: Greenwood Press, 1988) 10–21 and Samuel Swett Green, *The Public Library Movement in the United States 1853–1893* (Boston: The Boston Book Company, 1913) 60.

60. William F. Poole, "The Organization and Management of Public Libraries," in U.S. Bureau of Education, *Public Libraries in the United States of America: Their History, Condition and Management* (Washington: GPO, 1876) 479–80.

61. William A. Alcott, *The Young Man's Guide* (Boston: Perkins and Marvin, 1841) 5.

62. Leonard N. Neufeldt, *The Economist: Henry Thoreau and Enterprise* (New York: Oxford UP, 1989) 109.

63. Neufeldt 110.

64. "Library Reports," *The Life Boat* 5 (Sept. 1864): 31–32.

65. H. G. H., "Our Sea Libraries," *The Life Boat* 4 (Jan. 1862): 160.

66. "Loan Libraries," *Sailor's Magazine and Seamen's Friend* 64 (June 1892): 167.

67. *ASFS Loan Library Report. Library #1254, U.S. Gunboat Huntress, 1865*, Box 2, Folder 5, American Seamen's Friend Society Collection, Manuscript Collection.

68. David M. Hovde, "The Library is a Valuable Hygienic Appliance" in *Reading for Moral Progress: 19th Century Institutions Promoting Social Change*, University of Illinois Occasional Papers 207 (Urbana: GSLIS, 1997) 19–42.

69. Dorothy F. Deininger, "The Navy and Marine Corps System of Shipboard Libraries and General Libraries Ashore," in *Encyclopedia of Library and Information Science*, ed. Allen Kent and Harold Lancour, vol. 1 (New York: Marcel Dekker, 1968) 557.

70. Skallerup 221–46.

71. George Henry Preble, *U.S. Steam Sloop Narragansett's Circulating Library* (Norfolk, VA: Argus Print, 1860).

72. For a firsthand account of the field work of a delegate see Horice Quincy Butterfield, *A Delegate's Story* (Philadelphia: United States Christian Commission, 1863).

73. U.S. Christian Commission (New York Branch), *A Memorial Record of the New York Branch of the United States Christian Commission* (New York: J. A. Gray & Green, 1866) 52.

74. Taken from a USCC Commission form No. 2430 for a delegate named H. N. Rush dated June 13, 1864, and signed by George H. Stuart, private collection of Mark D. Jaeger, Lafayette, IN.

75. Bell Irwin Wiley, *The Life of Billy Yank* (Baton Rouge: Louisiana State UP, 1981) 153.

76. Lemuel Moss, *Annals of the United States Christian Commission* (Philadelphia: J. B. Lippincott, 1868) 685–86.

77. United State Christian Commission, "Library Book," *Second Report of the Committee of Maryland* (Baltimore: Sherwood & Co., 1863) 44.

78. Joseph C. Thomas, *Information for Army Meetings* (Philadelphia: United States Christian Commission, 1865) 30.

79. Joseph C. Thomas, "Loan Library System," *United States Christian Commission for the Army and Navy for the Year 1864: Third Annual Report* (Philadelphia: United States Christian Commission, 1865) 49.

80. Joseph C. Thomas, *A Reading for the Army and the Navy* (Nashville: n.p., 1863). The Reverend J. C. Thomas Collection, Manuscripts Division, Library of Congress, Washington, D.C.

81. Thomas, *A Reading*; Thomas, "Loan Library System," 49.

82. *Information* 31; Thomas, "Loan Library System," 47.

83. Thomas, "Loan Library System," 49.

84. Thomas, *A Reading*.

85. Joseph C. Thomas, *U.S. Christian Commission Loan Library System* (Evanston, IL: n.p., 1866). The Reverend J. C. Thomas Collection.

86. Moss 723.

87. U.S. Christian Commission (New York Branch), *A Memorial Record of the New York Branch* 44.

88. As of 29 November 1864, Thomas noted that twenty 125-volume USCC hospital libraries served the wounded and sick in the Nashville, Chattanooga, and Murfreesboro hospitals and forty more were on order; see Thomas, *Information* 30.

89. John Brougham, Letter to the Reverend J. C. Thomas, 14 February 1867, Letter file, The Reverend J. C. Thomas Collection.

90. David M. Hovde, "YMCA Libraries on the Mexican Border, 1916." *Libraries & Culture* 32 (Winter 1997): 113–24.

91. C. Howard Hopkins, *History of the YMCA in North America* (New York: Association Press, 1951) 455; William Howard Taft and Frederick Harris, *Service with Fighting Men* (New York: Association Press, 1924) 207.

92. Hovde, "YMCA Libraries."

93. J. G. Walker, *Catalog of Library Books Issued to Vessels of the U.S. Navy* (Washington, D.C.: Government Printing Office, 1886) 3.

94. Frank Barnard Heckman, "Libraries in the United States Army and Navy" *Library Journal* 32 (Feb. 1907): 68–69.

95. "Traveling Libraries in the Navy," *Library Journal* 37 (July 1912): 388–389.

96. Arthur P. Young, *Books for Sammies: The American Library Association and World War I* (Pittsburgh: Beta Phi Mu, 1981) 62.

97. "Plans for War Service by the A. L. A." *Library Journal* 42 (Aug. 1917): 613. Over forty such libraries were eventually established at U.S. Army training sites.

98. The Committee on Enlarged Program, *Books for Everyone: The Enlarged Program of the American Library Association* (Chicago: American Library Association, 1919).

99. "Papers and Proceedings: Colorado Springs Conference 1920," *ALA Bulletin* 14 (July 1920): 306–07; and Young 82.

100. *Statement of the Acting General Director to the War Service Committee*, 1 September 1919 American Library Association Archives, 89/1/52 Box 1, U of Illinois Archives, Champaign, IL.

101. Letter from J. I. Wyer, Jr. to Newton D. Baker, Secretary of War, 29 August 1919, *Minutes of the American Library Association—War Service Committee*, Richfield Springs, NY, 10 Sept. 1919, *American Library Association War Service Correspondence*, vol. 1. American Library Association Archives, U of Illinois Archives, Champaign, IL.

102. Carl H. Milam, "A.L.A. Library War Service Continuation Work." *Library Journal* 45 (15 Feb. 1920) 170.

103. Hovde, "YMCA Libraries" 113–124.

104. "Papers and Proceedings: Colorado Springs Conference 1920," *ALA Bulletin* 14 (July 1920) 307.

105. *Report of the Proceedings of the Executive Board of the American Library Association* (2 Apr. 1921). American Library Association Archives, 2/1/1 Box 2, U of Illinois Archives, Champaign, IL.

106. "Merchant Marine Library Association," *Library Journal* 46 (1 Apr. 1921): 304.

107. Report of the Proceedings of the Executive Board of the American Library Association (2 Apr. 1921). ALA Archives, 2/1/1 Box 2, U of Illinois Archives, Champaign, IL.

108. "Library Service to the Merchant Marine," *Library Journal* 48 (15 May 1923): 473–474.

109. James G. Neal, "The American Merchant Marine Library Association: The First Decade of Its Development 1921–1930." *The American Neptune* 41 (Jan. 1981): 9.

110. Franklin, "The Public Library of the High Seas," 229.

111. *Books: The Best Companions. Twenty-Sixth Annual Report* (New York: American Merchant Marine Library Association, 1947) 3; *Library Formula*, Book Club 1974 file, American Merchant Marine Library Association (AMMLA) Archives, New York, NY; personal correspondence, C. Elizabeth Leach, Director of Community Relations, United Seamen's Service, to David M. Hovde (3 May 1993).

112. George R. Berens of the S.S. *Flying Enterprise II*, Letter to the AMMLA, (27 Dec. 1959), AMMLA Archives.

113. J. W. Wilson of the S.S. *Flying Hawk*, Letter to the Executive Director, AMMLA, (14 March 1969), AMMLA Archives.

114. *Fifty-second Annual Report 1973*. (New York: American Merchant Marine Library Association, 1974), Charles S. Francis, Letter to the Members of the AAMLA Executive Committee (17 Apr. 1972), AMMLA Archives; and *Minutes of the Executive Committee Meeting, American Merchant Marine Library Association* (13 September 1972).

115. *Minutes of the Executive Committee Meeting, American Merchant Marine Library Association* (25 October 1972), AMMLA Archives; *Minutes of the Executive Committee Meeting, American Merchant Marine Library Association* (13 September 1972), AMMLA Archives.

116. *Minutes of the Executive Committee Meeting, American Merchant Marine Library Association* (13 September 1972), AMMLA Archives; *Minutes of the Executive Committee Meeting, American Merchant Marine Library Association* (4 Dec. 1972), AMMLA Archives. The United Seamen's Service is a social service organization with facilities in ports throughout the world. The USS began in 1942 with the American involvement in World War II. The organization's port facilities provide seamen with emergency assistance and legal aid, and acts as a liaison between seamen and local officials. In these facilities it also provides recreational activities, entertainment, postal services, and international phone services.

117. *American Merchant Marine Library Association 78th Annual Report* (New York: AMMLA, 2000) 12.

118. Hovde, "YMCA Libraries" 113–124.

119. Forrest B. Spaulding, "A Special Library that Encircles the Globe," *Special Libraries* 11 (Apr. 1920: 94.

120. In recent years the New York headquarters of the AMMLA has suffered tremendous setbacks. In 1993 it lost most of its library stock due to the bombing of the World Trade Center where its offices were located. Then on September 11, 2001, its entire facility was destroyed. Despite these losses, it continues to serve "[those] that go down to the sea in ships."

4. Valleys Without Sunsets: Women's Clubs and Traveling Libraries

Paula D. Watson

When Melvil Dewey became State Librarian and Secretary of the Board of Regents of New York, he developed an ambitious plan for advancing public libraries. Traveling libraries were an integral part of that plan. Dewey sent out his first library in February 1893. Almost immediately, the traveling library idea was taken up by the women's club movement, a phenomenon that was, itself, only just beginning to gather focus and momentum. Although women's clubs were not the only groups or individuals to become involved with traveling libraries, their contribution was unique and far-reaching. What they brought to the work that others could not was a massive, organized effort made possible by a national federation supported by a network of state federations composed of individual clubs in cities and towns of all sizes all over America. The mobilization of this army of women resulted in the rapid spread of the traveling library idea from state to state, in allocations of funds by state legislatures, and in the founding of thousands of public libraries from one end of the country to the other. This chapter will document women's club contributions to the public library movement through the promotion of traveling libraries and explore the motivations that inspired this enormous voluntary effort.

It is generally agreed that the public library movement began in 1876 with the founding of the American Library Association, the inauguration of the first library periodical, and the publication for the first time of detailed statistics on libraries by the United States Department of Education. A host of socioeconomic developments contributed to the growth of libraries. These included the spread of free public education, the conceptualization of libraries as adjuncts of the public schools, and the recognition that a flourishing democratic nation requires an informed citizenry.

Growing industrialization produced greater general prosperity and increased the time available for personal enrichment. Other contributing factors included the growth of the library profession, the formation of state library commissions to funnel state aid to libraries, the Carnegie gift program and, as recent research has shown, the organized work of women's clubs.[1]

There had been women's societies—church groups and charitable organizations—from colonial times. Around 1850, however, a new kind of female society began to emerge. Women started to form groups in noticeable numbers that focused on reading and study to meet their own needs for personal and intellectual growth. The number of study clubs increased steadily from 1860 to 1880; and, by the 1890s and into the new century, they were popping up all over the country. Since the business of the early women's clubs was reading, they often formed their own libraries or became interested in the founding of libraries in their communities. Nineteenth century women had begun to recognize that knowledge is power.

Despite the rapid growth in the number of libraries after 1875, there were still large numbers of people living in rural areas at the turn of the century who had no access to library services and, in some cases, little knowledge of books. Dewey saw the traveling library as a way to reach this population through means that seemed to him a natural evolution of the public library. Libraries started in larger cities in centrally located buildings. Branches were developed to reach more distant populations. Later, widely scattered delivery stations were established where, for example, a laborer could pick up and return a book on the way to work. Traveling libraries could reach people even further removed from the central service point. They were also an excellent application of Dewey's principle of "the best reading for the largest number at the least cost."[2] Building full service libraries in the hamlets, farming areas, lumber and mining camps, and all the other small settlements that dotted a vast nation was impractical and far too expensive. On the other hand, taking advantage of the new availability of quick and cheap transportation to bring books to people in such places had, in Dewey's view, a highly favorable cost-to-benefit ratio. Dewey also knew that libraries quickly grow stale without infusions of new material. "A library is like a reservoir of drinking water. It must have a constant fresh stream running through it or it will become stagnant and unusable." Traveling libraries provided an efficient way to enliven older libraries and keep them from withering away, as many had done over the years.[3] The first case of books that left Albany opened the way for thousands more to follow. Collections normally included from fifty to one hundred volumes packed in strong, wooden boxes designed to open out as bookshelves. They could be kept in a library or displayed in a country store, a school, or in the home of an interested individual—any place where people were welcome to browse, borrow, and return books.

FROM NEW YORK TO MASSACHUSETTS: WORK OF THE WOMAN'S EDUCATION ASSOCIATION OF BOSTON

Working within existing governmental structures, Dewey redirected the course of state aid to libraries in New York. A few years earlier, Massachusetts had created a different model for state support to library extension, a model that was to be emulated by many other states. In 1890 most towns in Massachusetts had public libraries, although not all were free. Nevertheless, legislation was passed in 1890 to create a state library commission, an appointed body of unsalaried citizens who would oversee a program to encourage public library formation. The statute provided that $100 worth of books would be offered to any town wishing to found a free public library. In 1892 the law was extended to include towns that already had libraries but wished to enrich their collections. Passage of the Massachusetts law led to what Henry S. Nourse, a member of the Commission, described as a kind of library epidemic. In a speech to the New York Library Association and the New York Library Club in 1896 he summarized the effect of the first commission as follows:

> It seemed as though a new microbe had been evolved—a library bacillus generated under the gilded dome of the Massachusetts statehouse, whose progeny had been wafted on the wings of the wind to the uttermost parts of the world to ferment and excite among all civilized peoples a craving for library privileges.[4]

The person behind the seminal Massachusetts legislation that released the "library bacillus" was a woman. Elizabeth Putnam Sohier was a member of an old Massachusetts family. Her brother, William Davies Sohier, who was Commissioner of Railroads and a member of the Massachusetts House, introduced the bill that she conceived.[5] In essence, Miss Sohier and the state of Massachusetts had decided that it was unacceptable for one hundred and three towns with six percent of the state's population to be without libraries. As Nourse observed in the same speech quoted above, the public library movement which found "its first home among the congenial hills of New York and New England" was to "spread state by state, westward, southward, through all the Republic, multiplying, by hundreds, by thousands, its little temples of learning, its storehouses of historic lesson and patriotic memory, every one of which is a pledge to the nation of unity, prosperity and peace." Massachusetts meant to lead the way with a "little temple of learning" in every one of its towns.[6]

Elizabeth Sohier was appointed to the Massachusetts Free Public Library Commission when it was established and served until her death in 1926. She was also a member of the Woman's Education Association of Boston. The WEA had been founded in 1872 to promote better education for women.[7] In 1890 the ladies fell into a bit of a slump. They noted that most of the projects they had struggled to start had matured into successful programs and been turned over to other established agencies to maintain. No new challenge seemed to present itself and the members gave serious consideration to disbanding. An urgent meeting was called to decide the question. It was the value of having an organized body ready to further educational causes as they arose that motivated them to go on:

> The Association was so valuable as an organized body, that it should continue to exist, ready to undertake educational work, which in an age and country like ours, must ever be coming to the front. The needs of today are very different from what they were when the Association was started, and it may be necessary, and probably will be, to broaden our lines of work....[8]

In 1892 a committee on libraries was formed, although no mention of it is made in the annual report. Miss Sohier was a member. The next year's report notes that, in March of 1893, the Committee brought in three speakers, including Samuel Swett Green, who spoke on the work of the Massachusetts Library Commission, and Caroline Hewins, who explained what the women could do to help in library work.[9] The books provided to towns by the state under the new library law were to be of a practical nature and of low cost so as to maximize their number. As explained in the 1894 annual report, the Association decided to supplement the state volumes with "more valuable," "otherwise unattainable" books.[10] It began by allotting twenty percent of its resources to create four libraries. By 1902 it had forty-one traveling libraries with almost 1,300 volumes read by seventy-five to 150 readers in the towns to which they were sent.

The women were thorough in their approach to library work. Members made regular visits to the towns receiving libraries and maintained correspondence with local contacts to keep in touch with the needs of the citizens. They studied circulation records carefully and adjusted the contents of the collections to the interests of the community. Noting the success of a picture exhibit on the Library of Congress that they had sent out, they put together more picture collections. Since travel books were popular, they assembled collections designed to satisfy the hunger for information on far-off places, supplementing books with photographs bought on their own trips abroad. They enjoyed the work more each year and developed an intense personal connection with the people in the towns they helped. Their descriptions of these towns eloquently illustrate the emotions that inspired them to continue. Their 1894 annual report, for example, speaks of a village nine miles from the nearest town "in a valley so deep that some of the children had never seen a sunset. When it is considered that there are at least three hundred similar villages in this state, though we hope that some have sunsets, the necessity for [our] work does not seem likely to die out."[11] One town reported to the Association in 1896 that the availability of books had caused a decrease in the incidence of drunkenness. The chair of the library committee observed:

> ...perhaps they are hardly to be blamed for drinking. The loneliness and confinement of these hill towns, especially in winter, is only to be compared with the solitary confinement that is being abolished in our prisons. But the inhabitants of Charlestown Jail are often better informed on the exciting events in the day than are their free brothers and sisters locked in the embrace of winter.[12]

The women were rewarded not only by letters of gratitude from readers, but with encouragement, praise, and requests for advice from other interested individuals and groups. Congratulations on the efficacy of their program came from California, Iowa, Indiana, Kansas, Missouri, Ohio, Wisconsin, and Pennsylvania. Inquiries came from women and library workers in these and many other states. When the library committee chair responded, women elsewhere caught the traveling library "bacillus." The WEA was directly responsible for exporting the traveling library idea to the Missouri Federation of Women's Clubs, which created its own program in 1898. The Missouri president's letter thanking the chair of the library committee is quoted in the 1898 report: "[Your letter] came just when we needed encouragement, as few of our ladies had any knowledge on the subject and that few had little conception of the benefits.... At our recent annual meeting, the traveling library was warmly endorsed. Now fifteen good libraries of fifty volumes each are provided for."[13]

When the secretary of a nearby club, the Cheerful Letter Exchange, asked what her group could do to help, the WEA chair suggested that the club send books to towns in Vermont and New Hampshire whose requests she had been unable to satisfy. Later, after two years of discussion, the chair visited the Woman's Club of Concord and work began towards a state-supported program in New Hampshire. News of the activities of the Boston women even found its way overseas to Italy. Mary Morison, the committee chair, found an article on traveling libraries in the Italian periodical *Nuova Antologia*. The author saw possibilities for a traveling library system but doubted the Italian government could afford to introduce one. The 1904 WEA annual report indicates that, in order to help get a system started in Italy, the library committee appropriated funds for an Italian language library. The plan was to give the library to an Italian women's club that would circulate it. Miss Morison resolved to find such a club during her summer trip to Rome.[14]

TRAVELING LIBRARIES AND THE STATE AND NATIONAL WOMEN'S CLUB AGENDA

In 1901 Dewey surveyed the progress of the traveling library idea in his "Field and Future of Traveling Libraries." The report summarized state-level activities nationwide and mentioned the initiatives of other organizations, such as the Grange and the American Seamen's Friend Society. Some individual private ventures were also described, including, for example, the libraries maintained by Senator J. H. Stout and by Mr. W. D. Witter in Wisconsin. It was women's clubs, however, that Dewey cited as "the most active promoters of the new system."[15] Ten years after the WEA sent out its first traveling libraries, an article by Mrs. Charles Perkins appeared in the *Federation Bulletin*, the national organ of the General Federation of Women's Clubs. Mrs. Perkins reported that there were 4,665 libraries with almost 350,000 volumes in thirty-four states with traveling library programs. She asserted that women's clubs were responsible for the creation of the programs in most of these states and for maintaining and increasing appropriations to them. Also in 1904, the librarian Helen Haines reported that clubs were sponsoring traveling libraries in every Southern state except Virginia: "In all, in thirty-one states[,] women's clubs have been and still are the moving spirit in traveling library development."[16] While many programs started by clubs had been taken over by state governments, according to Mrs. Perkins, club women still maintained over 1,000 libraries with almost 50,000 volumes on their own. These were mainly in states where the women had not yet been successful in securing legislation for state support. In Kentucky, club women taxed themselves ten cents per capita from membership dues to support their program; in Tennessee, the tax was five cents per capita. In Colorado, clubs contributed $5,000, or approximately the equivalent of $200,000 today.[17]

Groups of women working in isolation, however, would never have been able to initiate such a large number of traveling programs nationwide. The organized force of the General Federation of Women's Clubs (GFWC) inspired and magnified local efforts and aspirations. The Federation was formed in 1890 from a small core of well-established eastern clubs. Its first presidents, Charlotte Emerson Brown and Ellen Henrotin, saw clearly the potential for concerted political influence of a very large body of organized women working in common cause. They also recognized that creating state federations would make it possible to unite the many disparate clubs that were forming all over the country, and to involve them in a national progressive agenda. Ellen Henrotin, who was president of the GFWC for two terms, from 1892 to 1896, had a vision for the Federation: "The two great factors of modern civilization are cooperation and centralization. The value of one person's mind or one person's work is steadily diminishing. It is the associate mind that moves the world."[18] Central to this vision was the formation of state federations to organize women at the local level. She worked tirelessly to interest leaders in various states in the idea of federation, urging them to call local clubs together for meetings to which she could come to promote the idea.

The first two biennial meetings of the General Federation in 1892 and 1894 were devoted largely to organizing this new association of women. By the 1896 meeting an action agenda began to form, moving the Federation from an organization of groups devoted primarily to self-improvement to an organized force for social reform. Education was the theme of this third biennial and the proceedings record the passage of a resolution calling for clubs to exert their united influence to improve education from kindergarten to the university.[19] Maine women formed the first state federation in 1892, followed by women in Iowa and Utah in 1893. Club women in all three states soon became active in traveling library work. The first libraries were sent out in Maine by the Dial Club of Fairfield in 1894, just one year after its founding. In Iowa, by 1895, club women had secured legislation for a state library commission to take up traveling library work. The Utah Federation adopted traveling libraries as its first practical project in 1897.

The leadership of the General Federation encouraged this kind of grass-roots activity. President Henrotin personally urged Mrs. C. B. Buchwalter, the General Federation Chair of State Correspondence for Ohio, to pursue the traveling library idea as a means for "starting some good libraries in the State." When the Ohio Federation of Women's Clubs gathered for its first annual meeting in October 1895, Mrs. Buchwalter placed traveling libraries on the agenda as the primary item for discussion. She sent out a circular before the meeting regarding the "advisability of adopting a system of Traveling Libraries, similar to those in use in New York State." She also referred club women to an article by W. R. Eastman, the man in charge of the New York program.[20] A full morning session was devoted to lengthy discussion of the role the Ohio Federation might play in traveling library development. Mrs. Buchwalter observed that legislation would be required to appropriate the funds necessary for a successful program on the New York model. "If there were time," said Mrs. Buchwalter, "I should suggest that we confer at once with the State Librarian and ascertain the facts."

The convention report makes clear, however, that there was no time to consult because the federation leaders were so taken with the idea of traveling libraries that they wanted to move ahead immediately. Mrs. S. B. Sneath suggested that, if the Federation did not feel ready to request the necessary legislation, perhaps the membership could take up the work following the example of the Woman's Education Association in Massachusetts. There was some concern that Ohio clubs would be usurping the prerogatives of the Ohio Library Association, but a librarian in the audience assured the women that the OLA had not yet considered the matter. A resolution was passed endorsing "the idea of the formation of a system of traveling libraries in Ohio, beginning in a small way, under the auspices of the Federation, with the idea that this will be preliminary to a larger state effort later."[21]

Within a few months of this meeting, the OLA had, in fact, succeeded in lobbying for a new library law. The law established a State Library Commission to manage the State Library, opened the State Library collection to all the citizens of the state, and authorized the creation of a traveling library system. Later, the Ohio Federation of Women's Clubs joined with OLA to obtain an adequate appropriation for traveling libraries and to support the founding of public libraries in Ohio.[22] The first traveling library sent out in Ohio went to a woman's club. The Federation viewed the traveling library as a means to help found clubs in the country districts, where women would not otherwise have had books available for study. The State Librarian made every effort to accommodate club needs, and the clubs, in turn, founded numerous public libraries in towns across the state.

Several other state federations pledged themselves to programs at their first annual meetings in 1895. As reported in the *New Cycle* for December-January 1895-96, Minnesota women weighed two recommendations for work passed down from the General Federation: the first, to start a traveling library program; the second, to set up rest rooms equipped with reading matter for country women. Gratia Countryman, then Assistant Librarian at the Minneapolis Public Library, spoke forcefully in favor of the first proposal, and the delegates voted to take back from the convention the recommendation that their clubs start traveling libraries. The same issue of the *New Cycle* reported a speech in which the New Jersey Federation President, Mrs. Yardley, exhorted the first annual gathering of this organization as follows. "If we can interest the club women in traveling libraries, and, during my incumbency of this office, secure them for New Jersey and pledge ourselves to care for them (which by united action I feel sure we can do), we shall have done something worthy of ourselves."[23]

The New York State Federation was not formed until almost two years after Dewey sent out his first library. As recorded in the proceedings of the first annual meeting in November 1895, Myrtilla Avery, Dewey's assistant, spoke on traveling libraries and urged the creation of a correspondence bureau to promote their use. Her recommendations found a willing audience, since clubs already had active library work under way. The Allegheny County Federation of Women's Clubs, founded in the Spring of 1895 for the purpose of stimulating the formation of free libraries, held its first meeting one month before the State Federation's meeting.[24] As Dewey later reported in "Field and Future of Traveling Libraries," the New York State Federation, with Myrtilla Avery as chair of the library committee, developed an aggressive program in support of public library development. A key element of the program was publicizing the existence of traveling libraries.[25]

In state after state, club women made remarkable efforts on behalf of traveling libraries. In Kansas, in 1897, the women of the Social Science Federation, precursor to the Kansas State Federation of Women's Clubs, set themselves the goal of acquiring 3,000 volumes to circulate. They met the goal, with most of the volumes coming from individual women and clubs, and began distributing libraries in 1898. Impressed by what the women had been able to do through private philanthropy, the legislature established the Kansas Traveling Library Commission in 1899, and the Federation handed over its collection to the new agency. Lucy B. Johnston, who spearheaded the original Federation program, was appointed to the first Commission and remained a member for many years. In Delaware, the first state appropriations for traveling libraries went directly to the state women's club federation.

The efforts of Georgia clubs present a particularly striking example of women's work for library extension. Southern states were poorly equipped to participate in the public library movement. As a primarily agrarian region, the South did not have a strong library tradition, and economic recovery from the devastation of the Civil War was slow. Although the Georgia legislature established a library commission in 1897, no appropriation was granted until 1920. In the meantime Georgia club women, who had worked for the original commission legislation, used the traveling library to promote library development. They were particularly interested in eliminating illiteracy, not only among whites, but also among the black population. They were appalled that one-third of the population of the state could not read a ballot, that native-born white children in Atlanta had a far higher illiteracy rate than their peers in cities of similar size, and that half of the black population was illiterate.[26] The Atlanta Women's Club became a center of activity, fostering a plan to establish circulating libraries in the rural schools. Club women encouraged formation of library associations in towns with schools, and sent traveling libraries to these associations to stimulate interest. They got agreement from the county tax collectors to match local financial contributions to school library collections. When contributions totaled fifteen dollars (matched by ten dollars in tax money), they dispatched one of their own libraries to the town.[27]

Georgia women forged alliances not only with school and county administrators, but with other stakeholders as well. Mrs. E. B. Heard, chair of the Georgia Federation library committee, formed a particularly productive association not long after she began using her own home as a base of operations to send out libraries. The Seaboard Air Line railroad became interested in providing libraries to the people who lived along its line, which ran through Georgia, the Carolinas, and Virginia. The object, according to E. St. John, President of the company, was to provide books "relating to good farming and good housekeeping and also containing instructions as to how the people may improve their surroundings." St. John told Andrew Carnegie about his ideas and the program Mrs. Heard had begun. Carnegie, declaring her to be the "right woman in the right place," offered $1,000 in support. Mrs. Heard came to New York to use Carnegie's gift to outfit more libraries. She also received donations from interested publishers. Reporting on her visit, *The New York Daily Tribune* described the magnitude of her early, independent efforts:

> The work was begun by Mrs. Heard in her own home, Rose Hill, Middleton, Ga., where she collected as many books as she could, and began to distribute them. Since then the impetus given her effort by the free transportation granted by express companies and railroads has enabled her to send the boxes in all directions. Quantities of books have been given; and the rooms at Rose Hill which were used as a distributing headquarters are now overcrowded.[28]

In the interview with the newspaper about her work, Mrs. Heard displayed the generous attitude typical of club women:

> "I am glad to do it," she said yesterday. "Before I went into this work I felt that there were books too precious to be handled, that many of mine were too good to be lent to anybody; now I know that nothing is too good for the poorest reader, and I never send out a box that I do not try to put in some of my own choicest volumes."[29]

Like her Massachusetts colleagues, Mrs. Heard also did field work, traveling to any village where the exposure to books led to the desire to form an improvement association.

Georgia women worked closely with librarians too, especially with Anne H. Wallace, Director of the Atlanta Carnegie Library. Club women who were founding members and officers of the Georgia Library Association also held important posts on the Georgia Library Commission. Like their sisters in other southern states, Georgia women made prodigious contributions to library development. It was with justifiable pride that they reported their accomplishments over the years. In 1906, the tenth anniversary of the Georgia Federation, they boasted in the national *Federation Bulletin* that "Club women ... so systematized the library movement that not a country school in the State is without its library facilities."[30] The Georgia Federation *Yearbook* for 1914 reported: "There is an established or a prospective library in every town where there is a Woman's Club. Indeed, it is said that Women's Clubs have built more libraries than Carnegie."[31] Certainly many of these public libraries grew at least in part from the traveling libraries. Looking back on Mrs. Heard's accomplishments, the 1920 *Yearbook* reminded members of what a dedicated woman could do on her own. "Long years ago, one of the founders of the Federation, Mrs. Eugene B. Heard, started a traveling Library and today that library has 45,000 volumes and it requires two trained librarians to carry on the work."[32]

Local efforts in states like Georgia, Ohio, New York, Kansas, and Delaware fed into the General Federation's developing national agenda for libraries. Information on club involvement with traveling libraries was distributed at the 1896 biennial of the General Federation of Women's Clubs for delegates to take back to their clubs and state federations. At the 1898 biennial, a full evening's program was devoted to traveling library work. The session chair spoke on the remarkable growth of traveling libraries nationwide. She was followed by women from Ohio, Connecticut, Washington, New York, Idaho and Vermont, who all reported on accomplishments in their own states. State federations formed rapidly after 1895 and, initially, almost all had libraries as their highest priority. Although the General Federation and its state organizations took up many other important social and reform issues, libraries probably received more attention from more women over a longer period of time than any of the other worthy causes the Federation espoused.

MOTIVATIONS OF CLUB WOMEN

What was it that brought out this huge and prolonged outpouring of time, energy, money and devotion? There is obviously no definitive answer to this question or one that works for every club woman in every situation. To begin with, there was considerable variation in the backgrounds and circumstances of the women all over the country who shared the desire to do library work. The Boston aristocrats of the Woman's Education Association led lives quite different from the small town Michigan women trying to drum up interest in libraries in their districts. Women in densely populated areas could hardly imagine life on the far-flung ranches and mining camps of Colorado or North Dakota. Nevertheless, the idea of bringing books to people who did not have them appealed forcibly to all these women. As Frank Avery Hutchins, Chair of the Wisconsin State Library Commission, observed when he reported on traveling libraries at the ALA Conference in 1898:

> The great recent development of the work is due to that new but most powerful factor in our educational life—the women's club. In most of the states of the Union the women's clubs are doing more than the librarians to bring about the establishment and spread of traveling libraries. When they first commenced this work it was mainly for the purpose of sending special libraries to the weaker clubs, but the possibilities of the new plan as a means of helping women and children of isolated communities have appealed to them with such force that their money and their sympathy is flowing most freely to the destitute who are not of their own number.[33]

Untold hours went into selecting volumes, packing them into wooden cases, arranging for transportation, keeping records of circulation, maintaining voluminous correspondence, repairing damaged volumes, and placing libraries in new localities. In the transcript of the Federation meeting of 1904, the chair of the library committee in Illinois reported that she spent three hours each day on correspondence alone.[34] The value of this labor was viewed by all these women in simple and compelling terms. They believed that books made people's lives better and they knew that there were many people in remote places who had no access to them. Even in a state as compact and densely populated as Massachusetts, there were areas too poor and isolated to establish libraries. Every state had such enclaves: the pine woods of New Jersey, the mountain reaches in Tennessee, Georgia, and Kentucky. In the Western states, immense distances separated settlements. Almost every state had isolated farm families.

The situation of disadvantaged women and children, in particular, engaged the sensibilities of women who had access to books and libraries and could freely engage in the self-improvement fostered by reading circles and study clubs. "We are not content with having things ourselves," wrote the chair of the Illinois Federation of Women's Club library committee, "we want others to enjoy books as well as we."[35] The chair of the Kentucky delegation to the fourth biennial of the General Federation observed that club women felt the need to "better equalize things generally in the feminine world."[36] The "valleys without sunsets" to which Midwestern women were drawn to send books were the tracts of land where farm wives struggled through days of appalling drudgery and terrifying isolation. Club women were spurred to action by stories like the following repeated by Lutie Stearns, Secretary of the Wisconsin Library Commission and chair of the GFWC Library Extension Committee, at the twelfth biennial convention of General Federation:

> For many years I have lived on a farm on the cleared land of Northern Wisconsin, and I made an earnest study of the conditions that surround the lives of the average isolated farmer and his family. I have seen all of the loneliness and desolation of their lives, I have witnessed all the dreariness and poverty of their homes. I have been with them when our nearest railroad station meant a twenty-eight mile trip through bottomless mud...; when our nearest post office was eighteen miles away, over the same impassable roads and where we were often without mail for weeks at a time; when the nearest public library was sixty miles away; when the only element of culture or progress we possessed was the little backwoods school, housed in a tumble-down log shack and presided over by careless or incompetent teachers.[37]

Club women learned at their meetings that there were twenty million women on farms, that sixty percent of the inmates of insane asylums were from rural areas, and that most of these were farm women. How could they not be moved by an account like the following of a woman for whom "the loneliness was so great, the isolation so unendurable, the enforced idleness of long dreary winter so hideous, that she unpicked and remade, unpicked and remade her scanty wardrobe over and over again, unraveled and reknit her stockings, so as to keep the balance of her mind."[38]

Club women were concerned not only for the desperately needy who were separated from them by long distances, radically different topography, or social class. They were also interested in improving the lives of women just like themselves who had not yet been drawn into the widening world of opportunity they saw opening before them. As the library committee chair for New Hampshire wrote in her report for the 1914-15 *Yearbook*:

> Think for a moment what it would mean to you if you were deprived of the present day opportunities for pleasure, instruction and uplift given by books and magazines which are now taken as a part of your everyday life. Imagine, if you can, what it would mean to you if you had never had them, and from this effort to put yourself in the place of the woman who is not able to even have one book or magazine, may you gain a desire to help in any plan which may aid in making bright the dark places.[39]

Similar sentiments were expressed as aims for Ohio by the committee chair on library extension in the report of the fourth biennial of the General Federation:

> Our practical aim as a Federation, is to bring into existence to every woman in our state, no matter where she may live, the beneficial influences of a library and a club.... Every village, hamlet, agricultural district and city suburb ... has able women whose lives are isolated and purposeless, because there are no centers of intellectual and social stimulus within their reach.[40]

SEABOARD AIR LINE

Clubwomen often circulated traveling library books from their homes (1899). Pictured is Mrs. Willie Massey, head of Van Wyck, South Carolina's, circulating library. Reprinted with permission of the Duke University Rare Book, Manuscript, and Special Collections Library.

Women often felt a close personal tie with the people whose lives they believed they sweetened with the books they sent. In Atlanta, the traveling library committee chair reported: "Each club secures by every means possible, all the books and magazines it can and distributes them by hand, as loan libraries in remote districts through its own county. This saves carriage and gives the women of each club a personal interest which they could not feel if all the work emanated from one central head." Through sending traveling libraries into the "mountain fastnesses of Northern Georgia," "the sender and the receiver are ... being brought closer in sympathy and purpose, and bands of love are gradually bringing them in closer touch and acquainting each with the needs of the other."[41] When the chair of the WEA library committee could no longer justify sending books to a town that had successfully established a thriving library, she recorded her reluctance to sever the close ties that had developed:

> It requires some heroism to do this, as these are the towns with the largest circulation and most wide-awake and appreciative readers, while correspondence, and often acquaintance of several years, have made them seem like personal friends. They can still have the pictures and occasionally a special library but the feeling of regret at losing them from the regular list does not depart.[42]

The work also gave club women a heady sense of accomplishment. Inquiries directed to the chair of the library committee of the WEA addressed her as an expert who had the skills and experience to advise others. The women of the WEA were accorded what they saw as the honor of reviewing books for the Boston Public Library from 1895 to 1899. About twenty women were involved in this work each year, with each book read by two readers. During the time they engaged in this activity, the ladies read and reported on a total of four thousand books.

The thousands of club women in state federations who followed in the WEA's footsteps in traveling library work took deep and personal satisfaction from helping others. They saw themselves as part of an army bent on the intellectual and moral uplift of their community, their state, and, ultimately, their country. Some of them viewed this as a sacred trust and approached the task with an almost religious zeal. A conference paper reprinted in 1899 in *The Keystone*, the official magazine of the South Carolina Federation of Women's Clubs, captures the fervor of these missionaries of the book:

> Why not concentrate our work on our home libraries! Why send books out to people who may not always care for them? Why awaken all the craving and hunger for light and knowledge that can never be satisfied? They are possibly content as they are. It is easy to look at our work in this light, and natural; and yet, if that little band of men hundreds of years ago in Galilee and Jerusalem had faced their work in such a light, how poor, how pitiably poor, the world would be today.[43]

The General Federation of Women's Clubs and its state subsidiaries both enabled and stimulated the work. Delegates to the General Federation biennial meetings had the pleasure of reporting their own accomplishments and could hear what others were doing in other states that they could apply at home. The GFWC suggested goals for library work and offered practical advice through leaflets and circulars to the state federations. GFWC representatives attended state meetings and served as inspiring role models to local women. The Corresponding Secretary for Georgia, for example, wrote in *Club Woman's Magazine* in 1899 that when the GFWC Council met in Atlanta, the city had "never before been visited by so distinguished a body of representative women of note." After meeting Mrs. Henrotin and her entourage, "every woman present went to her home determined to engage vigorously in the work of organization," and "thus was a brand lighted in Atlanta which penetrated to every part of the state."[44]

The women were fueled by their own success. The more they accomplished, the more they wanted to accomplish. They found inspiration in the immensity of the task and the depth of commitment required for ultimate success. Reports stressed over and over again how much work there was to do, and how long it would take to do it. The idea that there was great and worthy work at hand, requiring years of planning and effort, and that it was theirs alone to accomplish, was a powerful motivator.

In 1899 Frances Le Baron, chair of the Illinois Federation library committee, predicted the decade of lobbying it would take to pass legislation establishing a state library commission, as well as the years of continued Federation support the Commission would require, when she wrote in 1899 as follows.

> During the next quarter century we hope to find that many farm neighborhoods and every school district will be ready to receive and enjoy the traveling library.... This will be slow work, with many disappointments, but we are working on long lines, with a firm faith in the future and in the value of our cause, and we hope eventually to carry the day with the enthusiasm of the women at each end of the line.[45]

Similar sentiments regarding long term commitment were expressed by the South Carolina library committee and reported in *The Keystone* in August 1899: "This is no fashionable fad that we have in hand; it is strenuous work. But—we women have the courage for it, the patience, the endurance; yes, and this is just between ourselves, we women have the brain for it."[46] Bringing books to those who did not have them joined club women in a great campaign. To stay the course together until victory was achieved was a challenge that gave them an enormous sense of purpose and an energizing feeling of competence.

The campaign also allied them with other women not of their number and placed them firmly in the march of progress. As the WEA library committee chair wrote in the 1899 report:

> Every year we grow to care more for our work and are spurred to greater activities by such letters as the following: "You can never know what a help it has been and is to know that there are so many ready to aid us in building up this library." To which answer can be made that it is a great pleasure to help where those who are aided are also working with all their might. When all libraries large and small are carried on in the same public-spirited fashion, the library millennium will be near to hand.[47]

CONCLUSION

The traveling library was one of the many ideas to influence the development of public libraries that sprang from the teeming mind of Melvil Dewey.[48] Within five years of when Dewey sent out his first case of books, twenty-two states had systems of traveling libraries, with an estimated 74,000 volumes.[49] By 1906 there were said to be approximately 350,000 traveling library volumes.[50] The traveling library idea had instant appeal for the class of women who were themselves just beginning to understand the value of self-improvement through reading. Club women had already started to share study collections with other clubs. Sending libraries to places where books were rare was a natural extension of the club practice of forwarding books gathered on a particular topic on to other clubs.

Women in reading clubs placed a high value on the changes books were making in their own lives and they were irresistibly drawn to the possibilities of improving the lives of others through reading. Although the WEA was not primarily a study club and never joined the General Federation of Women's Clubs or the Massachusetts State Federation of Women's Clubs, it nevertheless sparked interest in traveling libraries in both these organizations and, ultimately, in many other state federations.

Almost all the state library commissions that were created after the Massachusetts commission (with its "ladies' auxiliary" of traveling library organizers) established traveling library programs. Their reasons for doing so were the same as Dewey's when he sent out his first library in 1892. The commissions wanted to get books to people who had no access to libraries, so that those in remote places could have the same opportunities for education and enjoyment as those who lived in more settled areas. It was understood that some places were just too small to ever have an established library. For larger settlements, however, where a library could be a viable entity, the purpose for the traveling library was to stimulate public interest in library formation.

The table that begins on page 89 lists states in which women's clubs began traveling library programs before state agencies became involved. It illustrates clearly that club federations founded traveling library systems in most of the states where they came to exist. It also shows that in many of these states clubs were primarily or largely responsible for passage of the legislation to establish the state library commissions that carried on the programs the clubs had begun.

The table provides information on programs in thirty-eight states where clubs were in the vanguard in library extension. In nine other states, women's clubs either actively cooperated with state-established programs or helped in other ways to spread the public library idea. In Indiana and Pennsylvania, club women secured legislation to create the state library commission and cooperated enthusiastically with the state agency in library extension activities, particularly in the founding of libraries.

The State Librarian initiated traveling libraries in Michigan, but the club federation developed a close and formal relationship with the library commission early on, dividing the state into districts, each with club women assigned responsibility for stimulating interest in traveling libraries and in founding libraries. Information on Louisiana, Nevada, and Mississippi is fragmentary, but there is evidence that women actively supported library extension work in these states.

After Frank Avery Hutchins founded the state library commission in Wisconsin, he continued to rely on women's clubs for financial support and for help in expanding the library extension program. Dewey found New York club women to be staunch allies. Quite often clubs became acknowledged adjuncts of commissions in states where early club programs had been taken over by state agencies. Continuing club support took the form of lobbying for increased appropriations, gifts of money or books, or libraries sent out by individual clubs or federations to supplement state offerings.

It is difficult to make any kind of an accurate estimate of the total volumes clubs purchased or donated over the years for use on their own circuits or for libraries sent out by states. Sources documenting the work of state federations are fragmentary at best. To provide at least some idea of the magnitude and distribution of club work, the table gives a number of volumes in circulation at a point in time where documentation exists based on the assumption that each library contained the typical fifty volumes.

There can be no doubt that the number of volumes bought or contributed by women from the late 1890s to the late 1920s (in the case of some states), far exceeds the 70,000 volume total given in the table. In some states women provided only a short term initial impetus; in others, especially in the South and the West, they were the sole supporters of programs, in some cases continuing for as long as ten to twenty years.

It is obvious that club women had a natural affinity for the traveling library idea. At first the appeal was at a purely practical level: swapping libraries was an economical way for clubs to get source material for new areas of study. In Ohio, club women saw the traveling library, at least in part, as a means to start new clubs in rural areas and gain access to the resources of the State Library. Interest in starting new clubs, however, was not based simply on an urge to swell their numbers, but on the desire to open the lives of other women to new stimuli and greater usefulness. The women may have been drawn initially to the idea of helping other women and their children, but, as their understanding and idealism grew, their focus widened to encompass the general uplift of society.

As the General Federation of Women's Clubs solidified as an organization ready to look beyond itself, the leadership placed libraries close to the top of the national agenda. Ellen Henrotin, who was President from 1892 to 1894, extended the influence and strength of the GFWC by advocating the formation of state federations of clubs. Twenty state federations had been formed before the third biennial meeting of the GFWC in 1896. Most of these began library programs immediately, mainly focusing on traveling libraries. The official encouragement and practical support that flowed from the central organization on down through the state federations mobilized women at the local level. However, it was other, stronger stimuli that kept them going through long years of hard work. Certainly, they derived a deep sense of satisfaction from knowing in an abstract way that they were helping others. Personal connection through correspondence or direct contact was even more rewarding.

Most rewarding of all, however, was the gratification of feeling themselves grow from tenders of the hearth into effective citizens. Women learned, among other things, that they could organize, coordinate, respect each other's abilities, be relied on by others, and influence political outcomes. These lessons made them strong and proud and eager for more.

State Federations of Women's Clubs Traveling Library Work	Initial Date of Women's Work	Date of Agency	# of Club Libs.	Vols.	Years of Operation
Alabama Circulated, first unsystematically, by individual clubs and later taken up by the Federation.	1898	1907	?	1,000	8
Arkansas The first libraries of 20 volumes were sent out by the Quid Nunc Club of Little Rock to rural districts. A law was passed in 1921 authorizing the sending of books to schools, but no appropriation was made.	1898	1930	12 (1906)	600	?
California When the State Library began traveling library work, the Federation gradually phased out its own libraries, turning its efforts to publicizing the State Library program.	1899	1903	70 (1905)	3,500	4
Colorado[1] Traveling libraries were supported by a five-cent per capita tax on club dues. Club libraries were donated to the Traveling Library Commission the Federation had worked to establish.	1899	1903	122	6,100	4
Connecticut First traveling library was assembled by Norwalk Women's Club. Women's clubs later provided libraries to be circulated by the state commission.	1898	1903	63	3,150	?
Delaware The Federation received an appropriation from the state to support its traveling library program before their work resulted in the formation of a state library commission.	1895	1901	29	1,500	6
Florida The Florida Federation's traveling library collection began with two libraries donated by the Massachusetts Federation. This collection grew over the years until it was reorganized and handed over to the state commission.	1906	1926	26	1,000+	20
Georgia State Library Commission established in 1895, but not funded. Federation work finally procured an appropriation in 1921. Women's clubs filled the vacuum with their own library extension program.	1897	1921	?	?	23
Idaho First traveling library sent out by the Columbian Club of Boise. The Federation was responsible for passage of library commission legislation.	1899	1901	15	800	2

State Federations of Women's Clubs Traveling Library Work	Initial Date of Women's Work	Date of Agency	# of Club Libs.	Vols.	Years of Operation
Illinois While club women in Illinois worked for passage of a state library commission bill, they administered a system of traveling libraries. Their collection was turned over to the commission.	1898	1909	?	15,000	11
Iowa The Federation established the first traveling libraries and work for passage of a traveling libraries bill.	1895	1900	50 (1897)	2500	?
Kansas Club women gathered 3,000 volumes to form a traveling library, worked for legislation for a Traveling Library Commission, and then donated their libraries to the Commission.	1897	1899	34	3,000	2
Kentucky The Federation circulated traveling libraries while working for passage of a state library commission bill.	1896	1910	90 (1909)	5,000	14
Maine The movement was initiated by the Dial Club of Fairfield and later taken up as a Federation program. The Federation was responsible for passage of legislation establishing the state commission.	?	1899	?	?	?
Maryland First traveling library sent out by the Hythenam Club, which united its efforts with the Federation after it came into existence. The Enoch Pratt Library also sponsored traveling libraries and both the Federation and the Library cooperated with the State Library Commission once it was established.	1900	1902	?	?	?
Massachusetts The Woman's Education Association was the first club to take up the work, but the Massachusetts Federation also sent out traveling libraries, "school books by the thousand," and "barrels" of books, especially to rural areas of Southern and Western states.	1894	1890	200	8,000+	?
Minnesota Gratia Alta Countryman, Librarian of the Minneapolis Public Library, worked with women's clubs of the city to begin a traveling library program.	1898	1901	33	1,650	4
Missouri Federation established a Traveling Library Bureau.	1898	1907	26	1,300?	9

State Federations of Women's Clubs Traveling Library Work	Initial Date of Women's Work	Date of Agency	# of Club Libs.	Vols.	Years of Operation
Montana Federation circulated the first traveling libraries in the state and worked for a state library commission.	1910	1946	12 (1910)	600	?
Nebraska At its first annual meeting, the Federation decided to start a traveling library, primarily to serve needs of clubs. It worked for passage of state library commission legislation and founded nearly all the public libraries in the state.	1895	1901	?	?	?
New Hampshire The traveling library idea was exported to New Hampshire by the WEA, but a major program did not develop. After the Board of Library Commissioners was abolished in 1903, the Federation agitated for its re-establishment in 1917, and for initiation of a traveling library program.	1895?	1917	?	?	?
New Jersey Federation began work for a Traveling Library Commission in 1895. Individual clubs circulated traveling libraries. Later, the Federation sponsored a librarian and traveling libraries to reach the illiterate population of the pine woods.	1895	1899	?	?	?
New Mexico Worked for a state system of traveling libraries and secured legislation establishing the State Library Extension Service.	1913	1929	?	?	?
North Carolina Federation circulated traveling libraries and donated these to the state commission that was established as a result of its efforts.	1902	1909	92	4,600	?
Ohio The Federation became interested in traveling libraries especially for the purpose of increasing the number of clubs and worked for the speedy establishment of a state program.	1895	1896	0?	0?	?
Oklahoma Traveling libraries established when the Federation was founded. Maintained until it was felt that they were no longer needed, given the number of libraries that had been founded in the state.	1901	1919	?	1,000	17
Oregon The Federation was formed to address the need for public libraries	1901	1907	5	175	

State Federations of Women's Clubs Traveling Library Work	Initial Date of Women's Work	Date of Agency	# of Club Libs.	Vols.	Years of Operation
in the state and had a well-developed program before the state commission was established.					
Rhode Island A traveling library program was maintained until 1924 when the libraries were transferred to the State Board of Education.	1902	1924	?	40,000	22
South Carolina A Library Extension Committee was formed when the Federation was founded and a traveling library program begun.	1898	1943	105	7,875	
South Dakota A library committee was formed at the first annual meeting in 1900. The Federation resolved to work for a state library law and an appropriation for traveling libraries.	1904	1913	3	150	?
Tennessee Traveling library work was initiated by three separate clubs and then taken up by the Federation, whose libraries were turned over to the state library commission in 1910.	1897	1908	108	5,400	13
Texas A club woman from Waco fitted out ten cases of books to circulate in the county and various other clubs in the state followed suit. When the state library commission the Federation had worked for was established, its traveling libraries were donated and the Commission, in turn, asked clubs to furnish an additional 10,000 volumes.	1898	1909	65	3,250 + 10,000	11
Utah Federation secured free transportation from the railroads.	1898	1907	40	3,000	15
Vermont First traveling library in the state formed by the Morrisville Women's Club. The Federation worked for passage of a bill to establish a state commission that began its work with books donated by the clubs.	1897?	1900	12	600	3
Virginia Promoted traveling libraries and placed libraries in rural schools.	1920s		?	?	?
Washington Traveling libraries were an early work of the Federation, along with support of legislation for a state commission.	1897	1901	11	550	?

State Federations of Women's Clubs Traveling Library Work	Initial Date of Women's Work	Date of Agency	# of Club Libs.	Vols.	Years of Operation
West Virginia					
Federation established Committee on Traveling Libraries at second convention. Worked for the next thirteen years to establish state library commission.	1904	1923	15 (1909)	750	?
Wyoming					
Maintained traveling libraries and worked for a state commission.	?			?	?

TABLE NOTES

1. The Colorado Traveling Library Commission was composed entirely of members of the Colorado Federation of Women's Clubs. It had no state appropriation until 1912.

STATE TABLE SOURCES

Baldwin, Clara F. "The Public Library Movement in Minnesota, 1900–1936." *Minnesota Libraries* 14 (Dec. 1945): 385.

Blackman, Lucy Worthington. *The Florida Federation of Women's Clubs.* n.p. 1939.

Buffum, Hazel P. "Iowa Federation of Women's Clubs." *The Palimpsest* 34 (May 1953): 209–256.

Colorado Travelling Library Commission. *Report.* 1904; 1906.

Cottin, Sallie Southall. *History of the North Carolina Federation of Women's Clubs 1901–1925.* Raleigh, N.C.: Edwards & Broghton Printing Company, 1925.

Craighead, Lura Harris. *History of the Alabama Federation of Women's Clubs, 1895–1918.* Vol. 1. Montgomery: Paragon Press, 1936.

Davis, Gertrude S. "The Vermont Federation of Women's Clubs." *The Vermonter* 12 (1901): 415.

Dewey, Melvil. *Field and Future of Traveling Libraries.* Bulletin 40. University of the State of New York Home Education Department. September 1901: 112 (for Oregon).

Downs, Dorothy Gardner. *101 Years of Volunteerism.* Smyrna, Delaware: Shane Quality Press, 1997.

Foy, Mrs. Sidney S. and Mrs. C.K. Schnabel. "History of the California Federation of Women's Clubs 1900–1952." General Federation of Women's Clubs Archives, Washington, D.C. Typescript: unpaged.

General Federation of Women's Clubs. Tennessee Federation of Women's Clubs. *Woman's Work in Tennessee.* Memphis: Jones-Briggs Co.: 31–37.

Harcum, Mrs. Harry L., et al. *History of the Maryland Federation of Women's Clubs, 1899–1941.* Vol. 1. Federalsburg, Md.: J.W. Stowell Printing Co., 1941.

"History of New Mexico Federation of Women's Clubs" (typescript). General Federation of Women's Clubs Archives, Washington, D.C.

Kansas Travelling Libraries Commission. *First Biennial Report.* Topeka, 1901: 3–6.

Kentucky Library Commission. *First Biennial Report 1910-1911.* Louisville, 1912: 6–7.

Kenyon, Esther A. "South Dakota Federation of Women's Clubs: History." General Federation of Women's Clubs Archives, Washington, D.C. Typescript.

Knudsen, Adelia. "History of Utah Federation of Women's Clubs." GFWC Archives, Washington, D.C. (typescript).

Library Bulletin 2 (4). April 1933: 3.

New Hampshire Federation of Women's Clubs. *Yearbook* 1910; 1914–15; 1918–19.

New Mexico Library Bulletin 2 (4). April 1933: 3.

Official Report of the Fourth Biennial Convention of the General Federation of Women's Clubs. Louisville: John P. Norton & Co. 1898: 57 (for Arkansas).

Official Report of the Twelfth Biennial Convention of the General Federation of Women's Clubs. 1914: 340 (for Washington).

Oklahoma Library Commission. *Oklahoma Libraries.* Oklahoma City, 1937: 248–49.

Palmer, Maude G. comp. *The History of the Illinois Federation of Women's Clubs, 1898–1928. Part I.* Chicago: The Federation, 1928: 64.

Peattie, Ella W. "A Travelling Library in Nebraska." *Public Libraries* (1896): 269.

Public Libraries 1901: 227 (for Iowa).

Rhode Island Federation of Women's Clubs. *Golden Anniversary Yearbook 1945-46.* The Federation: n.d. 55–56.

South Dakota Federation of Women's Clubs. *Annual Report 1913-14.*

State of Washington First Biennial Report of the Superintendent of the State Traveling Library to the State Library Commission (1908): 5.

State Library Commission for the State of Delaware. *Bi-Annual Report 1901-02.*

"Traveling Libraries of Texas." *Texas Libraries* 1 (July 1914): 1.

Woman's Work: A Monthly Club Organ. Montgomery, Alabama. 1898–1900.

"Work of State Library Associations and Women's Clubs in Advancing Library Interests: Roundtable Meeting." *Library Journal* 26 (1901): 188–190.

Chapter Notes

1. Several dissertations and articles have discussed women's club contributions to libraries in limited geographic areas: Mary Edna Anders, "The Development of Public Library Service in the Southeastern States, 1895–1950," diss., Columbia, 1958; Donald G. Davis, Jr., "The Rise of the Public Library in Texas: 1876–1920," ed. Harold Goldstein, *Milestones to the Present: Papers from Library History Seminar V.* (Syracuse: Gaylord, 1978); Victoria K. Musmann, "Women and the Founding of Social Libraries in California, 1859–1910," diss., U. of Southern California, 1982. A recent monograph on Wisconsin women (based on a dissertation) that examines the relationship of the women's club movement to feminism and discusses Wisconsin club library programs is Janice C. Steinschneider, *An Improved Woman: The Wisconsin Federation of Women's Clubs 1895–1920* (Brooklyn: Carlson, 1994). The standard history of the General Federation, Mary I. Wood, *The History of the General Federation of Women's Clubs* (New York: The Federation, 1912) describes club library work, as do most of the published state federation histories. A general description of club involvement in traveling libraries is also included in Joanne E. Passet, "Reaching the Rural Reader: Traveling Libraries in America, 1892–1920," *Libraries & Culture* 26 (Winter 1991): 100–118. Anne Firor Scott mentions club library work in her important work book on women's voluntary organizations, *Natural Allies* (Urbana: U. of Illinois Press, 1991). In 1985, she stressed the need for more research in this area in her paper, "Women and Libraries," ed. Donald G. Davis, Jr., *Libraries, Books, and Culture: Proceedings of Library History Seminar VII. 6–8 March 1985. Chapel Hill, North Carolina* (Austin: Graduate School of Library and Information Sciences, 1986) 400–05. Two other papers by the present author were inspired by Scott's work: Paula D. Watson, "Founding Mothers: The Contribution of Women's Organizations to Public Library Development in the United States," *The Library Quarterly* 64 (July 1994): 233–269; and "Carnegie Ladies, Lady Carnegies: Women and the Building of Libraries." *Libraries & Culture* 31 (Winter 1996): 161–196.

2. Melvil Dewey, "Origin of the ALA Motto." *Public Libraries* 11 (1906): 55.

3. Melvil Dewey, "Field and Future of Traveling Libraries," in *Traveling Libraries*, University of the State of New York Home Education Department, Bulletin 40 (Albany: U. of the State of New York, 1901) 3–9.

4. Henry S. Nourse, "The Free Public Library Commission of Massachusetts." *Library Journal* (1896): 10.

5. Several sources name Elizabeth Sohier as the originator of the legislation that created the Massachusetts Free Public Library Commission. The most useful and detailed source is the article by her fellow commissioner, Hiller C. Wellman, "Elizabeth Putnam Sohier," *Pioneering Leaders in Librarianship*, ed. Emily Miller Danton (Boston: Gregg Press, 1972).

6. Henry S. Nourse, "The Free Public Library Commission of Massachusetts." *Library Journal* (1896): 13.

7. The Association made it possible for women to study on their own and take examinations at Harvard certifying their accomplishments. These efforts laid the foundation for Radcliffe College. The WEA also fostered programs to enable teachers and other women to take instruction in chemistry at the Massachusetts Institute of Technology and to study natural history at an institute that was the forerunner of the Wood's Hole Marine Biological Laboratory. The WEA also established the Boston Cooking School, the first of its kind, as well as nurse's training classes.

8. Women's Education Association, *Annual Report* 1890: 6.

9. Women's Education Association, *Annual Report* 1893: 5.

10. Women's Education Association, *Annual Report* 1894: 8.

11. Women's Education Association, *Annual Report* 1894: 16.

12. Women's Education Association, *Annual Report* 1896: 15–16.

13. Women's Education Association, *Annual Report* 1898: 20.

14. Women's Education Association, *Annual Report* 1904: 23. Ultimately, when library experts in Italy were consulted, they advised that their country was not yet ready for traveling libraries. The funds that had been collected were used instead for an Italian language collection for the West End branch of the Boston Public Library that had been founded earlier by the WEA.

15. Dewey, "Field and Future of Traveling Libraries" 10.

16. Helen E. Haines, "The Growth of Traveling Libraries," *World's Work* 8 (1904): 5233.

17. Mrs. Charles A. Perkins, "Library Extension Work," *Federation Bulletin* (1904): 188.

18. Ellen Henrotin, *General Federation Magazine* (March 1918): 38.

19. *Official Report of the General Federation of Women's Clubs Biennial Convention* 1896: 40.

20. W. R. Eastman, "A New Aid to Popular Education: Free Traveling Libraries," *Forum* [New York] (January 1895): 616–21.

21. *New Cycle* 9 (1895-96): 495.

22. At the OFWC's first convention, Mrs. Buchwalter urged club women to join the Ohio Library Association and, in 1899, the OLA constitution was amended to allow membership of women's clubs. Upon payment of dues of fifty cents, clubs could send a delegate to Association meetings who would have all the privileges of active membership including a vote; see *Public Libraries* (1899): 152.

23. *New Cycle* 9 (1895-96): 504.

24. Jane Cunningham Croly, *The History of the Women's Club Movement in America* (New York: Henry G. Allen, 1898) 953.

25. Dewey, "Field and Future of Traveling Libraries" 10–13.

26. Georgia Federation of Women's Clubs, Papers, Georgia State Archives, Atlanta.

27. Dewey, "Field and Future of Traveling Libraries" 79–80.

28. New York Daily Tribune 4 June 1899: sec. 3: 4. The photograph that accompanies this chapter appeared in the *Tribune* article.

29. *New York Daily Tribune* 4 June 1899: sec. 3: 4. Mrs. Heard later came to have a direct connection with her sisters in Boston. Like other library workers in other states, she became interested in replicating the WEA's program of traveling picture collections. The Boston club donated a collection for her to start with. Mrs. Heard, who was willing to send her finest volumes out on loan, was also happy to receive volumes that had been worn out in their travels through Massachusetts. The WEA report for 1906 mentions that cast-offs were sent down to her to be mended and dispatched to Southern readers.

30. *Federation Bulletin* (Feb. 1906): 234.

31. Georgia Federation of Women's Clubs, *Yearbook* 1914: 23.

32. Georgia Federation of Women's Clubs, *Yearbook* 1920: 35.

33. Frank Avery Hutchins, "Report on Travelling Libraries," *Library Journal* 23 (1898): 56.

34. *Official Report of the General Federation of Women's Clubs Biennial Convention* 1904: 30.

35. Illinois Federation of Women's Clubs, *Yearbook* 1898-99: 38.

36. *Official Report of the General Federation of Women's Clubs Biennial Convention* 1898: 100.

37. Lutie Stearns, "The Woman on the Farm," *Official Report of the Twelfth Biennial Convention of the General Federation of Women's Clubs* (1914): 210.

38. Haines 5234.

39. New Hampshire Federation of Women's Clubs, *Yearbook* 1914-1915: 61.

40. *Official Report of the General Federation of Women's Clubs Biennial Convention* 1898: 124.

41. Dewey, "Field and Future of Traveling Libraries" 79.

42. Women's Education Association, *Annual Report* 1900: 19.

43. *The Keystone: A Monthly Magazine Devoted to Women's Work* (August 1899): 5.

44. *Club Woman's Magazine* (1899): 98.

45. Frances Le Baron, "Traveling Libraries in Kane Co., Ill.," *Public Libraries* 4 (1899): 110.

46. *The Keystone* (August 1899): 4.

47. Women's Education Association, *Annual Report* 1899: 21.

48. Dewey never claimed to have invented the idea. A history of its antecedents is provided in an article by Myrtilla Avery included in Dewey's 1901 overview of the field, "Field and Future of Traveling Libraries" 43–45.

49. Hutchins 56.

50. Perkins 188.

5. The ALA Committee on Work with the Foreign Born and the Movement to Americanize the Immigrant

Plummer Alston Jones, Jr.

The American Library Association Committee on Work with the Foreign Born (ALA CWFB) was founded in 1918 during a period of free immigration to the United States and ended in 1948 during a period of restricted immigration based on a rigidly enforced quota system. Strangely enough, rather than being schizophrenic in its policies, the ALA CWFB remained throughout its thirty-year history a progressive body, ardently supporting the rights of the immigrant community to public library service.

LIBRARIANS' RESPONSE TO EARLY TWENTIETH CENTURY NATIVISM

In the first decade of the twentieth century, nativists, who had lobbied successfully for restrictions primarily to control immigration from Asia, now sought to exclude immigrants from southern and eastern Europe. These "new" immigrants were, according to the congressionally appointed Dillingham Commission of 1907, inferior to the "old" immigrants from northern and western Europe, who had arrived during the early and middle nineteenth century. Armed with the biased and unsubstantiated evidence provided by the Dillingham Commission, Congress would reverse the attitude toward immigration from tolerance to restriction with the passage of the National Origins Act of 1924. With one bold stroke of the legislative pen, the concept of America as the asylum for all was replaced by the concept of America as the haven for a select few.[1]

Surprisingly, while nativists and their representatives in the Congress clamored for immigration restrictions, librarians concentrated their efforts on the Americanization of immigrants already resident in the United States. Librarians, as a profession, defined Americanization simply as teaching English to immigrants and preparing them for naturalization. They viewed immigrants as Americans-in-the-making and themselves as active agents in the process. They called for a progressive laissez faire attitude toward immigration, including not only a tolerance for, but also an encouragement of cultural diversity.

AMERICANIZATION DURING AND AFTER WORLD WAR I

World War I was the first in a series of watersheds that shaped public opinion toward immigrants. Many librarians found themselves liberals in a conservative milieu, while others succumbed to the prevailing mood of xenophobia and to the edicts of state and local library boards to withdraw German materials from their collections. During the war public libraries embraced Americanization as a patriotic duty.

THE RED SCARE

During the years of the Red Scare following World War I, the American populace called for pulling in the reins on immigration and adopting a more isolationist posture in foreign affairs. While nativist-inspired Palmer raids were ferreting out politically radical immigrants for possible deportation, public librarians, who recoiled at their recent wartime exploits as purveyors of propaganda and perpetrators of censorship, rededicated themselves to Americanization, abandoning the urgency of patriotism for the former framework of tolerance. Avowing that all immigrants, even those of German ancestry, had unique "gifts" or contributions to make to American society, librarians were anxious to make them manifest to the general public through books and special programs.[2]

Librarians began to cry out for the replenishment of their foreign language collections, which had suffered during the war because of interruptions in the international book trade, wear and tear on the few titles available, attrition, and, in some cases, removal of censored titles. Increasingly, the demand arose for books in both foreign languages and simplified English about the United States—its history, customs, laws, values, industry, economics, agriculture, and ideals. While the need for such books was great, their availability in all the foreign languages spoken by the American immigrant community was limited.[3]

THE FOUNDING OF THE ALA CWFB IN 1918

John Foster Carr, a publisher and propagandist for Americanization, was convinced that the American public library was the most effective Americanizing force.

He joined the American Library Association in 1913, with the hope that American libraries would use his publications in their Americanization work with immigrants. A year later he founded the Immigrant Publication Society of New York, which published his guidebooks for immigrants as well as handbooks and pamphlets on Americanization topics for librarians and social workers.[4]

During the last months of World War I, Carr was employed by the ALA Library War Service to aid in the campaign to provide library books to men in the armed services. During the war, approximately $6,000,000 had been pledged to carry out varied programs of the ALA, over 4,000,000 books had been donated for the use of the armed services personnel, and over 700 librarians had served in war-related activities.

Working without an appropriation for advertising, Carr was able to collect almost single-handedly over 700,000 books in New York City alone during the course of fifteen months. He was able not only to assist the ALA Library War Service in its unprecedentedly expansive war work, but also to win the respect of the ALA Executive Board members and other influential librarians on matters relating to library work with immigrants.[5]

It seemed quite natural toward the end of the war that the ALA Executive Board appointed Carr as chairman of the newly formed Committee on Work with the Foreign Born, which officially began at the close of the war, in 1918. The fledgling ALA CWFB was charged with the mission "to collect from libraries and supply to them information on the desirable methods of assisting in the education of the foreign-born in American ideals and customs and the English language."[6]

The ALA Enlarged Program

The ALA, heady with the successes it had experienced in providing materials and services to the armed forces, was beginning to plan for a comprehensive program to extend library services to what were then identified as underserved populations, notably the immigrant community. In 1920 the ALA Executive Board proposed an ambitious Enlarged Program and launched a campaign to raise the needed revenue of two million dollars, $60,000 of which was to fund, over a three-year period, a program to enhance library citizenship activities. Carr, as chair of the ALA CWFB, was to administer these funds. He cited impressive statistics that more than 800 public libraries throughout the country had expressed an interest in this type of service, and more than 300 were already providing it.[7]

The missions of the ALA CWFB and the Immigrant Publication Society were mutually compatible, since Carr directed both. Indeed, during the fiscal years 1919 and 1920, when Carr chaired the committee, publication activity of the society was temporarily suspended and its work merged with that of the committee.

During his tenure as chair of the ALA CWFB, Carr worked closely with the leaders of the American library profession to determine the direction for the ALA during peacetime. The year 1919 was full of possibilities for a professional organization with a yearning to expand its mission. In May 1919 George B. Utley, ALA Secretary, announced plans for an open meeting of the ALA Council during the Asbury

Park (NJ) conference of the ALA, where potential peacetime initiatives for the ALA would be discussed.

The ALA Executive Board at the Asbury Park conference appointed a Committee on Enlarged Program for American Library Service. Carr, as chair of the ALA CWFB and spokesman for libraries and librarians in their work with immigrants, pleaded for funds to establish new initiatives and to sustain and expand existing citizenship programs.[8]

In October 1919 the Enlarged Program committee presented its preliminary report and recommendations regarding the areas of library service to be addressed. In December Carl Milam, ALA Executive Director, established headquarters for the Enlarged Program in New York. Carr, who had worked previously under Milam in the ALA Library War Service, was now assigned to the Enlarged Program headquarters, where his duties were in the areas of publicity as well as finance. Preparation of the budget for the Enlarged Program was largely his responsibility.

BOOKS FOR EVERYBODY CAMPAIGN

In February 1920, the Enlarged Program committee set into motion the wheels of the campaign to raise $2,000,000. To facilitate the massive fund-raising effort for the Enlarged Program, which was officially dubbed the "Books for Everybody" campaign, the country was divided into ten regions with a director appointed for each. In March 1920, Carr presented a proposed budget for the "Books for Everybody" campaign to the ALA membership. Of the $2,000,000 budget, $75,000 was budgeted for citizenship and other library programs for immigrants.[9]

To reassess the support of the ALA membership at large and to discuss the Enlarged Program further, a second special meeting of the membership was scheduled to be held in Atlantic City in late April and early May of 1920 in conjunction with the bi-state meeting of the New Jersey and Pennsylvania Library Associations. At this meeting the lack of unity among the ALA membership—regarding the risk of taking on more projects than could be handled and increasing criticism of the expansiveness of the Enlarged Program—seemed to presage the doom of the Enlarged Program.[10]

A compromise was struck at this meeting. The "Books for Everybody" campaign for the Enlarged Program would proceed as planned with the provision that half of the money raised would be set aside in an endowment fund. As a result of this compromise, Carr developed a new budget for the Enlarged Program that allowed for the $1,000,000 endowment. He presented a revised budget to the executive board in which the funds earmarked for the "citizenship" area were reduced from $75,000 to $60,000 over a period of three years.[11]

Carr would remain on the ALA payroll throughout the campaign and, as director of the Immigrant Publication Society, would assume personal responsibility for raising the $60,000 budgeted for the citizenship program. Carr, in a letter to Carl Milam, dated 14 April 1920, had also made it quite clear that, if the appeal was successful, the Immigrant Publication Society would assume the bulk of the responsibilities now vested in the ALA CWFB.[12]

The Colorado Springs annual conference of the ALA was held a few days later, on 7 June 1920. At that lackluster conference the Enlarged Program was surprisingly approved once again, although it was widely known that many members known to disagree with the Enlarged Program had refused to participate in the discussions, and others left the meeting before the final vote was taken.[13]

The date for the conclusion of the financial campaign, originally set for 30 June 1920, was extended. By September 1920 the prospects for a disappointingly unsuccessful conclusion to the campaign were foreshadowed. On 22 September 1920, in his address to the New York Library Association, Carr warned that the campaign was "on the verge of a spectacular failure and the disruption of the Association."[14] He made it clear that nothing short of a united effort of all ALA members could salvage the already weakened Enlarged Program.

Carr intended his Lake Placid address as a rallying cry for the failing Enlarged Program. Instead, response to his speech was as divided as the ALA membership over the issue of the Enlarged Program that nobody seemed to want anymore. The Enlarged Program campaign was terminated as of 30 November 1920. The final tally, after receipts and expenditures were reconciled, was a balance of approximately $80,000, barely 4 percent of the funds needed to carry out the Enlarged Program as planned. The share of proceeds of the campaign raised in conjunction with the joint appeal of the ALA and the Immigrant Publication Society was $2,000, out of $60,000 budgeted for the citizenship component.[15]

The handwriting was on the wall for the ALA CWFB. The only options were to exist on a shoestring budget or to disband. Although the committee chose to continue, Carr stepped down from his position as chair and terminated his membership on the committee.

ALA CWFB AND THE AMERICANIZATION MOVEMENT

In 1920, Eleanor (Edwards) Ledbetter replaced Carr as chair of the ALA CWFB. Carr's Immigrant Publication Society had published a Ledbetter pamphlet in 1918, *Winning Friends and Citizens for America; Work with Poles, Bohemians, and Others.* Carr was impressed by Ledbetter's work in the immigrant neighborhood surrounding the Broadway Branch of the Cleveland Public Library and anxious that her methods and philosophy, quite similar in many particulars to his own, be broadcast to libraries in communities throughout the country with large concentrations of immigrants.[16]

From 1920 through 1926, Ledbetter took full advantage of her position as chair of the ALA CWFB to disseminate practical advice on the education of librarians and library personnel working with immigrants. Ledbetter was acutely aware that library work with immigrants often proceeded without a sense of direction and without proper training of librarians entering the field. Under her leadership, the ALA CWFB became a national force for the continuing education of librarians by encouraging library schools to incorporate library work with immigrants into their regular courses.[17]

CONTINUING EDUCATION FOR LIBRARY WORK WITH IMMIGRANTS

The ALA CWFB also assumed the responsibility for providing informal avenues of education for librarians involved in work with the foreign born, who might not have the opportunity for formal courses in the various foreign literatures. Ledbetter corresponded widely with librarians from across the country about the lack of publications for immigrants and used the ALA CWFB as a clearinghouse to disseminate information on the availability of appropriate publications from a variety of sources. The committee, in turn, referred some requests to persons more qualified to offer suggestions and called for volunteers from the ranks of American librarians to assist with the fulfillment of others.[18]

Beginning in late 1921 and continuing through 1924, ALA CWFB members wrote a series of articles to introduce librarians to various ethnic and national groups of immigrants, to discuss their particular library needs, and to provide a common understanding upon which to base Americanization programs and library activities for immigrants. Each article presented information on a specific immigrant group's backgrounds and contributions to American society. The series, edited by Ledbetter and published in the *Library Journal*, included in-depth articles on Yiddish, Polish, Japanese, Romanian, Greek, Czechoslovakian, and Italian immigrants.[19]

The three articles on the Polish, Italian, and Greek immigrants were later revised, expanded, and published in pamphlet form by the ALA CWFB in its Library Work with the Foreign Born series. Ledbetter wrote the pamphlet entitled *The Polish Immigrant and His Reading*. She also wrote the introductions to the two remaining pamphlets published during her tenure as chairman, May M. Sweet's *The Italian Immigrant and His Reading* and Alison B. Alessios's *The Greek Immigrant and His Reading*.[20]

ALA CWFB COOPERATION WITH THE FOREIGN LANGUAGE INFORMATION SERVICE

At the beginning of Ledbetter's tenure as chair, the ALA CWFB worked closely with the Foreign Language Information Service (FLIS). Their cooperation was based on a common understanding of the needs of immigrants and informed by a mutual advocacy of cultural pluralism. The FLIS was originally created in 1918 as an agency of the federal government, but emerged as an independent agency by 1921. Throughout its years of service from 1918 to 1939, the FLIS perceived itself and was perceived by others as a liberal organization working for enlightened social and political reform. The leaderships of the ALA CWFB and the FLIS were not only convinced that their institutional missions were compatible, but also committed to working together to avoid duplication of efforts.

Ledbetter furnished the FLIS with a series of general articles, prepared in the form of news releases, on libraries and library work. These were translated subsequently into seventeen immigrant languages and disseminated widely by the FLIS to almost nine hundred newspapers published in the United States. One series of articles supplied by the ALA CWFB in 1926 was reportedly published 124 times in seven languages. In reciprocity for these news releases, the FLIS, through its various publications, particularly its periodical *The Interpreter*, drew their readers' attention to articles and publications produced by the ALA CWFB and library services available to immigrants.[21]

ALA CWFB AND THE ADULT EDUCATION MOVEMENT

From the passage of the National Origins Act of 1924 onward, the Americanization efforts of public libraries were no longer exclusively directed toward the eastern and southern European immigrant, but more and more toward the Western Hemisphere immigrant. An unexpected outcome of the drastic curtailment of European immigration was the acceleration of the Americanization of the earlier arrivals. With Western Hemisphere immigrants, Americanization was increasingly viewed as part of the adult education movement, which was attuned as well to the needs of illiterate American-born adults, including blacks and whites from the rural South.[22]

In response to this change in immigration and the stabilizing of the immigrant community, the ALA CWFB as early as 1928 began to question its organizational structure as a basically ad hoc committee established during free immigration and to explore the possibility of attaining section status, which would afford more flexibility and assure continuity of its mission during restricted immigration. Action was deferred while the ALA executive staff considered the feasibility of creating a department at ALA headquarters for work with the foreign born.[23]

The change in immigration had a more immediate impact on the public library community. The once distinctly separate goals of American public libraries—to Americanize immigrants as well as to educate the general populace—were merging into a single goal: imbuing a literate citizenry, composed of both foreign- and native-born Americans, with a spirit of internationalism. Although Americanization activities did not disappear, they continued to be centered at the local level with national coordination provided by the ALA CWFB.

Orlando C. Davis followed Ledbetter as chair of the ALA CWFB, but served only one term from 1926 through 1927. During his tenure, two important ALA studies sponsored by the Carnegie Corporation were published: *Libraries and Adult Education*, and *A Survey of Libraries in the United States*. The latter, based on the responses of approximately twelve hundred American public libraries, studied general library resources and services offered throughout the nation, including those specifically offered for immigrants.

Regrettably, the section of the *Survey* directly related to public library work with immigrants was based on responses from fewer than forty libraries. The section on book selection included statistics on the book stock in thirty-three foreign languages of twenty-eight public libraries, primarily in the Northeast and Midwest.[24]

From 1927 through 1933, Edna Phillips, secretary for work with the foreign born of the Massachusetts Free Public Library Commission, chaired the ALA CWFB. During Phillips's tenure, William Madison Randall, a professor at the Graduate

Library School of the University of Chicago, published "What Can the Foreigner Find to Read in the Public Library?," a study of foreign language materials in public libraries and their circulation per capita. Randall used the data presented on the foreign language holdings of the twenty-eight libraries in the 1927 *Survey* as well as the data on general library holdings from the 1927 *American Library Directory*. He found that the per capita ratio of foreign language books provided by public libraries to the foreign-born population was consistently lower than the ratio of English language books provided to the native-born population. Randall also discovered that there was no positive relationship between the number of foreign language books per capita and circulation per book, as there was for English books. He concluded that many libraries were failing to provide reading matter in immigrant languages that was as popular and attractive as that provided in the English language.[25] Responding to Randall's findings and the requests of the ALA membership at large, the ALA CWFB renewed its efforts as a clearinghouse for Americanization information.

Phillips's agenda as chair of the ALA CWFB was a reflection at the national level of what she was accomplishing at the state, local, and regional levels in Massachusetts and New England in the areas of public library service to immigrants and immigrant education. Under her leadership, the ALA CWFB compiled bibliographies that appeared in *Library Journal, American-Scandinavian Review,* and *Poland* throughout the 1930s. These bibliographies were produced while Phillips was chair both of the Massachusetts Library Club Committee on Work with New Americans and the ALA CWFB.[26]

The success of Massachusetts's public library programs and evening school Americanization classes for immigrants was made readily apparent in 1929, when the ALA CWFB published a handbook entitled *Reading Service to the Foreign Born,* "the first offered on the subject." Of the seven articles included in the handbook, three were directly related to library and Americanization efforts under Phillips's supervision in Massachusetts.[27]

Ironically, the publications of the ALA CWFB written after 1924 were limited exclusively to European countries, notably those of eastern and southern Europe, whose immigration quotas were comparatively small as a result of the National Origins Act. Nevertheless, the pamphlets filled a real need, particularly for librarians in the large urban centers of the Northeast and Midwest, where large concentrations of first-generation eastern and southern European immigrants lived and where Americanization was not an accomplished fact.

By 1935 the ALA CWFB members began to question the appropriateness of the phrase "work with the foreign born," since the majority of their work was for the benefit of American-born children of foreign descent, and very rarely for the foreign born themselves. Consequently, there was a second call to upgrade from committee to section status and to consider changing the name of the ALA CWFB to the ALA Section for Interracial Service. Neither came to pass. The fact that in 1941 the ALA CWFB met jointly with the ALA Adult Education Round Table was a further indication of the relatedness and overlapping of purpose of the organizations, but neither absorbed the other.[28]

THE ALA CWFB AND THE GREAT DEPRESSION

Throughout the destitute years of the Great Depression the ALA CWFB was led by Margaret Gabriel Hickman of the Los Angeles Public Library, who served from 1933 through 1938, and her successors, Esther Johnston of the New York Public Library, and Harland Abbott Carpenter of the New Bedford (MA) Free Public Library, who served from 1938 through 1941. The ALA CWFB concentrated its efforts on publishing bibliographies to aid in the selection and acquisition of foreign language books. The committee was particularly interested in books that would introduce immigrants to the United States, its politics and government, its economy and geography, and its cultural and educational opportunities. In cooperation with the editorial staff of *Booklist*, the ALA CWFB published bibliographies in nineteen foreign languages during the period from 1937 to 1941.[29] It also encouraged libraries to take advantage of new technological advances in non-print communications, most notably radio, for the purpose of library publicity, although printed signs, flyers, and brochures were not to be abandoned.[30]

ALA CWFB COOPERATION WITH ALA COMMITTEE ON REFUGEE LIBRARIANS

Beginning in the early 1930s and continuing after World War II, the plight of European refugees and displaced persons not only aroused deep-seated emotions among librarians, but also created a new, highly visible clientele. The employment of refugees and displaced persons was problematic throughout the United States, but most particularly in New York and other large urban centers. From 1941 through 1944, during her three terms as chair of the ALA CWFB, Jennie Maas Flexner, readers' adviser with the New York Public Library, worked in close contact with the ALA Committee on Refugee Librarians, which she also chaired. Under her leadership, both ALA committees made it their collective mission to identify, retrain if necessary, and place refugee librarians in suitable positions in American libraries.[31]

WORLD WAR II AND AFTER

The public library community was strangely silent on the topic of the internment of Japanese-Americans during the course of World War II, with one notable exception. In 1942 the Publicity Committee of the ALA Section for Library Work with Children sponsored a symposium that addressed the issue of library service to Japanese-Americans on the Pacific Coast during wartime. Responses from these children's librarians were a mixed bag, however, ranging from a serious questioning of the need for such drastic action to total agreement with the decision to isolate the Japanese immigrant community for the sake of national security. The ALA CWFB made no official statement regarding the internment of Japanese-Americans.[32]

At the end of World War II Edna Phillips began her second tenure as chair and served three successive terms from 1945 through 1948. During World War II, a critical shortage of labor occurred in the United States due to the redirection of American manpower away from domestic industrial and agricultural enterprises and toward support for the war effort overseas, as well as the lessened immigration from Europe. Since immigration from areas throughout the Western Hemisphere was unaffected by the National Origins Act of 1924, Phillips realized that the importation of migrant laborers from Mexico was the most viable solution to this labor shortage.[33]

ALA CWFB WORK WITH MEXICAN MIGRANTS

After World War II, the ALA attempted through the CWFB to provide library service for these Mexican migrant laborers, who were contracted during the war to work in railroad construction camps and on farms throughout the United States. Carl H. Milam, executive director of the ALA, asked Phillips to conduct a study of the labor situation with regard to Mexican migrants and to report on the feasibility of providing library service to them on a national basis.

In June 1945 Phillips sent Milam a memorandum outlining her findings. Phillips consulted with officials of the War Manpower Commission, the War Food Administration, and the U.S. Railroad Retirement Board; representatives of individual railroads hiring migrant laborers; and librarians and educators with experience working with them. She reported to Milam that as many as 75,000 Mexican migrant laborers were expected in the United States in July 1945.

Phillips suggested that the most feasible setting for the provision of library service to the migrant laborers was in the railroad construction and farm labor camps themselves. She called attention to work already in progress with migrant laborers in Ohio under the supervision of Edith Wirt, head of the Foreign Literature Department of the Cleveland Public Library and member of the ALA CWFB. Phillips recommended the continued support of such efforts as well as the establishment of library service points in other labor camps throughout the United States.

Phillips's memorandum was distributed to all U.S. library extension agencies that might possibly be in a position to provide library service to migrant labor camps. The migrant labor camp projects were continued on a local basis, but plans for national coordination under the ALA CWFB were abandoned.[34]

ALA CWFB DISBANDS IN 1948

During the three-year period from October 1945 through October 1948, the ALA CWFB accelerated the process of its transition from an organization promoting programs for the Americanization of immigrants into an organization working for the improvement of international and intercultural relations. Phillips kept the ALA CWFB membership informed regarding negotiations that were underway with ALA officials to bring about these changes. In October 1948 she reported that the ALA council had approved changing the name of the ALA CWFB to the ALA Committee on Intercultural Action. The new committee would have four basic functions:

(1) to foster tolerance and understanding among cultural groups; (2) to promote an appreciation for diversity among racial and ethnic groups; (3) to support the aims and work of the United Nations; and (4) to disseminate information on group dynamics and techniques for handling potential violence due to racial friction.[35]

Phillips was elected chair of the newly formed committee and served two terms from 1948 through 1950. The principal activity of the new Committee on Intercultural Action was the shipment of food and clothing to librarians in need in the countries serviced by CARE. Although the Committee on Intercultural Action was appointed and presumably met from 1950 through 1957, when its functions were absorbed by existing divisions of the ALA, there are no published minutes of or references to its activities.[36]

Ironically, Phillips, in her zeal to transform the ALA CWFB into an organization more in tune with the issues and trends of post–World War II American society, succeeded in administering the deathblow. The ALA CWFB, which had been engendered during the Americanization crusade following World War I, ceased to exist during the movement toward internationalism following World War II.

LEGACY OF THE ALA CWFB

What then was the enduring legacy of the alliance between the ALA CWFB and American public libraries? In their shared crusade to Americanize the immigrant, they found justification within the immigrant community itself. Since Americanization was the ticket to economic and social success in American society, immigrants did not shun it. Americanization became for librarians not an end in itself, but the means to allow immigrants to enter into the mainstream of American life. Librarians became more tolerant and responsive professionals, who instilled Americanization into eager immigrants while justifying the needs and rights of immigrants to the native-born community.

American immigration historian John W. Briggs affirms that "it is in the study of the educational function of the institutions which shape, perpetuate, and transfer culture that we may hope to find the means to expand our understanding of ethnic influences in America."[37] Truly, the American public library in alliance with the ALA CWFB, through their collective mission with the immigrant community, shaped, perpetuated, and transferred culture from the immigrant generation to successive generations. The sovereign alliance of these two institutions raised our national consciousness to the point where ethnic differences were not just tolerated, but more fully understood and respected.

APPENDIX

Chairs of the ALA CWFB, 1918–1948

John Foster Carr, Immigrant Publication Society, New York, 1918–1920 (2 terms)
Eleanor (Edwards) Ledbetter, 1920–1926, Broadway Branch, Cleveland Public Library (6 terms)
Orlando C. Davis, 1926–1927, Bridgeport (CT) Public Library (1 term)
Edna Phillips, Massachusetts Free Public Library Commission, 1927–1933 (6 terms)

Margaret Gabriel Hickman, Los Angeles Public Library, 1933–1938 (5 terms)
Esther Johnston, New York Public Library, 1938–1939 (1 term)
Harland Abbott Carpenter, New Bedford (MA) Free Public Library, 1939–1940 (1 term)
Esther Johnston, New York Public Library, 1940–1941 (1 term)
Jennie Maas Flexner, New York Public Library, 1941–1944 (3 terms)
Edna Phillips, Morrill Memorial Library, Norwood, MA, 1945–1948 (3 terms)

Checklist of ALA CWFB Publications

Alessios, Alison B. "Greek Books." *Booklist* 37 (15 July 1941): 554–56.
_____. *The Greek Immigrant and His Reading.* Library Work with the Foreign Born. Chicago: ALA, 1926.
American Library Association. Committee on Work with the Foreign Born. "Dealers in Foreign Books." *Library Journal* 47 (Aug. 1922): 647–48.
_____. "Norwegian Books for Libraries." *Library Journal* 59 (1 Feb. 1934): 117–18.
_____. Scandinavian Book Review Committee. "Danish Books for Libraries." *Library Journal* 58 (15 Feb. 1933): 173–74.
Andrews, Evelyn R. "Finnish Books." *Booklist* 34 (15 Feb. 1938): 238–39.
Barag, Esther. "Yiddish Books." *Booklist* 37 (1 July 1941): 517–19.
Bernhard, Josephine Butkowska. "Polish Books of 1937." *Booklist* 34 (1 Apr. 1938): 290–91.
_____. "Polish Books, 1938–1939." *Booklist* 36 (Oct. 1939): 49–50.
_____. "Suitable Books for Foreign-Born Readers." *Booklist* 31 (Jan. 1935): 149–52.
Bettencourt, Americo, and Anne Cabral. "Portuguese Books." *Booklist* 36 (1 Feb. 1940): 217–18.
Castruccio, Romilda. "Recent French Books." *Booklist* 34 (15 Sept. 1937): 36–37.
Coleman, Arthur Prudden. "Recent Polish Books." *Booklist* 33 (May 1937): 286.
Cowgill, Ruth. "Some Foreign Books of 1927 and 1928." *Library Journal* 53 (15 June 1928): 539–41.
Fritz, Ida M. "Recent German Books." *Booklist* 34 (15 Nov. 1937): 115–16.
Gratiaa, Josephine. "The Roumanians in the United States and Their Relations to Public Libraries." *Library Journal* 47 (1 May 1922): 400–4.
Horton, Marion. "Library Work with the Japanese," *Library Journal* 47 (15 Feb. 1922): 157–60.
Houghton, Cecile F. "Swedish Books." *Booklist* 36 (1 July 1940): 415–16.
Kiesler, Stefi. "French Books." *Booklist* 35 (1 Jan. 1939): 161–62.
Klancar, Anthony J. "Recent Serbian and Croatian Books." *Booklist* 33 (Mar. 1937): 222–23.
Korman, A. B. "Yiddish Books." *Booklist* 34 (1 Apr. 1938): 292–93.
Kovediaeff, Nadine. "Recent Russian Books." *Booklist* 34 (15 Dec. 1937): 159–60.
Lawson, Sarah, and Anne Kallio. "Finnish Books." *Library Journal* 60 (1 Jan. 1935): 32–33.
Ledbetter, Eleanor (Edwards). "The Czechoslovak Immigrant and the Library." *Library Journal* 48 (1 Nov. 1923): 911–15.
_____. *The Polish Immigrant and His Reading.* Library Work with the Foreign Born. Chicago: ALA, 1924.
_____. "The Polish Immigrant and the Library." *Library Journal* 47 (15 Jan. 1922): 67–70; *Library Journal* (1 June 1922): 496–98.
_____. "Slav Literatures: A List of Bibliographies." *Library Journal* 49 (1 June 1924): 553.
Linder, Greta. "Swedish Books for American Libraries, 1932–33." *Library Journal* 60 (1 May 1935): 401–2.
McLellan, Mary B. "Contemporary Fiction in Polish," *Library Journal* 61 (15 Feb. 1936): 154–55.
_____. "Recent Books in Swedish." *Library Journal* 61 (15 Dec. 1936): 961, 977.
Markowitz, Augusta. "Hungarian Books." *Booklist* 37 (1 Mar. 1941): 295–97.
Masse, Pauline. "French Books." *Booklist* 36 (Aug. 1940): 437–38.
Masters, Lydia W. "Armenian Books." *Booklist* 37 (15 Apr. 1941): 393–95.
Matz, Sol. "Bohemian (Czech) Books." *Booklist* 37 (15 Apr. 1941): 393–95.
Peschke, Melitta D. *The German Immigrant and His Reading.* Library Work with the Foreign Born. Chicago: ALA, 1929.
Pinski, David, and Jennie Meyrowitz. "Yiddish Literature." *Library Journal* 46 (1 Dec. 1921): 977–79.
Quigley, Margery. "Encouraging Use of Foreign Books," *WLB* 14 (Jan. 1940): 392.
_____. "The Greek Immigrant and the Library." *Library Journal* 47 (15 Oct. 1922): 863–65.
Reading Service to the Foreign Born. Compiled by the Committee on Work with the Foreign Born of the American Library Association. Chicago: ALA, 1929.
Sansone, Leonilda I. "Italian Books." *Booklist* 34 (1 Feb. 1938): 214–15.
Scoff, Theodora B., and Michel S. Abourjaily. "Arabic Books for Libraries." *Library Journal* 59 (Aug. 1934): 609–10.
"Some Recent French Books." *Library Journal* 57 (15 June 1932): 586–87.
Sweet, May M. "Italian Books for Public Libraries." *Library Journal* 58 (1 Sept. 1933): 699–701; *Library*

Journal 62 (15 Mar. 1937): 249; *Library Journal* 62 (1 Apr. 1937): 290–93; *Library Journal* 63 (15 Oct. 1938): 790–92; *Library Journal* 65 (1 Sept. 1940): 704–5.

_____. *The Italian Immigrant and His Reading.* Library Work with the Foreign Born. Chicago: ALA, 1925.

_____. "Italians and the Public Library." *Library Journal* 49 (15 Nov. 1924): 977–81.

Udell, Celia. "Danish Books." *Booklist* 35 (15 July 1939): 385.

_____. "Dutch Books." *Booklist* 34 (1 July 1938): 390–91.

_____. "Norwegian Books." *Booklist* 36 (Sept. 1939): 20.

Zubillago, Rosa E. "Spanish Books." *Booklist* 35 (1 Apr. 1939): 255–56.

NOTES

1. Maldwyn Allen Jones, *American Immigration* (Chicago: U of Chicago Press, 1960), 147–206, 251–53, 262–63, 266–70, 273–74, 276–77, 279–80; John Bodnar, *The Transplanted: A History of Immigrants in Urban America* (Bloomington: Indiana UP, 1985) 1–56; Dino Cinel, *From Italy to San Francisco: The Immigrant Experience* (Stanford, CA: Stanford UP, 1982) 71–100; John Higham, *Send These to Me: Immigrants in Urban America*, rev. ed. (Baltimore: Johns Hopkins UP, 1984) 71–80; and U. S. Immigration Commission, *Report of the Immigration Commission* (61st Congress, 2d and 3d sessions), 41 vols. (Washington: GPO, 1911), popularly known as the Dillingham Commission report.

2. "The Library's Part in Making Americans," *New York Libraries* 4 (Aug. 1915): 235–36; "The Public Library and Patriotism," *Minnesota Public Library Commission Notes* 5 (June 1917): 81–83; Faith L. Allen, "Children and Patriotism," *Wisconsin Library Bulletin* 14 (Feb. 1918): 46–47; Wayne A. Wiegand, *"An Active Instrument for Propaganda": The American Public Library during World War I*, foreword by Edward G. Holley, Beta Phi Mu Monograph no. 1 (Westport, CT: Greenwood, 1989) 87–112; Ida Faye Wright, "The Gifts of the Nations," *Library Journal* 45 (1 Mar. 1920): 215–16; Jessie M. Woodford, "How a Little Booth Helped a Big Movement," *Library Journal* 45 (1 Mar. 1920): 217; and Ernestine Rose, "How the Public Library Helps the Foreigner Make His American Contribution," in National Education Association of the United States, *Addresses and Proceedings of the Sixtieth Annual Meeting* (Washington: NEA, 1922), 1001–2.

3. Aksel G. S. Josephson, "Books for the Immigrants: I. Swedish," *Library Journal* 33 (Dec. 1908): 505; Caroline F. Webster, "Library Work with Foreigners," *ALA Bulletin* 9 (July 1915): 192–95; Josephine Gratiaa, "Making Americans: How the Library Helps," *Library Journal* 44 (Nov. 1919): 729–30; Mary L. Sutliff, "The Spirit of America," *Wisconsin Library Bulletin* 16 (Mar. 1920): 34–36; and "Americanization Work in Seattle Public Library," *Public Libraries* 25 (Oct. 1920): 448–49.

4. *Library Journal* 43 (Feb. 1918): 120; "John Foster Carr Is Decorated by Italy," newspaper clipping, John Foster Carr Papers, Manuscripts Division, New York Public Library; "Report of the Committee on an Enlarged Program for American Library Service," *ALA Bulletin* 14 (July 1920): 297–309; "American Library Association Enlarged Program: Trustees' Meeting Held at Boston Public Library," *Library Journal* 45 (1 June 1920): 506–7; and Dennis Thomison, *A History of the American Library Association, 1876–1972* (Chicago, ALA, 1980) 81.

5. Harry Varley, "Gauging the Sentiment Appeal in Selling Charity to the Crowd: The New York Library Book Campaign, a Study in Mob Psychology," *Printers' Ink* 107 (19 June 1919): 65–68; and Carr to Carl H. Milam, 14 Apr. 1920, Carr Papers.

6. *ALA Bulletin* 11 (Jan. 1917): 33 (quote); *ALA Bulletin* 11 (July 1917): 336; *ALA Bulletin* 12 (Nov. 1918): 405; and *ALA Bulletin* 13 (Sept. 1919): 451.

7. ALA Minutes, *Library Journal* 45 (1 Oct. 1920): 796–98; Alice S. Tyler, "Tolerance and Cooperation: A Message from the President of the ALA," *Library Journal* 45 (1 Nov. 1920): 890, reprinted in *Public Libraries* 25 (Nov. 1920): 518–19; and "A Mistaken Notion," *Public Libraries* 25 (Nov. 1920): 500–501. See also Carr's reply to Tyler: "A Greater ALA—A Letter to the President," *Library Journal* 45 (1 Dec. 1920): 979.

8. Thomison, *A History of the ALA*, 70–71; and George B. Utley, "Shall a Permanent Endowment Be Undertaken for Peace Time Work of the ALA?" *ALA Bulletin* 13 (May 1919): 92–93, also published in *Library Journal* 44 (June 1919): 382–83.

9. ALA Executive Board Minutes, *ALA Bulletin* 13 (July 1919): 359–61; ALA Council Minutes, *ALA Bulletin* 13 (July 1919): 361–71; *Library Journal* 44 (Oct. 1919): 625–26; "American Library Association Preliminary Report of Committee on Enlarged Program for American Library Service," *Library Journal* 44 (Oct. 1919): 645–63; *ALA Bulletin* 14 (Jan. 1920): 1; "The Enlarged Program Proceedings, January 1–3, 1920," *ALA Bulletin* 14 (Jan. 1920): 2–9; J. Randolph Coolidge, "Achievement Thru Conviction," *Library*

Journal 45 (1 Feb. 1920): 103–4 [text of speech delivered to the ALA special membership meeting in Chicago, 2 January 1920]; "The Opportunity and the Outlook," *Library Journal* 45 (1 Jan. 1920): 11–12; "At Chicago," *Library Journal* 45 (15 Jan. 1920): 55–56; ALA Council Minutes, *Library Journal* 45 (15 Jan. 1920): 76–79; Harold L. Wheeler, "That Two Million Dollars," *Library Journal* 45 (15 Jan. 1920): 82–83; "Look Down the Hill," *Library Journal* 45 (15 Feb. 1920): 165–66; Frank P. Hill, "Regional Directors of the ALA 'Books for Everybody' Appeal," *Library Journal* 45 (15 Feb. 1920): 173; "Proposed Budget for the ALA Two Million Dollar Fund," *Library Journal* 45 (15 Mar. 1920): 271–72; and *Library Journal* 45 (15 Mar. 1920): 274–75.

10. Scholasticus, "Is the ALA Attempting Too Much?" *Library Journal* 45 (1 Jan. 1920): 38; "A Plaint!" *Public Libraries* 25 (Feb. 1920): 73; M. E. A[hern], "The Called Meeting of the ALA," *Public Libraries* 25 (Feb. 1920): 80–82; *Library Journal* 45 (15 Mar. 1920): 274–75, *Library Journal* 45 (15 Apr. 1920): 361, *Library Journal* 45 (1 May 1920): 408; "Circular Letter on the Enlarged Program," *Library Journal* 45 (15 Apr. 1920): 363–64; "ALA Interests Concerning the Enlarged Program," *Public Libraries* 25 (June 1920): 328; and Thomison, *History of the ALA*, 80.

11. George B. Utley, "American Library Association: Atlantic City Special Conference, Colorado Springs Conference," *Library Journal* 45 (15 Feb. 1920): 177; *Library Journal* 45 (1 May 1920): 408; "Proposed Budget Plan Prepared by John Foster Carr, and Submitted as Information to the Joint Committee Appointed by the Executive Board of the American Library Association at Atlantic City on April 30th, 1920 [revised May 4th, 1920]," typescript, Carr Papers; *Library Journal* 45 (15 May 1920): 453; and ALA Council Minutes, *Library Journal* 45 (15 May 1920): 455–61.

12. Carr to Carl H. Milam, "Preliminary Draft of the Understanding between the American Library Association's Committee on Enlarged Program and the Immigrant Publication Society," 14 Apr. 1920, Carr Papers; Typescript form signed by F. C. Hicks, Frederick W. Jenkins, Richard R. Bowker, New York, 17 May 1920, Carr Papers; Carl H. Milam, Secretary, ALA, and W. N. C. Carlton, Chairman, Committee on Enlarged Program, ALA, to Raymond B. Fosdick, New York, 19 May 1920, Carr Papers; and "Statement," by Raymond B. Fosdick, Chairman, Executive Committee, American Library Association "Books for Everybody" Movement, in Greater New York, typescript, 26 May 1920, Carr Papers.

13. "John Foster Carr Is Decorated by Italy," Carr Papers; "Report of the Committee on an Enlarged Program for American Library Service," *ALA Bulletin* 14 (July 1920): 297–309; "American Library Association Enlarged Program: Trustees' Meeting Held at Boston Public Library," *Library Journal* 45 (1 June 1920): 506–7; and Thomison, *History of the ALA*, 81.

14. Carr, "A Greater American Library Association," *Library Journal* 45 (1 Oct. 1920): 775–8.

15. *Library Journal* 45 (1 Oct. 1920): 791; "The Status of the 'Books for Everybody' Campaign as Reported by the Regional Directors on July 15th," *Library Journal* 45 (1 Oct. 1920): 798–800; *Library Journal* 45 (1 Dec. 1920): 981–82; Typescript memorandum, 12 Jan. 1921, Carr Papers; and Thomison, *History of the ALA*, 81–84.

16. Carr, "Books in Foreign Languages and Americanization," *Library Journal* 44 (Apr. 1919): 246.

17. ALA CWFB Minutes, *ALA Bulletin* 16 (July 1922): 228–29, and *ALA Bulletin* 19 (July 1925): 220.

18. ALA CWFB Minutes, *Library Journal* 48 (1 May 1923): 406; *ALA Bulletin* 17 (July 1923): 209–10, *ALA Bulletin* 20 (Oct. 1926): 399–400; and Eleanor E. Ledbetter, "Books in Immigrant Languages," *Library Journal* 50 (15 Jan. 1925): 73–75.

19. See references to *Library Journal* articles by Gratiaa; Horton; Ledbetter; Pinski, and Meyrowitz; Quigley; and Sweet in Appendix—Checklist of ALA CWFB Publications.

20. Eleanor (Edwards) Ledbetter, *The Polish Immigrant and His Reading*, Library Work with the Foreign Born (Chicago: ALA, 1924); May M. Sweet, *The Italian Immigrant and His Reading*, Library Work with the Foreign Born (Chicago: ALA, 1925); and Alison B. Alessios, *The Greek Immigrant and His Reading*, Library Work with the Foreign Born (Chicago: ALA, 1926). The ALA CWFB also published in 1929 one other pamphlet in this series after Ledbetter's tenure, Peschke, *The German Immigrant and His Reading*, Library Work with the Foreign Born (Chicago: ALA, 1929).

21. Daniel Erwin Weinberg, "The Foreign Language Information Service and the Foreign Born, 1918–1939: A Case Study of Cultural Assimilation Viewed as a Problem in Social Technology," diss. U of Minnesota, 1973, 20–22, 261; Constantine Panunzio, "The Immigrant and the Library," *Library Journal* 49 (Nov. 1924): 969–73; ALA CWFB Minutes, *ALA Bulletin* 18 (Aug. 1924): 250, *ALA Bulletin* 19 (July 1925): 220, *ALA Bulletin* 20 (Oct. 1926): 400, 563; Sarka Hrbek [i.e., Hrbkova], "The Library and the Foreign-Born Citizen," 98–104; Ledbetter, "Books in Foreign Language," *Public Libraries* 27 (Dec. 1922): 599; Ledbetter, "Recent Development in Library Work with Immigrants," in *Proceedings of the National Conference of Social Work (Formerly National Conference of Charities and Correction) at the Fifty-First Annual Session...* (Chicago: U of Chicago Press, 1924) 589; *Library Journal* 51 (1 Nov. 1926): 979; *Libraries* 31 (Nov. 1926): 472; "Foreign Language Press Publicity," *Library Journal* 52 (1 June 1927): 603;

Ledbetter, "Channels of Foreign Language Publicity," *Christian Science Monitor*, 23 Mar. 1927, clipping, Ledbetter Papers, Cleveland Public Library, Archives; and various issues published between 1924 and 1926 of *The Interpreter*, vol. 1 (1922) through vol. 9 (Nov.-Dec. 1930) [all published].

22. Jones, *American Immigration* 279; Higham, *Send These to Me* 29–70; Maxine Seller, *To Seek America: A History of Ethnic Life in the United States* (Englewood, NJ: Jerome S. Ozer, 1977) 217–19; "A Hot Bed of Citizenship," *Wilson Library Bulletin* 2 (June 1924): 246–48; and Vera Morgan, "Expanding the Small Library's Contact with New Americans," *ALA Bulletin* 22 (Sept. 1928): 474–75.

23. ALA CWFB Minutes and ALA Council Proceedings, *ALA Bulletin* 22 (Sept. 1928): 473–75; *Library Journal* 53 (Aug. 1928): 669–70; and *ALA Bulletin* 23 (Aug. 1929): 269.

24. American Library Association, *A Survey of Libraries in the United States*, 4 vols. (Chicago: ALA, 1926–1927); and *Wilson Library Bulletin* 2 (Oct. 1924): 298.

25. William M. Randall, "What Can the Foreigner Find to Read in the Public Library?" *Library Quarterly* 1 (Jan. 1931): 79–88; ALA CWFB Minutes, *ALA Bulletin* 18 (Aug. 1924): 249–50, *ALA Bulletin* 19 (July 1925): 220–21, *ALA Bulletin* (Oct. 1926): 399–400.

26. Massachusetts Free Public Library Commission *Annual Report 1922/23*, 5, and *Annual Report 1923/24*, 3–4.

27. *Reading Service to the Foreign Born*, Compiled by the Committee on Work with the Foreign Born of the American Library Association (Chicago: ALA, 1929), 3, 29–35, 36–39, 56–60; and Edna Phillips, "A Plan for Cooperation in Work with Racial Groups," *ALA Bulletin* 26 (Jan. 1932): 29–30.

28. *ALA Bulletin* 27 (Mar. 1933): 151–52; *ALA Bulletin* 29 (Sept. 1935): 560, 731–33; *ALA Bulletin* 30 (May 1936): 420, (Aug. 1936): 617; *Library Journal* 63 (1 Sept. 1938): 644; *ALA Bulletin* 32 (15 Oct. 1938): 984–85; *ALA Bulletin* 33 (Sept. 1939): 618; *ALA Bulletin* 34 (15 Sept. 1940): 582–83; *Library Journal* 66 (1 Sept. 1941): 714; *ALA Bulletin* 35 (Sept. 1941): 157–59, (15 Oct. 1941): 620; *ALA Bulletin* 39 (15 Oct. 1945): 401; *ALA Bulletin* 40 (15 Oct. 1946): 386; *ALA Bulletin* 41 (15 Oct. 1947): 401–2; and *ALA Bulletin* 42 (15 Sept. 1948): 69–70, (15 Oct. 1948): 464.

29. See Appendix: Checklist of ALA CWFB Publications.

30. ALA CWFB Minutes, *ALA Bulletin* 18 (Aug. 1924): 250, *ALA Bulletin* 19 (July 1925): 220, *ALA Bulletin* 20 (Oct. 1926): 400, *ALA Bulletin* 30 (Aug. 1936): 827–28, *ALA Bulletin* 35 (Sept. 1941): 157–58; and Lisa Sergio, "The Importance of Interpreting America," *ALA Bulletin* 35 (1 Oct. 1941): 486–89.

31. ALA Refugee Librarians Committee Minutes, *ALA Bulletin* 35 (15 Oct. 1941): 644–46, *ALA Bulletin* 36 (15 Oct. 1942): 675, *ALA Bulletin* 37 (15 Oct. 1943): 371–72, *ALA Bulletin* 38 (1 Oct. 1944): 367–68, *ALA Bulletin* 39 (15 Oct. 1945): 388; Rudolf Hirsch, "The Foreigner in Library Service," *Wilson Library Bulletin* 14 (Sept. 1939): 50–51, 56; Jennie M. Flexner, "Readers' Advisory Work with the New Émigré," *Library Journal* 66 (July 1941): 593–95; and Franklin F. Hopper, "Jennie M. Flexner" [Obituary], *Library Journal* 70 (1 Jan. 1945): 37.

32. Zada Taylor, "War Children on the Pacific: A Symposium Article," *Library Journal* 67 (15 June 1942): 558–62.

33. Jones, *American Immigration* 276–79, 289–92.

34. Phillips to Miss [Julia Wright] Merrill, ALA, 27 June 1945, American Library Association, Archives, U of Illinois at Urbana-Champaign; Carl H. Milam, Executive Secretary, ALA, to Phillips, 28 June 1945, ALA Archives; ALA CWFB Minutes, *ALA Bulletin* 39 (15 Oct. 1945): 401, *ALA Bulletin* 40 (15 Oct. 1946): 386; Phillips to Carl H. Milam, Executive Secretary, ALA, 31 Mar. 1947, ALA Archives; Milam to Phillips, 7 Apr. 1947, ALA Archives; ALA CWFB Minutes, *ALA Bulletin* 41 (15 Oct. 1947): 401–2; and Milam to Phillips, 29 Mar. 1948, ALA Archives.

35. ALA CWFB Minutes, *ALA Bulletin* 42 (15 Sept. 1948): 69–70, (15 Oct. 1948): 464; and *Library Journal* 75 (15 Sept. 1950): 1430.

36. *ALA Bulletin* 44 (May 1950): 168, (June 1950): 221, (Nov. 1950): 406; *ALA Bulletin* 45 (Dec. 1951): 384; *ALA Bulletin* 46 (Dec. 1952): 384; *ALA Bulletin* 47 (Dec. 1953): 544; *ALA Bulletin* 48 (Dec. 1954): 619; *ALA Bulletin* 49 (Dec. 1955): 627; and *ALA Bulletin* 50 (Dec. 1956): 711, 717.

37. John W. Briggs, *An Italian Passage: Immigrants to Three American Cities, 1890–1930* (New Haven, CT: Yale UP, 1978), 278.

II. GOVERNMENT SUPPORTED PROGRAMS

6. Reachin' Behind Bars: Library Outreach to Prisoners, 1798–2000

Larry E. Sullivan and
Brenda Vogel

The library represents to every inmate the warden's desire that
every one of them should feel that an opportunity for newness
of life to them is open, and in such opportunity may be found
an ample encouragement of good purposes and well-meant
efforts. Better life, better men, hence a hope for the prevalence
of improvement.

> —*E. E. Byrum, Behind the*
> *Prison Bars (1901)*

What can I take with me? My idea was that I would read every
book I had ever wanted to. Then I found out that jail wouldn't
allow any book but the Bible.

> —*Susan McDougal (1999)[1]*

In 1986 John Gill, publisher of the *Crossing Press*, wrote a letter of complaint to
the New York State Commissioner of Corrections, Thomas Coughlin. New York
had recently issued a directive banning outside reading material coming into the prisons. Gill wrote: "I assume leisure time for prisoners can be spent in worthwhile reading. Denying books and magazines for prisoners is like turning out the lights and
saying 'spend your time in the dark—then when you go back to society you'll know
nothing about what has happened while you were in prison and adjust ever so much

better!'" Coughlin replied, "It is our belief, since all inmates have access to a wide variety of reading materials through the institution library and the extensive educational programs provided by each institution, the impact of this change will have a minimal effect...."[2]

The institutions charged or concerned with the care of convicts have attempted to improve character through reading since the inception of the penitentiary in the late eighteenth century. Reading is good for changing behavior—not all reading, but only that material approved by the keepers. This view, illustrated by the first quotation and the exchange between Gill and Coughlin above, was the prevailing philosophy of library outreach to prisoners until nearly the end of the twentieth century. To be sure, prison reading programs experienced watersheds during this history: the late nineteenth century with the Progressive Movement and the 1960s with the Civil Rights Movement. But in one way or another libraries were institutions exercising a hegemony that attempted to exclude whole categories of reading as demonic, irrational, heretical, or criminal.

The second quotation, from the Clinton Whitewater Case, represents perhaps another, but much different, philosophy of library outreach to prisoners. No books allowed.

Libraries, still in step with the ruling authority, follow the penal harm movement where pain is paramount. We are stepping away from any utilitarian moralism or even utilitarian pleasure, and just saying no. Let the chips fall where they may. Susan McDougal's experience was not an anomaly either. A federal court heard a case in Alabama where convicts confined to cells are not allowed to subscribe to magazines and newspapers and are allowed to read one religious book and one additional book from the prison library.[3] Many of our attitudes towards the reading in prison have not advanced considerably since the origins of the penitentiary. Let us look at the history of library outreach to prisoners and see how we got this way.

For most of its history the penitentiary has functioned under a consequentialist moral utilitarian ideology. This teleological philosophy operated under the belief that the means will lead to a beneficial end. It stressed the greatest good for the greatest number and focused on equitable and rehabilitative treatment for transgressors. Education played a major role in an offender's reformation. Ideally, reading materials would induce an ethical and moral change in the convicts. "Mental improvement" would teach convicts delayed gratification, a central tenet in the middle-class moral world. And reformers were nothing if not middle, usually upper middle, class. Cultural hegemony was a primary end of their library outreach efforts towards prisoners.[4]

Prison officials and reformers used a variety of means to achieve these goals. Early prison discipline was one of dread and terror, with all facets of the prison designed to remind the convict of the wages of sin. It is natural that prison reformers and prison officials' attitudes towards books and reading was intimately entwined with this harsh discipline. The reformative effects of prison were to be all encompassing, and any reading materials allowed should solely be for moral improvement. During the early years in the Philadelphia system the prisoner was permitted only the Bible for his solitary comfort.[5] Similarly in the Auburn, New York, system, reading was limited to a Bible and sometimes a prayer book.[6] Most prison libraries possessed a preponderance of religious and temperance works. The librarian was almost always the chaplain, a situation that continued well into the twentieth century.

Reformers attempted to mold the minds of deviants at a young age. As early as 1825, the New York House of Refuge, a juvenile institution, began a library to strengthen the character of the wayward urchins.[7] As one official remarked, "Prevention is better than cure, and with perseverance we shall save numbers of little devils from becoming big ones."[8] In the first thirty reports of the House of Refuge, the managers mentioned "instruction of the mind, or literary improvement" most often as a means of reforming their charges.[9]

By the mid–nineteenth century most penal institutions had libraries of some sort. And most books were supplied from outside sources. But almost without exception these libraries were homogeneous and designed to inculcate the moral and religious ideas of the hegemonic classes. The one great experiment at innovative library outreach came in the 1840s at Sing Sing prison in New York. This was the initial struggle over what was proper, moral reading for prisoners.

John Luckey, the Sing Sing chaplain, was a firm advocate of the prisoner's right to read. The archetypal prison chaplain of the mid–nineteenth century, he thought prisoners should read for moral improvement.[10] In 1844 a new matron of the women's department of the prison, Eliza Farnham, was appointed. Farnham had her own ideas about reading, however. Also a moral utilitarian, she nonetheless advocated new and different ideas concerning deviant behavior and prison etiquette. She was a participant in the phrenological craze, but her enemies also accused her of being a socialist, Fourierist, and an infidel. No matter what her "isms" might have been, Farnham's aim was the same as that espoused by other prison reformers. In 1845 she wrote, "It is my purpose, in the first place, to bring the women to a state of order and obedience. When that is accomplished, I shall endeavor to learn the state of their minds and their capabilities of improvement."[11] Upon arriving at Sing Sing she found a library consisting solely of seventy-five copies of Richard Baxter's *Call to the Unconverted Sinner.*[12] Farnham immediately set out to obtain different types of literature, including novels by Dickens, penny magazines, travels and voyages, the greatly popular works of E. D. E. N. Southworth and Catherine Sedgwick, as well as the phrenological works of George Combe and Orson Fowler. The purpose of these additions was not pure entertainment, but behavior modification. The first report on the female department at Sing Sing stated:

> The utility of well-adapted books to ignorant and immoral persons is beyond dispute. If there be any way to turn a man from evil deeds, it is to give him new thoughts. If he ought to think of things "pure, honest, lovely, and of good report," how shall he find ideas, or examples of such things in his own corruption, or superinduced blindness? We must alter the habits of thought before we can efficacy [*sic*] to new motives.[13]

Farnham held readings for her charges and supplied reading material for the cells. She also slightly altered the silent prison discipline by allowing occasional whispering, and she spent time on her phrenological work. Perhaps her regime would have worked had she not tread on the library preserve of the Reverend Luckey. The chaplain did not approve of inculcating a "love of novel reading averse to labor."[14]

And Mrs. Farnham was placing "immoral" works in Luckey's library. Luckey and his supporters could not stomach the idea of convicts reading Dickens' *Nicholas Nickelby* and the *Christmas Stories*, even though the matron had sufficiently bowdlerized them of 'immoral' passages. When it came to the point that Sing Sing was not big enough for both of them, Luckey lost the first round in the power struggle and was removed in 1846. One of his defenders bemoaned the low moral state of Sing Sing after the minister's departure by stating that Luckey's replacement was "said to be a Unitarian!"[15]

Luckey's supporters and Farnham's opponents sprang to the attack. One wrote sarcastically to Farnham's main protector on the Prison Board: "I will not vouch that there will not be an improvement in the moral of both matron and culprits after a free use of Fowler on sexual intercourse and such like virtuous books."[16] Another accused her of being an infidel and of introducing infidel books into the prison.[17] The Westchester *Herald* reported that the failure of the discipline at Sing Sing "has been generally attributed very justly ... to the defective management instituted and experimented on by the principal matron."[18] Finally, the New York State Board of Inspectors remarked that "the matron spent much of her time during her stay ... in the examination of heads, &c., to furnish, 'marked heads' and other material, in the form of notes to a new edition of an English phrenological work ... as a *vade mecum* for keepers."[19] The continuous attacks were too much for Mrs. Farnham, and early in 1848 she resigned and moved to Boston where she worked with the reformer Samuel Gridley Howe.

Thus ended the one great prison library outreach experiment of the first three-quarters of the nineteenth century. Farnham's choice of literature and her methods were too radical for her critics, although her goal was the same as the moral utilitarians'. One of her colleagues stated, "Our great desire was to control without punishment."[20] It would take many years and much effort before we would see a change in this view towards reading and behavioral control.

Beginning with the work of the New York Prison Association in the mid–1840s and gaining speed after the Civil War, penology became more and more "scientific." And to the post-bellum generation, knowledge was the key to social order, and social science was the key to this knowledge. It was at this time that the American Social Science Association first formed. The social sciences grew concomitantly with the natural sciences and the latter's method of classification. It is no coincidence that the rise of scientific classification of criminals occurred at this time. It is also not incidental that penologists and criminologist claimed to know the laws that governed criminal behavior. The new prison reformers were also part of a new wave of professional bureaucrats who prepared the way for twentieth-century environmentalism. This was the beginning of the long century of penal modernism, an age that strongly believed that a multifocal, positivist approach could manage and correct crime and criminals. Science would replace the normative system of law.[21]

Enoch Wines and Theodore Dwight's study of prisons, *Report on the Prison and Reformatories of the United States and Canada (1867)*, with seventy volumes of documentation, fueled a new reform movement which led to the National Prison Congress in 1870. The Congress delineated the basic principles of reform that would dominate the Progressive Period and beyond: rehabilitation rather than retribution;

classification of criminals; rewards for good behavior; probation; indeterminate sentences; and education. Education, of course, included the provision of well-stocked libraries. That prison libraries were still undernourished is evident from the New York Prison Association's summation of the 1870 Congress: "There is no well ordered plan of either buying or using books, and for want of it, the wise benevolence of the legislature in appropriating money has been and will continue to be shorn of its reformatory power."[22]

Thus began an age of active development of prison library outreach programs and the organization of libraries. Reformers praised the rehabilitative powers of good reading and enthusiastically crusaded for books for convicts. When Wines published his *State of the Prisons and of Child-Saving Institutions in the Civilized World* in 1873, all of the state prisons in the northern states had libraries for convicts. His survey of thirty-three state prisons showed a grand total of 50,663 volumes, or an average of 1,535 per prison, an increase from the 1,051 books recorded in 1868.[23] Other sources indicate fifty-three institutional libraries existing before 1876 holding 75,658 volumes, or an average of 1,427 per institution. The books were there, but we cannot determine the accuracy of the count.[24]

Reformers deemed convicts' reading habits paramount in reformative behavior. As one warden stated:

> All the prisoners who can read understandingly avail themselves of the privilege. The improvement from it is astonishing. Young men who two years ago were taught their first lesson here are now good readers; and it seems as if they had changed entirely in body and mind. They keep themselves now neat and clean, while they formerly were very filthy in their habits. They have better manners, and look more intelligent, more like human beings. Ignorance makes many convicts; education alone makes the man.[25]

Can we have a stronger statement for library outreach to the outcast class? Not only would reading modify one's behavior, but it would improve one's looks as well!

Beginning with the 1870 Prison Congress and continuing through the first half of the twentieth century, more and more prisons printed catalogs for their libraries, and various organizations issued pronouncements and standards for prison libraries. These catalogs were ephemeral documents passed out to prisoners and used for more than one reason. The earliest extant one comes from the Illinois State Penitentiary in 1877. Although several catalogs were published between 1870 and 1940, only ten or so reside or are recorded in repositories, and these include suggested reading lists.[26]

In 1876, the year in which the American Library Association (ALA) was formed, the New York Prison Association (NYPA) published the document *Catalogue and Rules for Prison Libraries*. The NYPA, ever in the forefront of penal reform, found approximately one thousand books suitable for prison reading. This list gives the first indication of officially approved reading material. Such books were "to fill the mind with noble aspirations, and not only to inspire substantial hopes and good purposes, but to point out the best ways of realizing them."[27]

The first decades of the twentieth century were busy ones for advocates of prison libraries. Florence Rising Curtis published her surveys of institutional libraries in 1912 and 1918. Between 1907 and 1918 the American Library Association made several reports on prison libraries, but not much came of them. In 1930 the Committee on Institution Libraries of the American Correctional Association issued a manual for prison libraries, and in the next year Austin MacCormick published *The Education of Adult Prisoners*. MacCormick adhered to a vision of the book as a powerful vehicle to change behavior. "The possible values of directed reading are almost limitless, especially in the field of adult education." Reading must be moral and "directed."[28] This sentiment, although dressed up in a Progressive liberal disguise, is not much different from the one Reverend Luckey of Sing Sing expressed in the 1840s.

MacCormick's study prompted the ALA and the American Prison Association (APA) to issue the *Prison Library Handbook* in 1932, for the purpose of "moral therapy." MacCormick's mind and the American Library Association's handbooks represented the culmination of progressive library ideology, and they state well the prevailing purpose of permitting reading behind bars—to persuade and control convicts to conform to the rules of the hegemony.

The history of reading in prison is rife with contradictions, as is reformative rhetoric itself. Prisons may have had library catalogs, handbooks, manuals, and other inducements and prescriptions to read, but many of the libraries did not have the actual books. One example out of many will suffice. Until 1932 the Illinois Penitentiary Library had approximately thirty thousand books. After a riot in that year, which completely destroyed the collection, the infamous murderer Nathan Leopold became the prison librarian and began rebuilding the library. Leopold used a variety of means of collection development, including his family's money, and the library eventually acquired more than sixteen thousand volumes.[29] But Paul Warren, an inmate there in the late 1930s, reported that "most of the books were discards from public libraries. There was a rule that all books that came in had to be okayed by the priest or Protestant minister."[30] He added that most of the good books, meaning sought-after novels, were smuggled in and sold or rented. Convicts not on the preferred list would receive the Bible or *Little Women*. During the same period in the Pontiac, Illinois, reformatory, the library contained only the Bible and works by Mary Baker Eddy.[31] Circulation statistics take on different meanings also. Austin MacCormick stated that one prison gave out two books per person per week, whether wanted or not, and then entered the figures into the annual report.[32] In Kentucky, the rules stated: "Those who can read are required books for perusal."[33] On the other hand, Frank Canizio, a convict in New York State's Dannemora Prison in the 1930s, complained that "if you ask about a book in the library they think about it for a month or two, or they forget it completely."[34] And in Alcatraz, not even newspapers were allowed in the prison.[35]

Only because of his dominance over and prestige among prison authorities and in the prison reform community did MacCormick succeed in convincing the APA to establish a standing Committee on Institution Libraries in 1938. The members of this committee worked with the American Library Association Committee on Correctional Institutions to lay the groundwork for the acceptance of professionally administered library programs in penal institutions.[36]

In that same year a prison library survey indicated that most of the federal prisons had their own library budgets. Eight of the twenty institutions responding to the survey reported that a civilian librarian was in charge of the program.[37] The federal prison library model did not take hold in most state prisons until decades later. Ironically, by the time many state systems finally developed library service in the 1970s, the federal program had collapsed. The federal prison rationale for libraries, outlined in the 1942 *Handbook of American Prisons and Reformatories*, became the universal clarion call:

> Self-sustained reading encourages sound habits of individual study and thought, because well established reading habits are likely to continue after release, and because library activities furnish the inmate with a means of maintaining alertness throughout his sentence and tend to counteract the development of prison stupor.[38]

The state of California initiated services to prisoners at the same time the federal system was codifying its policy. By 1940 the State Library of California was providing loan service to the state prison at San Quentin (then the second largest prison in the U.S.). This service was in addition to the facility library that contained 28,000 volumes. It was supervised not by a librarian, but by the full-time religious director. San Quentin also had a law library collection of 800 volumes. The books were purchased from the Inmate Library Fund, which was built with the interest on inmate accounts. The State Library provided inter-library loan at a postage charge to the inmate of one and a half cents. The library also received discarded volumes from the San Francisco City and county libraries.[39]

When the Objectives and Standards for Libraries in Adult Prisons and Reformatories were approved in 1943 and 1944 by library committees of both the APA and the ALA, the mantra thus provided would be included in state prison regulations until the century's end. Some objectives of the prison library were:

- To share with other departments of the institution the responsibility for useful social and vocational training of the prison population.
- To lessen the need for discipline and institute measures of mental hygiene by providing reading as a salutary release from emotional strain, as a healthy source for idle hours, as a positive aid in substituting acceptable new interests for undesirable attitudes.
- To broaden and support the rehabilitation program....[40]

This idea of reading as a basis for change in the individual and a mechanism for keeping their charges mentally alive was restated by the APA General Secretary, Edward R. Cass, in the 1950 preface to the APA *Library Manual for Correctional Institutions*: "The prison library provides a first line of defense against idleness, apathy, neglect, indifference, and human degradation ... the prison library has a very definite, distinct and worthwhile place in the essential rehabilitation program for selected offenders."[41] In this same *Manual*, MacCormick goes on to say:

> The proper function and true value of an institution library are clear-cut and incontestable. It is not merely a time-killing recreational device, although it provides recreation that for many men shortens the dreary days and years

immeasurably. It is not merely a slow-drip educational devise by which prisoners absorb a little "education" because they have nothing to do for many hours everyday but read, listen to the radio, or lie looking at the ceiling in their cells. Properly organized, directed and utilized, the institution library is an instrument of wholesome recreation, of direct and indirect education, and of mental health. Books are for many prisoners the bridge to the free world; over that bridge they can pass to a better world with a broader horizon than they ever knew before.[42]

The concept that reading would change (selected) inmates reigned supreme in the fifties and lasted until the end of the twentieth century. Both prison authorities and librarians, who always needed to appeal to the overarching interests of the state, found it necessary to attach specific reformation attributes to reading and library service. The mission of the public library as the arsenal for democracy or the teacher's intoxicated vision of reading as a molder of character did not hold a candle to the belief that books can reform the wicked or enable the deviant to become a law abiding citizen.

Court decisions in the forties paved the way for the prisoner's civil rights litigation of the 1960s, which later resulted in a federal court mandate to establish law libraries in prisons. Throughout the 1960s prisoners and human rights advocates bombarded the courts demanding court access. Marjorie LeDonne, in her landmark *Survey of Library and Information Problems in Correctional Institutions*, wrote: "During the period following *ex parte Hull* (1941) correctional agencies were not required to provide inmates with law books, but there was a recognized prohibition against the active intervention or denial of access to law books at hand."[43]

In the second half of the 1960s another branch of the federal government made a significant contribution to the development of prison libraries. In 1966 Congress added Title IV-A to the *Library Services and Construction Act* (LSCA), providing funding for institutional libraries. Before the LSCA, Federal funding to aid prison libraries was non-existent; thus "the real turning point in public library service to the institutionalized, ... came in the 1960s."[44]

Even though the amount of money set aside for prisons did not result in revolutionary or permanent changes in prison libraries across the board, there were ancillary effects of inclusion. In the library community it raised consciousness about prison library service and librarianship. As the distributors of these funds, the state library agencies became involved in lobbying for prison library service. Many added institutional consultants to their staffs.

The combination of institutional consultants and federal money enabled the state library agency to negotiate with prison authorities. The offer of funding provided the basis for the negotiation. The goal was to get them to recognize the need for service or, at least, to accept the underwriting of the service and, in many cases, to match the federal funds for their facility library programs. Some correctional agencies created professional library director positions with federal monies, and many began to hire professional librarians to manage the facility service. The state agency consultants provided training for the prison librarians and networked prison libraries to other library resources in their state. The LSCA certainly gave an important boost to the professionalization of prison librarianship.

THE RISE OF PRISONERS' RIGHTS

The political activism of the sixties provoked many organizations to focus on the plight of the inmate. In 1968 the American Association of Law Libraries (AALL) Committee on Law Library Service to Prisoners issued two publications: *Law Libraries Which Offer Service to Prisoners* and *Law Librarian Consultants to Correctional Institutions*. They also published the *Recommended Minimum Collection for Prison Law Libraries*. Judges and court masters relied on this list of federal and state law publications to enforce the law library agreements between the prison agencies and the courts.

Until 1969 the federal courts had been very reluctant to interfere in the administration of prisons. After that date the courts reversed the "hands-off" policy. This reversal in court policy fueled the prisoners' rights movement. It was this belief that prisoners did have rights that enabled librarians to separate their library goals from correctional agency goals.

The 1970s were the golden years of prison library service. It seemed as if everyone—prisoners, bar associations, criminal justice personnel, judges, academics, librarians, political activists, and Congress—was examining and challenging the "conditions of confinement," each in their own way.

In 1971 Congress passed the *Law Enforcement Assistance Administration Act* (LEAA), which provided funds for prison law libraries and for materials "to help prisoners prepare themselves for re-entry and for positive use of offender leisure time." In 1974 the Illinois Division of Corrections entered into an agreement with the state library and Illinois public libraries to provide library service to prisoners. In Ohio, the state library placed their catalog on microfilm at the Marysville, Ohio, Women's Reformatory, a prison which became one of the top five users of their inter-library loan service.

The 1970s were also exciting times of emergence and recognition for prison libraries. Three professional library periodicals devoted entire editions to correctional library service: *Illinois Libraries*, 1974; *Wilson Library Bulletin*, 1977; and *Library Trends*, 1977. Joan A. Stout and Gilda Turitz launched in October of 1974 *Inside—Outside; a Newsletter on Library Services to Youth and Adults in Prisons, Jails and Detention Centers*.

FROM REHABILITATION TO RETRIBUTION

While prisoners' rights issues, including the "right to read," gained popular support within and beyond the library community, there was a dark side brewing. An analysis of criminal justice literature marks this as a period of evolution from rehabilitation to retribution. Pro-punishment academicians, such as James Q. Wilson and Ernest van den Haag, called for incarceration to be an instrument of simple punitive action. Other academicians, led by Robert Martinson, attacked the concept of rehabilitation as a failure.

Prison authorities and correctional professionals were caught in a trend opposite to the trend being followed by librarians and library supporters. In 1977 Barratt Wilkins, Florida State Librarian, aptly summarized this confusion:

Maryland House of Correction, Maryland Correction Education Libraries, Jessup, Maryland. Credit: Brenda Vogel.

> While a majority of correctional officials believe that rehabilitation is a viable objective, the concept has come under increasing criticism by many responsible individuals involved in the correctional field. What remains, however, is that correctional library programs should be based on the provision of quality public library service.... This dichotomy of program philosophies may be partially resolved by placing stronger emphasis on another major assumption in the new correctional library standards, i.e. that services available to communities, including library services, must be available in correctional residential facilities.[45]

In the same year, amid the shift in correctional intent, the Supreme Court issued *Bounds v. Smith*, a decision that was the culmination of decades of inmate litigation. In *Bounds* the Court said that all state prisons must provide "meaningful access to the courts through people trained in the law or through law library collections."[46]

By the 1980s economic recession was taking its toll on library budgets. Although incarceration rates continued to rise, public library extension and special services to the institutionalized were terminated. Clara E. Lucioli captured the reality of outreach service at that time when she wrote: "Service and commitment to the institutionalized have shown no great stellar attributes; the here-and-there, off again, on-again treatment resembles more the flickering of a light bulb with a loose connection."[47]

After the *Bounds* decision, through the eighties and the nineties, prison authorities reluctantly, and only through court order, installed law library collections in their facilities. Too often the general prison library program was overshadowed, neglected, or terminated due to the law library mandate. Meanwhile, in the eighties construction of new correctional facilities flourished, with one thousand new beds added each week. The prison population more than doubled from the previous decade. The conflict over the goals of incarceration and the library's role in the incarceree's life did not abate. In many states, the general library was sustained only as long as LSCA money was obtained for its support.

In 1981 the ALA and the American Correctional Association (ACA)—formerly the APA—issued *Library Standards for Adult Correctional Institutions.* This publication cites "new developments in and new legal standards for the treatment and habilitation of adults" and increased "emphasis upon community involvement with the correctional institution" as reasons why the associations undertook to revise the old standards.[48] In 1982 the ALA Council adopted a "Resolution on Prisoners' Right to Read." It was based on California legislation, and it urged ALA state chapters to work toward getting similar legislation passed. The ALA, however, was never again involved in urging legislative or judicial support for prison libraries.

Meanwhile, the ACA was functioning more as an accreditation body than as an organization of reform. It no longer accepted standards for libraries developed by ALA. Its own standards for libraries were written with an eye toward keeping prison administrators out of court, rather than from a librarian's service perspective.

In the 1980s the ACA wholeheartedly supported dumping donated books on prison libraries without regard for how this action undermined the establishment of permanent library line item budgets or mocked collection management and development policies. Librarians began abandoning the notions of treatment and behavioral change that had already been ditched by the correctional community. Instead of focusing on the inmates' rehabilitation, prison librarians began to focus on providing resources to meet the informational needs and reading interests expressed by inmates.

In 1987 William Coyle's *Libraries in Prisons: A Blending of Institutions* flamed the debate about the purpose of the prison library. Coyle's argument harkened back to the treatment and rehabilitation philosophy of the nineteenth century. He reasoned that "inmates of state and federal prisons, unlike citizens of public library districts, are not the legitimizers of the services they receive. The state is, and the state's interests, reflected in the goals of correctional institutions, should therefore determine the nature and purpose of library service to prisoners."[49]

In the 1989 special-focus issue of the *Wilson Library Bulletin,* "Inside Prison Libraries," Daniel Suvak critiqued Coyle's premise: "He [Coyle] calls for a complete rethinking of the model on which prison library service is based, namely, the public library model.... By virtue of the name 'library,' this service is heir to a wealth of goals and ideals, not the least of which is the Library Bill of Rights."[50]

There was no evidence of fallout from the Coyle book in either the correctional or the library community. The philosophy of prison library service in the 1992 revision of ALA *Library Standards for Adult Correctional Institutions* revealed total opposition to Coyle's "change-based" model. The philosophy outlined in these standards was based on a prisoner's rights model: "Library services shall ensure the inmate's right to read and their right to free access to information. Services shall encompass the same variety of material, formats and programs as available in the outside community...."[51]

These standards too were completely out of step with political trends in the U.S. by the time they were published. The nineties were tumultuous for the prison industry. The number of people incarcerated was twice what it had been in the 1980s. In the final decades of the century, every politician from George Bush to local mayoral candidates ran as leaders who would be tough on criminals. "Lock 'em up and throw away the key" translated into legislation that did away with parole, demanded life in prison for three offenses ("three strikes and you're out"), and attempted to limit the federal court authority over prison conditions.

The *Prison Litigation Reform Act* (PLRA) lessened court oversight of prison conditions and set the tone for prison officials to begin the removal of privileges. This act was passed as an effort to limit "frivolous" inmate lawsuits and to return to the politics of "hands off" the prison authorities. At the same time, the Supreme Court modified the prison law library mandate. In the *Lewis v. Casey* (1996) decision, the Court made it clear that the right of access to the courts was not necessarily a right to a law library, but simply a right to get a claim to court. There were no amicus briefs filed by any library association on behalf of prisoners' rights to law libraries. As a result of this decision, the Arizona Department of Corrections put their law book collections up for sale. The Arizona Annotated Code was one of the titles removed from the facilities and placed on sale. The Department replaced this collection with about fifteen titles, including an unannotated edition of the code. Other states followed, dismantling their law book collections.

In 1997 the *Library Services and Construction Act* was replaced by the *Library Service and Technology Act* (LSTA). There was no mention in the LSTA of set-asides for institutions. State library agencies were no longer obliged to encourage the development of prison libraries. They could support, if they chose to, the use of computer technology in prison libraries through these federal funds.

Prison authorities, who were loath to provide computer technology for prisoners, were grateful for this new Act. By 2000 there was still no prison library on record permitting inmate access to the Internet. In an article in *American Libraries*, Sullivan summarized the issues surrounding the Internet and the prisoner at the beginning of the new millennium:

> Reading was and is reformative and helps develop critical thinking. The Internet accesses information only. Since we no longer hold fast to rehabilitative concepts, however, the use of the Internet fits right in with our new way of looking at imprisonment. Prison is to punish, and any rehabilitative or other consequentialist programs for inmates must help with their transition to a free society upon release.[52]

In many states, prison librarians were able to go online in the course of answering reference questions. To the inmate, the Internet was forbidden. Once again the need to control information in the guise of "a legitimate penological interest" prevailed against another contemporary ideology—to prepare prisoners for transitioning back to the community—and common sense.

Prison libraries had come full circle. For almost twenty years, under the protection of the court, many prison librarians had attempted to meet the needs expressed by their patrons, in spite of the ideologies of prison authorities. Toward the close of the twentieth century, prison libraries, which had become libraries not unlike those in the outside world, were at the mercy of a conservative Supreme Court and a political climate that supported long and hard incarceration. One may conclude that if prison authorities maintain their decision to exclude online access, it would likely mean that the nineteenth-century ethos of the keepers to control reading and information will frame prison libraries in the twenty-first century.

NOTES

1. Susan McDougal is the ex–Whitewater defendant acquitted of wrongdoing in the Clinton related real estate scandal. Her statement is found in "Ex-Prisoner's Dilemma," *New York Times Magazine* 25 April 1999:16.

2. Jerome Washington Papers. Sealy Library, John Jay College of Criminal Justice, The City University of New York.

3. *USA Today* 31 Aug. 1999: A7.

4. For a general overview of the utilitarian and deontological philosophies of prison discipline and their major proponents, see Larry E. Sullivan, *The Prison Reform Movement* (Boston: Twayne, 1990).

5. According to the Swedish visitor Frederika Bremer, the Pennsylvania Prison had a considerable library in 1850: "The library was large and contained in addition to the religious books, scientific treatises, travel books, and literary works, selected with discrimination. It was with no grudging hand that the seeds of learning were strewn to the prison's children." Quoted in Torsten Eriksson, *The Reformers: An Historical Survey of Pioneer Experiments in the Treatment of Criminals* (New York: Oxford UP, 1976) 71. The New York Prison Association, *Fifth Report* (Albany, 1850) 104 ff., mentions that the library was better than previously, yet still needed improvements. Negley Teeters and John D. Shearer, *The Prison at Philadelphia, Cherry Hill: The Separate System of Penal Discipline: 1829–1913* (New York: Columbia UP, 1957) 160, assert that the library volumes were primarily of a religious nature in the 1850s.

6. W. David Lewis, *From Newgate to Dannemora: The Rise of the Penitentiary in New York, 1796–1848* (Ithaca, NY: Cornell UP, 1965) 92.

7. Robert S. Pickett, *House of Refuge: Origins of Juvenile Reform in New York State, 1815–1857* (Syracuse, NY: Syracuse UP, 1969) 74–75.

8. Dorothy C. Barck, ed., *Letters of John Pintard to His Daughter, Eliza Noel Pintard Davidson, 1816–1833*, vol. 2 (New York: New-York Historical Society, 1937–1940) 257; Larry E. Sullivan, "Books, Power, and the Development of Libraries in the New Republic: The Prison and Other Journals of John Pintard of New York," *Journal of Library History* 21 (Spring 1986): 416, n. 48.

9. Pickett, *House of Refuge* 192.

10. For Luckey's life and views, see John Luckey, *Life in Sing Sing Prison, as Seen in a Twelve Years' Chaplaincy* (New York: N. Tibbals, 1860).

11. [Eliza Farnham], *First Report of the Female Department of the Prison Association of New York* (New York: W. Dean, 1845) 13.

12. Georgiana Bruce Kirby, *Years of Experience: An Autobiographical Narrative* (New York: G. P. Putnam's Sons, 1887) 193. Kirby was Farnham's assistant.

13. [Farnham], *First Report of the Female Department* 16.

14. Lewis, *From Newgate to Dannemora* 245.

15. Charles Halsey to Eliza Farnham, 3 Aug. 1846, John Bigelow Papers, New York Public Library. The new chaplain was Matthew Gordon.

16. J. M. Morse to John Bigelow, 10 Aug. 186, John Bigelow Papers, NYPL.

17. John Bigelow to T. W. Niven, 6 Aug. 1846, John Bigelow Papers, NYPL.

18. *Westchester Herald* 31, 22 Feb. 1848.

19. *Westchester Herald* 31, 22 Feb. 1848. The phrenological work was Marmaduke Sampson's book on criminal behavior, *Rationale of Crime*.

20. Kirby, *Years of Experience* 196.

21. In general, see Samuel P. Hays, *The Response to Industrialism, 1885–1914* (Chicago: U of Chicago Press, 1995); Robert H. Wiebe, *The Search for Order, 1877–1920* (New York: Hill and Wang, 1967); and

the bibliography in Arthur S. Link and Richard L. McCormick, *Progressivism* (Arlington Heights, IL: Harland Davidson, 1983).

22. New York State Prison Association, *Twenty-Sixth Report* (Albany, 1871) 41.

23. Enoch C. Wines, *The State of Prisons and of Child-Saving Institutions in the Civilized World* (1880; rpt., Montclair, NJ: Patterson Smith, 1968) 102.

24. Some sources of statistical information on prison libraries: S. J. Barrows, *Prison Systems of the United States. Reports Prepared for the International Prison Commission* (Washington: GPO, 1900); William J. Rhees, *Manual of Public Libraries, Institutions, and Societies, in the United States and British Provinces of North America* (Philadelphia: J. P. Lippincott, 1889); U.S. Bureau of Education, *Public Libraries in the United States of America* (Washington: GPO, 1876); U.S. Bureau of Education, *Report for the Year 1884-85* (Washington: GPO, 1886); "Annual Statistics and Quarterly News Items," *News Notes of California Libraries* 13 (October 1918): 452–810; Ray E. Held, *Public Libraries in California* (Berkeley: U of California Press, 1963); Katherine Sharp, *Illinois Libraries*, parts 1–4, *University of Illinois Bulletin* (Urbana, 1906–1908); Blake McKelvey, ed., *The History of Rochester Libraries* (Rochester, NY: Rochester Historical Society, 1937); Mirpah G. Blair, "Some Early Libraries of Oregon," *Washington Historical Quarterly* 17 (1926): 259–270. If we look closely at the above sources, we see that quoting average volumes per institution is meaningless. The prisons in Pennsylvania, Illinois, and New York had the largest numbers, while the majority had from three to five hundred volumes per institution. The statistics are also suspect. For wide variations in number, see Robert Gunn Crawford, "A History of the Kentucky Penitentiary System, 1865–1937," diss., U of Kentucky, 1955, 217.

25. Wines, *State of Prisons* 102–3.

26. Florence Rising Curtis in *The Libraries of the American State and National Institutions for Defectives, Dependents, and Delinquents* (Minneapolis: U of Minnesota, 1918) mentions twenty-three catalogs in 1912. Augustus Kuhlman in *A Guide to Material on Crime and Criminal Justice*, "corrected by Dorothy Campbell Culver" (Montclair, NJ: Patterson Smith, 1969), lists fifteen. Many of these can no longer be located in the repositories. Larry Sullivan has a number of prison library catalogs in his own collection and some are mimeographed and not even identified by institution.

27. New York Prison Association, *Catalogue and Rules for Prison Libraries to Aid in the Selection and Maintenance of Reading Matter in the Prisons and Jails* (Albany: Argus, 1877).

28. Austin H. MacCormick, *The Education of Adult Prisoners* (New York: National Society of Penal Information, 1931) 150.

29. Nathan Leopold, *Life Plus 99 Years* (New York: Doubleday, 1958) 215–21; "Head of a Prison Library," *Library Journal* 83 (Feb. 1958): 558–60.

30. Paul Warren, *Next Time Is for Life* (New York: Dell, 1953): 59.

31. Warren 152.

32. MacCormick, *Education of Adult Prisoners* 152.

33. Haynes McMullen, "Special Libraries in Ante-Bellum Kentucky," *Register of the Kentucky Historical Society* 59 (1961): 39.

34. Frank Canizio and Robert Markel, *Man Against Fate* (New York: Frederick Fell, 1958): 179.

35. James Henry Audett, *Rap Sheet: My Life Story* (New York: William Sloane, 1954): 159. On the other hand, the Kansas Penitentiary allowed the convicts to read newspapers much earlier; see Carl Arnold, *The Kansas Inferno: A Study of the Criminal Problem* (Wichita: Wonderland, 1906): 20. Regulations concerning newspapers varied widely, depending on time and location, and it is difficult to make generalizations. It is interesting to note that *The Prison Mirror*, the newspaper of the Minnesota state prison, had among its founders Cole Younger and his brothers, imprisoned there after the James-Younger gang's unsuccessful robbery of the Northfield, Minnesota, bank.

36. As the APA evolved into the American Correctional Association (ACA), the focus of the organization changed from an emphasis on prison reform to providing a "profitable" accreditation function. The Committee on Institution Libraries, at first vigorous, became obscure. In the 1990s, along with the acceptance of women and technology by the correction's community, it became the Committee on Libraries. Brenda Vogel, committee chair 1983–86 and again 1994–96, reported that the committee had very little clout within the organizations during the eighties and nineties. It was threatened with dissolution during the eighties, when she refused on behalf of her state to be a recipient of the donations of publishers' overstocks. An IRS regulation allowed the publishing industry to donate books to the nation's poor in exchange for a tax break. The non-profit ACA qualified to become a conduit for the distribution of the massive giveaway. Several state correctional agencies built warehouses and developed inmate warehousing training programs, expecting to receive tons of reading materials. Urban legend has it that the foundations of many prisons constructed in the eighties and nineties were laid upon heaps of Darryl Zanuck's biography.

37. Rudolf Engelbarts, *Books in Stir* (Metuchen, NJ: Scarecrow Press, 1972): 45–47.

38. *Handbook of American Prisons and Reformatories,* 5th ed., vol. 2 (New York: The Osborne Association, 1942) 47.

39. *Handbook of American Prisons* 243.

40. *Library Manual for Correctional Institutions: A Handbook of Library Standards and Procedures for Prisons, Reformatories for Men and Women and Other Adult Correctional Institutions.* Prepared by the Committee on Institution Libraries of the American Prison Association (New York: 1950) 103.

41. *Library Manual* vii.

42. *Library Manual* 4.

43. Majorie LeDonne, *Access to Legal Reference Materials in Correctional Institutions,* vol. 2 of *Survey of Library and Information Problems in Correctional Institutions, Final Report* (Berkeley: Institute of Library Research, 1974) 3. In *Ex parte Hull,* 312 U.S. 546 (1941), the court said that prison regulations may not abridge a prisoner's right to file a writ of habeas corpus. This was the first sign that the courts could back away from allowing that state prisons were the sole concern of prison administrators. Until this decision, and later in the mid-sixties, the courts maintained a "hands-off" state prisons policy.

44. Marcia J. Nauratil, *Public Libraries and Nontraditional Clienteles: The Politics of Special Services* (Westport, CT: Greenwood Press, 1985) 140.

45. Barratt Wilkins, "The Correctional Facility Library: History and Standards," *Library Trends* 26 (Summer 1977): 122.

46. No reform had a greater, more immediate effect on the balance of power between prison officials and prisoners than this Supreme Court decision. It devastated many prison library programs. For an overview on the effect of the decision, see Brenda Vogel, *Down for the Count: A Prison Library Handbook* (Metuchen, NJ: Scarecrow Press, 1995): 87–123.

47. Nauratil, *Public Libraries and Nontraditional Clienteles*: 144–45.

48. *Library Standards for Adult Correctional Institutions* (Chicago: Association for Specialized and Cooperative Library Agencies/ALA, 1981) 1.

49. William Coyle, *Libraries in Prisons: A Blending of Institutions* (New York: Greenwood Press, 1987); quotation from Coyle's "An Enabling Role for Prison Libraries," *Wilson Library Bulletin* 64.2 (Oct. 1989): 32.

50. Daniel Suvak, "'Throw the Book at 'Em': The Change-Based Model for Prison Libraries," *Wilson Library Bulletin* 64.2 (Oct. 1989): 31–32.

51. *Library Standards for Adult Correctional Institutions* (Chicago: Association of Cooperative and Specialized Library Agencies/ALA: 1992) 10.

52. Larry E. Sullivan, "The Least of our Brethren: Library Service to Prisoners," *American Libraries* 31.5 (May 2000): 58.

7. The Indiana Township Library Program, 1852–1872: "a well selected, circulating library as an educational instrumentality"[1]

Robert S. Freeman and
David M. Hovde

The Indiana Township Library program was approved by the Indiana legislature on 14 June 1852. It was one part of a three-part educational reform plan for Indiana. The other parts were the public schools and the state-supported institutions of higher learning. Over the years, the township library has received little attention in the literature and has become the least understood of the three parts. The main reasons for this neglect have been the relative success of the public schools and public universities, the failure of the township libraries, and the development of other, more successful public libraries. In this paper we describe the township library program, review the efforts to promote and sustain it, examine the values underlying it, and explain its failure.

The township library program continued the school district library movement that had begun in 1835. In that year the state of New York passed a law permitting voters in any school district to tax themselves up to twenty dollars in the first year and ten dollars in any succeeding years for the purpose of purchasing a library for the district. Several states followed New York's lead and passed similar legislation within the next six years: Massachusetts (1837), Michigan (1837), Connecticut (1839), Rhode Island (1840), the Iowa Territory (1840), and Indiana (1841).[2] By 1876 at least nineteen states had authorized some form of tax-supported library service in their school districts.

School district libraries were not what we would call school libraries.[3] They served the general population of a district, particularly the adults and adolescents, and contained relatively few books for children. In "The District-School Library, 1835–55," Sidney Ditzion notes that New York legislators were familiar with the idea of attaching general libraries to schools as early as 1812.[4] By the mid–1820s they were aware of Jesse Torrey's vision of "Free Circulating Libraries ... equally accessible to all classes of the community, including, particularly, the rising generation of both sexes over ten or twelve years of age."[5] By 1835 the legislators were ready to study and act on the innovative ideas of James S. Wadsworth, "the father of the school-district libraries of New York."[6] His proposals formed the basis of the first district library law. Like many other nineteenth-century reformers, he thought libraries and other educational institutions were necessary for stabilizing frontier communities and safeguarding democracy: "...the stability of government and the security of property in all republics, depend, in great measure, upon the information of the common people."[7]

After passage of the 1835 law it became clear that few voters in New York would take advantage of the opportunity to tax themselves for the full cost of a library. Therefore the legislature passed a more generous and forceful law in 1838, distributing $55,000 annually to the districts on condition that each district match its portion of the subsidy and spend the combined amount on a library.[8] The power over book selection, although vested in the districts' elected trustees, was now exercised by the superintendent of common schools. To guide the trustees, he distributed a list of titles acceptable for purchase. He also urged consideration of inexpensive libraries published by the American Society for the Diffusion of Useful Knowledge or by Harper & Brothers.[9] Despite complaints about the state's interference in what many thought a local responsibility, the new library program was remarkably successful. By 1846 there were approximately 1,145,250 volumes in 10,812 New York school districts, an average of 106 volumes per district.[10] Other states, too, revised their permissive library laws and began subsidizing school district libraries.

The reform movement that changed Indiana's approach to education resulted in large measure from the work of one man who approached his task with the zeal of a missionary. Caleb Mills was born on a farm near Dunbarton, New Hampshire, in 1806. His early education consisted of attending the Dunbarton Academy and following a course of reading in the town's circulating library. This experience is said to have fixed his taste for sound reading and for developing libraries.[11] In 1824 he entered Dartmouth College, which, like many other early American colleges, emphasized the training of ministers, missionaries, and teachers. There he met Edmund Otis Hovey, with whom he would eventually found the Wabash Teachers Seminary and Manual Labor College, later known as Wabash College, in Crawfordsville, Indiana. While students, Mills and Hovey became interested in frontier mission work.

In 1829 Mills entered Andover Theological Seminary. After one year, he left his studies to earn some money, and accepted a position with the American Sunday School Union (ASSU). In this position he was to survey the development and progress of Sunday schools in southern Indiana and Kentucky. One task for these church workers was to check up on the condition of the Sunday school libraries.[12] In 1832 Indiana had 276 ASSU schools.[13] At the same time, nationally, 79 percent of the 3,360 ASSU schools contained libraries averaging 91 volumes.[14] These free, circulating libraries, sometimes the only libraries in a community, contained standard religious works, easy-to-read moral tales for children, and other non-religious books. According to Edwin Rice, these libraries were successful in promoting good reading and popular education.[15]

Mills was born into the Second Great Awakening, the revival and reform movement that began among New England Protestant clergy in the late eighteenth century and introduced a reformist zeal into many aspects of American life—from education and literacy, through abolition and temperance, to women's and workers' rights. It produced a number of national organizations, including the American Bible Society, American Tract Society, American Seamen's Friend Society, and the Young Men's Christian Association. All of these organizations aimed at uplifting the individual, thus creating a moral, God-fearing society intertwined with capitalism and democratic ideas. Denominational mission societies as well as nondenominational organizations like the ASSU and the American Home Missionary Society came out of New England's colleges and seminaries in order to convert the Western population and save the frontier from undemocratic forces.[16] Mills was one of countless mission workers who proselytized the frontier of the new Republic.

THE CONDITION OF EDUCATION IN
EARLY NINETEENTH-CENTURY INDIANA

Despite their zeal, many New England missionaries were unprepared for the Indiana frontier. Their descriptions of Hoosiers were often less than complimentary:

> Ignorance & her squalid brood.... A universal dearth of intellect.... Of course there is no kind of ambition for improvement; & it is no more disgrace for man woman or child to be unable to read, than to have a long nose. I don't know of ten families who take any kind of paper, political or religious.... Need I stop to remind you of the host of loathsome reptiles such a stagnant pool is fitted to breed! Croaking jealousy; bloated Bigotry, coiling suspicion; wormish blindness; crocodile malice![17]

One commented that "all harmoniously unite in decrying education."[18]

Missionaries were not alone in their assessment. As early as 1790 the governor of the Northwest Territory noted Hoosiers' lack of enthusiasm for education: "They are the most ignorant people in the world."[19] According to William O. Lynch, it was widely held that education was not for the general public and rendered people unfit for manual labor.[20] Donald F. Carmony, in his study of the pioneer era in Indiana, adds that numerous families took the position that education was the responsibility of the parents or their church.[21] To be in favor of levying taxes to support common schools was political suicide for elected officials. In 1837 an Indiana legislator stated, "When I die, I want my epitaph written, 'Here lies an enemy to free schools.'"[22] In 1847 the *Indiana State Sentinel,* reporting on state funded education, commented that some legislators "hate colleges so cordially that they would go out of their way to kick a Sophomore, and would injure the school fund for the sake of ruining a college."[23]

Early Indiana schools were created through local interest. Oliver Johnson, who lived in what is now Indianapolis, recalled that "Pap and some neighbors got together and decided to build a schoolhouse and start some learnin for their youngsters."[24] The resulting log cabin, built in the 1820s, had an interior floor space of twenty square feet to accommodate a teacher and thirty children, without desks. The first teacher was a local man hired by the township trustees. The three-month school term cost fifty to seventy cents per pupil and the schoolmaster boarded at the homes of his students. Materials were scarce. Ink was derived from local flora. At times, the older students surpassed the teacher in subjects like arithmetic.[25]

The earliest official reference to education in what was to become Indiana is contained in the Ordinance of 1787, which established that "schools and the means of education shall forever be encouraged."[26] Vincennes University, the first institution of higher learning in Indiana, was incorporated by the territorial legislature in 1806. The funds for its creation and "procuring a library and the necessary philosophical apparatus" were raised through a lottery.[27]

Indiana's constitution of 1816 called for a comprehensive system of education that included township schools and a state university. Tuition would be free and equal to all. However, no tax was levied to support this mandate. Funds came from the sale of public lands, the collection of fines for violation of penal laws, and exemption payments from those who did not wish to participate in militia exercises.[28] A township school could be created at the request of at least twenty householders. An election would then take place to select three trustees who would make all the laws, rules, and regulations required to maintain and support the school.[29]

The Condition of Libraries

The earliest publicly funded libraries in the state developed out of provisions in the 1816 constitution allowing at least ten percent of the proceeds of the sale of town lots in a county seat to go to the development of a public library and the incorporation of a library company directed by seven trustees. To acquire materials, county commissioners could set aside twenty to twenty-five dollars. Numerous counties tried to establish libraries soon after the constitution was enacted, but few succeeded. Some libraries opened, but soon closed through neglect or lack of funds. Others merged with later entities. Funding for the Marion County Library began on 31 December 1821, with two percent of the revenue from the sale of town lots, but the money was turned over to the state and remained unspent for two decades. It was not until 8 January 1845 that the library officially opened, charging a seventy-five cent annual fee for families and fifty cents for individuals.[30] The lack of funds for building libraries during this period was also evident in the creation of the state legislature's library through money donated by the citizens of Harrison County in 1816.[31]

In 1824 the state legislature passed a comprehensive school law mandating a minimum school term of three months and dividing townships into school districts. Each district could have a school if at least twenty householders agreed. Three sub-trustees would direct each school.[32] They would also examine the teachers' qualifications. Furthermore, it was up to the district householders to decide on the level of support for the school and the teacher. The original provision of 1816 allowing the creation of library companies remained in force. During this period two libraries of note were founded: the New Harmony Library and the State Library. In larger towns one could find subscription libraries. The Indianapolis Library opened for business in 1828, selling shares at $5.00. It was kept in a private home and dissolved about five years later. Another group, the Young Men's Literary Society, opened a library in 1836 that lasted for fifteen years.[33]

ONE OF THE PEOPLE

As Indiana's population increased, so did the interest in common schools. In 1832 the governor observed that one hundred thousand school-aged children lacked access to a common school education. In 1833 members of the major political parties and Protestant denominations formed an Association for the Improvement of Common Schools and called for a seminary to train teachers. Another such meeting took place in 1837. While calling for improvements, the participants also recognized statewide "apathy in relation to the real value of a good education" as an obstacle to a common school system.[34] By 1846 one official claimed that 350,000 or sixty-four percent of school-aged children did not have the benefit of a common school education.[35] It was time for a firebrand to ignite the legislature. That firebrand was Caleb Mills.

In 1846 Caleb Mills, a Whig, wrote and delivered to the Indiana State Legislature the first of six annual epistles on the state of education in Indiana. Under the pseudonym "One of the People," he discussed the sad state of literacy in Indiana, the views on education in other states, tax support of schools, compensation of teachers, and other issues related to education at all levels. His missionary zeal is clear throughout these documents.

> I have examined the proceedings of the Legislature for the last twelve years in earnest expectation of seeing the subject of Education discussed and disposed of in some good degree as it deserves at the hands of the appointed guardians of the commonwealth. In this I have been disappointed, and I am not alone in my disappointment, for I often hear my fellow citizens expressing deep regret at the inefficient character of our common schools and the wretched condition of county seminaries, to say nothing of a want of a liberal and enlightened policy in respect to our higher Institutions of learning.... Here is indeed a humiliating fact, that one-seventh part of the adult population of a great and flourishing State is not able to read the charter of her liberties, or the votes cast in the exercise of their election franchise.[36]

He minced no words in lecturing the "gentlemen on this floor" who represented seventeen counties with an illiteracy rate of twenty to thirty-three percent of the adult population and two counties with a rate of almost fifty percent.[37]

According to the 1850 census, there were 151 libraries in the state not in private hands. This was most likely an underestimate, particularly in the area of Sunday school libraries, which were the principal source of juvenile literature in the state.[38] The census also reported sixty-one academies and county seminaries in the state, but this too was probably an underestimate.[39] One such institution was the Farmer's Institute founded in 1850 in Union Township of Tippecanoe County. Although the institute has long been closed, much of the library still exists on site and awaits study.

In his fifth message, which appeared in newspapers in 1850 and 1851, Mills discussed the "value of a well selected library in a district."[40]

> What scene could be more delightful to contemplate, than the children and youth in every school district in Indiana, acquiring a taste for reading and employing their leisure moments in perusing sterling and standard works of history, biography, travels, arts, science, and literature? The establishment of such libraries in our school districts would constitute an era in our educational history never to be forgotten by the present generation.[41]

He praised the New York and Massachusetts school district libraries and pronounced the series published by the "Harpers of New York, unequaled by any other house on the Western continent."[42] Based on expected revenue (with matching funds from the school districts) and the cost of the books, he hoped to put a library of 250 volumes into 4,000 school districts over a five-year period.[43] He mentioned several Harper titles in order to represent the quality and range of works available for such a library. Nevertheless, he would exclude

> all works of fiction, romance, and religion, the former as *worthless*, and the latter as unnecessary, since all such books could better be furnished from Sabbath school, parochial and private libraries, and thereby remove all occasion for sectarian suspicion and denominational bickering.[44]

In his sixth and final message, Mills continued to develop his vision of a statewide library program:

> It will require no protracted argument, no long array of facts to demonstrate the value of a well selected, circulating library as an educational instrumentality. The benefits of it are too obvious to admit a "moment" question. It may well be doubted, whether an equal sum expended in any other way, could accomplish so much for all the substantial purposes of education, intellectual and moral, as would be effected by the purchase of a good library of four or five hundred volumes.[45]

He recommended Harper's School District Library and invited the legislators to examine 208 Harper volumes he had placed in the State Library.

> It is no mercenary motive that prompts their recommendation, but a conviction of their intrinsic value and literary worth, and a strong desire to see our youth form a taste for such reading.... How many a farmer's boy, how many an artizan's apprentice, how many a widow's daughter, how many an orphan child, would thus have brought within their reach the richest thoughts of the most gifted minds, and by the perusal of such works in all departments of literature and science enlarge their capacity for enjoyment and usefulness in all walks of life?[46]

Here, for the first time, he spoke of township libraries rather than of school district libraries. Instead of 4,000 small, nearly identical district libraries, he now envisioned a larger library "of four or five hundred volumes" in each of Indiana's 872 townships. Each township would then divide its library "into as many divisions as there are districts in it and these divisions would necessarily vary with the number of children in the district."[47] He pointed out that one township library of 500 titles would be more economical than ten district libraries with ten copies of only fifty titles. Anticipating that readers would occasionally want new works, Mills proposed rotating the divisions, or turning them into traveling libraries: "One of these divisions is placed in each district to remain one year, or longer, if deemed best and then transferred to another.[48] To "guard against improper works being purchased through ignorance or any other cause," he proposed that "the Board of Education should be required to furnish a list of works suitable for such libraries and the law should restrict the purchase to such."[49] He concluded by reminding his audience of the positive effect reading could have on individuals and society:

> How highly would we all have prized in our boyhood, access to such a library as the proposed arrangement would place in every one of our eight hundred and seventy-two townships in Indiana. How many of you received the first impulses in that course that brought you to your present elevation, from the perusal of some stray volume that fell in your way when boys. How many, who have subsequently risen to eminence in the church and in the State, will date their first aspirations after knowledge awakened by some narrative of Indian wars or border strife? Such has been the starting point of many a one, now an ornament to society, a blessing to the land. Might we not hope that a similar result would follow from a like cause in our own beloved State? Are there not latent orators, dormant statesmen, slumbering poets, unawakened worth of every grade, that would be roused to life and activity, to honorable fame and a useful life, by access to such a library as I have submitted to your inspection? Such a mine opened in every township would yield products more rich and lasting than the mines of California.[50]

THE LIBRARY PROGRAM

Although historians have credited Mills with being the firebrand, he was not the only effective propagandist for libraries.[51] Samuel Hannah, the Superintendent of Common Schools, supervised a "Report of the Committee on Education, Accompanying the Common School Bill" and presented it to the legislature on 25 January 1848. Hannah discussed the New York program and the need for libraries attached to the schools. He also heavily quoted Horace Mann, Massachusetts's champion of common schools and libraries.[52] In 1851 Daniel Read, a professor at the State University, praised the library programs of New York, Massachusetts, and Michigan in his *Address on the Means of Promoting Common School Education*. He commented on his communication with the "Harpers of New York" regarding the costs of bringing such a program to Indiana, and stressed the importance of providing libraries to poor families in "remote and quiet neighborhoods." Such libraries "would be used in many a family by the light of hickory bark, and would be the means of bringing forth from poverty and obscurity, many who would otherwise never know their own powers."[53]

Caleb Mills, meanwhile, was doing more than writing epistles to the legislature. Sometime in 1851 or 1852 he traveled to New York, Connecticut, and Massachusetts. The only records of this trip are two pocket travel diaries that have no dates. "Call on the Harpers & solicit a complete set of their school libraries for the Vermont School," is one notation.[54] This, perhaps, is where he acquired the library mentioned in his messages. He then lists some of the books he examined. He met with other publishers, including Little, Brown, and Company of Boston and J. D. Dana of New Haven. He visited educators as well. In Albany he met with Christopher Morgan, the Superintendent of Common Schools and Secretary of State, and George R. Perkins, the Principal of the New York State Normal School. In Cambridge he called on Barnas Sears, Horace Mann's successor as Secretary of the Massachusetts Board of Education. Sears later would become president of Brown University.

The new Indiana constitution of 1851 and the revised statutes of 1852 brought significant changes to education in the state. One was the creation of the elected office of the Superintendent of Public Instruction. The new office had a two-year term. Prior to this the state treasurer had acted as the *ex officio* Superintendent of Common Schools. Another change was the new township library program.[55]

This new library law required a property tax of one quarter of a mill and a poll tax of twenty-five cents for the period of two years for the purchase of "township school libraries" by the Superintendent of Public Instruction, under the direction of the state Board of Education. The libraries distributed by the state were to be the responsibility of the township trustees, who were to "assess damages" and "adopt rules and regulations necessary for their preservation and usefulness." It was up to the voters to determine at an annual meeting where the library should be located, and the trustees were to appoint one of their own as librarian.

Interestingly, it was not Caleb Mills who would initiate the development of these new programs, but a political rival, William Clark Larrabee. Larrabee, a Democrat, was elected the first Superintendent of Public Instruction in November 1852. A Bowdoin College graduate, Larrabee had become a Methodist minister, revival preacher, professor, and, eventually, the acting president of Asbury College, now known as DePauw University, in Greencastle, Indiana. Like Mills, he had worked hard on pushing the 1852 education provisions through the legislature.[56]

In the first annual report of the Superintendent of Public Instruction, Larrabee used much the same rhetoric as Mills. He considered the township library program "one of the very best features in the whole system." He expressed concern for the poor rural elements of Indiana society, noting that "In the interior townships, readable books are very scarce, and difficult to be obtained." Like Mills, he saw the library program as a way to assure a stable society and democratic government: "It will elevate the standard of civilization. It will render children better governed, parents more intelligent, and citizens better qualified for the judicious discharge of social and public duty."[57] It fell on Larrabee, as Superintendent, to begin selecting books for the program. He promised a selection based on principles that would "make the library interesting and useful to all ages and classes of our community." The libraries would contain "sketches, travels, biography, history, and whatever else may promote taste and encourage habits of reading, and diffuse knowledge among the people." There would be "a few books of a special application to the practical pursuits," such as agriculture and "the mechanic arts of domestic life."[58]

It was Mills, however, who finished the job of distributing the first libraries. Elected Superintendent of Public Instruction in 1854, he finally had the opportunity to turn his dream into reality. In his annual report of 1856, he wrote that "One of the most prominent and characteristic events of the educational year just closed, is the reception and distribution of the last third of our six hundred and ninety-one libraries of three hundred and twenty-six volumes each."[59] It seems 77,392 volumes, the last third of the estimated 226,213 volumes originally ordered, had been delayed over the winter in New York. An appendix attached to the 1856 report reveals a total bill of $154,335 for expenses relating to the purchase and distribution of the libraries. Over $115,986, or seventy-five percent of the total, went to Harper & Brothers for "books, binding, printing, catalogues, circulars, rules and regulations, labels, boxes, packing, drayage, storage and insurance." The books were shipped by rail in 2,073 boxes from New York to Indianapolis.[60]

In the 1855 and 1856 reports, Mills indicated the intended audience for the libraries: the parent, the youth, the teacher, the man of science, and the artisan. He also outlined his "principles that govern and control the selection of books."[61] The books were "selected with reference to the intellectual development, literary tastes, and necessities of the various classes into which the masses are, by age and the employments of life, naturally divided."[62] There was one important caveat, however: the selection "should not contemplate the wants of any younger than twelve years of age."[63] Based on his experiences with the ASSU, he would likely have agreed with Jacob Dunn that juvenile literature for younger children was well supplied throughout the state in the Sunday school libraries.[64]

The books were of the "choicest character, both in sentiment, diction and design, for their perusal will modify, control and characterize, in no slight degree, the style, language and opinions of the rising generation; nor will they be without their influence on maturer years."[65] Three tenths of every one hundred books were aimed at the "moral and literary wants" of young readers between the ages of twelve and sixteen. Another three tenths were supposed to aid in the progress and attainment of those between the ages of sixteen and twenty. Two tenths were to "gratify the tastes and aid the pursuits of maturer minds.... In this way the important assistance could be rendered the parent, the teacher, the mechanic, the farmer, the merchant and the devotee of science." The remaining two tenths were devoted to general literature in order to "give symmetry and completion to the collection."[66] These libraries "were a rich source of moral and intellectual elevation" and an "aid to every great enterprise of the day."[67]

Mills's interest in a stable society is borne out in his conclusion that libraries would aid the cause of temperance, and "the youth of our commonwealth" would gain valuable lessons in American politics by reading the works of Joseph Story, George Bancroft, and Alexis de Tocqueville.[68] Biographies of Washington, Jay, Marshall, and others would "chasten the recklessness of their ardor and enthusiasm."[69] In the 1856 report he expanded on the importance of developing democratic ideals in youth.

No one who looks at the character of the times and the tendencies of the age will fail to perceive the desirableness and importance of deeply imbuing our youth with the spirit of those who laid the foundation of our government, shaped the national policy, and established the fundamental principles that have controlled and guided her subsequent development. How can either youth or age be brought into lively sympathy with those who achieved our emancipation from foreign thralldom, or those who subsequently reared our political fabric, without an intimate acquaintance with the history of our toils, privations and noble self-sacrifices? This knowledge can be obtained only by making themselves familiar with the standard histories of the times and the veritable biographies of those civic and military worthies prominent in colonial and revolutionary periods.[70]

In 1856 each library contained approximately 326 volumes at a cost of $213. The volumes were small (12mo, 16mo, and 18mo) and bound in uniform, natural leather cases with a heavily embossed oval containing the words "Indiana Township Library" on the front. Pasted on the inside of the front cover was a bookplate with "INDIANA TOWNSHIP LIBRARY" on the top line.[71] The second line had spaces for recording the volume number of the book and its cost. In the extant volumes examined, the cost was not recorded. The next line recorded the township and county. Below this were the "RULES AND REGULATIONS":

> The Library is in charge of the Trustees of the Township, who are accountable for the preservation of same.
>
> They may adopt rules and regulations necessary for the preservation and usefulness of the books, prescribe the time of taking and returning them, and assess damages done them by those entitled to their use.
>
> The Library must be kept open to all persons entitled to its privileges, throughout the year, without regard to school sessions.
>
> Every family in the Township is entitled to the use of two volumes at a time, and every tax-payer of the same, without family, to the use of one volume.
>
> No volume can be retained a longer period than __ days. [Examples range from thirty days in Fairfield Township in Tippecanoe Co. to ninety days in Wabash Township in Fountain Co.]
>
> That the Trustees may be able to make their Annual Report of the condition of the Library, and effect the necessary exchanges of the parts thereof in classified districts, all books must be returned to the Librarian __ days before the annual meeting. [Examples range from one day in Fairfield Township in Tippecanoe Co. to ten in Marion Township in Putnam Co.]

In the original Revised Statutes of 1852 the legislature had instituted a plan that undermined the objectives of Mills, Larrabee, and company. Section 141, for example, based the number of libraries each county received on the population of the county, not of the townships. These libraries were then broken up into smaller units of variable, undetermined sizes.[72] Mills denounced this modification in his 1855 report.[73] Later revisions provided for "existing inequalities to be corrected."[74] Making the best of a bad situation, Mills sent a series of circulars to county officials, outlining how the libraries should be distributed fairly. A total of 1,014 libraries were eventually distributed.

The Library Contents

In an appendix to his 1856 report, Mills listed the 228 titles that Larrabee had selected two years earlier.[75] The publishers and book dealers involved were Harper & Brothers, Charles Scribner, and J. S. Redfield, all of New York City; Sheets & Braden of Indianapolis; H. W. Derby of Cincinnati, and G. E. Warring. Harper & Brothers published approximately 145 titles, about sixty-four percent of the total; Scribner published over fifty titles, or twenty-three percent; and other publishers produced approximately thirty titles or thirteen percent.

The libraries were shipped to Indianapolis by rail and then delivered to the townships in three portable units. The list of books shows that boxes A, B, and C were not equal and were never intended to exist as independent units. They formed a balanced collection only when brought together. To show the distribution of subjects or genres in each box, we assigned our own broad subject or genre headings to each title. Box A contained sixty-seven titles in 107 volumes. Adult literature was the largest group with approximately nineteen titles. Juvenile literature had thirteen titles. World history and biography had ten each, description and travel five, and agriculture four. Science, self-improvement, and classical literature comprised the rest.

Box B had seventy-two titles in 107 volumes. Biography was the largest group with fifteen titles. World history had fourteen titles. Adult literature had nine titles and juvenile literature eight. Description and travel, agriculture, science, religion, American history, education, poetry, etiquette, and architecture filled the rest of the box.

Box C contained eighty-nine titles in 111 volumes. Juvenile literature was the largest group with thirty-six titles, many of which were written by Jacob Abbott. Biography had fifteen titles, travel and description nine, world history six, and poetry three. Rhetoric, art, agriculture, juvenile self-improvement, business ethics, religion, education, architecture, American history, mechanical arts, and science completed the box.

Larrabee, who was re-elected Superintendent of Public Instruction in 1856, provided a much longer list of titles approved for the township libraries in his 1857 Report. The 1,250 titles are listed, with prices, in a haphazard sequence.[76] Still, it is possible to identify most of the titles and the broad subjects or genres they represented. The largest group, with approximately 160 titles, was description and travel. Two topics within this group were especially important at the time. The first was the American West, with ten titles. Only a decade after the Mexican War and the resolution of the Oregon question, the country still had an expansionist mentality. The Kansas-Nebraska problem was also a major issue. Representative works are Francis Parkman's *The California and Oregon Trail: Being Sketches of Prairie and Rocky Mountain Life* and George Catlin's *Illustrations of the Manners, Customs, and Condition of the North American Indians*. The second topic was Arctic exploration, with eight titles. The geographic prizes of the Northwest Passage and the North Pole were the focus of many nationalistic ventures. *The U.S. Grinnell Expedition in Search of Sir John Franklin* by Elisha Kane is a representative title. In 1857 expeditions were still searching for Sir John Franklin and his men somewhere in the lower Canadian arctic.

Another large category, with approximately 140 titles, was history. Fifty-one titles related to American history and forty-six to European. Ancient history followed with twenty-nine. *Annals of Philadelphia* by John F. Watson, *History of Poland* by James Fletcher, *The Decline and Fall of the Roman Empire* by Edward Gibbon, and *A Popular Account of the Ancient Egyptians* by Sir John Wilkinson are representative. There were ancient historians from Herodotus to Tacitus and also a *Pictorial History of China*. Several titles, such as *History for Boys*, were aimed at a youthful audience.

Biography had approximately 110 titles. Several of these would be expected in a library created by men concerned with the survival of American democracy: *The Life of Washington* by James Paulding, *The Lives of the Signers of the Declaration of Independence* by Nathaniel Dwight, and *Sketches of the Life and Character of Patrick Henry* by William Wirt. There were also biographies of people from other cultures, including George Bush's *The Life of Mohammed* and Benjamin Bussey Thatcher's *Indian Biography*, a work on Native Americans.

Literature for adults consisted of about 120 titles. There were classics like *Don Quixote, Robinson Crusoe*, and an abridged, expurgated version of *The Arabian Nights' Entertainments*. There were newer American works by Irving and Hawthorne. Nearly thirty of the titles were religious and moralistic tales by Timothy Shay Arthur or Charlotte Elizabeth Tonna. Arthur, who wrote *Ten Nights in a Bar Room*, was one of the most prolific authors of the period, and Tonna, daughter of an Anglican minister and the author of *The Siege of Derby*, began her career writing tracts for religious societies.[77]

The children's literature section was just as extensive, despite Mills's original plan to exclude works aimed at children under twelve. Many of the works belonged to series, such as Jacob Abbott's *Rollo* series and Alice Haven's *Cousin Alice's Home Stories*.

Mills and Larrabee selected about fifty volumes of poetry. There were anthologies, including Halleck's *Selections from British Poets*, Bryant's *Selections from American Poets*, and Longfellow's *The Poets and Poetry of Europe*. These three writers and a few other Americans, such as John Greenleaf Whittier and James Russell Lowell, had volumes of their own poetry too. British poets who had their own volumes included Spenser, Milton, Goldsmith, Cowper, Crabbe, and Wordsworth; Shakespeare had six. There were also translations of Homer, Sophocles, and Virgil.

Science was represented by nearly seventy-five titles, such as Hugh Miller's classic *Old Red Sandstone*, Alexander Wilson's *American Ornithology*, and Matthias Jacob Schleiden's *Poetry of the Vegetable World*. There were also several works by Alexander von Humboldt, including *Cosmos*. Several volumes of the *Annual of Scientific Discovery* are examples of the series and serials found in the collection. A number of science titles were intended for a young adult audience, such as *Peterson's Familiar Science; or, The Scientific Explanation of Common Things* by Robert Peterson and Ebenezer Cobham Brewer.

Religion, centering on main line Protestantism, consisted of about eighty titles. Again, this conflicted with Mills's earlier statements against including sectarian works. Depending on the reader's point of view, there may have been even more religion books among the self-improvement, temperance, domestic science, science, business, education, adult and children's literature titles. There was *The Pilgrim's Progress*, the perennial classic of reformist literature, Charles McIlvaine's *The Evidences of Christianity in Their External or Historical Division*, and Henry Boardman's *The Bible in the Family*, all published by Lippincott, Grambo in Philadelphia.

Self-improvement literature had approximately thirty-four titles. About two-thirds of these were intended for a juvenile audience. Five of these were for boys, and five for girls. Examples are *Lectures to Young Men on the Formation of Character* by Joel Hawes and *The Young Woman's Friend, or, The Duties, Trials, Loves, and Hopes of Woman: Designed for the Young Woman, the Young Wife, and the Mother* by Daniel C. Eddy. There were also five temperance books in this area.

Agriculture had forty titles. These range from *Farm Implements, and the Principles of Their Construction and Use* by John Thomas, a Harper edition, to a number of titles published by C. M. Saxton of New York, including *The American Cattle Doctor* by George Dadd, *The American Poultry Yard* by Daniel Browne, and *Chemical Field Lectures* by Julius Stockhardt. Domestic science, with fifteen titles, featured another C. M. Saxton publication, *The Family Kitchen Gardener* by Robert Buist, and another Harper edition, Lydia Sigourney's *Letters to Mothers*.

Law and government were the subject of thirty-four titles, including Thomas Smith's *Elements of the Law*, a textbook on federal and state civil and criminal law, and Charles Goodrich's *The Science of Government as Exhibited in the Institutions of the United States of America*. Health and medicine had seventeen titles, ranging from professional treatises to home remedy handbooks. Examples included *Nature in Disease* by Jacob Bigelow and *Letters to the People on Health and Happiness* by Catharine Beecher. Education consisted of twenty-six titles, including Henry Barnard's *National Education in Europe*, Samuel Read Hall's *Lectures on School-keeping*, and David Page's *The Theory and Practice of Teaching: or, the Motives and Methods of Good School-Keeping*. The audience for most of these titles included teachers and those who oversaw their activities. The last major category was business and economics. The ten titles in this category were primarily guidebooks, including *Mercantile Morals* by William Van Doren and *A Practical Treatise on Business* by Edwin Freedley. Other subjects in the collection included architecture, particularly rural buildings, technology, the social sciences, and specific trades, including printing.

Clearly, Larrabee gave a great deal of thought to the library. His collection development went beyond the Harper's libraries and the school district libraries of many other states. Within the township libraries the relative proportions of description and travel, history, biography, and English and American literature were consistent with the collections found in public, mercantile, subscription, and benevolent society libraries of the day. Three other points should be made about the content of the township libraries. First, beyond the moral tales, self-improvement, and domestic science titles aimed at women were a number of works about women, such as Elizabeth Ellet's *Pioneer Women of the West* and Camilla Crosland's *Memorable Women, the Story of their Lives*. Second, there were a number of sets, series, and serials present in the collection. In addition to those mentioned above, there were a number of serials, including fifty volumes of *Littell's Living Age*, a literary magazine, and several series, including the Library of Entertaining Knowledge, totaling forty-one volumes, and Jardin's Naturalist's Own Library consisting of forty volumes. There were also plans to distribute sets of the *Encyclopædia Metropolitana* and the *Encyclopædia Britannica*.

Finally, while the libraries presented an impressive selection of reputable works that challenged and improved the minds of the adults and adolescents who read them, we must join Richard G. Boone in questioning

> the need or demand, in a pioneer State, with a school system scarcely two years old, of Macaulay's Essays or Hallam's Literature…. It is difficult to think there could have been much call for or use made of McCosh On Divine Government…. In general, it may be said the selection was made from the point of view of scholarly men familiar with great libraries, not from the experience of the readers of the books.[78]

COMMENTS FROM RECIPIENTS AND OBSERVERS

Period sources other than the annual reports of the Superintendent of Public Instruction offer little but complaints. The complaints reveal some of the causes of the demise of the program. One complaint came from a user of the Ripley Township library in 1857.

> We submit the question to every candid man whether a small, dingy room with only a plank partition between it and a vile doggery is a fit place to store away the rich mine of useful reading in which every family of the whole Township has an interest. Such is the case with the Ripley Township Library. One cannot select a book without hearing the horrid oath, and ribald song from the demons in the adjoining room at their bacchanalian orgies. Would our Township trustees desire to see their wives, sisters, or daughters enter such a den for the purpose of selecting a book? If not in the name of common sense remove it to some place where civil people may go without annoyance & where children may enter without danger of debasement.[79]

In 1865 *The New Albany Commercial* all but dismissed the local township library, when it noted that in a city of 18,000 people there was no public library "except the township library." The *Lafayette Weekly Courier* observed that the city had "Plenty of ten pins, billiards, and whiskey shops, but no facilities for literary culture."[80] It also noted problems with accountability:

> The Library of the township is in rather a dilapidated condition. Large numbers of books have been taken out and never returned. The negligence of someone makes it difficult, if not impossible, to fix the individual responsibility for the books where it properly belongs.[81]

Annual Reports

Comments in the annual reports of the Superintendent of Public Instruction echoed these concerns but continued to express hope for the system until the second decade of the twentieth century. In the 1855 report Mills quoted a township official: "Nearly all the books have been drawn out as much as twenty-five times, many of them oftener, and quite a number of the books are not permitted to remain in the library an hour before they are withdrawn."[82] This same report foretold problems with the system. It noted that in 1852 the property and poll tax levied to support the program lasted only two years. This tax fell almost $10,000 short of the amount needed to fully support the effort. Another similar levy was enacted in 1855 for one year. Mills observed that "uncertainty incident to such legislative restriction is enough to damage the reputation and interest of even the best causes."[83] The 1859 report noted complaints about the libraries not being replenished and damaged books not being repaired: "In some townships ... individuals have read nearly or quite every book ... and call loudly for more."[84] There were also complaints about sectarian bias, location of the library, and the competence of the librarian.[85]

During the Civil War the libraries were largely neglected. Even if lawmakers had been interested in levying taxes to continue the program, the legislature was not in session. The radical Republican governor had sent the Democratic controlled legislature home and ruled the state as a virtual dictator for two years. The annual reports noted continued interest in the library program and called for new taxes and better reporting by the township trustees. The 1865 report commented on the declining use of the libraries since the beginning of the war. It blamed this on lack of new material and the township officials' neglect of the program.[86] In 1865 the legislature authorized another tax to support the program for one year and, for the first time in several years, to purchase new books. Eighty-eight titles were selected, amounting to 28,291 volumes. Of twenty subject areas, religion now ranked first with fourteen new titles. Self-improvement literature was second with nine. Education, young adult literature, law and government, and politics supplied eight titles each. Six titles related to the Civil War.[87] The new law based the distribution of the books on "school population." This meant that some townships received only two books while others received hundreds.

Leaving the libraries in the hands of the township trustees was a major defect in the program. By law the trustees were required to preserve the libraries, place them in convenient locations, and make them available to all. This was not done in many places, and yet there is no evidence that any trustee was ever punished. The negative attitude and behavior of many trustees toward education is clearly evident in the complaint of a county official:

> Trustees under the old system always felt that when they had built a house and hired a teacher their work was done. All that was to follow belonged to the teacher and the Director. Nor do they so much as occasionally visit the school to see about either the competence or fidelity of the teacher. They simply turned over the school house and children to the care of the new teacher, and then turned their backs on him....[88]

In his 1868 report the Superintendent of Public Instruction noted the repeal of the tax levy. He pleaded the continued need for new books, because "Science and art are constantly making new contributions to learning."[89] Further, he stated that the libraries "serve as a desirable antidote to the light, cheap, fictitious and often demoralizing literature which is everywhere spread out before the reader in the rail car, the news stalls, and too often on the counter of the book store."[90] In that year, due to the new titles added in 1867, readership rallied from a circulation of 90,000 in 1865 to over 140,000. However, this boost to the program was short lived as the readership dropped again in 1870 to 99,000. The acquisition of books declined steadily to only 922 in 1872, and readership slipped to 92,622.[91] The 1872 report continued to call for new money. It raised concern over the plight of poor children, noting that access to good books will "exert an elevating influence over their tender minds and hearts" and form their "habits for life," saving them from "the many ways that lead to ruin and degradation."[92]

In the 1878 report County Superintendent G. W. Ramage of Monroe County continued the rhetoric of support and lamented the neglect of the libraries and the loss of books. He also attacked the oft referenced township trustees as the culprits in the poor condition of the libraries. He noted they had done little to advertise the existence and location of this "very important element for good."[93] He renewed the call for legislation to hold the trustees accountable. In the report for the following year, County Superintendent J.C. MacPherson of Wayne County commented on a survey of the township libraries in his county which showed that the books suffered more from neglect than from use. The survey indicated that the libraries were "broken and scattered." The spines of some books were broken and many showed little or no use. Others had disappeared without a trace and still others had reappeared at second hand furniture sales. He concluded that the program was "a palsied member, a withered branch, of our educational system."[94] In the 1888 Report, Fremont Goodwin, the Warren County Superintendent, who considered the libraries among "the first steps in the educational progress in our state, and ... the greatest of these," lamented that "these libraries are forgotten" and the "books are now too old."[95]

In the 1894 Report, the Superintendent of Public Instruction, Hervey Vories, discussed a survey of school libraries in the state. In that year only 439 libraries remained of the 1,014 that once covered the state. Many of these were no more than a handful of books in a trustee's barn. In the forty years since the beginning of the library program, little had changed: "Think of the number of families who have no books in their homes except the Bible and a few school text-books, and some idea of the neglected condition of the school children in the townships may be had." Vories reported that fifty-seven percent of the state's children did not have access to any library.[96] Frustrated, he observed that a library tax approved by the legislature permitted the trustees to enact an annual levy of one cent on the dollar of property, but only when a library valued at over $1,000 was established in the township by private donation.

The annual reports of the Superintendent of Public Instruction continued to mention the existence of some township libraries into the World War I era. They also proposed replacing the program with another because of the continuing need for libraries in the rural areas of the state.

Conclusion

The Indiana Township Library program was a failure. This seed of grassroots education did not find fertile ground in Indiana. It had little chance of success. First, it was largely invisible compared to the other two parts of Indiana's educational enterprise, the state supported universities and public schools, which attracted the attention of the public and politicians. The benefits of these institutions were obvious and support was easy to gain and maintain.

Second, unlike the other two institutions, the libraries were left in the hands of non-professionals who seem in large measure to have been hostile to their responsibility. To Mills, Larrabee, and their successors, the libraries were a self-evident good. Yet they put little effort into a structure of accountability and maintenance. There is no record of any trustee punished for failing to secure fines for lost or overdue books. What money was collected did not support a program for repair or replacement. Furthermore, no one was rebuked for failing to make the library available to the public or for neglecting to advertise its location.

Third, the collections, carefully selected by scholarly gentlemen, did not contain a high enough proportion of books for unskilled readers or children under the age of twelve. Also, due to the lack of continuous funding for new purchases and the absence of a plan to rotate titles among different townships, the collections became stagnant and no longer attracted curious readers. Finally, after 1870, Indiana began to develop legislation that would lead to the establishment of modern public libraries. As this process continued, the township libraries were discarded, absorbed, or forgotten.

Notes

1. The subtitle is from "One of the People [Caleb Mills]," *Sixth Annual Address on Popular Education to the Legislature of Indiana* (Indianapolis, 1852), rpt. in Charles W. Moores, *Caleb Mills and the Indiana School System*, Indiana Historical Society Publications vol. 3, no. 6 (Indianapolis: West-Weaver, 1905) 622.

2. In the case of Indiana, a few secondary sources mention school district library legislation occurring as early as 1837, but we have found no evidence of this in the Indiana laws; see Richard G. Boone, *A History of Education in Indiana* (New York: D. Appleton, 1892) 338–39. For an overview of "school library" legislation in the seven states mentioned and fourteen other states, see "School and Asylum Libraries," chap. 2 in U.S. Bureau of Education, *Public Libraries in the United States of America: Their History, Condition, and Management: Special Report*, vol. 1 (Washington, D.C.: GPO, 1876) 38–58. For discussions of school district libraries in the context of American library history, see Carleton Bruns Joeckel, *The Government of the American Public Library* (Chicago: U of Chicago Press, 1935) 8–14; David Kaser, *A Book for a Sixpence: The Circulating Library in America*, Beta Phi Mu Chapbook 14 (Pittsburgh: Beta Phi Mu, 1980) 86–88; and Jesse H. Shera, *Foundations of the Public Library: The Origins of the Public Library Movement in New England, 1629–1855* (Chicago: U of Chicago Press, 1949) 181–84. For useful summaries of journal articles of the period, see the section on school district libraries in the U.S. in Haynes McMullen, ed., *Libraries in American Periodicals Before 1876: A Bibliography with Abstracts and an Index* (Jefferson, NC: McFarland, 1983) 54–59.

3. In the introduction to his *American Libraries Before 1876*, Beta Phi Mu Monograph Series 6 (Westport, CT: Greenwood, 2000) Haynes McMullen explains the omission of certain types of libraries from the main part of his study. He omits both school libraries and school district libraries, asserting the latter were more for children than for adults. He does not omit township libraries, however, asserting that they were intended for adults; see McMullen 2, 34, 124–25, 169–71.

4. Sidney Ditzion, "The District-School Library, 1835–55," *Library Quarterly* 10 (1940): 545.

5. Jesse Torrey, *The Intellectual Torch* (1815; Woodstock, VT: Elm Tree Press, 1912) 9; quoted in Ditzion 546. In his *Annual Report* for 1837, John A. Dix, New York's superintendent of common schools, wrote that the purpose of the school district libraries was "to disseminate works suited to the intellectual improvement of the great body of the people rather than throw into school districts, for the use of the young, books of a merely juvenile character;" quoted in Ditzion 555.

6. Ditzion 550.

7. [Barnard's] *American Journal of Education* 5 (1858): 395; quoted in Ditzion 550.

8. Ditzion 553.

9. In 1839 New York's Secretary of State, John C. Spencer, met Fletcher Harper in Albany and proposed that Harper & Brothers, which had already begun publishing Harper's School District Library, supply the books for the district libraries. See J.C. Derby, *Fifty Years Among Authors, Books and Publishers* (New York: G. W. Carleton, 1884) 101–04.

10. State of New York, *Messages from the Governors*, vol. 4 (Albany: J. B. Lyon, 1909) 264.

11. James Insley Osborne and Theodore Gregory Gronert, *Wabash College; the First Hundred Years, 1832–1932, Being the Story of Its Growth from Its Founding in the Wilderness to the Present Day* (Crawfordsville, IN: R. E. Banta, 1932) 31.

12. An example of this can be seen in the Home Missionary Society Papers, 1816–1894, Series I, Incoming Correspondence—Indiana 1832 A–J, Amistad Research Center, Dillard University, New Orleans. It contains a form entitled "Home Missionary—Extra. Statistics for the Annual Report." A missionary by the name of James Chute reported that there were 150 volumes in the Fort Wayne, Indiana, Sabbath School Library.

13. Anne M. Boylan, *Sunday School: The Formation of an American Institution, 1790–1880* (New Haven: Yale UP, 1988) 31.

14. Boylan 50.

15. Edwin Wilbur Rice, *The Sunday-School Movement 1780–1917 and the American Sunday School Union 1817–1917* (New York: Arno Press, 1971) 147; Sidney Mead, "The Nation with the Soul of a Church," *Church History* 36.3 (1967): 262–283.

16. David G. Vanderstel, "To Meet the Needs of the West: Edmund Otis Hovey and the Founding of the Wabash College," *American Presbyterians: Journal of Presbyterian History* 69.2 (Summer 1991): 71.

17. Colin Brummitt Goodykoontz, *Home Missions on the American Frontier* (Caldwell, ID: Caxton Printers, 1939) 191.

18. Goodykoontz 192.

19. Moores 363.

20. William O. Lynch, "The Great Awakening," *Indiana Magazine of History* 41.2 (June 1945): 108.

21. Donald Francis Carmony, *Indiana, 1816–1850: The Pioneer Era* (Indianapolis: Indiana Historical Society, 1998) 363.

22. Carmony 363.

23. "Common Schools," *Indiana State Sentinel* 5 Jan 1847: 2.

24. Oliver Johnson, *A Home in the Woods* (Bloomington: Indiana UP, 1991) 46.

25. Johnson 48, 54–55.

26. Jacob Piatt Dunn, "Growth of Libraries in Indiana," *Twenty-third Biennial Report of the State Superintendent of Public Instruction* (Indianapolis: Wm. B. Burford, 1906) 61.

27. Dunn, "Growth" 62.

28. Carmony 363. The use of militia fines, "collected from persons conscientiously scrupulous of bearing arms," was not a reliable source of revenue. These fines collected between 1818 and 1841 generated a total of $445.40. See Douglass Maguire, *Annual Report of the Treasurer of the State of Indiana to the General Assembly* (Indianapolis: John D. Defrees, 1947) 57–58. The militia laws in Indiana were never strictly enforced, particularly after 1832, and few militia roles were turned into the state's adjutant general. See William J. Watt and James R. H. Spears, *Indiana's Citizen Soldiers: The Militia and National Guard in Indiana History* (Indianapolis: Indiana State Armory Board, 1980) 32–33.

29. Carmony 364.

30. Jacob Piatt Dunn, *Greater Indianapolis*, vol. 1 (Chicago: Lewis Publishing Co., 1910) 511.

31. Charles Kettleborough, *Constitution Making in Indiana*, vol. 1: 1780–1851 (Indianapolis: Indiana Historical Commission, 1916) 127.

32. Carmony 366.

33. Dunn, *Greater Indianapolis* 510.

34. Carmony 371–73.

35. Carmony 379.

36. Moores 398, 401.

37. Moores 402.

38. Dunn, "Growth" 63.

39. James Albert Woodburn, *Higher Education in Indiana*, Bureau of Education Circular of Information No. 1, Contributions to American Educational History (Washington: GPO, 1891) 47–48.

40. "Education No. 3," *Indiana Statesman* 20 Nov. 1850: 3.

41. "Education No. 3" 3.

42. "Education No. 3" 3.

43. "Education No. 3" 3.

44. "Education No. 3" 3.

45. One of the People [Caleb Mills], *Sixth Annual Address on Popular Education to the Legislature of Indiana* (Indianapolis: J.P. Chapman, 1852), rpt. in Moores 622.

46. Mills, *Sixth Annual Address* 622–23.

47. Mills, *Sixth Annual Address* 625.

48. Mills, *Sixth Annual Address* 625.

49. Mills, *Sixth Annual Address* 626.

50. Mills, *Sixth Annual Address* 625–26.

51. F. A. Cotton, *Education in Indiana* (Indianapolis: William B. Burford, 1904) 20.

52. Committee on Education, "Report of the Committee on Education, Accompanying the Common School Bill presented January 25, 1848," *The Report of the Superintendent of Common Schools to the General Assembly 1847* (Indianapolis: John D. Defrees, 1848) 371–73.

53. Daniel Read, Address on the Means of Promoting Common School Education: Delivered in the Hall of the House of Representatives, at Indianapolis, on the Evening of December 30, 1851 (Indianapolis: Jean-Pierre P. Chapman, 1852), rpt. in *Indiana Documentary Journal* (1851-52): 356–85.

54. Information about this trip was gleaned from two small, uncataloged daybooks that are part of The Caleb Mills Collection, Robert Ramsay Archival Center, Lilly Library, Wabash College, Crawfordsville, Indiana.

55. "An Act to Provide for a General and Uniform System of Common Schools, and School Libraries, and Matters Properly Connected therewith [Approved June 14, 1852]," *The Revised Statutes of the State of Indiana Passed at the Thirty-sixth Session of the General Assembly*, vol. 1 (Indianapolis: J. P. Chapman, 1852), chap. 98, sec. 138–46.

56. William Warren Sweet, *Indiana Asbury-DePauw University 1837–1937: A Hundred Years of Higher Education in the Middle West* (Greencastle: DePauw University, 1962) 32.

57. William C. Larrabee, *First Annual Report of the Superintendent of Public Instruction for the State of Indiana to the General Assembly* (Indianapolis: J. P. Chapman, 1853) 27–28.

58. Larrabee, *First Annual Report* 28–29.

59. Caleb Mills, *Fourth Annual Report of the Superintendent of Public Instruction*, in *Reports of the Officers to the State of Indiana to the Governor*, Second Part (Indianapolis: William J. Brown, 1856) 252.

60. Caleb Mills, "Appendix Number VI," *Fourth Annual Report of the Superintendent of Public Instruction for the State of Indiana* in *Reports of the Officers to the State of Indiana to the Governor*, Second Part (Indianapolis: William J. Brown, 1856): 351–55. No two published sources agree on the exact number of volumes distributed or the costs of purchase and distribution. All original documents of the superintendent of public instruction for the period have been lost. We use numbers from the published sources cited.

61. Caleb Mills, *Third Annual Report of the Superintendent of Public Instruction*, in *Documents of the General Assembly of Indiana at the Thirty-Eighth Session*, Second Part (Indianapolis: Austin H. Brown, 1855) 841.

62. Mills, *Third Annual Report* 841.

63. Mills, *Third Annual Report* 841.

64. Dunn, "Growth" 63.

65. Mills, *Third Annual Report* 841.

66. Mills, *Third Annual Report* 841.

67. Mills, *Third Annual Report* 841.

68. Mills, *Third Annual Report* 842.

69. Mills, *Third Annual Report* 842.

70. Mills, *Fourth Annual Report* 253.

71. In some specimens, the Indiana Township Library bookplates are pasted over labels that read "Indiana School Library;" evidence of early confusion about the official name of the program. The 1852 law establishing the township libraries refers to them as "township school libraries;" see *Revised Statutes* (1852) 456.

72. *Revised Statutes* (1852) 456.

73. Mills, *Third Annual Report* 842.

74. "An Act to Provide for a General System of Common Schools, the Officers thereof, and their Respective Powers and Duties," *Laws of the State of Indiana passed at the Thirty-eighth session of the General Assembly* (Indianapolis: Austin H. Brown, 1855), chap. 86, sec. 132.

75. Mills, "Appendix Number VI" 351–55.

76. William C. Larrabee, "Statement No. 4," *Sixth Annual Report of the Superintendent of Public Instruction, for the State of Indiana* (Indianapolis: Joseph J. Bingham, 1857): 127–35.

77. David James O'Donoghue, "Tonna, Charlotte Elizabeth," in *The Dictionary of National Biography*, ed. Sir Leslie Stephen and Sir Sidney Lee, vol. XIX (London: Oxford UP, 1950) 961–62.

78. Boone, *History of Education in Indiana* 344.

79. "Ripley Township Library," *Montgomery Weekly Journal* 5 Feb. 1857: 1.

80. "Township Items," *Lafayette Weekly Courier* 19 Sept. 1865: 3.

81. "Lafayette Township Library," *Lafayette Weekly Courier* 19 Sept 1865: 2.

82. Mills, "Appendix No. VI" 351.

83. Mills, "Appendix No. VI" 351.

84. Samuel L. Rugg, *Eighth Annual Report of the Superintendent of Public Instruction for the State of Indiana* (Indianapolis: John C. Walker, 1860) 209.

85. Rugg, *Eighth Annual Report* 209.

86. George W. Hoss, *Fourteenth Report of the Superintendent of Public Instruction for the State of Indiana* (Indianapolis: Samuel M. Douglass, 1866) 38–42.

87. The books purchased in 1865 were bound by Shurtleff & Macauley, Binder of Indianapolis, in the same style as the first books. The books themselves were purchased through Merrill & Co., a printer and bookseller in Indianapolis. This information is taken from bookplates of the 1865 collection.

88. M. M. Campbell, "Monroe County," in Alex C. Hopkins, *Twenty-second Report of the Superintendent of Public Instruction* (Indianapolis: Sentinal, 1874) 213.

89. B. C. Hobbs, *Sixteenth Report of the Superintendent of Public Instruction for the State of Indiana* (Indianapolis: Alexander H. Conner, 1869) 28.

90. Hobbs, *Sixteenth Report* 29.

91. Milton B. Hopkins, *Twentieth Report of the Superintendent of Public Instruction for the State of Indiana* (Indianapolis: R. J. Bright, 1872) 146.

92. Hopkins, *Twentieth Report* 146.

93. G. W. Ramage, "Care and Management of Township Libraries," in James H. Smart, *Twenty-sixth Report of the Superintendent of Public Instruction of the State of Indiana* (Indianapolis: Indianapolis Journal Co., 1879) 213.

94. J. C. Macpherson, "Township Libraries," in James H. Smart, *Twenty-eighth Report of the Superintendent of Public Instruction of the State of Indiana* (Indianapolis: Carlon & Hollenbeck, 1880) 75.

95. Fremont Goodwin, "What Shall Be Done with the Township Libraries," in Harvey M. La Follette, *Thirty-sixth Report of the Superintendent of Public Instruction* (Indianapolis: Wm. B. Burford, 1888) 275–76.

96. Hervey D. Vories, *Fortieth Report of the Superintendent of Public Instruction* (Indianapolis: Wm. B. Burford, 1895) 67–68.

8. The Adult Collection at Nashville's Negro Public Library, 1915–1916

Cheryl Knott Malone

The historical practice of restricting library access by race, common in the U.S. South until the middle of the twentieth century, complicates notions of extension and outreach. In the South of the early twentieth century, white librarians seldom reached out with collections and services for blacks. The outreach efforts that did exist almost always conformed to the prevailing norm of racial segregation: separate and unequal.

Although a complete history of racially segregated public libraries has yet to be written, the topic has interested a number of researchers over the years.[1] Such work has made crucial contributions to U.S. public library history. Still, there are gaps in our understanding, particularly regarding the collections available in the branches for black readers. The public library collection offered to a town's readers can reveal a great deal about library officials' sense of the appropriate and the acceptable, as Christine Pawley's work on the print culture of Osage, Iowa, and Wayne Wiegand's on Sauk Centre, Minnesota, have demonstrated.[2] In a more recent case, William D. Boyd evaluated collections at selected public libraries in three Southern states in the early 1990s and found that large urban public libraries had more books by or about African Americans than did those serving smaller communities, even when the smaller cities had relatively high numbers of black residents.[3] A similar evaluation of holdings, but for an earlier time period characterized by segregated rather than integrated service, is attempted here for the adult collection at Nashville's Negro Public Library.

The Carnegie Library of Nashville opened in 1904, but African Americans were not allowed inside. Barred from access, black community leaders worked for several years to secure a Carnegie grant for a separate branch and to convince city officials to support it.[4] While the building was still under construction, Margaret Kercheval, the white librarian in charge of the Carnegie Library, hired Marian Hadley, a local black resident, to head the branch. Upon accepting the job, Hadley made a temporary move to Louisville in the fall of 1915 to participate in a two-month-long apprenticeship at the Western Colored Branch of the Louisville Free Public Library.[5]

In Hadley's absence, Kercheval ordered books for the Negro Public Library, or the Negro Branch, as it was sometimes called. In the summer of 1915, the white library board had authorized Kercheval to purchase $2,000 worth of books with which to stock the branch. She ordered books throughout the late summer and fall of 1915. Ordering ceased at the end of 1915 and did not begin again until April of 1916, when Hadley was on the job. At the Negro Library's opening in February of 1916, the books on the shelves were those Kercheval had selected. The Nashville Public Library Negro Branch Accession Book, 1915–27, is available at the Metropolitan Government Archives in Nashville, and the records recorded in it provide a glimpse of what one early twentieth century white librarian considered suitable for the local African American reading public.[6]

The extant accession records of the Negro Public Library appear in a standard bound volume designed and sold by the Library Bureau. The accession book served as the librarian's record of items received. A staff member would log each item on a separate line in the ledger, recording in abbreviated form the author, title, place of publication, publisher, year, supplier, cost, and related information. Also recorded, in the case of Nashville, was either the Dewey Decimal class indicating the broad subject of the work or a code designating the genre, such as F for fiction. Although the Negro Library's accession book includes several years of orders, the focus here is only on the collection as received by opening day, February 10, 1916. This essay describes the collection and analyzes it in comparison to the books by or about African Americans that were in print and available for purchase while Kercheval was placing her orders. Opening day was a pivotal moment in the library's history because that is when the leaders of the African American community and other potential users of the library acquired their first impression of the new facility that had taken so long to materialize. Some 1,000 individuals registered as borrowers between February 11 and April 27; the opening day collection did not change until ordering began anew in April.[7]

The opening of a branch catering to African American readers would appear to be an opportunity to create a special collection of books written by African Americans or about black life and culture.[8] Kercheval apparently did not see it in quite that way. Instead, judging by the titles she ordered, Kercheval saw it as an opportunity to intermingle the classics of Western literature with some of the lighter reading popular at the time. Such a collection building strategy left a gap, an almost total absence of titles by or about African Americans.

By opening day, the accession book included records for 2,027 volumes (1,782 individual titles) covering an array of topics. Table 1 shows the breakdown of titles by the subject classes and form categories to which the librarian assigned them, with the exception of four volumes that received no designation. These categories grouped works either by the Dewey Decimal class indicating the broad subject of the work, such as "8" for literature or "9" for history, or by one of four codes designating the genre: F for fiction, B for biography, JN for juvenile non-fiction, and JF for juvenile fiction.

It was clear by the time Nashville established its Negro Public Library that patrons of public libraries generally favored fiction over other reading material. Christine Pawley's study of circulation records in Osage, Iowa, in the 1890s found that "[a]lmost without exception, Osage users charged out novels."[9] In 1908 the Librarian of Congress, Herbert Putnam, criticized public librarians who purchased what he considered a disproportionate amount of light fiction because they knew it would boost the circulation statistics they reported to city officials in their annual reports. He suggested "a lopping off of the supply of current light literature by our libraries."[10] In 1915 some members of the New York Public Library board considered the library's fiction circulation rate of fifty to sixty percent of total circulation to represent an inappropriate expenditure of tax dollars on books for entertainment rather than for education. Librarians and library supporters rallied; their assertion of the cultural importance of imaginative works marked a turning point in the profession's sense of its purpose.[11] At the same time, urban public librarians recognized that branch libraries in particular might have to stock popular fiction to attract individuals who had not customarily used libraries.[12]

In the Negro Library's accession book, adult fiction represented the largest single category with 409 volumes accounting for twenty-three percent of the total collection and about thirty-seven percent of the adult collection. Including the 379 volumes of juvenile fiction, the 788 fiction titles totaled about forty-four percent of the collection. The "literature" category included 241 titles, almost fourteen percent of the collection. Together, adult fiction and literature totaled about thirty-seven percent of the collection, and made up almost sixty percent of the books for adult readers. Dewey class 3, for materials on sociology, law, education, and economics, was the next largest single category of reading for adults, with 103 titles accounting for approximately six percent of the total collection.

Juvenile fiction and juvenile non-fiction made up more than one third of the collection. For the youth collection, Kercheval ordered eighteen works by Joel Chandler Harris and seven by Thomas Nelson Page. Both men revealed their fondness for the traditional Old South in their books. She also ordered Helen Bannerman's *The Story of Little Black Bobtail*, *The Story of Little Black Quasha*, *The Story of Little Black Quibba*, and *The Story of Little Black Sambo*. Also on the children's shelves were books such as Thomas Aldrich's *The Story of a Bad Boy*, with its portrayal of Aunt Chloe as a contented slave.[13] Despite the significance of the juvenile collection, the books at an adult reading level outnumbered those for children.

Since Kercheval had no existing collection on which to build, she began establishing the Negro Public Library's collection with orders for multi-volume sets that would serve as a foundation or core. Among the first titles Kercheval acquired for the new branch were reference sets such as the thirty-five volume *Encyclopedia Britannica*, the eighteen volume *New International Encyclopedia*, the five volume *Dictionary of the Bible*, the seven volume *Cyclopedia of Engineering*, and the seven volume *Cyclopedia of Applied Electricity*. She also ordered Charles Dudley Warner's *Library of the World's Best Literature* in thirty volumes. Other sets included the ten volume

Speaker's Garland, the five volume *Short Studies on Great Subjects*, Woodrow Wilson's five volume *History of the American People*, and Rossiter Johnson's twenty volume *Great Events by Famous Historians*.

Notwithstanding a modest level of library funding, the Negro Library collection included multiple copies of a few titles and multiple titles by a few authors. Kercheval purchased eight copies of the Bible. She also bought two copies each of Jane Addams's *Twenty Years at Hull-House*; Shakespeare's plays and sonnets; Sir Walter Scott's *Ivanhoe*; and William Henry Elson's *History of the United States of America*. In some cases, the librarian obtained two copies of a single title and designated one for the adult and one for the children's section of the library. Examples of this practice included four works by James Fennimore Cooper: *The Deerslayer*, *Last of the Mohicans*, *The Pathfinder*, and *The Prairie*, all of them best sellers when first published in the 1820s and 1840s.[14] In all, Kercheval ordered sixteen titles by Cooper. Other authors she favored were Henry James, with twenty titles; Sir Walter Scott and Mark Twain, with nineteen titles each; Kipling, fifteen; Louisa May Alcott and George Eliot, ten each; and Tolstoi and Austen, four each. Consistent with her profession's reverence for the classics of Western literature, she ordered Homer's *The Iliad* and *The Odyssey*, Dante's *Divine Comedy*, Rousseau's *Emile*, and Macaulay's *History of England*. She also purchased multi-volume works of the abolitionist-poet James Russell Lowell and of the popular poet James Whitcomb Riley. Perhaps a bit more daring were her acquisition of Darwin's *Descent of Man* and *Origin of Species* and William James's *Principles of Psychology* and *Pragmatism*.

Kercheval purchased other books she apparently thought would be of interest to black readers, including twenty-three Thomas Nelson Page titles such as *In Ole Virginia* and *The Old South: Essays Social and Political*. Also listed in the accession book were two copies each of Joel Chandler Harris's *Uncle Remus and His Friends: Old Plantation Stories, Songs, and Ballads, with Sketches of Negro Character*, *Uncle Remus, His Songs and His Sayings*, and *Nights with Uncle Remus*. Apparently one copy was intended for adults and one for children. The Library accessioned fourteen additional Harris titles by opening day. Kercheval ordered three books by the popular African American poet Paul Laurence Dunbar, known for his deft handling of black dialect. Two were collections of his poetry, but one, *In Old Plantation Days*, was a collection of short stories. First published in 1903 by Dodd, Mead, the collection depicted a nostalgic view of slavery, but a few of the stories included subtle elements of protest.[15] Considered in the context of Kercheval's acquisitions, the emphasis on plantation and dialect can also be read as evidence of a stereotyped view of black life and expression.

Such an interpretation is reinforced by some of the other choices apparent in the accession log. Only six books in the library's collection had some form of "Negro" in the title. Of those, three were by Booker T. Washington: *The Education of the Negro, Negro Education Not a Failure*, and *The Story of the Negro* in two volumes. Also on the shelves was Andrew Carnegie's *The Negro in America*, which Washington's secretary, Emmett Scott, had helped research.[16] Frederick Jerome Work's *Folk Songs of the American Negro* and Charles Jones's *Negroland or, Light thrown upon the Dark Continent* were available as well.

Additional books penned by Booker T. Washington were in the library's collection: *Character Building*, a collection of speeches; *The Man Farthest Down*, based on Washington's observations during a trip to Europe; *My Larger Education*, a follow-up to his earlier autobiography, *Up From Slavery*; and *Tuskegee and Its People*, a volume describing the work of the school Washington had founded. Washington had made himself acceptable to whites by advocating black acquiescence to the status quo even as he worked secretly for change.[17] Kercheval apparently felt that Washington's message of accommodation was a desirable one for her clientele.

Other African American writers who worked openly for change did not appear in Kercheval's records. She did not acquire James Weldon Johnson's *Autobiography of an Ex-Colored Man*, anonymously published in 1912. She purchased nothing by W.E.B. Du Bois or Charles Chesnutt. Also absent from the log were books by sympathetic whites such as Mary White Ovington and Ray Stannard Baker.

The omissions in Nashville were not the result of a lack of availability. By checking the *Publishers' Trade List Annual* it is possible to discern which titles were in print while Kercheval was placing orders for the Negro Branch. The *PTLA* was a reference book that compiled major publishers' catalogs. Included were those listing published books by or about African Americans, such as Appleton; Doubleday, Page; Holt; Macmillan; Neale; and Charles Scribner's Sons. Table 2 lists a selection of the titles by or about African Americans in the *PTLA* in 1915 but not accessioned by the library's opening day. Among the titles the *PTLA* listed were five by Charles Chesnutt, including *The Conjure Woman*, a collection of seven short stories published by Houghton Mifflin in 1899. The stories were set on plantations but did not conform to the romanticism of other plantation fiction, particularly in their depiction of malicious masters rather than benevolent ones.[18] Other works by Chesnutt still in print in 1915 were *The House Behind the Cedars*, a story of a mixed-race woman who passes for white; *The Marrow of Tradition*, a novel portraying the recalcitrance of unreconstructed small-town Southerners; and *The Wife of His Youth and Other Stories of the Color Line*, with race mixing as a central theme.

Also still in print in 1915 was former Vice President Henry Wilson's three-volume *Rise and Fall of the Slave Power in America*, first published in the 1870s when Wilson was a Radical Republican in the U.S. Senate. George Washington Williams's *A History of the Negro Troops in the War of the Rebellion, 1861–1865*, originally published in 1888 by Harper & Brothers, was also available. The book argued that black soldiers had helped save the Union.[19]

Popular works in print in 1915 included Matthew Henson's *A Negro Explorer at the North Pole* and Ray Stannard Baker's *Following the Color Line*. A bit more scholarly were W. E. B. Du Bois's *The Negro* and *The Souls of Black Folk*, both listed in the *PTLA*. Howard University sociologist Kelly Miller had two books in print in 1915, *Out of the House of Bondage* and *Race Adjustment*.

It is difficult to interpret why Kercheval did not order these titles. None of the extant evidence can suggest her motives. It is likely that she relied on the same selection criteria she used to develop the white collection. Kercheval may not have been well-informed about the availability of books by or about African Americans and may have missed some works out of ignorance. She also may have consulted the *A.L.A. Catalog* published in 1904 and edited by Dewey, Seymour, and Elmendorf, and its supplement for 1904 to 1911, edited by Bascom. The *Catalogs* were intended to guide librarians who were building public library collections.[20] Of the 35 titles in print but not ordered by opening day (Table 2), only eight were listed in the *A.L.A. Catalog* and its supplement: Archer's *Through Afro-America*; Baker's *Following the Color Line*; Chesnutt's *The Conjure Woman*; Du Bois's *The Souls of Black Folk*; Hart's *The Southern South*; Ovington's *Half a Man*; Spears's *The American Slave-Trade*; and Stephenson's *Race Distinctions in American Law*. These eight indicate where Kercheval diverged from the recommended acquisitions. But for the remaining 27 titles not recommended in the *A.L.A. Catalog* and its supplement and not ordered for the Negro Library, Kercheval's decisions were in alignment with those of the librarians and other experts who compiled the catalogs of recommended books.

In some cases, however, especially that of Du Bois, the omissions seem not the result of ignorance or of professional consensus. They seem instead to reflect the values of local dominant culture. By 1915 Du Bois was well known by whites as well as blacks, and white Nashville was certainly aware of him. He had been a student at Fisk University in the 1880s. When *The Souls of Black Folk* appeared in 1903, the Nashville *American* editorialized that it was "dangerous for the negro [*sic*] to read."[21] Du Bois's work to help found the National Association for the Advancement of Colored People, his editing of its magazine, *The Crisis*, and his continuing criticism of Booker Washington (even in his obituary in the December 1915 issue of *The Crisis*) furthered Du Bois's national reputation.[22] The lack of his work in the library suggests active avoidance of works by a Northern-born black intellectual intent on agitating for empowerment.

Although more works by and about African Americans would appear on the shelves over the next several years under Marian Hadley's direction, the opening day collection reflected Margaret Kercheval's sense of what was standard and suitable. And African American readers no doubt welcomed the opportunity to consult a variety of reference works and to take home selected classics as well as lighter popular fare. It would be foolish to suggest that the availability of the classics was a kind of indicator of the collection's inadequacy. To some degree, public libraries exposed all of their users to the Western literary tradition. But was it possible for readers relegated to separate physical spaces to experience a shared literary culture? It seems unlikely in the context of the early twentieth-century South.

In his discussion of the classical liberal education valued by African Americans in the post–Civil War period, historian James D. Anderson has noted that "the classical course was not so much the imposition of an alien white culture that would make blacks feel inferior as it was a means to understanding the development of the Western world and blacks' inherent rights to equality within that world."[23] Anderson offers as an example the testimony of black educator Richard Wright before the U.S. Senate Committee on Education and Labor in 1883. Wright cited Humboldt and Herodotus as authorities to counter the notion of black racial inferiority. White Southerners did not interpret the classics in the same way black educators such as Wright did.

Only by having access to the Western canon could black readers begin to interpret its texts. And only by having access to texts by or about blacks could readers be exposed to a fuller spectrum of perspectives. Readers could wring meaning only from what was available to them, and for those readers who relied on the public library, what was not available to them was as significant as what was.

Table 1. Number and percentage of titles by class in the Nashville Negro Public Library Accession Book, July 1915–January 1916.

Class	Class Description	No.	%
0	General works	4	.22
1	Philosophy	35	1.98
2	Religion	40	2.25
3	Sociology	103	5.79
4	Language	8	.45
5	Natural science	41	2.31
6	Useful arts	57	3.21
7	Fine arts, music, sports	26	1.46
8	Literature	241	13.55
F	Fiction	409	23.00
9	History	48	2.70
910	Travel	31	1.74
B	Biography	48	2.70
JF	Juvenile fiction	379	21.32
JN	Juvenile non-fiction	308	17.32
Total		1,778	100.00

Table 2. Selected books by or about African Americans in print but not ordered for the Negro Public Library, 1915.

Author	Title
Archer, William	*Through Afro-America: An English Reading of the Race Problem*
Bailey, Thomas Pearce	*Race Orthodoxy in the South and Other Aspects of the Negro Question*
Baker, Ray Stannard	*Following the Color Line*
Brawley, Benjamin	*A Short History of the American Negro*
Cable, George Washington	*The Negro Question*
Chesnutt, Charles	*The Conjure Woman*
	The House Behind the Cedars
	The Marrow of Tradition
	The Wife of His Youth, and Other Stories
Cooney, Dotia Trigg	*A Study in Ebony*
Dowd, Jerome	*The Negro Races*
Du Bois, W.E.B.	*The Negro*
	The Souls of Black Folk
Evans, Maurice Smethurst	*Black and White in the Southern States*
George, James Zachariah	*The Political History of Slavery in the United States*
Hart, Albert Bushnell	*The Southern South*
Henson, Matthew	*A Negro Explorer at the North Pole*
Holtzclaw, William Henry	*The Black Man's Burden*
Johnson, James Weldon	*The Autobiography of an Ex-Colored Man*
Merriam, George S.	*The Negro and the Nation*
Miller, Kelly	*Out of the House of Bondage*
	Race Adjustment

Ovington, Mary White	*Half a Man*
Page, Thomas Nelson	*The Negro: The Southerner's Problem*
Price, John Ambrose	*The Negro, Past, Present, and Future*
Randle, Edwin Henderson	*Characteristics of the Southern Negro*
Reed, John Hamilton	*Racial Adjustments in the Methodist Episcopal Church*
Siebert, William Henry	*The Underground Railroad from Slavery to Freedom*
Spears, John R.	*The American Slave-Trade*
Stephenson, Gilbert Thomas	*Race Distinctions in American Law*
Wheatley, Phillis	*Poems and Letters, First Collected Edition*
Williams, George Washington	*A History of the Negro Troops in the War of the Rebellion, 1861–1865*
Wilson, Henry	*History of the Rise and Fall of the Slave Power in America*
Woodson, Carter Godwin	*The Education of the Negro Prior to 1861*
Work, Nathan Monroe	*Negro Year Book*

NOTES

1. Eliza Atkins Gleason wrote about segregated libraries before the era of widespread desegregation in *The Southern Negro and the Public Library* (Chicago: U. of Chicago Press, 1941). E. J. Josey and Ann Allen Shockley have edited a *Handbook of Black Librarianship* (Littleton, CO: Libraries Unlimited, 1977) that includes historical sketches of libraries serving African Americans. Josey has also discussed civil rights activism and its impact on segregated libraries in "The Civil Rights Movement and American Librarianship: The Opening Round," *Activism in American Librarianship, 1962–1973*, eds. Mary Lee Bundy and Frederick J. Stielow (Westport, CT: Greenwood Press, 1987) 13–20. The *Encyclopedia of Library and Information Science*, eds. Allen Kent, Harold Lancour, and Jay E. Daily, 35 vols. (New York: Marcel Dekker, 1968–83) has several entries on libraries and segregation: Joseph H. Reason, "Library and Segregation," vol. 16, 22–26; Casper L. Jordan, "Library and Segregation: Contemporary and Controversial Aspects," vol. 16, 27–43; and Doris Hargrett Clack, "Segregation and the Library," vol. 27, 184–204. Rosemary Ruhig Du Mont has surveyed the history of librarians' attitudes toward African American librarians and library users and outlined the development of library education for African Americans in "Race in American Librarianship: Attitudes of the Library Profession," *Journal of Library History* 21 (Summer 1986): 488–509. Robert Martin and Lee Shiflett have focused on the establishment of separate library schools in "Hampton, Fisk, and Atlanta: The Foundations, the American Library Association, and Library Education for Blacks, 1925–1941," *Libraries & Culture* 31 (Spring 1996): 299–325. James Carmichael has considered the establishment of Atlanta's branch for blacks in "Tommie Dora Barker and the Atlanta Public Library, 1915–1930: A Case Study in Female Professionalism," *Atlanta History* 34 (Spring 1990): 24–41. Klaus Musmann has drawn on key publications to provide a historical overview of library segregation up to 1950 in "The Ugly Side of Librarianship: Segregation in Library Services from 1900 to 1950," *Untold Stories: Civil Rights, Libraries, and Black Librarianship*, ed. John Mark Tucker (Champaign: Graduate School of Library and Information Science, U. of Illinois, 1998) 78–92. Cheryl Malone has used primary sources to document the founding and development of segregated libraries in Louisville, Houston, and Nashville; see "Books for Black Children: Public Library Collections in Louisville and Nashville, 1915–1925," *Library Quarterly* 70 (April 2000): 179–200; "Autonomy and Accommodation: Houston's Colored Carnegie Library, 1907–1922," *Libraries & Culture* 34 (Spring 1999): 95–112; "Louisville Free Public Library's Racially Segregated Branches, 1905–35," *Register of the Kentucky Historical Society* 93 (Spring 1995): 159–79. Andrea L. Williams has consulted original materials to reconstruct the history of some segregated libraries in Texas in "A History of Holland Public Library, Wichita Falls, Texas, 1934–1968," *Untold Stories*, 62–77. Dan Lee has traced the development of library services for blacks in South Carolina in "From Segregation to Integration: Library Services for Blacks in South Carolina, 1923–1962," *Untold Stories*, 93–109; and Patterson Toby Graham has done the same for Alabama in "Segregation and Civil Rights in Alabama's Public Libraries, 1918–1965," diss., U. of Alabama, 1998. Clarence W. Hunter has recounted the desegregation of the Mississippi Library Association in "The Integration of the Mississippi Library Association," *Mississippi Libraries* 56 (Fall 1992): 68–71; and Kayla Barrett and Barbara A. Bishop provide a history of "Integration and the Alabama Library Association: Not So Black and White," *Libraries & Culture* 33 (Spring 1998): 141–61.

2. Christine Pawley, "Reading on the Middle Border: The Culture of Print in Osage, Iowa, 1870

to 1900," diss., U. of Wisconsin–Madison, 1996, 231–51; Wayne A. Wiegand, "Main Street Public Library: The Availability of Controversial Materials in the Rural Heartland, 1890–1956," *Libraries & Culture* 33 (Winter 1998): 131–32.

3. William D. Boyd, "African-Americans and Public Library Collections in the South: A Preliminary Investigation," *Research Issues in Public Librarianship: Trends for the Future*, ed. Joy M. Greiner (Westport, CT: Greenwood Press, 1994) 56–61.

4. Cheryl Knott Malone, "Accommodating Access: 'Colored' Carnegie Libraries, 1905–1925," diss., U. of Texas at Austin, 1996, 159–73; Bobby L. Lovett, *The African-American History of Nashville, Tennessee, 1780–1930: Elites and Dilemmas* (Fayetteville: U. of Arkansas Press, 1999) 126.

5. Cheryl Knott Malone, "Quiet Pioneers: Black Women Public Librarians in the Segregated South," *Vitae Scholasticae* (Spring 2000): 80.

6. Cheryl Knott Malone, "Books for Black Children: Public Library Collections in Louisville and Nashville, 1915–1925," *Library Quarterly* 70 (April 2000): 185.

7. Malone, "Accommodating Access" 184. A fuller discussion of the Negro Public Library's registered borrowers is found in Malone, "Reconstituting the Public Library Users of the Past: An Exploration of Nominal Record Linkage Methodology," *Journal of Education for Library and Information Science* 39 (Fall 1998): 282–90.

8. The preface to the *A.L.A. Catalog, 1904–1911* suggested that a library might diverge from the Catalog's recommendations to satisfy local needs or to build a special collection related to the interests of a particular reading community; see Elva L. Bascom, *A.L.A. Catalog, 1904–1911* (Chicago: ALA, 1912) 7.

9. Pawley 272.

10. Putnam, quoted in Evelyn Geller, *Forbidden Books in American Public Libraries, 1876–1939* (Westport, CT: Greenwood Press, 1984) 21.

11. Esther Jane Carrier, *Fiction in Public Libraries, 1900–1950* (Littleton, CO: Libraries Unlimited, 1985) 73–74.

12. Linda A. Eastman, *Branch Libraries and Other Distributing Agencies* (Chicago: ALA, 1911) 8.

13. Malone, "Books for Black Children" 188–90.

14. Frank Luther Mott, *Golden Multitudes: The Story of Best Sellers in the United States* (New York: R.R. Bowker, 1947) 305–6.

15. Doris Lucas Laryea, "Paul Laurence Dunbar," *Dictionary of Literary Biography, Volume 50: Afro-American Writers Before the Harlem Renaissance*, ed. Trudier Harris (Detroit: Gale, 1986) 119.

16. Louis R. Harlan, *Booker T. Washington: The Wizard of Tuskegee, 1901–1915* (New York: Oxford UP, 1983) 82.

17. Harlan vii–ix.

18. William L. Andrews, "Charles Waddell Chesnutt," *Dictionary of Literary Biography, Volume 50: Afro-American Writers Before the Harlem Renaissance*, ed. Trudier Harris (Detroit: Gale, 1986) 40–41.

19. Linda O. McMurry, "George Washington Williams," *Dictionary of Literary Biography, Volume 47: American Historians, 1866–1912*, ed. Clyde N. Wilson (Detroit: Gale Group, 1986) 341.

20. Analyses of the predecessor to the *A.L.A. Catalog* and its 1904–1911 supplement, *Catalog of "A. L. A." Library: 5000 Volumes for a Popular Library*, appear in Geller, *Forbidden Books* 54–56, Pawley 243–51, and Wayne A. Wiegand, "Catalog of 'A. L. A.' Library (1893): Origins of a Genre," *For the Good of the Order: Essays in Honor of Edward G. Holley*, ed. Delmus E. Williams, et al. (Greenwich, CT: JAI Press, 1994) 237–50.

21. Quoted in Herbert Aptheker, introduction, *The Souls of Black Folk*, by W. E. B. Du Bois (Millwood, NY: Kraus-Thomson, 1973) 17.

22. David Levering Lewis discusses the decline of Washington and the rise of Du Bois up to 1919 in his *W. E. B. Du Bois: Biography of a Race, 1868–1919* (New York: Henry Holt, 1993) 408–434, 501–02.

23. James D. Anderson, *The Education of Blacks in the South, 1860–1935* (Chapel Hill: U. of North Carolina Press, 1988) 30.

9. Historical Overview of Tribal Libraries in the Lower Forty-Eight States

Lotsee Patterson

The title of this collection, *Libraries to the People: Histories of Outreach*, indicates that there have been multiple attempts to extend library service to underserved population groups. With American Indian populations, however, there has been a historical absence of these efforts. Although there are exceptions, such as services provided by the state library agencies in New York, New Mexico, and Alaska and by a few large public libraries, outreach to tribes has been notably non-existent. Not to justify the past or excuse this oversight, there are reasons why this has been the case.

Most tribes are located some distance from urban areas where public library or regional library systems might have otherwise attempted outreach services. State librarians have frequently taken the stance that tribes are federal responsibilities and, therefore, the state library is not obligated to provide services to them. In addition to these two common circumstances, it may be that often library personnel just don't know what to do with tribes in terms of library services and programs. Thus it was a matter of simply not knowing how to go about it rather than not wanting to provide services. Above all, through, it is hoped the reason is not the one expressed to the author by a high level federal government political appointee, who was at the time responsible for library programs in the U.S. Department of Education, when she said, "Indians don't need libraries, they can't read anyway."[1]

If library outreach services have not reached American Indian tribes, what has been the status of library services on Indian reservations? This is the subject of this paper. Only services on tribal lands are addressed, not services to urban Indians.

Foundations of Tribal Libraries

Most tribal libraries began as small donated collections of assorted materials which later, with assistance from various sources, gained the impetus to organize, grow and become genuine libraries. Many obstacles were faced, however, not the least of these being a stable source of funding and trained personnel.

While formidable problems existed, there was never any doubt on the part of tribal leaders or members that a library in their community was highly desirable. Education is valued by native people living on reservations and they often view having a library within their community as an important avenue to attaining it. As a Santo Domingo Pueblo tribal official stated to the author:

> Our high school students are bussed off the reservations to public schools, sometimes as far as forty miles. They cannot stay after hours to use the library. They are placed at an unfair disadvantage because they have no access to library materials after school. Most of them do not have these kinds of materials in their homes. They need a place to study and they need resources that they can use in their studies in writing reports and so forth.[2]

What tribal leaders did not know was how to start, organize, and maintain a library. Fortunately, over the past forty years, assistance has been slowly coming their way. Heightened awareness in America of the country's disreputable treatment of minorities may be credited with creating a climate more favorable toward the Nation's First People. The results have been several milestones occurring over the past forty years which have had an enabling effect on tribes. Perhaps the most significant of these was the passage of the Indian Self-Determination and Education Assistance Act in the mid–1970s. This federal legislation encouraged self-governance by enabling tribes to contract with the Bureau of Indian Affairs to manage their own affairs.[3] Prior to this, the U.S. Department of Interior's Bureau of Indian Affairs had oversight responsibilities for the education and welfare of most tribes which included the administration of rules and regulations that governed them. For the most part, tribes were passive entities in their own operations. Many did not even have a building in which to manage their affairs. A tribal librarian illustrates this dramatically:

> Small wonder that so much of the tribe's culture, traditions, and history was lost. The Miami Tribe did not have its own office building until 1978. Prior to that, the Chief's office was his car. The tribal secretary/treasurer kept the typewriter and one filing cabinet at her home.[4]

Over the past thirty years many tribes have not only contracted for management of all or part of their operations, they have also expanded their tribal facilities. This fact alone has been the impetus for the establishment of a number of tribal libraries.

Another milestone in the development of tribal libraries was Title II B of the Higher Education Act. In the late 1960s and early 1970s the U.S. Department of Education began funding competitive programs targeted for training and educating minorities through this piece of legislation. Many of the Native American librarians practicing today were recipients of Title II B fellowships. Other funds from this source were used to set up research and demonstration projects. A significant number of the tribal libraries in operation today got their start under the auspices of these projects.[5]

A third major piece of legislation affecting development of tribal libraries was the revision and extension of the Library Services and Construction Act enacted in 1984. A rewritten Title IV of this Act was targeted for tribal libraries and the amount of money available was a percentage set aside of Titles I, II, and III of the Act. This action was a direct outcome of the 1979 White House Conference on Libraries and Information Services and, more indirectly, of the 1978 Native American Pre-Conference.[6] At the 1978 Pre-Conference an omnibus bill promoting library services for American Indians was produced. Accepted and passed in its totality by delegates to the 1979 White House Conference, the bill led to the first legislation that designated funds specifically for tribal libraries. Although the amount of money awarded is not enough on which to operate a tribal library, the Act remains an important source of revenue for tribal libraries. Originally administered through the U.S. Department of Education, it is now a responsibility of the Institute of Museum and Library Services.

From the early 1980s until the mid–1990s, The National Commission on Libraries and Information Science took the lead in championing tribal libraries. The Commission had a Native American Committee that gathered information and documented the need for library and information services on reservations. In addition to site visits to reservations, the Commission held hearings throughout the country and listened to testimony about the dire need for library services in Indian country. The most recent of these resulted in a massive report, *Pathways to Excellence: A Report on Improving Library and Information Services for Native American Peoples.* Released in December 1992, it was accompanied by a smaller summary report by the same title.

The larger report includes a strategic plan for development of library and information services to Native Americans as well as summaries of the site visits and testimony given by individuals at each hearing. The Summary Report lists ten major challenges to be considered by "all concerned in order to initiate a process for dramatically improving library and information services for Native Americans."[7] To date no new initiatives have been taken by any federal agency to address the challenges outlined in the Reports.

Other federal agencies have programs which offer competitive grants that complement library programs. Notable among them are those available through the National Historical Publications and Records Commission (NHPRC), part of the National Archives and Records Administration. The NHPRC funds projects to preserve, publish, and encourage the use of documentary sources relating to the history of the United States. A number of tribes have used funds from these grants to collect and preserve documents of their history and to archive materials.

Although priorities for federal programs adjust to new government initiatives, the programs and agencies mentioned above have been, and continue to be, the primary force for development of tribal libraries on Indian reservations. Some state library agencies have also been active partners in assisting tribal libraries, as have some regional or public libraries near reservations.

Tribal Library Initiatives

The evolution of tribal libraries is not well documented. A study conducted in 1980 indicates that literature on library services to Native Americans was a recent phenomenon and appeared to have a direct relationship to federal funding, with 85 percent of it appearing from 1969 to 1976. The study further reports that traditionally library service to Native Americans consisted of that provided by bookmobiles. Comments and data gathered in the study reveal that the role of governments in providing library and information services to Native Americans was undefined and that questions of jurisdiction arose continually.[8]

It is known that as early as 1958 the Colorado River Tribal Council of Parker, Arizona, had established a library on their reservation. Since this library is still in operation today, it may hold the record as the longest continually operating tribal library. The early 1960s saw the St. Regis Akwesasne Mohawks in New York State and the Shoshone-Bannocks on the Fort Hall Reservation in Idaho initiate efforts to establish libraries. In New Mexico, Volunteers in Service to America (VISTA) gathered donated materials and organized small collections for tribal members to read. Libraries in Laguna and Acoma Pueblos started in the same way. While Acoma has never successfully maintained a library over an extended period, the library at Laguna has been continually operating and growing since 1974, when the author assisted tribal officials in setting up the library and in training a tribal member to manage it.

With the influx of federal dollars into training, research, and demonstration projects in the early 1970s, outside agencies such as universities began to reach out to the tribes and assist them with library development. Possibly the largest of the initiatives was a multi-year study conducted by the University of Minnesota that focused on information needs of selected tribes. Later taken over by the National Indian Education Association, then located in the Twin Cities, the project purchased books and other resources to place in three different types of environment in three geographically dispersed tribes. On the St. Regis Mohawk Reservation in upper New York State, materials were placed in a tribal library in a government building near the center of tribal activity. At a second site, in Rough Rock, Arizona, on the Navajo Reservation, books were placed in a school library with the understanding that any tribal member could use them. At a third site, on the Standing Rock Sioux Reservation in North Dakota, materials were given to a newly founded two-year tribal college library and to local schools. The study attempted to assess usage of these materials by tribal members and examine how well the resources filled their information needs. It also evaluated which of the environments—school, tribal college or separate tribal library—enhanced usage of the materials. One interesting conclusion of the study was that the lack of trained professionals in all of the sites limited the usefulness of the library to fill information needs.[9]

Training library aides in the pueblos was a primary goal of programs initiated by the author while a faculty member at the University of New Mexico from 1973 to 1978. Using grants from the Higher Education Act Title II B Research and Demonstration monies, aides were selected by either school or tribal officials. A secondary objective was the establishment of libraries. Working with fifteen of the nineteen pueblos, libraries were started either in the local school operated by the Bureau or in the pueblo. None of the pueblos or schools had ever had a library. Training personnel first proved to be the key to maintaining the library after the federal grants ended. Today, some twenty-five years later, six of the original eight tribal libraries are flourishing. They are in the pueblos of Zuni, Laguna, Isleta, Cochiti, Santa Clara, and Jemez. Others, Acoma and Santo Domingo, periodically open and close depending on circumstances. In addition, at the Pueblo of Zia, where a school was used as the site, the library has expanded to become the tribal library.

One of the librarians hired to do training in the last two years of these grants was a doctoral student, Ben Wakashige, who is now the State Librarian in New Mexico. With his intimate knowledge of the pueblo libraries and his concern for serving the unserved, he has been a strong and effective advocate for tribal libraries. Wakashige now heads an agency that established the Native American Libraries Project at the State Library. Funded by the state's legislature for two years in 1994, the Project focused on technology and the Internet. In 1997 the State Library, again with funding from the state legislature, established a resource and training center on the Navajo Reservation and placed computer equipment in thirty-three communities. This outreach service includes fourteen pueblos, several communities on the Navajo reservation, and the state's two Apache tribes, the Jicarilla and the Mescalero. The State agency's strategic plan includes increasing efforts in library development in tribal communities and continuing to focus on improving Internet access in these communities. State funding will be used for library acquisitions, library skills training workshops, professional consultation on meeting library standards, and an annual summer institute that addresses funding issues, tribal archives, Internet searching, and related topics. With strong support from the New Mexico State Library and the state's legislature, the tribal libraries in the state have a promising future.

One other important factor in the success of the New Mexico tribal libraries was the formation of a Native American Tribal Libraries Round Table within the state's library association. Formed in 1976 or 1977 with the original students in the training grants at the University of New Mexico, this Round Table has grown into a group of more than thirty members. Now identified as the Native American Libraries Special Interest Group (NALSIG), it consists of dedicated librarians who lend support and encouragement to each other. It is believed this interest group is unique among state library associations.

Another state that has demonstrated exemplary progress with its native people and libraries is New York. In 1977 the state legislature enacted a law providing permanent support for Indian libraries by enabling those libraries to become full members of the public library system. Since that time several million dollars have supported four libraries on three reservations: the Mohawk's Akwesasne Library and Cultural Center in St. Regis; the Seneca Nation's Library, serving residents of the Allegany Reservation in Salamanca, the Cattaraugus Reservation in Irving, and the Tonawanda Community Library, serving the Seneca Nation members in Akron.

Other state library agencies have also supported tribal libraries in recent years. Arizona and Montana have, depending to some degree on leadership at the state level, been inclusive when working with tribes. The state library agency in Alaska provides enormous and enthusiastic support for its native people.

The most promising recent development for tribal libraries has been the tribal college movement on reservations. Beginning in the 1970s, with their number growing considerably in the 1980s, the now nearly thirty tribal colleges are having a great impact on library services in rural areas where many numbers of Native Americans live. Located primarily in large states in the western half of the country, these colleges have libraries that function not only as college libraries but also as public libraries. They have been given land-grant status by the U.S. Congress, which enables them to receive funding directly from federal appropriations. As accredited institutions, they must have qualified librarians managing the libraries. This mix of stable funding and qualified library directors is resulting in better library services in these communities.[10]

Summary

The history of tribal libraries is a narrative that must continue. If the libraries are to be more than just a blur in the evolution of tribal development, they must have some dependable source of funding, sustained training opportunities, and improved internet-ready facilities and equipment. Tribal officials strongly support the concept of a library for their reservations, but they have few financial resources to support them. As several of the libraries grow, others cling to survival. Hopefully, these will not become another relic among the already too many relics associated with tribal histories.

Notes

1. A. Mathews, personal communication (January 1986).

2. Lotsee Smith, "Statement of Lotsee Smith," American Indian Policy Review Commission, Task Force #5, Indian Education Hearings (Albuquerque, NM: April 23, 1976).

3. Lotsee Patterson, "Native Americans," in Alex Boyd, ed., *Guide to Multicultural Resources 1997/1998* (Fort Atkinson, WI: Highsmith Press, 1997) 316.

4. Kay Alexander, "The Little Archives That Could!" *Annotation* 27.4 (1999): 8–9.

5. Lotsee Patterson, "History and Status of Native Americans in Librarianship." *Library Trends* 49 (2000): 189.

6. United States, National Commission on Libraries and Information Science, "Self Determination Requires Information Power: The Report of Record on the White House Pre-Conference on Indian Library and Information Services on or Near Reservations" (Denver: October 1978) ERIC, ED186170, RC011987.

7. Richard G. Heyser and Lotsee Smith, "Public Library Service to Native Americans in Canada and the Continental United States," *Library Trends* 29.2 (1980): 353–68.

8. Richard G. Heyser and Lotsee Smith, "Public Library Service to Native Americans in Canada and the Continental United States," *Library Trends* 29.2 (1980): 353–68.

9. University of Minnesota, Bureau of Field Studies, *A Summary of the National Indian Education Association Library Project* (St. Paul, MN: University of Minnesota, 1972) ERIC, ED066194.

10. Lotsee Patterson and Rhonda Harris Taylor, "Tribally Controlled Community College Libraries: A Paradigm for Survival," *College Research Libraries,* 57 (1996): 316–29.

III. INNOVATIVE OUTREACH SERVICES

10. Electronic Outreach in America: From Telegraph to Television

John W. Fritch

It is difficult to quantify early outreach activities in American libraries, largely because the term "outreach" did not exist with its present meaning until the mid–1960s.[1] The heading "Outreach programs" did not appear in *Library Literature* until 1970-71. An earlier heading that encompassed what we now refer to as outreach was "Library extension." This included a broad range of activities: building more branch libraries, providing service to non–English speaking immigrants or rural residents, and reaching new constituencies via electronic technologies. Even though the meaning of "Library extension" was broad, it was not all-inclusive. Early bibliographies, for example *Library Work: A Bibliography and Digest of Library Literature* (1912), used seventeen *See Also* headings under the phrase.[2] Additional headings not referenced under "Library extension" also covered outreach activities, including "Telephone," "Radio," and "Television." To conduct a thorough search for early outreach activities, a researcher must compile a long list of terms and yet never be sure that the list is comprehensive.

The Concise Dictionary of Library Science (1996) defines "Outreach service" as "service aimed at a potential user group that cannot visit a library or information service in person."[3] "Electronic library outreach" will be defined in this essay as the extension of library information via electronic media to patrons not physically present in the library. The focus will be on early innovations in electronic library outreach in America and on selected sources that describe these innovations. This essay is not intended to be a comprehensive compilation.[4]

Although it may be acknowledged that the concept of library outreach has been clouded by semantic difficulties over the years, John Colson reminds us that

[t]he public librarian in the United States has long held a strong sense of his mission to serve the unserved ... from the founding of A.L.A. in 1876 to the enactment of the Library Services Act in 1956, the principal goal of public librarians was to make their institutions available to every citizen.[5]

Kathleen Weibel, too, in *The Evolution of Library Outreach 1960–75 and Its Effect on Reader Services* (1982) posits that public libraries have always been closely tied to outreach.[6] She cites Ernestine Rose's work *The Public Library in American Life* (1954) as documenting the close affiliation between public library development and extension activities.[7]

In the history of American libraries, the concept of extending services to underserved populations was often perceived as a matter of establishing new libraries or branch libraries in places without library service; the concept of "technology," as it related to libraries, often meant a new method of shelving books or generating catalog cards. Yet, in the late nineteenth and early twentieth centuries, as electronic communication began to be commonplace in America, many librarians utilized electronic technology to assist them in getting information to the public.

TELEGRAPH AND TELEPHONE

The electric telegraph had a remarkable impact on the transmission of information in the late nineteenth century, but in the early stages of its development it was regarded as a scientific novelty.[8] In 1844, the initial year of commercial telegraph service in the United States, the public was able to send messages free of charge, but few took advantage of the opportunity.[9] Yet within a few years the public embraced telegraphy, and by 1850 there were 12,000 miles of telegraph wires operated by over twenty companies.[10] An indication of the power of the telegraph was the quick demise of the Pony Express after a transcontinental telegraph link was established across the United States in 1861.

The telegraph became an important and widespread communication device, but not in libraries. In his 1954 doctoral dissertation, "The Development of Reference Services in American Research Libraries," Samuel Rothstein mentions telegraph service in only one library by 1905, a special legislative library that used telegraphy to relay crucial information to legislators.[11] Telegraphy was never common in libraries, possibly because operating a telegraph required special training and a great deal of practice.[12]

The invention that revolutionized electronic outreach for libraries was the telephone. The earliest reference to the telephone in Cannons' *Bibliography of Library Economy* (1927) is to the second volume of the *Library Journal*, published in 1877, only one year after the invention of the telephone.[13] The article reveals that interest centered on the particulars of telephone operation, detailed costs and associated expenses of the telephone, and an announcement that the Boston Public Library had telephone connections between its branch libraries and the main library.[14] The usefulness of these telephones was limited; early systems typically had a range of no more than twenty miles.[15] Telephone usage and the number of telephones grew exponentially after 1893 due to increased competition following the expiration of Alexander Graham Bell's original telephone patent.[16] As prices dropped and capabilities expanded, articles in library periodicals discussed the practical uses of telephones in libraries. An article in *Public Libraries* mentioned books being renewed by telephone as early as 1900.[17]

By 1908 the telephone was touted in *Library Journal* as one of the "most effective" means of library publicity through reference service, especially when patrons needed information in a timely manner.[18] Yet many patrons preferred not to use the telephone or did not have convenient access to one. A letter published in *Public Libraries* in 1908 states that the Newark Free Library had

> not found it easy to increase as much as we would like the use made of the telephone by the public in asking questions of the library, despite the fact that telephone calls are welcome has been quite well advertised in the local papers and the telephone number has been printed on much of our stationary and many of our blanks.[19]

In later decades, telephone use in libraries became widespread. In June 1922 *Public Libraries* received a letter calling for a uniform telephone number for libraries so that access would be easier.[20] Telephone use was so heavy in the 1920s and 1930s that articles warned against advertising too much for fear that librarians would be unable to handle the deluge of questions.[21] Some authors also recommended that certain types of questions should not be answered over the phone, especially genealogy and contest questions, and those involving medical and legal issues.[22] The telephone was viewed as a device that enabled librarians to reach out to new constituencies such as businessmen who might not have enough time to come to the library to have their queries answered. Businessmen were perceived to be a very influential group in terms of their ability to promote public support of libraries.[23]

The usefulness of the telephone in outreach was evident by the mid–1930s and early 1940s, when articles began discussing special "telephone service desks" and the use of switchboards in libraries. A brief article in *Library Journal* noted that a switchboard with a library assistant serving as "interpreter-hostess" could help in identifying and sorting information requests, and in transferring calls to the proper department efficiently.[24] In separate articles published in *Library Journal* and the *Wilson Library Bulletin*, Florence Gifford and Emily Garnett identified materials required for telephone service desks, including essential reference books, atlases, city directories, and telephone directories for cities across the United States and Canada.[25] The Cleveland Public Library estimated that it answered 25,000 telephone queries in 1940, and anticipated doubling that number in the following year with the addition of a new telephone reference desk. The new desk would notify workers of incoming calls by a system of lights rather than traditional bell-rings, which would allow "better concentration for our readers and for the staff."[26]

By the mid–1940s, the telephone had become a regular part of reference service. Reference service textbooks, such as Margaret Hutchins's *Introduction to Reference Work* (1944), discussed purchasing the "best telephone equipment" and forms for telephone reference, as well as hiring knowledgeable switchboard operators if more than one department offered the service.[27] Meanwhile, the frequency of journal articles discussing telephone service decreased. From 1942 to 1948 there were only two articles listed under "Telephone information service" in *Library Literature*.

Radio

The first radio broadcast "program" took place in 1906; the first radio news broadcast in 1920; and the first commercial radio programs followed soon thereafter. Radio quickly developed an avid following among librarians and educators. Many thought it would revolutionize the way that Americans gained access to information and education—from live news broadcasts, to books being read over the air, to detailed educational programs and entire curricula delivered exclusively via radio. During the 1920s more than 100 radio stations were granted licenses, and most of these went to colleges and churches.[28] Librarians quickly stepped forward to make some of the educational thrusts of radio a reality, despite a concern that radio might reduce the popularity of reading and ultimately cause the demise of the book.

Many early radio broadcasts featured works of literature either reviewed or simply read on the air. This practice prompted copyright discussions and the idea that a new type of authors' rights, "first radio rights," might be necessary. It also generated speculation that new methods would be discovered to directly charge radio listeners a "few cents a night," rendering radio programs "immensely" profitable.[29] *Publishers Weekly* contained several articles in the early 1920s that discussed copyright and broadcasting the content of published works.[30]

Concerns about radio negatively impacting the quantity and quality of people's reading and their interest in literature were quite common. However, in an article published in 1988, Dave Berkman indicates that the relationship between early broadcasters and authors was synergistic: authors received free publicity for their literary works, while broadcasters received free programming.[31] Berkman cites a 1922 article in the *New York Times Book Review* by John Walker Harrington as the first in the periodical press to mention the risks involving "radio literature."[32] Berkman also notes the possibility of some unhappiness among both listeners and authors: authors perhaps felt demeaned by having to "peddle" their books, while listeners opined that many "literary" people highly regarded for their writings were terribly dull speakers.

There was also a good deal of speculation about the positive impact of radio on literature. According to an article in the *New York Times* (12 October 1924):

> It is claimed that radio, with its millions of listeners, its ability to pierce the remotest parts of the country and the great distance it covers, can do for literature what it already has done for music. It has already been demonstrated that broadcasting can create an interest in literature.[33]

It was observed that radio reviews were being used at the meetings of literary clubs in the metropolitan district. The writer also discussed letters sent to Columbia University's broadcasting station from listeners enamored with a series of radio lectures on Robert Browning.[34]

One of the first library radio broadcasts cited in *Library Literature* occurred in 1922, only two years after the first news broadcast. Announced in *News Notes of California Libraries* under the title "First Library Talk by Radio," the program was basically an advertisement for library services in California's Sutter County, with encouragement for every "man, woman, and child" to take advantage of local library services.[35] Another "library speech" was given in the same year at the invitation of the *St. Louis Post-Dispatch* and heard "at all receiving stations within 200 miles." This broadcast is documented in "Radio and Library Service," an article published in *Public Libraries* (May 1922), which expressed the promise of radio in terms of library outreach: "It is not too much to expect that before very long, those who cannot go to the lectures, to church or to story hours will be served in their own homes by means of radio contrivances."[36] By October of that same year, librarians from the Carnegie Library of Pittsburgh were broadcasting children's stories on the Westinghouse Company's radio station that were heard as far away as Galesburg, Illinois.[37]

Several other libraries made radio broadcasts early in the 1920s. A questionnaire sent out by the *Library Journal* in 1924 indicated that libraries in Boston, Indianapolis, Newark, Portland (Oregon), Schenectady, St. Louis, Seattle, and Tacoma had some ongoing radio presence, with many having multiple program offerings each week.[38] Local radio stations often solicited topics and speakers from public libraries, providing even small libraries a perfect opportunity to reach an eager listening public. One reason radio stations approached librarians was that stations had a great deal of air time to fill with local programs prior to the predominance of network programming in the mid–1920s. Another factor was the Radio Act of 1927, which stipulated that the Federal Radio Commission (precursor to the Federal Communications Commission) assign licenses based partly on whether stations operated in "the public interest, convenience, and/or necessity."[39]

There was an early call for radio outreach in 1926 in the *Papers and Proceedings of the 48th Annual Meeting of the American Library Association* under the title "Some Objectives for Agricultural Libraries." Charles H. Brown of the Iowa State College Library noted that most colleges had broadcasting stations that could be used for more than agricultural extension. He posed the question: "How far are we using this opportunity for talks on home libraries and children's books?"[40] Since many libraries already had radio programs on the air, or were planning to have them in the near future, the American Library Association (ALA) acknowledged the importance of radio by forming a Library Radio Broadcasting Committee (LRBC) in 1926.[41]

Dissatisfaction with the way that libraries were utilizing radio was occasionally voiced. Librarian Ethel Fair submitted an "open letter" to the LRBC that was published in *Library Journal* in 1928. She complained that although many libraries were offering broadcast programs, their purpose seemed to be advertising for the libraries involved, rather than service to the public. In a published response, the Chairman of the LRBC, Charles H. Brown, maintained that service had largely been the focus of library radio broadcasts, but also indicated that he doubted whether "the public is especially interested in hearing from librarians." Brown emphasized that trained radio broadcasters had skills to hold and entertain an audience that the majority of librarians lacked.[42]

At the beginning of the 1930s a general interest in educational radio programs prompted the founding of several organizations.[43] The Institute for Education by Radio convened in June 1930 at Ohio State University and began publishing yearly proceedings under the title *Education on the Air*.[44] It is somewhat surprising, given librarians' ready utilization of radio for educational purposes, that they were represented by only a single chapter in the Institute's first proceedings.[45] The National

Committee on Education by Radio was also founded in 1930. The purpose of this Committee was to protect and promote broadcasting by educational institutions, and one of its first acts was to lobby for a minimum number of radio "broadcasting channels" to be reserved exclusively for educational organizations.[46] The same year saw the establishment of the National Advisory Council on Radio in Education, a non-partisan organization of fifty "representative citizens interested in education."[47] It was hoped that this group would assist in organizing and coordinating educational radio efforts.[48]

Realizing that librarians could marry the public interest in radio with local discussions and library events, Francis K. W. Drury, the Executive Assistant in Adult Education of the ALA, compiled "The Broadcaster and the Librarian; How the Radio Station and the Library Can Help Each Other." Issued by the National Advisory Council on Radio in 1931, this bulletin explored why radio broadcasting needed library cooperation, how commercial radio stations and libraries could cooperate, and how reading could be stimulated through cooperative broadcasts.[49] In 1932 the *Bulletin of the American Library Association* recognized the publicity that public libraries generated for themselves by posting commercial broadcast schedules on their bulletin boards. Luther Dickerson, then Chairman of the LRBC, also pointed to opportunities for successful tie-ins between national radio broadcasts and local discussion groups in public libraries. The Indianapolis Public Library had just sponsored one such program in which a group met in the library to hear background information on a speaker (John Dewey), listened to a scheduled broadcast by the speaker, and then discussed the content of the speech.[50]

One early task of the LRBC was to survey libraries about their radio broadcasting activities. The results of this survey were made public in the *Bulletin of the American Library Association* in 1930.[51] They indicated that a number of libraries had experimented with broadcasting and come to the conclusion that it was not a worthwhile investment of time. The negative respondents provided four reasons why library broadcasting was not fruitful: the crowding out of library programs in favor of commercial programs; the reorganization of commercial radio stations; the allotment of unpopular hours to library broadcasts and subsequent lack of response from the public; and the prevalence of library programs that reviewed only the most recent books, stimulating demand for specific titles which libraries could not meet. In 1932 the LRBC set several goals for itself: a series of nationally sponsored book talks, a children's hour of entertainment (closely allied with books and reading interests), and increased support by libraries of educational radio activities.[52]

In subsequent years the LRBC was especially interested in promoting radio broadcasts for youth. At the 55th Annual Conference of the American Library Association in 1933, the LRBC met with the ALA's Section for Library Work with Children to discuss what was being broadcast and what should be broadcast for children. Luther Dickerson indicated that both the National Broadcasting Company (NBC) and Columbia Broadcasting System (CBS) were willing to give free air time to the ALA if a "good program" that would hold the attention of the audience could be developed. It became clear that such a program would be expensive and would require professional talent, direction, and supervision. Dickerson reported that the ALA had been in contact with several organizations to ascertain current satisfaction with radio programs for children and, possibly, to collaborate in securing funds for a comprehensive series of children's programs.[53]

During the 1930s, commercial radio saw the emergence of dramatic series such as *The Shadow* and popular daytime serials or "soap operas" such as *Ma Perkins* and *The Romance of Helen Trent*.[54] The popularity of these programs reinforced radio's role as a prime source of entertainment in American society.[55] The number of "radio sets" (receivers) continued to grow, and by 1938 more American homes had radios than had indoor plumbing, automobiles, or telephones.[56]

Two major works on library broadcasting, each by an LRBC member, appeared in the late 1930s. In *Radio Roads to Reading: Library Book Talks Broadcast to Girls and Boys*, Julia Sauer provided the transcripts of radio book talks presented by the Rochester Public Library over a five-year period.[57] The talks were directed at students in the fifth to eleventh grades and were heard in school during school hours. Sauer recommended orienting broadcasts for children toward a particular age group, rather than trying to use one book talk for all ages, and focusing on only one book per broadcast due to the short attention spans and recollection abilities of children. In *The Library and the Radio*, Faith Holmes Hyers explored four areas delineated in the table of contents: The Librarian Cooperates with Educators on the Air; The Librarian as Broadcaster; The Librarian Experiments with Radio Programs; and A Look Ahead.[58] Hyers bemoaned the lack of a nationwide broadcast sponsored by the ALA, and looked ahead to a time when professional library broadcasts could be recorded, distributed, and aired as appropriate or convenient in each library's local area.[59]

Libraries were able to collaborate with commercial radio stations with increasing frequency. Educational Directors and other executives from NBC and CBS participated in the 1938 ALA conference in Kansas City. Six local Kansas City station directors were commended for their help in broadcasting twenty-eight conference programs. Commercial broadcasters also agreed to work cooperatively with libraries to send advance announcements of educational programs to libraries, to print reading lists along with the announcements (titles probably to be selected by the New York Public Library), and to "mention libraries as a source of reading enjoyment for interests stimulated by radio programs." A final step in cooperation was to be the establishment of radio "listening rooms" in libraries as a means of supplying books and discussion partners to complement broadcasts, while at the same time encouraging listeners to tune in to radio programs in a social setting.[60]

The great popularity of radio during its "golden age" in the 1930s and 1940s was due, at least in part, to the Depression and to the fact that receivers were inexpensive and the programs were free. People continued to enjoy radio entertainment and information even in times of great financial hardship.[61] During the thirties, the number of American homes with radios increased from twelve million to thirty million. It became obvious over time that radio was not the threat to reading that some had imagined; in fact, *Library Literature* even indicated the success of "wireless" book clubs.

One such club, the Radio Book Club at Iowa State College, got its start in 1930. This was five years after the college library had begun broadcasting book reviews, and two years after it had begun reading books over the air. The Club possessed its own library and loaned copies of books it recommended via the U.S. Postal Service for an average cost of less than twenty cents per book. The Club was financially self-supporting, even though it often purchased seven or eight copies of a book. Although membership was limited by postal zone to those living within 300 miles of Ames, Iowa, the Club boasted that 1,200 members in ten states had taken advantage of the service by 1933.[62]

Other libraries coupled radio outreach with home delivery but did not use the appellation "radio club" or require membership. The Kansas City Public Library used its broadcasts to advertise its existing holdings and services. Programs such as *Questionnaire of the Air* and science broadcasts, which were billed as "news reel[s] of the latest scientific discoveries and experiments which directly affect your life and mine," were designed to pique patron interest. Listeners could then telephone the library and request the "author, title, or subject desired." Home delivery was accomplished via Western Union on the same day the patron request was received. A small fee of ten cents was charged to cover costs on the transport of up to six books.[63]

The growth of commercial dramas, daytime serials, quiz shows, and other popular radio programs caused new concerns among librarians about cooperation with radio stations. These concerns prompted Frances Henne to author "Library-Radio Relationships" for *The Library Quarterly* in 1941. In this lengthy article, Henne maintained that although library radio activities had waned, many staunch supporters for library broadcasting still existed. She observed that two hundred known libraries were presenting radio programs and suggested that "the actual number probably far exceeds that number."[64] She grouped radio programs into six categories: Book Talks, Library Publicity, Interviews, Guest Speakers, Novel Reading, and Question and Answers. Henne posed two fundamental questions regarding collection development: should libraries purchase low-level fiction when radio programs provided its equivalent to a large audience, and should book selection be altered due to the popularity of radio programs and consequent changes in reading interests and demand?

Henne also offered some common sense advice for would-be library broadcasters: librarians should thoroughly examine and understand their goals before attempting to present radio programs. Henne called for systematic evaluation of library radio programs already on the air, noting that measurements of this sort had "rarely been attempted." She observed that when librarians claimed that circulation increased for particular books due to a radio broadcast, they typically had no hard data to back those claims.[65] Finally, she speculated that radio might prove somewhat transitory and eventually succumb to television or some other medium.

Many libraries were using radio in an attempt to increase the public's desire for books and to inform listeners about library services. *Library on the Air*, published in 1940, contained transcripts of successful radio programs that the author, Marie Loizeaux, had requested from libraries across the country.[66] Noting that children had received much of the attention of library broadcasts in the past, she planned her book to help libraries reach an adult audience. She had secured permissions from the programs' authors for any library to use the transcripts verbatim, thus essentially providing templates for adult library radio broadcasts. The transcripts were comprehensive; even things like sound effects, music, and stage directions were specified. Public library, academic library, and school programs were all represented in Loizeaux's book, although public library programs comprised the greatest number of offerings.

An examination of the types of programs represented in *Library on the Air* reveals the range of successful library broadcasts offered throughout the 1930s. Loizeaux presents seven types of program: Libraries in General, The Wheels Go Round (an explanation of staff and library functions), The Reader is Served (this category is further broken down into Juvenile, Readers' Advisory, and Reference), Books About One Thing or Another, Authors on the Scene, Book Reviews, and Random Ideas.

As a new decade began in 1940, the ALA's Library Radio Broadcasting Committee was merged along with the Visual Methods Committee into a single, new Audio Visual Committee.[67] This transition reflected the growing importance of educational films and the advent of television as a broadcast medium.[68] Although television began to compete with radio as a mass attraction by the late 1940s, libraries increased their radio activities throughout the decade.[69] A summary of library radio broadcasting activities covering most of the 1940s is presented in Frances Nunmaker's book, *The Library Broadcasts,* published in 1948.[70]

MOTION PICTURES AND SLIDES

Although the visual media of motion pictures and slides were not extensively used in early electronic library outreach, they did play a role in general outreach, at least in terms of advertising and publicity. Due to the popularity of motion pictures during the first half of the twentieth century, some librarians embraced film technology as a way to promote interest in libraries, not only within libraries, but also within theaters. Musmann relates that the Binghamton Public Library in New York used intermission periods at a motion picture show to display slides with catchy slogans advertising the library in at least two theaters.[71] In 1915 the *Library Journal* reported that another library filmed the opening of its branch library and the children's hour, and then showed the film at a local theater.[72] It is not known how successful such advertising campaigns were, but they did get libraries mentioned at events that were often considered to be in competition with libraries and reading.

PHONOGRAPH RECORDINGS

Thomas Edison was attempting to find a method of mechanically repeating telegraph messages when he invented the phonograph. First patented in 1878, Edison's phonograph utilized tin foil wrapped around a metal cylinder as the recording medium. He used his device to make acoustical recordings of significant men of the time, including Browning and Tennyson. These rare, early recordings were designed for coin-operated machines that were rented to various businesses. In 1887 Emile Berliner, a German living in America, patented a recording disc and began manufacturing "gramophone" equipment. Many of the early gramophone recordings were of opera singers and classical music. Electrical recording developed around

1925. This raised the quality of sound reproduction and lowered the price of records.[73]

Some libraries embraced musical recordings and hosted "phonograph concerts" as early as 1914.[74] In August 1915 the *Library Journal* published a special issue to help "stimulate the work of American public libraries in the collection and promotion of good music." One means of doing this involved the circulation of "record discs."[75] The professional literature reflects the growing interest in recordings over time. Articles emphasized the cataloging and care of records while collections were being built in the 1920s and 1930s. In the 1940s the emphasis shifted to methods of circulating record collections and how this could enhance the appeal and patronage of libraries.

TALKING BOOKS

Thomas Edison, in his original patent application for the phonograph, had mentioned that the blind might someday listen to recorded books. It took many years and advances in technology before this idea could be realized. In 1933 Congress passed Public Law Number 439, which provided monies for books on "sound-reproduction records." The law passed after the American Foundation for the Blind offered to pay for 1,200 special phonograph machines to play the recorded books. The Library of Congress inaugurated its talking books program in 1934, offering free delivery of records to visually impaired patrons. Among the first works recorded were the Bible, the Constitution, the Declaration of Independence, and Shakespeare's poems and plays. Twenty-four distribution centers were located across the United States.[76]

Many hurdles had to be overcome before talking books could be used efficiently. Records had to be manufactured with enough recording time to be practical. Early twelve-inch records played at seventy-eight revolutions per minute for only five minutes. They were made of shellac and were expensive, extremely heavy, and easily broken. By 1937 standards for talking books had been developed which specified a twelve-inch vinylite record, 33⅓ revolutions per minute, a recording pitch of 150 grooves per inch, and a spiral lead-in groove to allow a listener to place the needle on the record before starting the turntable. Records were mailed to patrons via the U.S. Postal Service in sturdy, cardboard containers with labels in both print and Braille. Even with these advances, however, book-length recordings were still unwieldy. *Gone with the Wind* required eighty records and had to be shipped in four containers, each holding up to twenty-two records.[77]

Special record players, originally called "talking-book reproducers," were available in both electric and hand-cranked, spring-driven models. During the Depression, manufacture of these machines became a Works Progress Administration (WPA) project at the urging of Helen Keller and the American Foundation for the Blind. After the advent of World War II, no new machines were produced, which made machine repair an essential activity. WPA workers made repairs until 1942, when the WPA was discontinued. Congress then authorized special funds that allowed machine repairs to continue during the War. From the opening of the manufacturing plant in 1935 until its closing in 1942, over 25,000 talking book machines were produced, in addition to thousands of phonograph needles, pickup arms, and record containers.[78] An extensive history of talking books can be found in Marilyn Lundell Majeska's *Talking Books: Pioneering and Beyond* (Washington: Library of Congress, 1988).

LIBRARY OF CONGRESS LIVE CHAMBER MUSIC BROADCASTS

The Library of Congress has long had an affiliation with music, developing collections of copyrighted musical compositions as early as 1846 and forming a music "department" in 1897. Over time the Library developed a musical outreach program for radio listeners. In 1924 Elizabeth Sprague Coolidge gave funds for an auditorium devoted to chamber music.[79] The potential for outreach was recognized long before construction began: "While Washington will be the immediate recipient of all these advantages [of the new auditorium], the proposed activities will have an influence all over the country. The recitals need not be limited to Washington. There is also the radio and other ways of reaching out."[80] The Library's first "festival of chamber music" took place in the Coolidge Auditorium in October 1928. The first broadcast of a Library chamber music concert went out over the airwaves in 1935.[81] A little over a decade later, the Library began sponsoring weekly chamber music broadcasts.[82]

TELEVISION

Although crude technologies essential for television broadcasting had been demonstrated as early as 1901, capabilities for broadcasting programs of high quality took many years to develop.[83] By the early 1930s sporadic experiments in early television broadcasting were being conducted. Under the Communications Act of 1934, Congress dissolved the Federal Radio Commission and established the Federal Communications Commission (FCC) to regulate television as well as radio.[84] Modern television, which incorporated a device called an iconoscope, was patented in 1938. Introduced to the general public at the 1939 World's Fair, television was slow to become popular in American homes. This was partly due to the high cost of television sets and meager initial programming, and partly due to World War II. During the war the FCC placed a ban on new television licenses, which temporarily halted the number of broadcasting stations at ten.[85] It was also during the war that "Television" first appeared as a heading in *Library Literature.*

A letter regarding television published in the *Wilson Library Bulletin* in 1940 encouraged librarians to embrace the new medium both as a publicity device and as medium that could convey useful information. The letter also expressed concern that television could become an efficient competitor to libraries if libraries did not make it an ally. The author warned: "There are many angles to think over NOW before television is as common as the newspapers."[86]

In 1945 Lawrence Lowman of CBS pointed out the changes that would be necessary for television to become successful after the war: larger pictures (standard at the time was 7.5" by 10"), clearer pictures with higher definition, color, reliable pictures without "ghosting," and cheaper television sets.[87]

The New York Municipal Library had one of the first television studios located in a library. Announced in *Special Libraries* in December 1945, it was designed to be an instructional studio featuring classes sponsored by the City College of New York. These classes were open to the public and included an introduction to television programming and production. The goal of the classes was to create a balance "between the technical and creative aspects of television." Students were expected to create and produce their own television programs. There was also a plan to add donated television "receivers" to each branch library in the New York Public Library system.[88] Demand for television increased dramatically after the War, and receivers were present in over 1,000,000 American homes by 1949.[89] By the late 1940s interest and activity in television broadcasting prompted the Library Public Relations Council of the ALA to publish *The Use of Television by the Public Library*, a transcript of a panel discussion which took place in New York in November of 1948. The panel was comprised of individuals representing television production, network programs, entertainment, and libraries. Discussion ranged from the technical aspects of television to the popularity of current programs to potential collaborations between libraries and television networks.[90]

Librarians were certainly aware of the explosive popularity of television, and the professional literature reflects that television prompted a concern similar to that which surfaced with the introduction of radio: fear that television might cause a decline in reading. In this case, however, television was indeed partly responsible for a drop in reading, although it was not cited as the only factor.[91] Surveys of public libraries conducted during this time reflected declines in the circulation of books, especially books of light fiction and other recreational reading materials. Librarians proposed various responses to the impacts of television: greater attention to individual needs; special activities for the elderly; musical events; book discussions; and better service.[92]

Librarians overcame initial concerns about television, and in 1953 held a preconference on television prior to the ALA annual meeting in Los Angeles. The preconference dealt with programming concepts and library-television relationships, and sparked interest in new opportunities for libraries to utilize television. Librarians' enthusiasm, however, was relatively short-lived. By the end of the decade, few original ideas regarding television were being offered by librarians.[93] Rather, most library involvement concerned the abilities of libraries to utilize the popularity of commercial programs already being broadcast. A considerable amount of information on the impacts of early television on libraries is available in Gene Lanier's *The Library and Television; A Study of the Role of Television in Modern Library Service* (1959).[94]

Despite librarians' enthusiasm and early collaborative efforts with television networks, Musmann indicates that "television has not played an important role in the history of the library's technology."[95] Even educational television (prior to public television), which fit the missions of libraries well, was considered by 1972 to have had only a minor impact.[96] In 1978 Harold Goldstein concluded: "A large variety of programs have been aired for listening and viewing; but libraries and librarians have not effected major changes in library objectives and services as a result of these newer forms of communication." Yet Goldstein remained optimistic about the future: "As networks develop and as libraries become more closely intertwined in their activities, perhaps broadcast services will result which will utilize material resources and human skills more fully and in more innovative aspects than in the present era of mass communication."[97] Goldstein's comments seem to have anticipated the development of more advanced networks, such as the Public Broadcasting Service (PBS) and the Internet.

CONCLUSION

Many electronic media showed great early promise and have had enormous societal impacts over time. The telephone especially provided a new way for librarians and library users to communicate. Radio had an immense educational and public relations impact early on, and still exists as a popular medium for entertainment, advertising, and education. And television, from its inception, seemed to be a medium with excellent potential for library outreach.

Today, electronic library outreach continues to flourish, and while much attention is focused on the Internet, many of the early media discussed in this essay are still serving the needs of individuals and libraries. Outreach is still achieved via telephone, radio, sound recordings, films, and television. Library outreach activities are perhaps most visible to the general public through national educational television programs. The ALA collaborates with the PBS on series such as *Reading Rainbow* and *Between the Lions*. Such programs, along with the Internet, offer evidence of the fulfillment of the promise of early electronic outreach: that libraries can truly become organizations without walls that reach out to provide information to individuals wherever electronic technologies are found.

NOTES

1. Kathleen Weibel, *The Evolution of Library Outreach 1960–75 and Its Effect on Reader Services*, University of Illinois Graduate School of Library and Information Science Occasional Papers 156 (Urbana: GSLIS, 1982) 5.

2. Anna Lorraine Guthrie, ed., *Library Work: A Bibliography and Digest of Library Literature* (Minneapolis: H. W. Wilson, 1912).

3. Stella Keenan, *Concise Dictionary of Library Science* (London: Bowker Saur, 1996) 153.

4. For an extensive view of early library devices, some of which are neither electronic nor oriented toward outreach, see Klaus Musmann's *Technological Innovations in Libraries 1860–1960: An Anecdotal History* (Westport, CT: Greenwood, 1993). For an overview of early library outreach activities, one can start with John Colson's 1975 article "The United States: An Historical Critique," in *Library Services to the Disadvantaged*, ed. by William Martin (Hamden, CT: Linnet Books, 1975) 61–82.

5. Colson 61.

6. Weibel 5.

7. Ernestine Rose, *The Public Library in American Life* (New York: Columbia UP, 1954).

8. Tom Standage, *The Victorian Internet: The Remarkable Story of the Telegraph and the Nineteenth Century's On-Line Pioneers* (New York: Walker Publishing, 1998) 49.

9. Alvin F. Harlow, *Old Wires and New Waves: The History of the Telegraph, Telephone, and Wireless* (1936; New York: Arno Press, 1971) 105.

10. Standage 58.

11. Samuel Rothstein, "The Development of Reference Services in American Research Libraries," diss., U of Illinois at Urbana–Champaign, 1954, 131.

12. Musmann 131.

13. H. G. T. Cannons, *Bibliography of Library Economy: A Classified Index to the Professional Periodical Literature in the English Language Relating to Library Economy, Printing, Methods of Publishing, Copyright, Bibliography etc., From 1876 to 1920* (Chicago: ALA, 1927) 221.

14. Justin Winsor, "The Telephone," *Library Journal* 2 (1877–78): 22.

15. Ithiel de Sola Pool, et al., "Foresight and Hindsight: The Case of the Telephone," *The Social Impact of the Telephone*, ed. Ithiel de Sola Pool (Cambridge, MA: MIT Press, 1977) 132.

16. John R. Pierce, "The Telephone and Society in the Past 100 Years," *The Social Impact of the Telephone*. ed. Ithiel de Sola Pool (Cambridge, MA: MIT Press, 1977) 161.

17. "News from the Field," *Public Libraries* 5 (1900): 25.

18. Marilla Waite Freeman, "The Relation of the Library to the Outside World; or The Library and Publicity," *Library Journal* 33 (1908): 492.

19. "Use of Telephones in Libraries," *Public Libraries* 13 (1908): 361.

20. Julia A. Robinson, letter, *Public Libraries* 27 (1922): 329.

21. Emily Garnett, "Reference Service by Telephone," *Library Journal* 61 (1936): 911.

22. Garnett 910; Rosemarie Riechel, *Improving Telephone Information and Reference Service in Public Libraries* (Hamden, CT: Library Professional Publications, 1987) 2.

23. Garnett 911.

24. "The Switchboard," *Library Journal* 61 (1936): 330.

25. Florence M. Gifford, "Telephone Service Desk," *Wilson Library Bulletin* 15 (1941): 827; Florence M. Gifford, letter, *Wilson Library Bulletin* 16 (1941): 15; Garnett 909.

26. Gifford, "Telephone Service Desk," 827.

27. Margaret Hutchins, *Introduction to Reference Work* (Chicago: ALA, 1944) 174.

28. Mark J. Braun, "Noncommercial Radio," *History of the Mass Media in the United States: An Encyclopedia*, ed. Margaret A. Blanchard (Chicago: Fitzroy Dearborn, 1998) 472.

29. "'First Radio Rights for Authors," *Literary Digest* 20 January 1923: 29.

30. Harold Goldstein, "Radio-TV and the Library," *Encyclopedia of Library and Information Science*, eds. Allen Kent et al., vol. 25 (New York: Marcel Dekker, 1978) 53.

31. Dave Berkman, "Letters, Libraries, and Broadcasting—They Go Back a Long Way," *Public Library Quarterly* 8.3-4 (1988): 20–21.

32. John Walker Harrington, "Risks of Radio Literature," *New York Times Book Review* 6 August 1922: 12.

33. "Book Reviews Now Broadcast," *New York Times* 12 October 1924 sec. 9: 15.

34. Covered in "Radio Prompts Listeners to Read Books," *New York Times* 25 May 1924 sec. 9: 15; and more comprehensively in Hoxie Neale Fairchild, "Broadcasting Books," *Publishers Weekly* 24 May 1924: 1671–1673.

35. Edna Hewitt, "First Library Talk by Radio," *News Notes of California Libraries* 17 (1922): 266–67.

36. "Radio and Library Service," *Public Libraries* 27 (1922): 279.

37. "A New Kind of Story-Telling," *Public Libraries* 27 (1922): 502.

38. "The Use of Radio by Public Libraries," *Library Journal* 49 (1924): 581–82.

39. Louise Benjamin, "Federal Radio Commission," *History of the Mass Media in the United States: An Encyclopedia*, ed. Margaret A. Blanchard (Chicago: Fitzroy Dearborn, 1998) 215.

40. Charles H. Brown, "Some Objectives for Agricultural Libraries," *Bulletin of the American Library Association* 20 (1926): 475.

41. "Committees and Boards," *Bulletin of the American Library Association* 27 (1933): H-25.

42. Ethel M. Fair, "An Open Letter to the A.L.A. Committee on Radio Broadcasting," and Charles H. Brown, "Mr. Brown's Reply," *Library Journal* 53 (1928): 357–58.

43. Faith Holmes Hyers, *The Library and the Radio* (Chicago: U of Chicago Press, 1938) 2.

44. Josephine MacLatchy, ed., *Education on the Air: First Yearbook of the Institute for Education by Radio* (Columbus, OH: Ohio State University, 1930).

45. Frances Clarke Sayers, "The Relation of the Library to Radio Education," *Education on the Air* 180–90.

46. "National Committee on Education by Radio," *School and Society* 33 (1931): 49.

47. "National Advisory Council on Radio Education," *School and Society* 31 (1930): 666–67.

48. "Radio Broadcasting Round Table," *Bulletin of the American Library Association* 24 (1930): 465–66.

49. "Radio and the Library," *Bulletin of the American Library Association* 25 (1931): 156.

50. "Library Radio Broadcasting Round Table," *Bulletin of the American Library Association* 26 (1932): 584.

51. "Radio Broadcasting Round Table," *Bulletin of the American Library Association* 24 (1930): 463.

52. "Library Radio Broadcasting Round Table," *Bulletin of the American Library Association* 26 (1932): 584.

53. "Second Session," *Bulletin of the American Library Association* 27 (1933): 794.

54. Ronald Garay, "Radio Entertainment," *History of the Mass Media in the United States: An Encyclopedia*, ed. Margaret A. Blanchard (Chicago: Fitzroy Dearborn, 1998) 564.

55. Goldstein 52.

56. Frank J. Chorba, "Golden Age of Radio," *History of the Mass Media in the United States: An Encyclopedia*, ed. Margaret A. Blanchard (Chicago: Fitzroy Dearborn, 1998) 239.

57. Julia Sauer, *Radio Roads to Reading: Library Book Talks Broadcast to Girls and Boys* (New York: H. W. Wilson, 1939).

58. Faith Holmes Hyers, *The Library and the Radio* (Chicago: U of Chicago Press, 1938).

59. Hyers 85, 88.

60. "Library Radio Broadcasting," *Bulletin of the American Library Association* 32 (1938): 655–56.

61. Godfrey 567.

62. Edward S. Allen, "Radio Library," *School and Society* 38 (1933): 508–09.

63. D. W. Kohlstedt, "Library Opportunities," *Library Journal* 61 (1936): 939, 969.

64. Frances Henne, "Library-Radio Relationships," *The Library Quarterly* 11 (1941): 450.

65. Henne 456.

66. Marie D. Loizeaux, *Library on the Air* (New York: H. W. Wilson, 1940).

67. "Committee on Committees," *American Library Association Bulletin* 34 (1940): P-41.

68. Goldstein 52.

69. Garay 564; Goldstein 54.

70. Frances G. Nunmaker, *The Library Broadcasts* (New York: H. W. Wilson, 1948).

71. Musmann 175.

72. "Motion Pictures," *Library Journal* 40 (1915): 451.

73. Jay E. Daily, "Nonprint Material," *Encyclopedia of Library and Information Science*, eds. Allen Kent et al., vol. 20 (New York: Marcel Dekker, 1977) 101.

74. "Library Extension Work," *Library Journal* 39 (1914): 870.

75. Introduction, *Library Journal* 40 (1915): 561.

76. Marilyn Lundell Majeska, *Talking Books: Pioneering and Beyond* (Washington: National Library Service for the Blind and Physically Handicapped, Library of Congress, 1988) 1–5.

77. Majeska 7–14.

78. Majeska 18.

79. John Y. Cole, *For Congress and the Nation: A Chronological History of the Library of Congress* (Washington: Library of Congress, 1979) 89, 91, 92.

80. "New Opportunity for Library of Congress," *Public Libraries* 30 (1925): 144.

81. Cole 100.

82. "Forty Years of Concert Broadcasts From the Library of Congress," *Library of Congress Information Bulletin* 46 (1987): 468.

83. Robert T. Jones, "Educational Television," *Encyclopedia of Library and Information Science*, eds. Allen Kent et al., vol. 7 (New York: Marcel Dekker, 1972) 557.

84. Marvin R. Bensman, "Federal Communications Commission," *History of the Mass Media in the United States: An Encyclopedia*, ed. Margaret A. Blanchard (Chicago: Fitzroy Dearborn, 1998) 214.

85. Bensmann 214.

86. Frederick L. Myers, letter, *Wilson Library Bulletin* 15 (1940): 82–83.

87. Lawrence W. Lowman, "Television—A Major Postwar Industry," *Special Libraries* 36 (1945): 273–74.

88. Douglas Hudelson, "Television Comes to the Library," *Special Libraries* 36 (1945): 478–80.

89. Chorba 240.

90. American Library Association. Library Public Relations Council. *The Use of Television by the Public Libraries* (New York: Printmasters, 1949).

91. Musmann 187.

92. Musmann 187–88.

93. Goldstein 55.

94. Gene Daniel Lanier, *The Library and Television; A Study of the Role of Television in Modern*

Library Service, thesis, U of North Carolina, 1959 (Rochester: U of Rochester Press for the Association of College and Research Libraries, 1959).

95. Musmann 183.

96. Jones 557.

97. Goldstein 57.

11. "On the Roof of the Library Nearest You": America's Open-Air Libraries, 1905–1944

Gerald S. Greenberg

When the concept of freely circulating books among the reading public was first initiated, there was significant concern that the health of readers was being placed at risk. Could not infectious disease be spread among unsuspecting readers, especially those who routinely licked their fingers in order to facilitate page-turning? Should not books in the possession of sick readers be sterilized before returning them to the collection? Or perhaps it would be best to destroy them altogether. The epidemics that regularly ravaged congested cities at the time inspired enough fear to threaten the very existence of public libraries.[1] Rumor attributed the premature death of at least one librarian to infection-by-book, and in 1900 book circulation was terminated in Scranton, Pennsylvania, rather than risk the spread of scarlet fever. Despite the panic engendered by such reports, cooler heads eventually prevailed. Yes, science told us that bacteria was present in books, and infection was a theoretical possibility, but the probability of this occurring was low. Public libraries survived the scare, although the health question lingered for decades.

Even if books were unlikely to infect readers, might not readers infect each other? Crowded together in close quarters, the residents of America's immigrant neighborhoods lived in conditions conducive to the spread of tuberculosis and other fearful diseases. Libraries, like schools, were viewed as places where disease was likely to be spread. Wouldn't the health of readers and students benefit from exposure to fresh air? Such treatment was regarded as *de rigueur* in management of tuberculosis. The open-air school movement promoted outdoor education worldwide as the proper method for instructing "delicate" children.[2] The National Tuberculosis Association published the *Journal of Outdoor Life* (1904–1935) in order to provide a forum for open-air treatment. In Great Britain the open-air schools flourished during the first three decades of the twentieth century as that nation addressed its tuberculosis problem. Surely, outdoor reading rooms would help protect the health of readers. City parks would serve the purpose. If real estate was in short supply, rooftops might suffice.

Treatment of disease did not represent the only reason for open-air libraries. Moving outdoors was the only logical response to summer heat in the days before air conditioning. The heat captured by and contained within city buildings during the summer months made it difficult for readers to enjoy their literature. Why not permit the patrons of the public library to read out of doors and escape the heat? It would not be possible for the library to meet the needs of researchers in the open air, but the casual reader of popular literature might be accommodated. Surely the library would attract many more regular users by providing a relatively comfortable atmosphere in which readers might enjoy their visit.

Open-air libraries also provided a more aesthetically pleasing setting for readers. Gardens replete with fountains and statuary framed the Cervantes outdoor reading room in Seville, Spain, credited by many as the first such facility. Although few of America's open-air libraries could match the tiled floors and bookcases found in Spain's outdoor reading room, the trees could provide shade and filter sunlight in a manner that Thoreau would have admired. Open-air libraries could be established on the waterfront of lakes, at beaches, on manicured lawns, and amidst diverse botanical surroundings populated by a variety of birds and other wildlife. Such diversion was especially welcome at times when a crumbling world economy had plunged a nation into despair.

Roof Gardens

In 1905 the new Rivington Street branch public library on New York City's lower east side was constructed with an open-air reading room on its roof.[3] The library, seeking to remedy a traditional decline in patronage during the hot summer months, noticed that the roof of the nearby University Settlement building had been converted into a garden which was extremely popular with neighborhood residents seeking relief from the heat. Accordingly, they incorporated a 40-foot-square roof garden in the plans for their new branch library. It featured a tiled floor, iron railings, and an awning. During the day, the reading room hosted 40–50 children who read their favorite books while seated at wooden tables. Library staff limited the number of children using the facility by issuing "library tickets." This practice was necessitated by the attempt of many children to bring their baby brothers and sisters up to the roof with them. Once each week one hundred children were accommodated for a "story hour." In the evenings, from 6 to 9 P.M., the rooftop was reserved for adults. Under strings of electric lights, men and women were able to enjoy their reading in the cool night air. The roof garden attracted nearly 7,500 readers during the first summer.

So popular was this new design that architects were instructed to incorporate roof gardens in the plans for three new east side branches.[4] By 1910, five branch libraries featured rooftop reading rooms: Hamilton Fish Park, William Seward Park, St. Gabriel's Park and Columbus, in addition to Rivington Street. The newer branches were more spacious than the Rivington facility. Consequently, library staff did not need to be quite as strict regarding their admission policy. It was anticipated that non-readers, such as women doing their sewing, would be welcome to enjoy the facility as well. The number of visitors to the roof gardens was incredibly high. From May 1 through October 12 in 1909, the Rivington Street branch attracted 28,586 persons — 8,240 in July alone. The Hamilton Fish branch welcomed over 16,000 that same year. Promotional posters proclaimed: "After the heat and noise of the day's work, why not enjoy the books and magazines on the roof of the library nearest you."[5] Photographer Lewis Hine documented the popularity of the facilities during the 1910 season in his pictures of users at the five open-air branches. The New York Public Library's newsletter indicates that the roof gardens remained in use through 1920.[6]

During the Great Depression the public library in Evanston, Illinois, also adopted this concept. Lacking space at ground level, the roof of a one-story addition to the library was converted into an open-air reading room replete with awnings and spring metal chairs which were special-purchased.[7]

PARK LIBRARIES

Open-air library historians have credited Spain with creation of the first park libraries during the early years of the twentieth century. Stone and tile bookcases, whose volumes were supervised by park attendants, welcomed outdoor readers in several cities throughout the country. Prominent among such facilities were the María Luisa Park library in Seville honoring the literary achievements of playwright Serafín Alvarez Quintero and his brother Joaquín Alvarez Quintero, and the Cervantes library in the Paseo de las Delicias in Seville where circular tiled benches depicted scenes from *Don Quixote*. The Cervantes library in the gardens at Chapultepec Palace in Mexico City, a gift from Spain, featured bronze likenesses of Don Quixote and Sancho Panza. Blue and yellow picture tiles decorated four seats which formed a circle around a central fountain. These Spanish facilities were conceived as memorials to great cultural figures, and were often located in areas that had been frequented by these national heroes. Such was the case in yet another Seville park where shelves of books were placed beside a favorite tree beneath which the famed poet Gustavo Adolfo Bécquer liked to read. Because they were established as a tribute to Spain's literary giants, aesthetics were an important consideration. The health benefits of outdoor reading rooms, however, were not lost on one visitor to Chapultepec. After viewing an inscription at the entrance to an outdoor library that read, "Books are Doors to Fairyland, Guides to Adventure, and Comrades in Learning," she suggested the addition "and Pathways to Healthland."[8] The actual number of volumes offered to Spanish readers were limited, frequently restricted to the holdings of a single bookcase. Library personnel expressed guarded optimism in making even these few books available to the outdoor reader, as evidenced by the inscription carved into the stone shelf of a park library in Madrid. It read, "these books which belong to everyone are placed in everyone's care." Rather informal at first, Spain's approach to the outdoor reading room became increasingly regulated over time. Library staff replaced park attendants, and the facilities were viewed more as extension libraries than museums.[9]

The first park library in America was established in 1932. Inspired by the Spanish models, legendary Boston mayor James Michael Curley arranged for the city Park Department to circulate books and magazines on Boston Common. The effort did not involve the city's libraries, but its popularity, enhanced no doubt by Curley's personal charisma, served to focus attention on the idea throughout the nation. Curley's initiative served to provide diversion to many of Boston's citizens idled by the Depression. While circulating up to 100 books per day between June and October, the library also served as a social service distribution point where articles of clothing were provided to the needy. Few books were lost during the library's operation, and the experiment was deemed a success. Nevertheless, it was not repeated the following summer.[10] Instead, New York City adopted the concept three years later.

On 17 August 1935 the New York Public Library's Extension Division opened what *New Yorker* magazine characterized as "an eccentric little branch" in Bryant Park, adjacent to the city's main library at Fifth Avenue and 42nd Street. The park, named after William Cullen Bryant, was already equipped with benches that were regularly occupied by residents seeking respite from their daily job-hunting—potential readers all. The paved central terrace, bordered by sycamore trees and English ivy, constituted a natural reading room. Mobile book racks were obtained from a defunct organization of unemployed women called the "Hop-light Ladies" who had sold books outside the library. A waterproof chest was available in which to store

New York Public Library's Bryant Park Open-Air Library (1937). Reprinted from *Hygeia* (June 1938: 538), with permission of the American Medical Association. © 1938 American Medical Association.

the library's literature in the event of rain. Nevertheless, when park employees wheeled out their books and magazines at 10 A.M., they were greeted by "stony indifference."[11] Ruth Wellman, Superintendent of the Extension Division, and four employees of the Works Progress Administration (WPA) staffed an umbrella-shaded table for thirty minutes before the first patron appeared—Edna S. Lewis of the New York Adult Education Council. Setting the example she hoped others would follow, Lewis seated herself beneath a tree-shaded bench with a borrowed copy of Joseph Conrad's *Lord Jim*. Gradually, others followed her example, and by 3 P.M. over a dozen readers had availed themselves of this new opportunity. Wellman sent aides throughout the park to advertise the new service, thus sparking additional interest. By day's end the experiment was showing signs of promise.

In order to maximize the chances for success, rules and regulations were kept at a minimum. Readers were not required to remain in the vicinity of the book racks with their literature, but were free to roam throughout the park. Every effort was made to avoid embarrassing the impoverished or homeless: when signing out a book, no address was required. Fiction, especially murder mysteries, proved more popular than academic volumes. Given the lingering Depression, it was understandable that works on economics would be in high demand. Because Bryant Park's supply of information in this area was insufficient, most readers seeking such material had to be referred to the main library. One single-tax proselytizer, disappointed by the absence of literature on Henry George and his ideas, vowed to contribute his personal holdings to the park's shelves. Wellman planned to encourage such donations by sending library trucks to solicit contributions. Library hours were set at 10 A.M. to 7 P.M. The library remained open through mid–October. During its thirty-seven days of operation, 9,777 items were circulated. Eighteen books and twelve periodicals were lost.

When the park reading room reopened in May 1936, it was apparent that the open-air library had attracted a wide variety of New Yorkers. Office workers in the vicinity frequently spent their lunch hours with a book and a cigarette in the park. For this reason, the hours between noon and 2 P.M. were the most busy. Because there were no nearby residential neighborhoods, men comprised approximately 70 percent of the library's patrons, and children were seldom seen. The reading room was forced to resort to a reserve system for the most popular books: Somerset Maugham's *Of Human Bondage* (1915, given new popularity by the 1934 motion picture featuring Bette Davis) and William Makepeace Thackeray's *Pendennis*, which was reportedly finished by one reader during the course of seven lunch periods. Thanks to the generosity of periodical publishers, the shelves boasted gift-subscription issues of magazines such as *Esquire, Literary Digest, New Republic, Reader's Digest,* and *Scribner's*. These publications were among the park's most popular. Mysteries and westerns were the most frequently circulated books, but more substantial fiction also found a readership. Controversial literature, such as *Spoken Word* (the official publication of the clergyman-demagogue Father Divine) was accepted for its "sociological interest."[12] Reference service was limited to the questions that could be answered by an English-language dictionary and the *World Almanac*. On the other hand, patrons of the main library were not infrequently referred to the park in order to locate issues of magazines that were unavailable at the indoor facility because they had been sent to the bindery. With 1936's circulation totaling 65,000 and losses limited to seventy items, the outdoor reading room was deemed a success.

On 19 August 1940 the New York Public Library Director, Harry Miller Lydenberg, presided over a celebration of the open-air reading room's fifth anniversary.[13] Lydenberg, past president of the American Library Association (1932–1933), was an administrator experienced in coping with the hardships imposed by the Depression. Under his leadership the library was able to increase circulation and continue to display modest growth despite economic hardships. The open-air library was symbolic of Lydenberg's achievements. Innovative yet cost-efficient, it created goodwill through outreach. The WPA library workers manning the park reading room were federally funded, and much of the outdoor collection was donated. The service they offered was practically regarded as an official harbinger of the summer season, much like the Decoration Day holiday.

The open-air reading room expanded the extent of its outreach during World War II. Many servicemen were stationed in the mid-town Manhattan vicinity, and the library had been advised of the fact that a considerable number of them were interested in obtaining reading material. In response, the library advertised its Bryant Park location at servicemen's recreation centers, and prepared the park's WPA workers to receive increased military patronage. Poised to welcome a record number of visitors, the open-air reading room encountered disaster on opening day in 1942. Ordinarily, rain was the bane of open-air libraries, causing workers to rush books and magazines into the safety of waterproof shelters. On 1 May 1942 a careless cigarette ignited a dry wooden book bin, causing a fire. By the time extinguishers could be retrieved from the main building, books and magazines had suffered damage.[14]

By 1943 the Depression was subsiding as the wartime economy boomed. The number of idle visitors to Bryant Park had greatly declined. Many of those who had frequented the reading room in the past were either gainfully employed or serving in the military overseas. Nevertheless, the open-air reading room resumed operation in May, although two weeks later than usual. Hours were also reduced: noon to 5 P.M., Monday through Friday. In addition, members of the American Women's Voluntary Services replaced the WPA workers as attendants.[15] The Bryant Park library's ninth season was to be its last. Citing staff shortages, the New York Public Library's acting head of circulation, Esther Johnston, announced that the outdoor reading room would not open in 1944.[16] Official announcement was postponed until the third week in June, indicating that the library was reluctant to announce the official demise of the service.

The Bryant Park open-air library, in its nine seasons of existence, had become a warm weather fixture in mid-town Manhattan. Much like Central Park, it provided welcome relief from the urban, business landscape. While not as green a setting as Central Park's meadows, Bryant Park offered a healthy, refreshing, aesthetically pleasing environment within which to cultivate the mind. By adopting an unorthodox approach to outreach, the library was able to assist in lifting the spirits of Depression-era New Yorkers, help occupy the time of war-bound servicemen, and present an interesting lunchtime option for Manhattan workers.

The relative success of New York's experiment with a park library encouraged other systems throughout the nation to adapt the concept to their own circumstances. In 1938 the library in Montclair, New Jersey, placed book racks along the sidewalk adjacent its building, but the summer sun's heat and glare proved uncomfortable. The books were then moved onto the library's lawn. Shaded by hemlock trees and enclosed by the city's Swedish Congregational and Unity churches, the scene proved fresher, quieter, and more popular with readers.[17]

Los Angeles established three successful park libraries in the 1930s, taking advantage of the large number of potential readers in the vicinity who cited their dislike for the regular library's indoor atmosphere. Very few of these potential readers were cardholders. They were repelled by library routines, red tape, and dress conventions. In response, the libraries brought books and magazines out to them. The main library, just outside the central business district, used an adjacent park, as in New York. Tables and umbrellas were added to the existing benches. Patronage increased enough to warrant establishment of a second such facility at Pershing Square in the center of the business district, traversed by an estimated 100,000 persons on a daily basis. The 2,500 seats contained in the location were never enough to accommodate the pedestrians who provided an audience for soapbox orators. The library offered those interested in calmer diversion the chance to peruse the written word in a quieter setting. Sheltered by banana plants, book stands and tables were installed. Many readers responded positively. A third park library was established in Lafayette Park near a branch library. All three locations were staffed by WPA workers who kept the park libraries open from 9 A.M. until 4 P.M. The reading material consisted of approximately 250 magazines and 150 books at Pershing Square, the most popular location. All the books had either been withdrawn from the regular collection due to excessive wear, or were duplicate copies. Patrons were not required to sign out the material. Books and magazines were freely distributed to anyone who asked, yet losses were few. Total circulation for the three libraries was 56,204 books and magazines for the period 1 June 1937–31 May 1938. These open-air facilities had the obvious advantage of maintaining operation year-round.[18]

The semitropical climate of southern Florida as well as Hawaii's tropics were especially conducive to open-air libraries. School librarians in Florida availed themselves of the idyllic climate in establishing study halls outdoors. The Harris School in Miami allowed their female students to recline in deck chairs or seat themselves upon waterproof pillows while completing reading assignments. The sunshine, palm trees, hibiscus, and bougainvillea created a picturesque setting. Perhaps demonstrating that their commitment to open-air reading was not limited to the balmy environment, the school held yearly camp sessions in the mountains of North Carolina where mornings were typically frosty. Nevertheless, outdoor study hall was held at 10 A.M. along a sunny hillside protected from the wind.[19]

Many civic buildings in Honolulu were built with open-air courtyards attached, including the Library of Hawaii. Readers were invited to enjoy books and magazines under the open sky, surrounded by tropical foliage, as if they were relaxing on their own patios. Visitors from the mainland, accustomed to hot, cramped indoor facilities illuminated by artificial lighting, were occasionally moved to establish open-air reading rooms in their own libraries. Because it would be impractical to construct permanent courtyards as part of the library in most sections of the continental United States due to the colder climate, imaginative use of existing lawns and porches was called for. The Education Library of Central Washington College in Ellensburg, Washington, adapted its patio in just such a manner, putting to good use the campus's natural rural beauty.[20]

Most park libraries were established in areas well-suited for the purpose. The reading rooms might well have been created years earlier if anyone had thought of it. In some instances, however, considerable labor was needed to be employed in order to convert a long-neglected yard or garden into an outdoor reading room. Such was the case with Goucher College's open-air facility. The small, private college was founded in 1885. Located in Baltimore, its library building stood at the corner of two city streets. As is the case at most schools, when spring fever arrived, it was difficult for the faculty to keep the students' minds on their studies. The librarian decided to undertake the task of converting a vacant lot into a park library. The narrow plot of ground adjacent to the library was piled high with scrap lumber that had been removed from the library building when it had been converted from dormitory use. A brick wall and rickety board fence enclosed the yard. The library staff worked weekends to accomplish the necessary transformation. After removing the lumber, two small dogwood trees were planted, surrounded by lilies-of-the-valley, violets, irises, and wild geraniums. Ivy was donated to plant along the brick walls. A long bench was moved in from another part of campus, and the Goucher Alumnae Association purchased seat cushions, garden chairs, and a table. The most challenging aspect of the renovation consisted of creating an entrance to the garden where there had been none. It was decided to construct steps inside and outside of a ground floor library window in order to permit access to the yard. This represented a less-expensive alternative to creation of a doorway. It was also suggested that climbing out a window added to the impression that the students were indeed escaping from the indoor library. Signs placed at the second floor circulation desk advertised the outdoor reading room each spring, and flowers grown in the yard were placed at the desk to attract student notice. The yard was a reading room only, for books and periodicals were not placed outside. The experiment was deemed a success when it was observed that students chose to read in the open-air even in the rain.[21]

In 1938 the Pingree School in Ogden, Utah, created a similar facility for their grade-school students on the west lawn of their campus. Book cases were moved out among the lilac bushes, chairs were provided, and the "Alice Reading Room" was established. The path leading to the open-air library was dubbed "Thru the Looking Glass," and statues of Alice and Peter Pan were planned as additions.[22] Clearly, the concept of enjoying literature in natural surroundings had wide appeal.

BEACH LIBRARIES

During the summer of 1936 two communities experimented with waterfront libraries. Pursuant to a suggestion of a library staff member, the Glencoe, Illinois, Public Library secured the cooperation of the community's Park Board in operating a small library from a beach house on the shores of Lake Michigan. The library viewed the venture as a challenge in book selection. Short, light fiction proved most popular with reader-bathers. Selections on travel and humor were included, as well as a sampling of juvenile literature. The presence of a few storybooks, suitable for reading aloud, ensured that groups of children could be entertained. Volumes in need of repair or those recently mended were selected for display. It was suggested that these volumes probably suffered less damage than those in the regular collection that were routinely wrapped in wet towels when transported to and from the shore. The collection was changed weekly to ensure variety, but reserves were accepted for popular books. The volumes were displayed on a counter in the beach house, and signs along the shore invited bathers to become readers as well. A beach attendant who monitored the library required borrowers to register their name and the date. Books were due back at the close of the day. Because use of the beach was restricted to residents of Glencoe, simple security measures were deemed adequate. In addition to the popularity of the experiment, the exercise was viewed as an example of positive library outreach and cooperation between village authorities.[23]

The Public Library of New Rochelle, New York, motivated by the idea of bringing its literature to the people, rather than requiring them to come indoors during the summer, inaugurated a "Sun Tan Library" at Hudson Park adjacent to a beach on Long Island Sound. Borrowers could choose to read either on the grass or in the sand. Most users were bathers who took their selections to the shore and returned them at closing. Organizers of New Rochelle's beach library concurred with other open-air promoters who considered informality an essential quality for successful outreach of this sort. Accordingly, books were assembled on pushcarts that had been ingeniously fashioned from discarded baby carriages. Large wooden trays were mounted on the vehicles, which were painted in bright colors. Each cart held approximately one hundred books. A large beach umbrella shaded the circulation attendant. The library included books on sailing and swimming in their offerings along with the usual mysteries, westerns, and short stories. Magazines were also offered. The "Sun Tan Library" was open during July and August from 10 A.M. until 4 P.M. on Tuesdays and Saturdays, and 1 to 4 P.M. on Thursdays. Over 2,000 items were borrowed during the season, an average of approximately ninety per day. The day of highest circulation saw 207 books and magazines borrowed. Borrowers were permitted to take their selections home if they so desired. Several applications for library cards were processed, and reserves for specific titles were accepted. In this manner, the New Rochelle beach library functioned more like a regular branch than other open-air facilities. Operators of the library reported that many patrons at first assumed that they were conducting a book sale, so novel was the idea of using the beach as an extension library. Plans to continue the service into September were abandoned when an infestation of large black flies accompanied the arrival of cooler weather. The "Sun Tan Library" was reopened for a second season in 1937.[24]

Conclusion

The open-air library represented a response to a number of societal influences. It can be seen as integrally related to the open-air school movement and the worldwide effort to defeat diseases such as tuberculosis through fresh-air measures popularized by sanitariums. Although it has never been clearly demonstrated that fresh air was effective in curing tuberculosis, the belief in its value impacted heavily on the manner in which schools and libraries chose to operate, especially during the summer when warm weather presented administrators with outdoor options. It is also noteworthy that open-air libraries virtually disappeared in the mid–1940s, coinciding with the discovery of drug therapies effective in the eradication of tuberculosis.

Before the widespread use of air conditioning in the 1950s, libraries watched in dismay as the summer heat effectively reduced the numbers of patrons visiting their facilities. Imaginative outreach advocates adopted strategies for bringing the books to the public outside. In gardens, on lawns, at the park, and on the beach, books and periodicals were delivered to the people where reading could continue in more comfortable surroundings. During the Great Depression, this service was especially necessary and appreciated. In America's communities, idleness and resulting despair seriously disrupted the lives of its citizens. Library extension programs such as the open-air reading rooms performed a social service function, attempting to renew the spirit as much as the intellect.

Aesthetes had long received inspiration from nature. The beauty found under a blue sky surrounded by summer's blooming foliage may be augmented by man-made fountains, tiled benches, and sculptured statuary. One need not be a classical philosopher to find such an atmosphere conducive to the acquisition of knowledge. Spain's open-air libraries were monuments to national literary heroes. Urban Americans treasured any lawn or park that provided a green setting in which they could enjoy a favorite book or magazine.

In an age when America's institutions effectively control the environment of its indoor spaces, and modern medicine has largely eradicated communicable diseases that once ravaged cities, open-air libraries represent a historical phenomenon. Yet, bookmobiles still provide valuable outreach services, especially in rural America, and other nations remain in need of the very same innovative programs that open-air librarians brought to Americans earlier in this century.

On 22 December 1948 the Chief Librarian of Hagi Library in Yamaguchi Prefecture, Japan, loaded thirteen chairs, a desk, and two magazine display racks upon a two-wheeled handcart. A large sign advertised the establishment of the "Blue Sky Library," its holdings limited to American magazines provided by the occupying army. Although the weather was cold and most readers didn't understand English, business was brisk. Most were amazed that "free library" meant, in fact, that no fee was required. Others were impressed by the quality of the paper and binding ("No wonder we were defeated," commented one patron). Two hundred and seventy four persons stopped to browse; ninety-one sat and read. Not one magazine was lost.[25] It is certain that there will remain places and times that call for the initiation of open-air libraries.

NOTES

1. Gerald S. Greenberg, "Books as Disease Carriers, 1880–1920." *Libraries and Culture* 23 (1988): 281–94.

2. Ernest Bryant Hoag and Lewis M. Terman, *Health Work in the Schools* (Boston: Houghton Mifflin, 1914). Chapter XII discusses the open-air school phenomenon from the first experiment in Charlottenburg, Germany, to its appearance in England (1907) and America (1908). The innovation is hailed as a great success in the education and treatment of tubercular children.

3. "An Open-Air Reading Room," *The World's Work* 12 (1906): 8025.

4. "Open-Air Libraries for the City's Poor," *New York Times* 24 April 1910: 8.

5. Undated poster, New York Public Library, Research Library Archives.

6. NYPL's *Staff News* featured articles on rooftop garden reading rooms in the issue of June 1918: 82; and specifically on the Hamilton Fish branch in the issues of 24 July 1919: 100, and 22 July 1920: 85.

7. Cora L. Keagle, "Outdoor Libraries," *Hygeia* 16 (1938): 540.

8. Keagle 540.

9. Ruth Wellman, "Open-Air Reading Rooms," *Library Journal* 61 (1936): 667.

10. Wellman 668.

11. "Park Sitters Shun Open-Air Library," *New York Times*, 18 August 1935: 1.

12. Wellman 670.

13. "Library Cuts Cake for 'Open-Air Reading Room,'" *New York Times* 20 August 1940: 17.

14. "Reading Room in Park Opened at Library," *New York Times*, 2 May 1942: 13.

15. "Outdoor Library Ready," *New York Times*, 17 May 1943: 17.

16. "Public Library Abandons Outdoor Reading Room," *New York Times*, 21 June 1944: 23.

17. Keagle 540.

18. L.H. Sweetser, "Outdoor Reading Rooms in Parks," *American City* (October 1938): 91–93.

19. Iris Grannis, "Outdoor Study Hall," *Wilson Library Bulletin* 18 (1938): 458.

20. Catharine Bullard, "Take Your Book Out of Doors," *Library Journal* 65 (1940): 822; "An Outdoor Reading Room," *Wilson Library Bulletin* (1941): 719.

21. Martha G. Hall, "The Library Garden is Open," *Wilson Library Bulletin* 14 (1940): 733, 738.

22. Cleo Pierce, "The Alice Reading Garden," *Wilson Library Bulletin* 12 (1938): 676–77.

23. Helen Beckwith, "A Beach Library," *Wilson Library Bulletin* 11 (1937): 606.

24. Aubrey Lee Hill, "A Beach Library," *American City* 52 (July 1937): 97, 99.

25. Takeichi Mura, "Japan's Blue Sky Library," *Library Journal* 75 (1950): 1461–63.

12. The Use of Radio to Promote the Municipal Reference Library of the City of New York

Barry W. Seaver

In 1922, two years after the first regular radio broadcast, the editor of *Radio Broadcast* magazine stated that a radio station could be built and operated for less money than was needed to run an average-size public library and claimed that the station would provide the local community with greater educational benefits. He also commented that radio stations could be financed by individuals who wanted to rid themselves of excess wealth, like Andrew Carnegie had done by funding public library construction.[1] A few years later a librarian, Rebecca Browning Rankin, the director of the Municipal Reference Library of the City of New York, seized upon radio broadcasting as an inexpensive means of reaching her client populations in order to bring them into her library and to communicate information from the library's collection directly to them.

Municipal reference libraries were established in the first decades of the twentieth century as part of a movement to reform city government in the United States.[2] Their mission: to collect and disseminate information to improve policy decision-making, increase the efficiency of public administration, and create a politically educated electorate.[3] However, elected officials, employees of city government, and the citizens they served had to be convinced of the need for the information municipal reference libraries could provide.

In New York the City Comptroller established a library in 1913 to serve the business community and Finance Department employees, but there was little demand for a centralized source of information about local government and public administration. A year later the Finance Department transferred its library to the New York Public Library (NYPL), which assumed responsibility for the newly named Municipal Reference Library (MRL) in March 1914.[4] For the next fifty-five years the municipal reference librarians directed its operations as an independent division of the NYPL while maintaining a relationship with the local government that varied as administrations and politics changed.[5]

Demands on the MRL from city officials and the citizens of New York increased or decreased depending on political issues, elections, investigations, and emergencies. Under reform administrations during World War I and the Depression, the library staff was called upon to provide information to assist local government programs and to report on these activities to the public. At these times the MRL received support in the form of favorable legislation and funding for publications. However, from 1918 to 1934 the municipal reference librarians had to struggle with cuts in appropriations, threats to the library's existence, criticism of its services and policies, and general neglect from its clients in City Hall who were allied with the local Democratic party machine. During both times of use and neglect the librarians employed available media to promote the MRL and its mission with varying degrees of success.

PROMOTION OF THE MRL

In the fall of 1914 the municipal reference librarians began a program of publicity primarily to attract city officials and employees to the MRL, but also to guide them in the use of its collection. They used publications such as a weekly bulletin, *Municipal Reference Library Notes*, printed bibliographies, and municipal yearbooks to communicate with prospective customers in the local government and their constituents. Funding for such publications, which depended on the financial and political situation in New York City, was unreliable. To relieve this problem, the staff of the MRL received permission to produce broadcasts at no cost on the municipally owned radio station, WNYC. They used this opportunity to educate the citizens of New York about their local government and to make them aware of the information services available at the library.

Rebecca Browning Rankin became the municipal reference librarian in February 1920 and assumed responsibility for *Notes*, which she continued to publish weekly until budget cuts during the Depression forced her to reduce it to a monthly publication.[6] Rankin experienced satisfaction and recognition as the editor of the MRL's newsletter, despite budget reductions which forced her to economize and keep most issues to four pages. In *Notes* she published a monthly list of New York City government publications received by the library and a "Current Civic Literature" section that included annotations on publications about the efforts of other cities in the fields of planning, education, traffic control, housing, and public health.

To supplement the MRL's publicity program and outreach services, Rankin developed a series of weekly broadcasts for WNYC. She began using the new medium to announce the fifteenth anniversary celebration of the MRL in March 1928.[7] On the evening before the MRL's birthday Rankin stood stiffly before the WNYC microphone and spoke to the people of New York about their government and the library.[8] Her slightly high-pitched but clear, strong voice encouraged them to visit the Municipal Building where the MRL and most of the administrative departments were located. Rankin told them that after a visit "you would have an increased feeling of pride in your City [because] the running of your City is a huge undertaking, admirably done. You can afford to give the government machinery more attention and study."[9]

Rankin also defined the purpose of the MRL and listed what she believed to be its priorities. For her the primary mission of the library was to aid elected officials by providing them with detailed facts about what the local government had done and how it was done, as well as about the experiences and practices of other cities. She told her radio audience that "our ideal is to have such information that will help the city official or commissioner of the department so that he may intelligently adopt the best policies for the governing of the City."[10]

Rankin's second goal was to assist all public employees in the daily performance of their jobs. She stressed the library's dependability as the most important aspect of its service. She also referred to the MRL as a reference library for anyone interested in politics and government and as the agency that makes "the City of New York known to citizens all over the world."[11] She gave her listeners a detailed description of the collection and concluded her invitation to visit the MRL by telling them that the library was the "fact centre" for officials as well as for all New Yorkers.[12]

Rankin heard praise for the broadcast and her radio voice from Harry Lydenberg, Acting Director of the NYPL.[13] She also received glowing reviews in the newspapers. The MRL, according to one review, "got another very nice boost last evening … from Miss R. B. Rankin."[14] The birthday celebration for the library was a success despite a late winter blizzard. The *New York Times* reported that the "fifteen hundred people [who] attended the modestly planned reception in honor of that event attests to its significance."[15] The newspaper also mentioned Rankin's nine-year tenure as the director of the MRL and claimed that "[i]f the City Government still falls short of the ideal it is not her fault."[16]

THE MRL TAKES TO THE AIR

Rankin's radio broadcast celebrating the library's birthday generated enough interest that the director of WNYC asked her to do a regular radio program.[17] She consulted Lydenberg about the offer and received his approval to become involved in using the new technology to communicate with the city's employees and citizens.[18] In January 1929 the MRL took to the air with fifteen minute broadcasts on Friday evenings.[19] Rankin assigned different topics to her senior staff to research and write about depending on their interests. They were instructed to emphasize the resources of the library in their reports and to deliver their speeches to the radio audience.

Margaret Kehl, one of the MRL reference librarians and a native New Yorker, presented speeches about "How New Yorkers Keep Cool," and "Fires that have Startled New York."[20] Kehl described the broadcasts as "popular chats" and acknowledged that "[o]ur prime purpose was to appear so wide-awake that everyone would want to visit the library. We were anxious to make a name for the Municipal Reference Library as surely as any commercial advertising program."[21] Kehl's broadcast of "Where New Yorkers Eat," in late May 1929, received the biggest response with letters and reporters inquiring about her story, particularly the anecdote placing the invention of chop suey at the Waldorf.[22]

Over the next nine years Rankin delivered the majority of the library's weekly radio broadcasts. The broadcasts began as part of her publicity strategy for the MRL, but they became an outreach service that featured year-long programs, such as "Civics-in-Action," which was produced to coincide with subjects taught in high school civics classes during 1930-31. Other series were: "Highlights in Municipal Government," "New York Advancing," and "What the City Does for You." These broadcasts provided New Yorkers with vital information during the Depression, while competing against commercial programs like "Amos and Andy" and "The Goldbergs."[23]

The MRL Assists the Administration of Mayor La Guardia

In the fall of 1933 Rankin went on the air and called for greater citizen involvement in the political process. During voter registration week, she told her listeners that the act of voting was "a moral and a political trust" and attacked the tendency to ignore this obligation. Rankin pointedly asked the radio audience: "Are you among the apathetic and indifferent element of citizens which is altogether too large if democracy is to be a success?"[24] Her radio speech, part of a campaign to get out the vote, brought record numbers to the polls and helped elect Fiorello La Guardia to the second toughest job in the world—Mayor of the City of New York.[25]

Rankin was a supporter of La Guardia but she did not abandon the role of radio commentator that she had developed during the series "What Our Cities Are Doing." Rankin continued to survey solutions attempted by other municipal governments to problems that were plaguing New York, while indirectly expressing her opinion on the local situation. She was particularly concerned about the lack of revenue to pay for unemployment relief. In the fall of 1934 research performed by the MRL helped to shape the Emergency Sales Tax that raised money to pay for programs that helped unemployed New Yorkers survive the Depression.[26]

Changes in Radio Programming for the MRL Staff

Rankin and her staff continued to fill a weekly radio spot during the winter months of 1934-35, but they added a twist to their new series, "Your City's Government."[27] Previously they stood alone before the microphone and delivered a fifteen minute address, but now they wrote scripts requiring the participation of the regular announcer at WNYC. Kehl recalled that in an interview format "it was necessary for us to use the announcer as a foil—to put words in his mouth, so to speak."[28]

Rankin designed the new radio series to inform the average citizen about the services available to them as well as to provide instruction on civic responsibilities, while acquainting the audience with the resources of the MRL.[29] She hoped to answer questions a typical New Yorker might ask about their local government and featured one department or agency each week. "Often the department heads or representatives ... came to the broadcast [which] cemented the feeling between the library and the departments," Kehl stated later.[30] However, according to Kehl, the fifteen minutes of air time did not allow the interviews to develop or provide much information to the public because "it [was] difficult to break up a thought with questions and at the same time cover a large territory in such a short time."[31]

RANKIN PROMOTES THE MRL AND THE ADMINISTRATION OF THE CITY OF NEW YORK

In September 1936 Rankin published an account of Mayor La Guardia's administration, *New York Advancing: A Scientific Approach to Municipal Government*. She also produced a new series of radio speeches to inform the citizens of New York about his accomplishments in office.[32] "Starting in December of 1936, Miss Rankin began a solo series of [weekly] broadcasts based on and amplifying her own compilation, *New York Advancing*," Kehl recalled.[33] On the first Wednesday of the month at 4:30 P.M. Rankin reintroduced herself to WNYC's audience and called attention to La Guardia's aid to taxpayers through his efforts to balance the budget.[34] She also read

Rebecca Rankin delivering a speech in the WNYC studio, October 1934. Photograph courtesy of the Municipal Archives of the City of New York.

extensively from the introduction to *New York Advancing* and quoted reviews that had found fault with her restrained writing but praised the purpose and integrity of La Guardia's administration.

Rankin used the next two broadcasts to explain to New Yorkers how a new charter would affect their local government and how proportional representation, a weighted system of voting commonly referred to as PR, was expected to work.[35] Both proposals, referendums on the City Charter and PR, had received the electorate's approval at the polls in November 1936.[36] Her comments on the new system of voting emphasized PR's fairness.[37] Rankin stated that it guaranteed each borough representation equal to its voting population without the need to resort to the politics of reapportionment. She also told her radio audience that "under proportional representation you may vote for a minority candidate with the full assurance that the vote will not be wasted. In an ordinary election such is never the case. Under proportional representation every party has a share in government according to its numerical strength. Every voter has an equal share in his government."[38]

The radio speeches on the Charter and PR generated such a large and enthusiastic response, Rankin was asked by the Director of WNYC to repeat them at the later hour of 6 P.M. when a greater number of working people and businessmen could tune in.[39] Rankin, in her relaxed, conversational manner, delivered the fifteen minute addresses for the second time in February 1937.[40] She also had her explanation of proportional representation recorded, and it was rebroadcast by the city's radio station and lent to groups attempting to educate their members about the new method of voting.[41]

In the election of November 1937 La Guardia became the first mayor of New York ever to be reelected without the support of Tammany Hall, and City Council members were chosen by the proportional representation system. PR strengthened the presence of Republicans and minor parties on the city's legislative body, and the dire warnings made by local Democratic politicians, that it would be too complicated for voters, proved to be exaggerated and unfounded.[42] New Yorkers, with the help of an educational campaign that included radio broadcasts by Rankin, were able to adapt and vote by ranking their choices to serve on the Council.[43] "The predictions of its opponents that many people would not vote at all, and that fifty percent of the ballots would be invalid has fortunately failed to come true," Rankin stated in a *Notes* article on the use of PR in the fall election.[44]

RANKIN FULFILLS HER DESIRE TO TEACH

Rankin continued her efforts as an educator in early 1938 with a series of broadcasts that explained "How the New Charter Works."[45] On the first two Thursday evenings in February she spoke to radio listeners about the City Council and its election by PR, which she contended had "proved itself and elected a higher type of city councilmen and a more representative body" than the Board of Aldermen it replaced.[46] During these broadcasts Rankin attempted to decipher for her audience the chaotic early meetings of the evenly divided Council, which had earned it the title "The Greatest Show in Town."[47]

Rankin completed the first two broadcasts of 1938 by expressing the hope that the Council meetings would "continue to air all issues of vital importance to the citizens of New York."[48] Kehl presented the broadcast the following week and spoke about the city's new Administrative Code—the local ordinances Rankin later referred to as the "leftovers" from the research performed at the MRL to revise the Charter.[49] Rankin assumed responsibility for the remainder of the weekly programs, which she ended on the last day of March. She recounted the innovations in the local government and told the radio audience that "none of the modern changes will work satisfactorily and to the benefit of the city unless they are backed by the citizenry. The officials not only need to be honest and efficient but also understanding of citizen requirements. If there is ... close cooperation between citizens and officials the new Charter has a great opportunity."[50] On 31 March 1938 she signed off by stating that the "Municipal Reference Library strives to serve as the bureau of information for both citizen and official and to help each one understand the problems of the other."[51] This speech ended the library's decade long experiment in civic education through radio broadcasts.

The Radio Venture Ends but the MRL Remains in Demand

During the first week of March 1938, which marked the MRL's twenty-fifth anniversary, Rankin described in detail the creation of the City Planning Commission over WNYC and invited her listeners to use the resources of the library for further study, yet she neglected to mention its birthday.[52] Ten years earlier she had inaugurated the radio broadcasts and held an elaborate celebration to commemorate the fifteenth anniversary of the MRL and to call attention to its collection and services. However, in the fifth year of Mayor La Guardia's administration the library was so busy that she felt the same type of publicity was no longer needed.

Before the final broadcast Kehl conceded to a meeting of librarians in New York that "considering the number of talks given the direct response was small. But please remember we were not giving away samples. We were simply inviting the public to delve into our treasure house" of information.[53] She cited requests for copies of speeches from the "Civics-in-Action" series and broadcasts reprinted in the *New York Times* as examples of positive responses to the use of radio to reach out to larger audiences. "Statistics show that the demands on the Municipal Reference Library have grown consistently in the past years," Kehl continued and asked: "Isn't it possible that radio has helped?"[54]

Conclusion

The MRL staff prepared and presented over three hundred radio programs between 1928 and 1938 as part of their publicity program and outreach service. Many of the broadcasts were repeated by WNYC announcers and brought attention to the library in the form of newspaper articles and interviews. The use of this modern mass communication medium also attracted patrons to the MRL. The statistics to which

Kehl referred recorded the number of people visiting the library and show an increase in attendance for every year during the decade. After the staff of the MRL began its broadcasting service the increase in visitors to the library averaged five thousand per year, while prior to employing radio the yearly increase had been under a thousand. However, during La Guardia's first year as mayor, the number of people coming through the doors of the library jumped by twenty thousand. Following his first year in City Hall six thousand more patrons visited the MRL each year until the war years of 1942–45.[55]

During Mayor La Guardia's three administrations (1934–1945) the MRL became an effective and vital adjunct of the local government. In his first year, research performed by the library staff helped to shape the Emergency Sales Tax which provided revenue to pay for the City's unemployment relief efforts.[56] During La Guardia's second term Rankin used her close relationship with the mayor to convince him to find a way to provide pensions for the public librarians in New York City. She also helped mediate negotiations between local government officials and the Board of Trustees of the NYPL, which led to the inclusion of the librarians in the New York State Employees Retirement System.[57]

Rankin persuaded La Guardia of the need to establish a municipal archive and he appointed her chair of the Mayor's Municipal Archives Committee.[58] Under her leadership the MRL assumed archival and records management functions for the City of New York. After La Guardia's last term, Rankin appealed to the new administration to continue her appointment and the work of the Municipal Archives Committee. Due to the favorable political conditions produced by post-war management studies in both federal and municipal governments, her request was granted and, before her retirement in 1952, she was able to create the Municipal Archives and Records Center of the City of New York.[59]

In 1946 Rankin considered a proposal for reviving the library's radio broadcasts in a book review format.[60] However, she was dealing with unprecedented staff turnover, including the retirement of her assistant librarian, Margaret Kehl, and decided that the new reference staff did not have enough experience with the demands of their work to attempt broadcasting at the same time.[61] Instead, Rankin published a third edition of *New York Advancing* and several revised editions of her *Guide to the Municipal Government of the City of New York* to serve as the primary outreach service of the library.[62]

The use of radio by Rankin and her staff succeeded as a publicity strategy by bringing more patrons and requests to the library, and as an outreach service by communicating information directly to the audience of WNYC. The broadcasts began as a public relations stunt and continued to provide publicity for the MRL, but the speeches about voting procedures, policy issues and governmental assistance programs developed into a civic education service.[63] Because of the specialized nature and mission of the library, the staff became subject experts who were able to organize information, analyze research, and set forth authoritative conclusions about public administration and local government activities. They used the radio broadcasts to communicate their knowledge to listeners who were able to learn and form their own opinions about civic affairs and current events.[64]

NOTES

Much of the material in this chapter is covered more extensively in Barry W. Seaver, "Rebecca Browning Rankin Uses Radio to Promote the Municipal Reference Library of the City of New York and the Civic Federation of Its Citizens," *Libraries & Culture* 36.2 (2001): 289–328.

1. J. H. Morecroft, "Radio Currents," *Radio Broadcast* 1 (1922): 3.

2. *National Municipal Review* 4 (1915): 176–7.

3. *Bulletin of the American Library Association* 2 (1908): 193.

4. *Bulletin of the NYPL* 19 (1915): 222.

5. The NYPL oversaw the operations of the MRL until 1969 when local government under Mayor John Lindsay took control of the library and the municipal archives and records center, which had been established in 1952 as part of the MRL. See Barry Seaver, "Legacy of Reform: The Municipal Reference Library of the City of New York," *Biblion: Bulletin of the New York Public Library* 1 (1992): 154.

6. Rebecca Browning Rankin directed the MRL from 1920 to 1952. She served in many key policy-making positions, both on mayoral committees and in professional organizations. She was president of the New York Special Libraries Association, 1920–22, president of the Special Libraries Association, 1922–24, and served as its executive secretary, 1930–34.

7. Rankin, "Invitation to MRL's 15th Anniversary Celebration, March 8–9, 1928," Municipal Archives of the City of New York (MA) Box 5609 MRL's 15th Anniversary.

8. MA Box 15 Rankin's Personal Correspondence. Picture of Rankin before the WNYC microphone in the studio on the 25th floor of the Municipal Building.

9. Rankin, "A Fact Center for Municipal Information," *Special Libraries* 19 (1928): 66–8. Reprint of Rankin's speech given over WNYC on Wednesday 7 March 1928 at 9:45 P.M.

10. Rankin, "A Fact Center."

11. Rankin, "A Fact Center."

12. Rankin, "A Fact Center."

13. Harry Lydenberg to Rankin, 9 March 1928, MA Box 5609 MRL's 15th Anniversary.

14. *Brooklyn Daily Eagle*, 8 March 1928: 2.

15. *New York Times*, 23 March 1928: 20.

16. *New York Times*, 23 March 1928: 20.

17. "Broadcasting Municipal Affairs by the MRL," *American City* 41 (1929): 161. Announcement of the MRL's talks over WNYC at the invitation of Albert Goldman, the Commissioner of the Dept. of Plant and Structures, which oversaw WNYC's operations.

18. Lydenberg to Rankin, 26 May 1928, NYPL Archives Box 14 Director's Office Correspondence.

19. "List of MRL Radio Speeches for 1929," MA Box 8 MRL Radio Talks. Broadcasts began on 18 Jan. 1929 and were presented at 5:50–6:05 P.M. every other Friday through most the year.

20. MA Box 8 MRL Radio Talks. Margaret Kehl delivered "Cool," 16 Aug. 1929 and "Fires," 8 Nov. 1929.

21. Margaret Kehl, "Nine Years of Broadcasting," 19 Nov. 1937, MA Box 16 Rankin's Personal Correspondence. Kehl presented a speech on the history of MRL's radio activities to a monthly meeting of New York Special Libraries Association.

22. Kehl, "Where New Yorkers Eat," 24 May 1929, MA Box 8 MRL Radio Talks. For an editorial summarizing Kehl's radio broadcast, see *New York Sun*, 25 May 1929: 20.

23. Kehl, "Nine Years of Broadcasting."

24. Rankin, "Voting and Citizenship," 9 Oct. 1933, MA Box 8 MRL Radio Talks.

25. *New York Times*, 8 Nov. 1933: 1.

26. Barry Seaver, *The Career of Rebecca Browning Rankin, the Municipal Reference Librarian of the City of New York, 1920–1952*, diss. University of North Carolina at Chapel Hill, 1997 (Ann Arbor, MI: UMI, 1997) 269–72.

27. MA Box 8 MRL Radio Talks. The series, "Your City's Government," began 9 Oct. 1934 and continued until 25 June 1935. Rankin delivered half of the thirty-four speeches.

28. Kehl, "Nine Years of Broadcasting." Kehl stated that the interview format was derived from a radio series, "You and Your Government," which was presented over NBC in 1932 by the National Advisory Council on Radio in Education and the American Political Science Association.

29. *Bulletin of the New York Public Library* 39 (1935): 256. This is MRL's annual report for 1934.

30. Kehl, "Nine Years of Broadcasting."

31. Kehl, "Nine Years of Broadcasting."

32. MA Box 9 MRL Radio Talks. Rankin delivered a series of radio speeches under the title "New York Advancing" from Dec. 1936 to June 1937.

33. Kehl, "Nine Years of Broadcasting."

34. Rankin, "New York Advancing," 2 Dec. 1936, MA Box 9 MRL Radio Talks.

35. Rankin, "New Charter," 9 Dec. 1936, MA Box 9 MRL Radio Talks.

36. *New York Times* 4 Nov. 1936: 1.

37. Rankin, "Proportional Representation," 16 Dec. 1936, MA Box 9 MRL Radio Talks.

38. Rankin, "Proportional Representation."

39. Christie Bohnsack, Director of WNYC, "Press Release," 28 Jan. 1937, MA Box 9 MRL Radio Talks.

40. MA Box 9 MRL Radio Talks. Rankin repeated the radio speeches the "New Charter," 11 Feb. 1937 and "Proportional Representation," 18 Feb. 1937.

41. MA Box 9 MRL Radio Talks. Rankin had the Radio Recording Company of New York record the radio speech "Proportional Representation" for $5. The silver acetate disk recording of Rankin runs for almost twenty minutes and remains in excellent condition. WNYC rebroadcast the recording on 11 March 1937.

42. George McCaffrey, "Proportional Representation in New York City," *American Political Science Review* 33 (1939): 847–8. Thirteen of the twenty-six members of the first City Council were Democrats while five American Labor Party candidates and three Republicans won seats along with three Fusion Party candidates and one independent Democrat.

43. McCaffrey 847–8. In the 1937 election, out of the total ballots cast for councilmen, 87.7 percent were valid and 9.1 percent were not, while 3.2 percent were blank.

44. Rankin, "Proportional Representation," *Municipal Reference Library Notes* 23 (1937): 97–8.

45. Seymour Siegel, Director of WNYC, to Rankin, 25 Jan. 1938, MA Box 10 MRL Radio Talks. Siegel sent Rankin an official notice that WNYC would broadcast the library's series "How the New Charter Works" on Thursdays at 6–6:15 P.M. from 3 Feb. to 31 March 1938.

46. Rankin, "The City Council," 3 Feb. 1938, MA Box 10 MRL Radio Talks.

47. Rankin, "The City Council," 3 Feb. 1938. See McCaffrey 847. The thirteen "regular" Democrats on the Council were opposed by an equal number of members who formed a coalition to block the election of a City Clerk and the selection of committee chairs in early 1938.

48. Rankin, "The City Council," 10 Feb. 1938, MA Box 10 MRL Radio Talks. Rankin presented a second speech on the Council and attempted to answer questions the MRL had received after her initial broadcast.

49. Kehl, "The Administrative Code," 17 Feb. 1938, MA Box 10 MRL Radio Talks. See Rankin, "City Librarian Looks Over Twenty-four Years of Service," *NY World Telegram* 24 Sept. 1944: 13.

50. Rankin, "Various Departmental Improvements," 31 March 1938, MA Box 10 MRL Radio Talks.

51. Rankin, "Various Departmental Improvements," 31 March 1938.

52. Rankin, "The City Planning Commission," 3 March 1938, MA Box 10 MRL Radio Talks.

53. Kehl, "Nine Years of Broadcasting."

54. Kehl, "Nine Years of Broadcasting."

55. MA Box 5608 MRL Statistics 1914–57.

56. Seaver, *Career of Rebecca Browning Rankin* 269–72.

57. Seaver, *Career of Rebecca Browning Rankin* 332–46, 375–9.

58. Jason Horn, "Municipal Archives and Record Center of the City of New York," *The American Archivist* 16 (1953): 311–20.

59. Horn 311–20. In 1947 President Truman appointed Herbert Hoover to chair the Commission on the Organization of the Executive Branch which recommended a system of records management to control government documents. William O'Dwyer, who succeeded La Guardia as mayor of New York, instituted a similar study and reactivated the Municipal Archives Committee with Rankin as its chair in 1948.

60. James Katsaros, Assistant to the Municipal Reference Librarian, to Rankin, 30 April 1946, MA Box 8 MRL Radio Talks. Katsaros proposed that the library staff review books on WNYC.

61. Rankin to Katsaros, 1 May 1946, MA Box 8 MRL Radio Talks. Kehl left her position earlier in the year to become a professor of library science at Drexel University.

62. Rankin published *New York Advancing: A Scientific Approach to Municipal Government*, 1936; *New York Advancing: World's Fair Edition*, 1939; and *New York Advancing: Seven More Years of Progressive Administration in the City of New York*, 1945. She published *Guide to the Municipal Government of the City of New York* (Brooklyn: Eagle Library Publications, 1936); and revised editions in 1938, 1939, 1943, 1948, 1950, and 1952.

63. Faith H. Hyers, *The Library and Radio* (Chicago: U of Chicago Press, 1938) 61–75. Hyers reported on the results of a 1934 survey of public libraries by American Library Association. Forty libraries responded that they had attempted radio broadcasts, but few had developed regular programs.

These continuing radio series were devoted primarily to book reviews and discussions, storytelling for children, and publicity for library services. The radio broadcasts of the MRL were the only ones focused on the broader objective of disseminating information about local government activities and political issues.

64. Columbia University, Bureau of Applied Social Research, *The People Look at Radio; Report on a Survey Conducted by the National Opinion Research Center* (Chapel Hill: U of North Carolina Press, 1946) 42–3. Paul Lazarfeld, the director of the Bureau, analyzed the results of the survey and concluded that radio broadcasting was instrumental in stimulating women and less-educated citizens to take a greater interest in current affairs and informed them about politics.

13. *Synergy,* Social Responsibility, and the Sixties: Pivotal Points in the Evolution of American Outreach Library Service

Toni Samek

In the late 1960s a number of American librarians argued that library collections lacked balance, that a purist moral stance on intellectual freedom was an example of hands-off liberalism, and that the library served mainstream social sectors, not the whole community. As a result, they had little faith in the establishment stance of library "neutrality" and its accompanying vision of intellectual freedom. Instead, they believed that the library should become an active agent for social change and that the concept of intellectual freedom should incorporate the premise of social responsibility.

Librarians who advocated social responsibility used the issue of the alternative press to redress a perceived imbalance in library collections, to provide enhanced information services to a broader public, to make the library more relevant to a changing society, and to show that long-standing library practices put the library profession in conflict with its own Library Bill of Rights—the American Library Association's (ALA) policy statement on intellectual freedom. Much of this activity emanated from San Francisco Public Library's Bay Area Reference Center (BARC), established in 1967. The experimental Center provided support reference services to seventeen North Bay Cooperative Library System libraries scattered across six counties. BARC occupied a small room just off the Main library's general reference department and communicated with most of the cooperative institutions via facsimile transmissions, nationwide communication systems, and photocopying equipment. To find information on new areas of interest, BARC looked to non-commercial book publishers and in 1967 began publishing its own monthly newsletter, *Synergy*, to disseminate news of the project and to serve as a reference tool. *Synergy's* "Update" section listed outstanding new additions to the San Francisco Public Library reference collection, while another section included a bibliography of topical importance "not obtainable through usual channels."[1]

San Francisco was a hotbed of social activity in 1967. From the city's 65,000 person anti-war demonstration held concomitantly with the Spring Mobilization Committee's New York City protest, to the influx of thousands of people for the "Summer of Love" activities, the Bay community manifested social change.[2] Celeste West, *Synergy's* first editor, commented on the relationship between San Francisco's transformation and the local library scene. She described the city as "a trend-mecca—whether it be communal living, campus riots, gay liberation, independent film making ... you name it and we've got it." But what San Francisco had, she argued, was not reflected in library collections unless somebody took the time to pull together "the elusive printed material."[3] Thus, *Synergy* began to examine the nature of library card catalogs, indexes, and selecting tools because its staff believed that such tools were mostly "rear-view mirrors" that provided little or no bibliographic access to the public's current information needs.

Synergy's staff believed that because librarians were not sufficiently trained to create access to or learn about where to find many forms of information, they were unable to fulfill their professional mandate to present balanced and multiple points of view. The passive nature of library practice, grounded on a myth of "neutral" service, understated this problem. Because librarians were followers and not leaders in the information marketplace, alternative press topics received attention only when big publishers sensed profit. To illustrate this point, West tracked the lag time between discussions of women's liberation in the alternative press and their appearance in mainstream library literature. The mainstream library press, she noted, "slumbered along" for nearly five years before recognizing it in about 1970.[4]

Synergy consistently included information about neglected topics. The April-May 1968 issue, for example, criticized conventional library literature's lack of attention to subjects like astrology, Native Americans, the women's liberation movement, ecology, the drug revolution, library service to prisoners, the occult, the family, the underground press, and criticisms of the establishment. In subsequent issues, *Synergy* provided coverage of these and other topics. But *Synergy* stood for more than just information access. Under West's direction, it called on librarians to become "pivotal agents to enforce" the Library Bill of Rights, to support a free press, and to develop a new professional attitude by shifting from "conserving and organizing" information to "generating or promoting it."[5] *Synergy* defined an alternative library culture that worried less about the library as a keeper of the cultural record, and more about the library as an active agent for change.

SOCIAL RESPONSIBILITY AND THE ALA

By the summer of 1967, other librarians began adopting *Synergy's* philosophy. For example, at ALA's conference in San Francisco a group of librarians picketed a meeting cosponsored by the Adult Services Division and the Council on Foreign Relations, where Maxwell D. Taylor delivered a pro–Vietnam War speech. Approximately 150 people (students, hippies, and librarians) rallied outside the conference hotel waving signs that read "Books Not Bullets" and "This is a Taylor-made Demonstration." Inside, librarians demonstrated at the entrance to Taylor's banquet room.[6] The protest showed an emerging political movement within librarianship in general, and ALA in particular.[7]

Then, in December, library educator Mary Lee Bundy published a report in *Wilson Library Bulletin* on factors that influenced public library use, and concluded that the profession had failed to meet its responsibility to a changing society. While "extraordinary educational, political, economic, social and technological changes" had occurred and the culture in which libraries functioned had "dramatically altered," the public library had "stood still, caught in the straitjacket of its traditional view of itself and the world, by its historical commitments, and by its clienteles."[8]

While *Synergy* exemplified the important connection between the new librarianship and the social message of the alternative press, it was not sufficiently influential to carry the movement forward. And while library activists had a common interest in the alternative press and often made contacts and connections through it, they still lacked a mechanism for organizing their more general social justice efforts. By 1968 Dorothy Bendix, Kenneth Duhac, and eight other ALA members began informally meeting to discuss an alternative library agenda within the association structure.[9] They called themselves the Round Table on Social Responsibilities of Libraries (RTSRL) which was renamed Social Responsibilities Round Table (SRRT) in 1971.

Although at the 1967 ALA annual conference in Kansas City "some councilors expressed strong antipathy to the very idea of the round table," six months later RTSRL received unanimous support.[10] And eventually, on January 30, 1969, at ALA's midwinter conference in Washington, D.C., the Council voted unanimously to approve the formation of RTSRL. But the ALA administration's spirit of accommodation had limits. An official ALA report on aids to collection-building published in the *ALA Bulletin* failed to mention *Synergy*.[11] That may have been an oversight. But other incidents occurred that convinced library activists that intellectual confrontations would have to take place within ALA in order to define the library's role in society.

At the University of Maryland, School of Library and Information Studies (SLIS), students and faculty were meeting over the issue of inner-city recruitment, and at about the same time thirty students from ten library schools had gathered "to identify themselves and their ideas to one another."[12] For two days in March 1969, students discussed how library schools and library education needed to change, diversify, and become more relevant to society. Their aim was to organize a national conference of library school students and other like-minded librarians. James C. Welbourne (President, Maryland SLIS Student Group) initiated action and circulated a letter of concern to fourteen other library schools.[13]

Before the library school representatives met in Washington in June, a spring symposium on "Public Library Service to the Black Urban Poor" held at Wayne State University issued the "Friday the 13th Manifesto." This document stated that "the social crises of the cities have brought people into conflict with the Establishment," that librarianship "reflects the values and attitudes of the Establishment," and that "present" priorities were established in response to the articulated needs of the power structure, not the unarticulated needs of those outside the power structure. The missive concluded that because "the library profession has been neither neutral nor objective," it must immediately adopt a "philosophy of *advocacy* in every respect of its service to the urban poor."[14]

> As a result of the College Park meeting, the "Friday the 13th Manifesto," and "discussions and the confrontations going on at other campuses," the Congress for Change (CFC) was born.[15] On June 19, 1969, *Wilson Library Bulletin* noted, 180 "youngish people dedicated to smashing the status quo" came to Washington, D.C., from library schools in New York, Pennsylvania, and Maryland. About 30 years old on the average, the "shaggy-faced, long-haired, or wide-eyed [students] behind giant, steel-rimmed, tinted sunglasses,"[16] jammed into "a plasticplush meeting room" in the "mangy" Manger-Annapolis Hotel.[17]

Wilson Library Bulletin noted "there was not a potted palm or silver punch bowl" in the hotel, and that it was "a welcome change just to be talking about poverty and the disadvantaged without being surrounded by cut flowers and Hiltonian opulence that have come to form the setting for most library conferences."[18] The group participated in general sessions, workshops, and all-night discussions on how social movements applied to library education and careers. In particular, the unstructured meeting included among its topics the Berkeley Free Speech movement, Vietnam, anti-ballistic missile systems, ALA election reform, library education, and recruitment. On all issues, delegates expressed a diversity of opinions and agendas. Despite their differences, however, they agreed on a set of statements to be presented at ALA's upcoming Atlantic City Membership meeting, and called themselves the CFC.

Unlike RTSRL, CFC was neither intended to become part of ALA's structure, nor to be an ongoing pressure group. Rather it was a one-time event designed to bring concerned individuals together. As RTSRL member Carolyn Forsman put it: CFC "was more an experience than an organization."[19] Its purpose was strictly to make waves in Atlantic City.

On 25 June 1969, between 3,000 and 4,000 people flocked to the first Membership meeting at the convention hall's Grand Ballroom to hear a long discussion on ALA's structure and purpose. While Albert P. Marshall and Lester Stoffel presented parallel motions on the establishment of a committee to study the association's goals and future, incoming ALA President William S. Dix announced that such a committee—the Activities Committee for New Directions for ALA (ACONDA)—had already been recommended to him by the Executive Board in their June 23 meeting. After "the basic issues involved in changing the ALA were sunk in a malodorous parliamentary quagmire,"[20] ACONDA's statement of purpose and committee selection procedures were established. The Executive Board would nominate twelve members. The President would select the first six on his own and another six from the Junior Members Round Table and RTSRL nominations. The President would also appoint a thirteenth person as ACONDA's chair. In effect, the committee's composition would be a curious mixture of ALA's "radicals" and "mossbacks."[21] As a result, ACONDA was soon called the "Dix Mix."[22]

Wilson Library Bulletin reported that, although probably few CFC/RTSRL members knew it, Dix "shared most of their concerns." He had fought McCarthy's attacks on libraries, chaired the Intellectual Freedom Committee from 1951 to 1953, and chaired the joint committee with the American Book Publisher's Council that drafted the "Freedom to Read Statement."[23]

After the ACONDA announcement, outgoing President Roger H. McDonough presented CFC to the packed general Membership meeting. Welbourne then introduced CFC delegates, some of whom read statements that revealed that the CFC, like RTSRL, would not separate politics from work when it came to "race, violence, war and peace, inequality of justice and opportunity."[24]

ACONDA's initial discussion on the association's future obligations and priorities took place at ALA's headquarters in Chicago on September 26 and 27. Both ALA President Dix and Executive Director David H. Clift attended the two-day Chicago sessions and Frederick Wagman (former ALA president and Director of Libraries, University of Michigan) presided over the group.[25]

ACONDA identified the following as areas needing ALA's attention: (1) ALA's social responsibilities, social relevance, and its commitments to fundamental values such as library service to the disadvantaged and international concerns; (2) Manpower, library education, ALA membership's welfare, and recruitment with an emphasis on people interested in service to disadvantaged minority groups; (3) Intellectual freedom, including the development of better procedures for the support of librarians under pressure or attack for upholding the Library Bill of Rights; (4) Further democratization of ALA, including more participation by younger members, in particular, and greater responsiveness to members' concerns, in general; (5) Legislation; and (6) Planning and research.[26] Because ACONDA had to prepare a preliminary report for ALA's midwinter conference, it determined that the first draft of this report be completed and disseminated by January 1 to the whole body for study. Accordingly, ACONDA organized itself into various subcommittees, each concerned with one of its priorities for action. George J. Alfred of the Walden Branch Library in San Francisco was named chair of the Social Responsibilities Subcommittee.

Meanwhile, the H. W. Wilson Company gave *Synergy* the Library Periodical Award "for a highly contemporary, off-beat, consistently communicative, NOW-oriented publication which, in imaginative format and sprightly content, matches its milieu, while giving useful service to its clientele."[27] *Synergy* staff used the positive publicity to continue driving their message home. Issue 24 (December 1969) covered the women's liberation movement and provided commentary on the New Left's exploitation of women, the objectification of women by underground papers, and the "low and sinking status" of women in the library profession.[28]

As the year drew to its close, *Synergy* continued with its alternative press and library culture activities, and RTSRL (already the largest ALA round table with 1,013 members) pressed forward and planned for ACONDA. Thus, two years after a small group of Bay area librarians began to spur interest in the alternative press and argue that librarians needed to address social issues, ALA had a formal conduit for its members to tackle social responsibility.

The issue of social responsibility was prominent at ALA's midwinter 1970 meeting in Chicago, where approximately 1,800 members checked in at the aged Sherman House Hotel.[29] *Wilson Library Bulletin*'s "Month in Review" summary stated that the "atmosphere of tension, hostility, and polarization in the City of Law and Order was almost as visible to conferees as the steam and soot trapped in the frozen air of the Loop."[30] The ongoing Trial of the Chicago Eight/Seven was just four blocks away from the Sherman House. The National Call for Library Reform, a coalition which evolved from CFC and Atlantic City conference activism, braved the cold and staged a protest march to the Federal Building, where dissenting librarians called for the "right, principle, and constitutional guarantees of free speech and due process," and cited many examples of free speech infringements, including police brutality against demonstrators at the 1968 Democratic National Convention, the Chicago Eight/Seven trial, oppression of Black Panther members, the "apparent" murder of Fred Hampton, and the mishandling of Bobby Seale's due process rights. They called on ALA not to meet in Chicago or any other city that "exemplified the repressive forces" of society. Meanwhile, underground press worker and ALA member Tom Forcade "haunted the conference, an apparition in Yippie garb." And police intervened at the Chicago Public Library, where Illinois RTSRL sponsored a film about local police riots and where guerilla theater performers acted out several scenes. Thus, a local newspaper headlined, "Librarians get good look at cops in action."[31]

But the midwinter conference also included some new ALA business. At its January 20 meeting "Council passed a motion to set aside a fund of up to $50,000" to expedite ACONDA's recommendations. ACONDA presented its *Interim Report of the Activities Committee on New Directions for ALA,* with attendant Subcommittee background papers, to the members. The committee then asked the membership to "come tell us what you think." The unstructured discussions that followed lasted three days.[32]

Meanwhile, the creation of the Task Force on Intellectual Freedom constituted RTSRL's most important accomplishment because it inter-related the concepts of intellectual freedom and social responsibility, and caused some ALA members to wonder whether the association should shift its focus from institutions to individuals. ALA retained the stance that social responsibility and intellectual freedom were dichotomous, and that it should retain an institutional membership focus. RTSRL members disagreed. They wanted ALA to be more responsive to the needs of librarians, including female, minority, gay, and lesbian librarians. They were also involved in organizing library school students and librarians in their intellectual freedom disputes.

ALA's Council had commissioned ACONDA's Subcommittee on Social Responsibilities of Libraries to explore improved library service for the disadvantaged and report its recommendations at the Detroit conference. George J. Alfred and his colleagues interpreted this directive as an opportunity to disseminate a broader social responsibility agenda. To some extent, social and political conditions such as "a favorable job situation, the availability of federal funding, and pressures on institutions from outside" helped to facilitate the climate in which the library movement could find expression.[33] For example, Bundy and Stielow argue that the idea of improving library service to the disadvantaged was a part of the "War on Poverty" and "The Great Society" discourse of the Kennedy and Johnson administrations.

The federal government "bypassed" local governments and set up spending programs for poor urban communities, while libraries also established their own poverty programs. The Library Services and Construction Act (first passed in 1956 as the Library Services Act) and the 1965 Higher Education Act were key sources of funding for library services to the disadvantaged. E. J. Josey noted that the advent of new programs for minority communities that resulted from federal funding programs was a major impetus for library activism and the increasing concern for social responsibility in libraries.[34]

With respect to library service to the disadvantaged, the Subcommittee decided that a comprehensive definition of intellectual freedom was insufficient, and that the omnibus term "social responsibility" also needed defining. George J. Alfred, A. P. Marshall, and Shirley Olofson collaborated on a three page ACONDA document entitled *Subcommittee Report: Social Responsibilities*, in which they identified two conflicting definitions of social responsibility held by ALA members. The first reflected a traditional interpretation in which the library functioned as a provider of factual material on all sides of issues. In this interpretation, the library housed and preserved information and kept, but did not promote, ideas. The second reflected the new, activist interpretation—"the relationships that librarians and libraries have to non-library problems that relate to the social welfare" of society. Because the group believed that intellectual freedom complemented rather than opposed social responsibility, it opted to use the second definition to begin the process of improving library service to the disadvantaged. The group agreed that ALA needed to "re-think and re-allocate traditional library sources of income" and improve legislation, information, practical advice on topics such as workshops, publications, and recruitment, and finally consulting services.[35]

But because many ALA members considered the demand that ALA demonstrate a sense of social responsibility towards many issues—"specifically non-library issues"—controversial, the Subcommittee recognized that the new activist interpretation of social responsibility would prove highly problematic.[36] For example, many librarians were reluctant to abandon librarianship's claim to a "neutral" stance and they were afraid of the social, financial, and legal repercussions that could result from ALA's involvement in social issues. The Subcommittee resolved that it needed to find ways to allay these two fears.

With respect to library "neutrality," the Subcommittee noted that because librarians reacted subjectively to many issues (e.g., intellectual freedom and racial integration) it saw no reason not to validate the activist definition of social responsibility. Furthermore, it asserted that the old definition was unrealistic and served to shelter libraries from rather than expose them to social changes. With respect to involving ALA in social issues that threatened ALA's tax-exempt status, the Subcommittee set out to determine if this fear was justified. Because the American Association of University Professors (AAUP) also enjoyed a tax-exempt status, the Subcommittee contacted AAUP and found out that it experienced no threat to its tax-exempt status, despite a 1969 Internal Revenue Service review of its activity in defending faculty member's rights (academic librarians included). The Subcommittee decided there was no reason to fear that ALA's tax-exempt status would be jeopardized by helping librarians threatened with loss of academic freedom or political interference. Ultimately, ACONDA's *Subcommittee Report: Social Responsibilities* urged that ALA's social responsibilities "be defined in terms of the contribution that librarianship as a profession can make in the effort to ameliorate or even solve the many critical problems of society." Here the report outlined both direct and indirect action, both programming and making "freely available the full range of data and opinion on all aspects of such problems."[37]

At the 2 July 1970 Membership session at ALA's annual conference in Detroit, David K. Berninghausen (Director, University of Minnesota library school) took exception to Recommendation 4a(1)(c)—that ALA "define the broad social responsibilities of ALA in terms of (c) the willingness of ALA to support the guidance and support of its members on critical issues"—and moved that the words "of direct and demonstrable relevance to librarianship" be included. This suggestion triggered a lengthy debate about ALA's role in society. Eventually, members settled a second revised version of Recommendation 4a(1)(c)—"define the broad social responsibilities of ALA in terms of (c) the willingness to take a position on current critical issues."[38]

When Membership reconvened the next afternoon, Tyron D. Emerick immediately moved that all approved agenda items not yet considered by Membership be scheduled for ALA's midwinter meeting. The motion passed. Thus, only after three days of meetings and "a great deal of squabbling and parliamentary maneuvering," ACONDA proposals were on their way to the Council.[39]

A key issue at the Atlantic City conference was whether ALA should "take a stand;" but in Detroit the question became "on what" should ALA take a stand."[40] Paul Bixler (Antioch College) was puzzled that while social responsibility "was clearly the source" for ACONDA's "inauguration and the stimulus for its enormous labors, the Subcommittee statement came at the tag end of the whole report, not as an introduction."[41] And when Council debated 4(a)1(c), which allowed ALA to take positions on current issues, Ervin J. Gaines (Director, Minneapolis Public Library) proposed a statement that would limit items to those involved with libraries and library service. Margaret Monroe (University of Wisconsin) proposed a simpler substitution—require position statements to indicate relevancy to librarianship. Her amendment passed roughly 100 to 35, although she and approximately 35 other Council members opposed it.[42]

Ultimately, the Council resisted "the idea of an office devoted to social responsibilities," although, *Wilson Library Bulletin* pointed out, "a few hours before they had named that as one of the Association's priorities."[43] Instead, the Council approved an Office for Library Service to the Disadvantaged and Unserved, but gave it no specific charge or money.[44] It also accepted only the general ACONDA statements of principle, but deferred those requiring implementation. It then established its own ALA Ad Hoc Council Committee on New Directions (ANACONDA) to discuss the remaining items in *ACONDA's Final Report*, directed ANACONDA to submit a report by midwinter, and voted not to take final action on the complete ANACONDA report until late fall, 1971. Thus "professionalists" successfully deflected *ACONDA's Final Report*. Although ACONDA's life would be short, it had already left a legacy. It had held hearings at midwinter and solicited a wide spectrum of views. It had published its preliminary document in *American Libraries*, and held "open" meetings. But ACONDA tried to focus on new directions, and this "enraged the establishment." "Probably nobody knows," the *Bulletin* surmised, "the true effect of the delay," or the impact of confusion surrounding "TAX EXEMPT STATUS."[45]

But issues of social activism preoccupied more than just Membership and Council meetings at the Detroit conference. Discussions on new directions also dominated RTSRL, the RTSRL-affiliated Intellectual Freedom Committee and Black Caucus meetings, as well as the President's Program. Rooms were made available for a "blacks-only Caucus," a "late-night women's liberation meeting," and a meeting of homosexual and bisexual librarians, "which, like so many fugitive groups, was under RTSRL's wing." Whereas the RTSRL meetings drew, to some extent, an elitist and exclusive underground group in Atlantic City, the "enlarged and wide-open RTSRL meetings, [programs,] and receptions" drew thousands in Detroit.[46]

EXTENDING THE REACH OF THE ALTERNATIVE PRESS

In Detroit, RTSRL members elected Patricia Schuman (New York City Community College) as the new Action Council Coordinator and she immediately welcomed volunteers for a new Task Force on Alternative Books in Print. The Task Force evolved out of RTSRL's interest in the effects of the Radical Research Center, a non-library organization founded in 1969 at Carleton College in Northfield, Minnesota. While ACONDA had been preparing its paperwork the Radical Research Center published the first volume of the *Alternative Press Index* in February 1970. It showed librarians and non-librarians that standard library tools like *Books in Print* gave only limited access to current alternative media. Library activists were embarrassed that librarians and library schools had done nothing to address the pressing need for indexes to non-mainstream periodicals. Jackie Eubanks, for example, spoke about her embarrassment that the *Alternative Press Index* began outside ALA.[47] As an active RTSRL member, a volunteer indexer for the Radical Research Center, and a veteran in the alternative press movement, Eubanks took a leadership role in the new Task Force on Alternative Books in Print.

The Task Force began working on a strategy to make libraries and their collections relevant for their publics.[48] It proposed to compile a list of non-serial publications available from underground movement presses and allied organizations left out of *Books in Print* by creating an adjunct to regular reference tools. This adjunct would enhance library and bookstore access to media produced by nonprofit, anti-profit, counterculture, Third World, and other activist groups.

Mary McKenney, a trained librarian who worked for the Radical Research Center, expressed pleasure that at last like-minded people across the nation were connecting the social responsibility movement in librarianship to the alternative press movement.[49] For others, however, the alternative press remained a mystery. In May 1970 James O. Lehman published a survey of what 101 American colleges used as selection tools. He found that librarians favored *Choice, Library Journal, New York Times, Saturday Review, Publishers Weekly, Booklist,* and *Wilson Library Bulletin* as selection aids. Survey respondents seemed unaware of the alternative press review media, such as *Synergy,* as a tool for the library selection process.[50]

RTSRL had an ally in *Synergy*. *Synergy*, for example, complemented efforts of the alternative press by covering ALA's gay liberation movement and by providing a bibliography of gay periodicals in its October issue. It also addressed job discrimination based on sexual orientation, homosexuality as a topic within conventional classification schemes and subject heading lists, freedom and equality for other minority groups within ALA, and bibliographic resources for marginalized groups.[51] Furthermore, as part of its effort to provide information about the alternative press and alternative library activity, *Synergy*'s staff lobbied for the "Great Unreviewed," which constituted "60%+ of all books published."[52] Because standard reviewing journals like *Kirkus Reviews*, *Publishers Weekly*, and *Choice* did not cover the alternative press, *Synergy* tried to fill the void. It encouraged subscribers to read intensively in their areas of specialty and to get involved in self-publication.

When *Synergy*'s October issue went into distribution, Eubanks and fellow New Yorker Mimi Penchansky of Queens College had just completed a letter campaign to over 1,500 organizations, many of which had been listed in the *Directory of the American Left*. They had identified 250 non-serial materials for the Task Force on Alternative Books in Print's proposed publication project, *Alternatives in Print*. Next, they adopted the *Alternative Press Index* subject headings and persuaded Ohio State University Library Director Hugh Atkinson to get the university press to publish it.[53]

The Task Force opted for an academic publisher for several reasons. First, commercial publishers judged the proposed publication unprofitable and not sufficiently market tested. Second, alternative press publishers did not have enough start-up capital to get the project off the ground. Third, ALA's publishing procedures were too arduous for a project intended to move quickly. RTSRL member Joan Marshall was especially angry with ALA for not picking up projects rejected by commercial publishers. She believed ALA needed to support the alternative press.[54]

RTSRL members like Marshall, Eubanks, and Penchansky were deeply committed to providing access to the alternative press because they recognized librarians' traditional inability to balance collections by ignoring relatively inaccessible materials. They had no illusions about the profession's "neutrality" and believed that ALA-accredited library schools trained students to build collections using mainstream selection tools and venues. In their view, the Task Force on Alternative Books in Print offered an opportunity to counter the effect of conventional training.

With Eubanks at the helm, the Task Force lobbied to get small and alternative presses into the standard library indexes, catalogs, and bibliographic references. Second, it planned to revise ALA exhibit policies which reinforced the concept that "the biggest are best" and which charged "too much for the small publisher to afford to exhibit at ALA meetings."[55] To this end, the Task Force launched a campaign to change ALA's policies on the leasing of exhibit-hall space so that ability to pay would replace set fees. Because small presses had less money to spend on booth space they were often excluded from library conferences. Large commercial publishers were a regular presence.[56] Initially the Task Force used RTSRL as a vehicle for setting up small press displays at ALA conferences. On varying occasions, displays at RTSRL's exhibit-hall booth were regarded as a part of RTSRL's programs. Eventually the Task Force succeeded in getting ALA's approval for a special section of less expensive exhibit space where small presses could afford to exhibit.[57] The Task Force also set up exhibits at smaller regional library conferences, at meetings of the American Booksellers Association, and at the National Women's Studies Association.

While the Task Force on Alternative Books in Print stood out as the RTSRL group most involved with the alternative press, RTSRL's general goal—to make libraries more relevant to the public—provided the impetus for other task forces to address issues of access. The Ethnic Materials Task Force (later an ALA round table) sought to make ethnic materials by and for Blacks, Puerto Ricans, American Indians, Asian Americans, and Chicanos more accessible to patrons and better known to other librarians. Other task forces focused on literature for women, gays and lesbians, labor workers, political prisoners, migrant workers, and other groups. And for the next several years, all benefited from the efforts of the Task Force on Alternative Books in Print, which functioned as a central part of both RTSRL's structure and mission.

By spring 1973, *Alternatives in Print* was going into its third edition, which covered publications by 800 groups and small presses—only one hundred of which had appeared in *Books in Print* and only fifty of which were cited in the *Small Press Record of Non-periodical Publications.*[58] Other evidences of unbalanced collections continued to surface. For example, when the Philadelphia area SRRT's Intellectual Freedom Committee surveyed materials in neighborhood libraries, it found that: (1) "relatively favorable book budgets are no guarantee that the library's collection will include controversial materials in any significant quantities;" (2) the "values of the institution and the librarian inevitably come into play;" and (3) "some librarians with modest budgets and a sense of social and artistic adventure are building more contemporary and provocative collections than others, who have more money at their disposal but suspect or dislike the unorthodox or feel compelled to ignore it because of institutional policy."[59] Where these signs of unbalanced collections came to light, the larger library social responsibility suffered visibly as well.

The profession's general neglect of the alternative press was symptomatic of ALA's broader status quo politics. Within just a few short years, the library social responsibility movement began to show signs of its political effect. At the annual ALA conference in Las Vegas in June 1973, ALA established its first Intellectual Freedom Round Table. But *Sipapu* publisher Noel Peattie commented that "many saw it as an attempt to co-opt the dissidents from ALA's intellectual freedom 'club,' and certainly later experience has shown that headquarters control of this supposedly grass-roots group is as strong as it is with any intellectual freedom activity in ALA."[60] It was during this organizational change that, despite its influence on the profession, the social responsibility movement began to suffer. Ultimately, the library counterculture mirrored the larger world where the 1960s counterculture became institutionalized or incorporated into the "slick-surfaced, mass-produced" cultural scene of the 1970s.[61]

By 1973, the nation's mood for activism had waned. Gitlin notes that as the Vietnam War subsided, so too did "the urgency of politics." The "vision of One Big Movement dissolved."[62] Not unexpectedly, impetus for agitation in librarianship lessened as well. SRRT had also alienated many mainstream librarians by its inability to define social responsibility in a way which appealed to the majority in ALA. On 30 September 1973, for example, alternative library publisher Samuel Goldstein wrote library activist Sanford Berman that he feared too many activist librarians were "stuffy about how un-stuffy" they were and lamented the fact that the social responsibility library movement only addressed itself to a relatively small portion of ALA's membership. In his view, if the movement wanted to effect change it would have to learn to compromise rather than simply "turn off the faucet of the larger library constituency."[63] Goldstein believed that the social responsibility library movement depended upon its usefulness to library practitioners, not its rhetoric.

Another blow to the struggling social responsibility library movement came in August 1973 when the *SRRT Newsletter* announced that California State librarian Ethel Crockett was terminating federal funding for *Synergy*—the journal that jump-started the library social responsibility movement in 1967. Crockett maintained that Title I of the Library Services and Construction Act funded demonstration projects for not more than two years and because *Synergy* had already received five, she told it to seek financial assistance elsewhere.[64] But while Crockett initially claimed she notified the Bay Area Reference Center (BARC) of the funding cut on April 26 and followed it up with a May 4 memorandum to "Persons Interested in the Future of *Synergy*," she later admitted that somehow the "information was not given to the *Synergy* staff, so that the announcement that funds would, indeed, be cut off after this June 30 came as a shock." Celeste West maintained that the abrupt notice left little time to save *Synergy* and, disgusted with the funding flap and tired of hassles, she resigned. In her resignation letter, West asked, "WHAT DOES THE STATE LIBRARY HAVE IN ITS CROCK O'RELEVANCE?" She believed *Synergy*'s many bibliographies and reviews on topics such as feminism, Native Americans, unions, children's liberation, occultism, head comix, radicals in the professions, free schools, and independent publishing were very "relevant" to the contemporary library world.[65]

The San Francisco Public Library talked publicly of taking over the magazine, but BARC feared censorship. BARC members recognized the library press was not free. In general, it was monopolized by a blend of associations and institutions and controlled by particular publishing interests. Even *Synergy*, for example, was financially dependent on a federal grant and each issue required San Francisco Public Library's approval before publication. The library had previously "bollixed five different reprint offers which might have brought in money," West argued, "choked creativity on the bone of prior censorship," and suppressed "protesting editorials." West maintained she had to kidnap the final *Synergy* issue from the printer just to get it published. Other staff members complained of "odd military-school-like reprimands" and threats that they would be denied legal salary increases.[66]

Ironically, in its last year of existence *Synergy* received its second H. W. Wilson Library Periodical Award and sold 2,000 copies per month. In hindsight, West argued (without providing evidence) that Crockett's real objection to the high-impact periodical was not a question of money. Instead, she asserted, California governor Ronald Reagan had appointed Crockett state librarian, and in West's view, directed Crockett "to kill" *Synergy*—the flagship alternative library publication that fostered an attitude for change in the profession, gave rise to a wave of alternative library literature, provided a ground for library activists to express their opinions and make connections, and "upped the ante on library periodicals" at a time when most librarians remained the "purveyors of Reader's Digested Status Quo print."[67]

Revolting Librarians

Sanford Berman once noted that although some of the "most committed and influential library-cats nationwide" produced core alternative library literature, they were often "heavily shit upon" by the establishment. He believed that alternative library publishers were targeted precisely because the literature they produced tightened connections between the alternative library movement and other movement groups and had the potential to make libraries "more like the social catalysts they should be—rather than the Establishment ass-lickers that most of them [were]."[68] In late 1973, he supported West's venture to publish a new library journal free of institutional restrictions under the Booklegger Press banner, an independent publishing house which West had founded in 1972.[69] The first book that came off the new press was titled *Revolting Librarians* (1972), an anthology of provocative essays edited by West and Valerie Wheat that took the field by storm with its savvy coverage of such topics as the librarians' image, the library press, library schools, and professionalism. *Revolting Librarians* was reviewed in numerous library publications ranging from *Library Journal, College & Research Libraries,* and *Library Resources & Technical Services* to *Library Union Caucus Newsletter* to *School Media Quarterly.* Eugene Darling's *Library Union Caucus Newsletter* review said, "We have in this book some very vivid and accurate pictures of what's wrong with libraries." Charles W. Conaway's *Library Resources & Technical Services* review said the book deserved "at least selective reading by all librarians and particularly by administrators and library educators, the groups with whom the revolting librarians have the most difficulty in communicating." Georgia Mulligan's *College & Research Libraries* review recommended that "you at least *look*" at *Revolting Librarians.* And in *Library Journal* John Berry wrote, "Get the little red book!"[70]

West called the new journal *Booklegger Magazine* and, like *Revolting Librarians,* intended it to take on the library establishment and assist librarians in taking power over their working lives. Soon after *Booklegger Magazine*'s first issue, a bimonthly Toronto journal called *Emergency Librarian* appeared as a sister publication. Edited by Canadian librarians Sherrill Cheda and Phyllis Yaffe, *Emergency Librarian* emerged from a surge of feminist interest at the 1972 Canadian Library Association conference. Together the two journals became the first "women-owned and published library magazines ... in a profession run by women but still ruled by men."[71] As the mouthpieces for some of the profession's leading feminist voices, *Booklegger Magazine* and *Emergency Librarian* blended the 1960s women's, alternative press, and library movements.

The library movement's (1967–1973) impact on American librarianship continues today. *Synergy*—the periodical that *Library Journal* called "a vital acquisition for ... feminist views ... and a superb ... example of lively, liberated library journalism"—paved the way for other alternative library publications, including *Sipapu, The Unabashed Librarian, Revolting Librarians, Booklegger Magazine, Emergency Librarian, Alternative Library Literature, Progressive Librarian,* and *Librarians at Liberty.*[72] Today, library association groups such as the Alternatives in Print Task Force of SRRT (publisher of *Counterpoise: For Social Responsibilities, Liberty and Dissent*), independent library groups such as the Progressive Librarian's Guild (self-described as "left-wing" of SRRT and publisher of the *Progressive Librarian*), independent library publishers such as CRISES Press (publisher of *Librarians at Liberty* and *Alternative Publishers of Books in North America)*, and a broad range of electronically based forums such as *Anarchist Librarians Web, Street Librarian, Library Juice,* and *librarian.net* carry on the work started by *Synergy* more than thirty years ago.[73] But *Synergy*'s staff did more than spur interest in the alternative press. The Bay area librarians also urged library professionals to address social issues. Within just a few years of *Synergy*'s inception, ALA had a formal conduit for its members to tackle issues of social responsibility. RTSRL/SRRT was the foundation for subsequent round tables for intellectual freedom, for women, for international relations, for government documents, for exhibits, and other topics. And from these roots grew ALA's Office for Library Service to the Disadvantaged and the Unserved—the forerunner to today's Office for Literacy and Outreach Services.

NOTES

Parts of this chapter are covered in the more extensive monograph: Toni Samek, *Intellectual Freedom and Social Responsibility in American Librarianship, 1967–1974* (Jefferson, NC: McFarland, 2001).

1. Richard Cronenberg, "Synergizing Reference Service in the San Francisco Bay Region," *ALA Bulletin* 62.11 (December 1968): 1379, 1384.

2. Edward P. Morgan, *The Sixties Experience: Hard Lesson About Modern America* (Philadelphia: Temple University Press, 1991) xix–xx.

3. Celeste West, "Stop! The Print is Killing Me," *Synergy* 33 (1971): 3.

4. The April 1970 issue of *American Libraries* included an article titled "The Disadvantaged Majority: Women Employed by Libraries" by Anita R. Schiller, *American Libraries* 1 (April 1970): 345–49. And in May 1970 *Library Journal* ran a feature by Janet Lois Freedman, "The Liberated Librarian?: A Look at the *Second Sex* in the Library Profession," *Library Journal* 95 (1 May 1970): 1709–1711.

5. Celeste West, "Stalking the Literary-Industrial Complex," *American Libraries* 13 (1982): 299; "A Conversation with Celeste West," *Technicalities* 2 (April 1982): 3–6.

6. "San Francisco '67," *Library Journal* 92 (August 1967): 2708.

7. Carolyn Forsman, "Up Against the Stacks: The Liberated Librarian's Guide to Activism," Affiliates, List of Correspondence, 1970–1973, ALA's Social Responsibilities Round Table Papers (SRRT), Box 11, University of Illinois at Urbana–Champaign, University Archives.

8. Mary Lee Bundy, "Factors Influencing Public Library Use," *Wilson Library Bulletin* 42 (December 1967): 382.

9. The group included Dorothy Bendix (Drexel Institute of Technology, Graduate School of Library Science), Bessie Bullock (Brooklyn Public Library), Verner Clapp (President, Council on Library Resources Inc., Washington, D.C.), Kenneth Duhac (Division of Library Extension, Maryland State Department of Education), Norman Finkler (Montgomery County, Maryland, Department of Public Libraries), Rachel Gross (Huntington Valley, Pennsylvania, Public Library Trustee), Allen T. Hazen (Columbia University, School of Library Service), Evelyn Levy (Enoch Pratt Free Library), H. Thomas Walker (Maryland Division of Library Extension), and Benjamin Weintraub (Rutgers, Graduate School of Library Service).

10. "Wait 'Til Atlantic City," *Library Journal* 94.6 (15 March 1969): 1104–1105.

11. "*Know Your ALA: Services to Members and Aids to Collections,*" *ALA Bulletin* 63 (January 1969): 54–57.

12. "The ALAiad, or, A Tale of Two Conferences," *Wilson Library Bulletin* 44.1 (September 1969): 80.

13. Mary Lee Bundy and Frederick J. Stielow, *Activism in American Librarianship, 1962–1973* (New York: Greenwood Press, 1987) 125.

14. Correspondence, Clearinghouse, 1969–70, ALA's SRRT Papers, Box 7.

15. Correspondence, Clearing House, 1969–70.

16. "The ALAiad" 80.

17. Bundy and Stielow, *Activism* 123.

18. "The ALAiad" 81, 80; *Proceedings 1969 of the Midwinter Meeting Washington, D.C. January 26–February 1, 1969 and the 88th Annual Conference Atlantic City June 22–28, 1969* (Chicago: ALA, 1969) 58.

19. Forsman, "Up Against the Stacks" 11.

20. "The ALAiad" 82, 89.

21. Boris Raymond, "ACONDA and ANACONDA Revisited: A Retrospective Glance at the Sounds and Fury of the Sixties," *Journal of Library History* 14 (Summer 1979): 357.

22. "A Great Show—In Two Parts and a Cast of Thousands," *ALA Bulletin* 63 (July-August 1969): 947.

23. "The ALAiad" 91.

24. Kenneth Duhac, "A Plea for Social Responsibility," *Library Journal* 93 (1968): 2798.

25. The group included Albert P. Marshall (Director of Libraries, Eastern Michigan University), David Kaser (Director of Libraries, Cornell University), Glenn F. Miller (Assistant Director, Orlando Public Library), Katherine Laich (Assistant City Librarian, Los Angeles Public Library), William Hinchcliff (Media Services, Federal City College), Arthur V. Curley (Director, Montclair [NJ] Public Library), Keith Doms (Director, Free Library of Philadelphia), George J. Alfred (by now with the Walden Branch Library, San Francisco), Shirley Olofson (Librarian, Information Center, University of Kentucky), J. Maurice Travillian (Director, Marshalltown [IA] Public Library), and John G. Lorenz (Deputy Librarian of Congress). Alfred, Curley, and Hinchcliff represented RTSRL. Laich, Miller, and Olofson represented JMRT.

26. "Activities Committee on New Directions for ALA," *ALA Bulletin* 63 (November 1969): 1383.

27. *Synergy* 24 (December 1969): 25.

28. Peggy Barber, "Ladies in Waiting," *Synergy* 24 (December 1969): 24.

29. *American Library Association Proceedings of the Midwinter Meeting Chicago January 18–24, 1970 and the 89th Annual Conference Detroit June 28–July 4, 1970* (Chicago: ALA, 1970) 5.

30. "The Month in Review," *Wilson Library Bulletin* 44 (March 1970): 687.

31. "The Month in Review" 687, 690.

32. *American Library Association Proceedings* (1970) 6.

33. Bundy and Stielow, *Activism* 7.

34. Bundy and Stielow, *Activism* 7, x.

35. "Subcommittee Report: Social Responsibilities," DeJohn Correspondence, 1969–70, ALA's SRRT Papers, Box 1.

36. "Subcommittee Report: Social Responsibilities."

37. "New Directions," *American Libraries* 1 (September 1970): 747.

38. "Another Opening, Another Show: Detroit, 1970," *American Libraries* 1 (July-August 1970): 670–671.

39. "ACONDA Revised Recommendations on Democratization and Reorganization: A report presented for consideration of Council and Membership, Midwinter Meeting, January 1971," *American Libraries* 2 (January 1971): 81–92.

40. "Another Opening" 677.

41. Paul Bixler, "On Taking a Stand," *American Libraries* 1 (April 1970): 329.

42. "The Month in Review" 689–90.

43. "On Taking a Stand" 681.

44. The Office for Library Service to the Disadvantaged and Unserved is the forerunner to ALA's current Office for Literacy and Outreach Services.

45. "ALA 1970: Notes and Comments," *Wilson Library Bulletin* 45 (September 1970): 19, 22.

46. "ALA 1970: Notes and Comments" 16–17.

47. ALA Meetings, 1969–70, SRRT-ALA General Meeting Proposal for an Alternative "BIP" National Task Force, ALA's SRRT Papers, Box 8.

48. Noel Peattie, *A Passage for Dissent: The Best of Sipapu, 1970–1988* (Jefferson, NC: McFarland, 1989) 138.

49. Mary McKenney to Sanford Berman, 1970, Mary McKenney, 1970–72, ALA's Sanford Berman Papers.

50. James O. Lehman, "*Choice* as a Selection Tool," *Wilson Library Bulletin* 44 (May 1970): 960.

51. Celeste West, "The Body Politic," *Synergy* 29 (October 1970): 3–5.

52. West, "Stop!" 3.

53. "Librarians in Action," *Workforce* (March-April 1973): 20–23.

54. "SRRT-ified Action: Reports on the Programs, Plans, and Projects of SRRT Task Forces," *School Library Journal* 97.4 (1972): 734–35.

55. Jackie Eubanks to Martha Ann Kollmorgan, 25 March 1974, ALA's SRRT Papers, Box 7.

56. Jackie Eubanks to Martha Ann Kollmorgan.

57. Betty-Carol Sellen (1970–87), Getting Library Attention, ALA's SRRT Papers, Box 11.

58. *Books in Print* (New York: Bowker Co., 1948–); Len Fulton, *Small Press Record of Non-periodical Publications* (Paradise, CA: Dustbooks, 1969–1975). In 1975 *Small Press Record of Non-periodical Publications* became *Small Press Record of Books*.

59. S. J. Leon, "Book Selection in Philadelphia," *Library Journal* 98 (1 April 1973): 1089.

60. Bundy and Stielow, *Activism* 50–51.

61. Hugh Fox, *The Living Underground: A Critical Overview* (Troy, NY: Whiston Publishing Co., 1970) 11. Many small presses joined organizations like the Committee of Small Editors and Publishers (COSMEP), the Alternative Press Syndicate, and the Coordinating Council of Literary Magazines. And "for many of the underground poets," for example, "even COSMEP" became too "efficient," too much an "institution" or "computer," noted Abe Peck. Alternative publishing had clearly shifted course. Fewer underground papers existed and among these publications were more topical—feminist, environmental, etc. *Sipapu* 5 (January 1974): 16.

62. Todd Gitlin, *The Sixties: Years of Hope, Days of Rage* (Toronto: Bantam Books, 1987) 421–422.

63. Samuel Goldstein to Sanford Berman, 30 Sept. 1973, CALL/Sam Goldstein, 1973–74, 1977, ALA's Sanford Berman Papers.

64. *Synergy* (1973), ALA's Sanford Berman Papers. See also Edward Swanson, "*Synergy* Protest" *American Libraries* 4 (July/August 1973): 408; Noel Peattie, "The Fortunes of *Synergy*," *Sipapu* 4 (July 1973): 8–10.

65. "*Synergy* Editor Resigns," *American Libraries* 7 (July/August 1973): 412.

66. "Celeste West on Synergy," *Sipapu* 4 (July 1973): 71.

67. "A Conversation with Celeste West" 3–6.

68. Sanford Berman to Mr. Brian Kirby, March 1971, Libraries to the People, 1971–1973, ALA's Sanford Berman Papers.

69. Celeste West, Elizabeth Katz, eds., *Revolting Librarians* (San Francisco: Booklegger Press, 1972) iii.

70. Eugene Darling, "Are Librarians Revolting?" *Library Union Caucus Newsletter* 2 (January 1973): 5; John Berry, "Little Red Book," *Library Journal* 98 (15 February 1973): 515; Georgia Mulligan, *College & Research Libraries* 34 (March 1973): 165–166; Charles W. Conaway, *Library Resources and Technical Services* 18 (Summer 1974): 294–295; and, *School Media Quarterly* 1 (1974): 227 [reviews of *Revolting Librarians*, eds. Celeste West and Elizabeth Katz].

71. "A Conversation with Celeste West" 3–6.

72. "SYNERGY," *Library Journal* 96 (1 September 1971): 2593.

73. *Alternative Publishers of Books in North America* 4 was produced by the Alternatives in Print Task Force of the Social Responsibilities Round Table of ALA, but published by CRISES Press.

14. For the Love of Books: Eddie Lovett and His Backwoods Library

Emily J. Branson and
John Mark Tucker

> I conceded my ignorance a long time ago, and have tried to
> overcome it. And you want to know something? Reading a book
> is still the only way to do that.
>
> — *Eddie Lovett*

The *Oxford English Dictionary* defines a hero as one "who exhibits extraordinary bravery, firmness, fortitude, or greatness of soul, in any pursuit, work, or enterprise;" one admired for "achievements" and "noble qualities."[1] Society tends to bestow the designation of hero on people who are famous or especially excellent at what they do, but not necessarily on people of excellent character. Eddie Lovett, who died in June 2000 at the age of eighty-four, certainly qualified for the *OED* definition, if not necessarily contemporary usage of the term. Lovett was not wealthy and he had little formal education. He was known beyond his immediate neighborhood primarily because Charles Kuralt presented a profile of him. Yet, Lovett had a purpose in mind for himself; he pursued that purpose with single-minded intensity; and he succeeded in ways that have inspired all who have heard his story.

Lovett's fame resulted from his having built a private library of about 4,000 volumes. He constructed the library at his home in Bradley County, Arkansas, near the village of Banks. Building the library was not an unusual feat in itself, but clearly unusual for a black sharecropper's son with only an eighth-grade education. We have been inspired by Lovett's library and by his desire through the library to improve himself and the lives of his children. He had decided to "declare war on [his] igno-rance,"[2] reading books that many formally educated people balk at. As he grew older, he devoted more and more of his time to his children and his library, the latter becoming an "oasis for the unrestrained pursuit of knowledge."[3]

COLLECTING, TEACHING, AND OUTREACH

In considering the impulses and ideas involved in *Libraries to the People*, the work of Eddie Lovett came immediately to mind. We thought of him because of the multiple factors that make his story so compelling. Foremost among these were, of course, his limited economic and educational resources. People who spend their lives sharecropping or raising watermelons in rural communities tend not to build substantial private libraries. For the most part, the history of private libraries begins with stories about the cultural and intellectual tastes of individuals of vast wealth. Moreover, such wealth tends to accumulate in powerful urban centers like New York, Chicago, or Los Angeles, which have become centers for rich, specialized research collections. And while Eddie Lovett's library was not one of these, it grew out of a moral purpose equal to, if not surpassing, the ideals that stimulated the growth of great libraries like those of J. Pierpont Morgan or Henry Huntington.

Lovett wanted to teach. He wanted to teach himself and to teach his children. He wanted to read to his children as his father had read to him. The task of train-ing the young would not be left to the public school alone. When he was in his forties, Lovett's second wife died, leaving him with five children twelve years of age and younger. Amidst the challenges presented by single parenthood, Lovett's devo-tion to his children lay at the very heart and core of his determination to build a pri-vate library. Lovett's friends and neighbors wanted to know why he did not let someone else rear his children, let someone else take responsibility for them. He responded, "No, Lord," and chose his own way, finally concluding, "I've tried my best to develop their minds because I know they are going to need it. They most cer-tainly will that."[4]

But Lovett was also exceedingly generous; he did not intend that his collection of books would serve only himself and his children. He wanted to share it with oth-ers. And his expressions of frustration about why people did not make more exten-sive use of his library were the expressions common to the most mission-oriented of American library workers. He said that "a lot of [people] ask why children in the area don't use the place more—don't come around and browse. Well, it's open to the public. Anybody—student, teacher, or otherwise—would be more than welcome. I'm here every day."[5]

> I've known some people who would look me in the eye and declare they wouldn't waste five minutes with any book. Most blacks around here don't even know about this place. A white man drove up here the other day and asked for a beer. He looked at the sign and thought it was a tavern.[6]

Undaunted, and living in what many would describe as deep poverty, Eddie Lovett built a library, a powerful instrument intended for the intellectual growth and economic potential of his family, and he sought to share it with neighbors and friends and, indeed, with anyone traveling from near or far.

The Impulse to Build

Eddie Lovett overcame numerous obstacles to become, as he called himself, "Eddie Lovett, Polyhistor and Philologus." He spent much of his early years helping his sharecropping parents in the fields. What little schooling he was able to obtain fired his imagination to such a point that when he entered the Army, he carried a duffel bag of books from place to place. He married Lucille Sheppard on 1 May 1940 when his possessions consisted only of a trunk that contained two pairs of khaki pants, a few shirts, and several books. Eddie was optimistic about his future, but his marriage did not survive his initial tour of duty with U. S. Army engineers in Europe and North Africa. Following her divorce from Eddie, Lucille took their son, Lawrence, and moved to Indiana. Eddie enlisted again in the Army and toured Japan. Upon his return, he married Nelsie Lee Jones, the mother of a two year old, and Eddie and Nelsie then had four children of their own. Along the way, Lovett re-enlisted in the Army in order to fight in the Korean War; it was during this tour that his book collecting began in earnest. His blue denim barracks bag often included as many as fifty books; he would wait until late in the evening and read in latrines (where lights remained on), underscoring passages and making marginal notes. During various tours he visited libraries in Belgium, England, France, Germany, Holland, and Italy, and he became interested in ancient and European history. He also took courses offered by the Army, including one on East Asian history when he was stationed in Guam. By the time he had mustered out at Fort Gordon, Georgia, with bibliophilic interests running high, he invested $506 for a rare history of the slave trade published in 1860.[7]

When Lovett decided to build a library for his growing collection, he cleared an acre of land about three miles from Banks, Arkansas. He paid $40 for an abandoned building across from the general store in Banks. He tore down that structure, hauled the lumber to his property, and constructed a library building, 14×28 feet, with wooden walls, sheet metal, a tin roof, double-hung doors, and a wood-burning stove. He called it the Hippocrene Library (from Greek mythology, meaning "fount of inspiration"). As he began collecting his books, teaching his children, and expanding his interests, he could not resist the urge of self-expression, and he began writing letters to the editor of the local newspaper, the *Eagle Democrat*, published in Warren, Arkansas. As news of Lovett's library and his intellectual and reading interests entered the stream of mass media, he was eventually discovered by Charles Kuralt, whose *On the Road with Charles Kuralt* television series of human interest stories reached the furthest corners of the national consciousness, providing Eddie Lovett and his library with national visibility. Kuralt labeled his newfound subject "Scholar of the Piney Woods" and fondly described Lovett's library and his reading tastes as sources of happiness. He cited the quotation over Lovett's library door, "Hic Habitat Felicitas—here lives happiness."[8]

THE ORIGINS OF HAPPINESS

Lovett's intellectual interests were fresh and personal. He was not a man of letters but rather, a man of learning. As a child, Eddie had been inspired by his father, Bertram "Shoat" Lovett. Bertram Lovett was a man of minimal means and education, yet, with high hopes for his family and after a full day of laboring in cotton fields, he taught his children to recite poetry and memorize passages from the Bible. Bertram read to his children from a large picture-filled tome that Eddie remembered as *Daniel and the Revelation.* The family studied "blueback" spellers and McGuffey readers, and a love of books, reading, and learning was instilled deep in Eddie's heart.

Eddie could read by age four, and he attended school at age six. Yet, in his separate but unequal society, he and others of his race were forced to work cotton fields as a first priority. A typical school year involved no more than three months of instruction, and blacks were not allowed to continue beyond the eighth grade. But the love of learning was like seed which would soon germinate. Lovett wanted not only to read books but to own them as well.

His first acquisitions were intensely practical. As he later recalled, he had been splitting rails, cutting cordwood, working cotton, and bailing hay, earning about $2.60 per week, when he saw an advertisement for a book about mathematics. The book was designed to help the reader weigh, measure, and calculate. It would teach Lovett how to convert figures in areas and sizes, and would surely come in handy while sharecropping beans, corn, or cotton. Dredging up the memory, Lovett recalled he could scarcely contain his enthusiasm. When the package arrived COD, the postman honked his horn from the road in front of Lovett's house. Eddie ran out to the mailbox and gave the mailman almost a week's pay for a copy of *Ropp's Commercial Calculator,* but did not take time to enjoy his purchase immediately. He had been dredging a log pond with a mule and slip-an [*sic*] iron shovel, and he returned to his task. He caught his foot under the slip, cutting into a joint to the bone. He was taken to a doctor who clamped the tendons together, dressed the wound, and prescribed pain medication. When Eddie returned home with an unplanned respite from his labors, he reverently thumbed through his new acquisition, and penned in the date of September 8, 1934.

As Lovett began to save money, he added to his collection. He bought *A Carpenter's Guide,* a leather-bound four-volume set for $6.00, which he paid for at $1.00 per month. Eddie was working 12 to 14 hours a day and, as he recalled, when lunch time arrived, his coworkers were eating and talking under a shade tree while he was reading. Thus, he expanded his interests and bought *Astronomy for Amateurs,* a book that contained instructions for building a crude telescope. Many nights he climbed barn rooftops to study the stars and he told his disbelieving friends and neighbors that one day men would be able to walk on the moon. He bought *The Educator's Library,* an eight-volume set on ancient, European, and American history. Reading these books and books like these, he discovered heroes of his own. He told Charles Kuralt that his favorite authors included Socrates, Shakespeare, Descartes, and James Baldwin.

As Lovett saved more money he continued to add to his library. History emerged as his most important subject, guiding and informing his acquisitions, but that subject was only one of many in which he collected. He acquired the writings of Dante, Voltaire, Rousseau, and Thomas Jefferson. Among historical works were Will and Ariel Durant's *The Story of Civilization*; Edward Gibbon's *The Decline and Fall of the Roman Empire*; the collected writings of Abraham Lincoln, Woodrow Wilson, Bruce Catton, and Shelby Foote; and the U.S. Department of the Army history of the Civil War in 120 volumes.

Since Lovett pursued knowledge rather than academic degrees, his was an untrained mind. A voracious reader, he consumed at least 10,000 volumes in multiple fields of study. His tastes became broad, deep, eclectic, and idiosyncratic. A roll call of his own heroes indicates something of his range:

Queen Anne	Gandhi	Marco Polo
Susan B. Anthony	Geronimo	Eleanor Roosevelt
Anita Bryant	Hannibal	Franklin D. Roosevelt
Confucius	Ho Chi Minh	Socrates
Prudence Crandall	Robert E. Lee	Spartacus
Jane Fonda	Mary Magdalene	The Venerable Bede
Benjamin Franklin	Thurgood Marshall	

He made personal applications from the lessons and lives of those he admired, and so he named his children after important people. He named one child Sophocles, another Joanna (after one of the women at Jesus's tomb), also Enima (suggested by Nietzsche) and Yuri (for Soviet cosmonaut Yuri Gagarin). Lovett did not like Alexander the Great, Julius Caesar, Sigmund Freud, or Napoleon. He held firmly to his belief in the Bible as the most important book, having read from Genesis through the Revelation eight times.[9]

Lovett's taste in music proved as eclectic and unpredictable as his reading tastes. He collected Beethoven, Brahms, Handel, Mozart, and Tchaikovsky, as well as Blind Lemon Jefferson, Chet Atkins, Johnny Cash, Merle Haggard, and Elvis Presley. Other favorites included Roy Acuff, Eddy Arnold, Red Foley, Tennessee Ernie Ford, and Hank Williams, as well as Duke Ellington and large samplings of bluegrass, the blues, spirituals, and slave songs from the Smithsonian collections.

EDDIE LOVETT AS AN AUTHOR

As often happens with voracious readers, the impulse to write, to put one's own thoughts into print, becomes equally voracious. Lovett wrote numerous letters, perhaps hundreds, and took them to the editorial offices of the *Eagle Democrat*. This local newspaper faithfully published these in its "letters to the editor"; thus the paper served as *de facto* publisher for the things Lovett wanted to say.

Examining a small fraction of his letters, we found them to be engaging yet rambling, fun to read, and, ultimately, full of his interests and enthusiasms. He peppered his readers with strong rhetoric filled with exclamation marks. His patterns of communication ranged from balanced and closely reasoned arguments to sarcasm and stately, memorable aphorisms. Among the letters we read, the topics Lovett treated fell into broad subject categories as follows: history—12; education—10; racial issues—7; crime—4; and religion—3. Yet he treated no subject in truly discrete ways; he mixed and mingled topics as he assembled seemingly unrelated facts into his missives.

At times, he appeared simply as a responsible history teacher. He described the life of George William Bush, a free African-American who fought alongside Andrew Jackson in the Battle of New Orleans and explored the Oregon Trail.[10] He reviewed the problems of Haiti, describing it as the oldest Negro republic in the world.[11] In discussing issues of crime and education, he appealed to analysis provided by nineteenth-century historian Thomas Babington Macauley.[12] His overview of the prospects for peace in the Middle East cited the special role of Jerusalem and began with the division of the Northern and Southern kingdoms as described in the Old Testament.[13]

Lovett wrote often of education. In one letter he observed that he had lived under fifteen presidential administrations from Woodrow Wilson to Bill Clinton and had never seen such a corrupt and permissive society as now (1999). Responsibility for training the young belonged in the home; schools could not do it alone. He, himself, had been taught at home by his father and his stepmother. Moreover, support and problem-solving for public education belonged at the local level rather than the federal level.[14] Lovett penned a special letter on 17 May 1997, exactly forty-three years after the U.S. Supreme Court's decision to outlaw segregated public schools. "Eddieisms" on this occasion were memorable.

> Your children's first teachers are their parents. Their first classroom is their living room. The desire to learn does not come from sitting beside white students nor riding in the same bus at the same time. It comes from that 'burning desire from Within the student and his parents.'
>
> There are two aristocracies: the aristocracy of culture and the aristocracy of wealth ... the aristocracy of culture is far superior....
>
> Students do not carry guns, knives, and drugs to school. Good students carry books, pencils, notebooks....[15]

Lovett presented the secret of success in life.

> I must tell you dear students this one thing: there is one and only one key that will unlock the doors of opportunity ... and that is the key of education, and your common denominator is your common sense.[16]

He took great pride in the educational achievements of his family.

> I do not have any illiterate, retarded, low I. Q. children. I have four sons who are mentally alert, and two very beautiful daughters and highly intelligent, educated daughters.... My sons all have a high school education from an NCA accredited school at Hermitage, Arkansas. We have something to be thankful for, proud of too![17]

Lovett was never afraid to make tough, courageous statements on racial topics. His last letter to the *Eagle Democrat*, dated 1 March 2000, examined the history of world slavery and key events in the American civil rights movement. He added:

> The greatest sins and misdeeds that have ever been done to the black race [were] done to it by the "Black Kings" of Africa who sold millions of their people into slavery....[18]

Other racial pronouncements were more placid.

> A good deed is good regardless [of] what race it comes from. A bad deed is bad and harmful regardless [of] what race commits it.[19]

> Let us celebrate Black History every month of the year by educating ourselves and our children.[20]

Some statements seemed iconoclastic.

> Getting along does not mean "racial integration." No one in his or her right mind wants "racial integration." God almighty did not ordain it, period! ... No one on the face of this planet can dispute this plain truth. But we are all members of the human family....

> And stop looking at too many "soaps" and listen to the "firebell" in the night that Mr. Thomas Jefferson told us about. "Hatred" will never, never, never solve any problems. It will only intensify them to your detriment and sorrow.[21]

An analysis of Lovett's thoughts and ideas would require fuller explication from a much larger sample. Suffice it to say that his historical interpretations were fact-laden and nuanced, but his conclusions were often unpredictable. To label him, as to label many others, as inconsistent would seem fruitless and inappropriate. But a richly learned mind (rather than a richly lettered mind) is bound to produce something that more traditional scholars find puzzling. Yet, his most powerful legacy, a well-educated family (supported by his library), grew out of deeply held values, faithfully and consistently articulated—that strong family ties would be nurtured, parents would teach their children, and books and reading would become life-blood essentials.

A Library for the Next Generation

Lovett's love of reading and knowledge seem to have been exceeded only by his love for and devotion to his family. He once told a reporter,

> I taught my children. I taught them right here, by the fireside, and later when they were in school, to get a good education, and to try to make useful citizens, good, decent, law-abiding.[22]

Such instruction often came at a high price. He would not take his knowledge and his national visibility and turn them into tools for personal fame or self-aggrandizement. He committed himself to rearing his children as his "greatest monument." He endured the mountain of paperwork and financial stress of adopting his stepson; he once sold his car to cover medical expenses; and he lived quite modestly on Social Security income, veterans' benefits, and small farm profits.

But the prices to be paid for a good education and for an appreciation of reading and learning were far higher than financial ones. They involved rituals of family organization and personal sacrifice. When his children arrived home from school, Lovett had dinner on the table, after which he supervised homework. He kept TV out of the house, aware of that medium as a source of some good programming but, in his own words, mostly trash. Often his children prepared their lessons in his library, which was heated (apparently for a number of years the house was not). Once lessons were completed, the children used his library to study other subjects. The 10:00 P.M. bedtime was strictly enforced, but during weekend evenings the children often remained in the library until midnight. When Lovett's daughters were dating, he enforced the 10:00 P.M. curfew with no difficulty. The children awoke to breakfast and a hot bath (in a portable bathtub or one of several washtubs). They recited lessons as they bathed and dressed for school. Lovett's goal was never to let them leave for school without being fully prepared.

And Lovett succeeded admirably. Enima and Joanna were class salutatorian and valedictorian respectively, becoming college graduates; and Joanna earned a master's degree. All the Lovett children were successful students whose grades ranged from good to excellent. Only one son adopted a system of values at odds with that promoted by his father. Thus, the life of crime chosen by Sophocles was truly a riddle to the whole family, the only tarnish on the otherwise stellar educational achievements involving Lovett, the public school system, and his library.

Where his children were concerned, Lovett refused to compromise. He showed no interest in the public displays of African-American non-violent protest mounted by leaders of the American civil rights movement. The movement was at its peak during the time his children were coming of age and his library was reaching new levels as an instructional instrument. Lovett and his family might have been tempted to join a freedom march, but he would have no part of that. On behalf of his children, however, he was adamant that they would have the best education available. Thus, he told members of a nearby school board that his children would not attend a separate, inferior, all-black school. And when his third-grader, Joanna, and his first-grader, Sophocles, along with a neighbor's child, journeyed twelve miles to an elementary school in Hermitage, Lovett had quietly but effectively integrated that school.[23]

Not surprisingly, Lovett lived to see the day when his influence extended to the generation beyond that of his children, a fact corroborated eloquently by his grandson, Edwin L. Kolen. In a touching memoir, Kolen wrote that

> He made a profound and lasting impression on me. His patriotism and pride for serving in World War II and the Korean War contributed to my desire to continue the family tradition of serving in the military…. I will always remember his humor, affection, and good meals that he prepared, but [also his] encouraging me to be the best that I could dream by 'reaching for the astros.'[24]

THE HIPPOCRENE AND THE PHOENIX

The day of 7 January 1975 dawned quite cold and Lovett went out to the library to stoke the stove. Not long after returning to his house, he looked out the back door and noticed the smoke. Sparks had blown out through unwelded joints in the chimney, caught in the attic, and burst into flames. The lumber had been very old pine and the building and most of the contents were soon engulfed. Once the books had begun to burn, it took nearly four days for the fire to run its course. Eddie and his children were devastated. They had been able to make just a few quick runs into the inferno without risking serious injury. They had saved an adding machine and a few photographs of Lovett's family and his heroes. Little evidence remained of an effort — forty years in the making — to build a library for his family and his neighbors. The Hippocrene Library had been reduced to ashes.

Charles Kuralt soon learned of the Lovett family's distress and talked about it on the CBS Evening News of 23 January 1975. Lovett's national reputation, in combination with Kuralt's publicity, laid the groundwork for a new library. The Phoenix Library, like a bird rising from the ashes, would replace the Hippocrene. Lovett bought more lumber, this time for a slightly larger building. The structure, 20 × 48 feet, was wooden with wooden roof and sheet metal, four sets of double doors, and stairs, and was constructed on exactly the same location as the Hippocrene. Lovett chose tough green oak and estimated that construction would require between three and four months. He received offers to help but chose to do all the work himself. He added a globe and crafted small reading tables from Honduran mahogany.

Lovett acquired the materials using money sent by television viewers and admirers throughout the nation. He claimed that every nickel and every penny that had been contributed were used to support the library and its construction. He sent donors statements of how he had spent their particular contributions. Lovett had no insurance and knew, of course, that the Phoenix Library had depended on the largesse of numerous well-wishers. Among donations was a four-foot-tall bird, fashioned like a phoenix by high school students and, of course, books by the truckload.[25]

Lovett's library grew, and estimates of its size ranged as high as 40,000 volumes in paper and hardcover. These volumes did not result from acquisitions of Eddie's tender loving care. Rather they came as an outpouring of respect and admiration for one whose love of books and learning deserved rich rewards. Gone were his rare history of the slave trade and other specialized items. In their place were thousands of volumes delivered directly from publishers. Contemporary and retrospective authors included:

Martin Buber	Jack London
Pearl Buck	William Manchester
Robert Caro	Golda Meir
Bruce Catton	Merle Miller
Will & Ariel Durant	Carl Sandburg
Edward Gibbon	Arthur Schlesinger, Jr.
Tom Hayden	William Shakespeare
Josephus	Margaret Truman
	Walt Whitman

Trucks arrived frequently; 20,000 volumes came from Milwaukee alone. Eighteen-wheeled rigs had difficulty navigating the dirt road to the Lovett farm. Truckers could not find the space to turn around and so were forced to negotiate the last mile in reverse. Lovett's new structure could not accommodate the burgeoning volumes of books, so he began housing books in his home, finally turning that building over to library purposes and constructing a new building for his residence.

Years later, Lovett was still gratefully acknowledging the support and generosity of admirers throughout the nation. Nearly two decades after the fact, he noted that people from across the U.S.A. and several foreign countries had sent or brought multiple volumes, new and old. He seemed especially delighted with new sets of the *Encyclopædia Britannica*, the *World Book Encyclopedia*, and *American Heritage*, which he described as treasure troves worth thousands of dollars.

> All these books were an out right gift to me. Why did [people] do this? Because they knew I was trying to help myself and they came to my rescue. I am talking from practical experience. They knew I would cherish them [the books] and burn the midnight oil by studying them.[26]

He took special pride in the Bibles, commentaries, and other biblical and religious reference works he had been given. These included the King James Version, the *New American Bible*, the *Harper's Bible Dictionary*, multiple commentaries on Daniel and Revelation, the Koran, the Torah, histories of Israel, the works of Josephus, also *Who's Who in the Old Testament* and *Who's Who in the New Testament*.[27] He added a continuing refrain to the effect that there was no short-cut to a [high] quality and well balanced education. And as recently as two years before his death, he wrote a letter to thank S/Sgt. Shirley Clark of Fort Polk, Louisiana, for the gift of *Baptism Day*, a 16" × 20" print by Polly Mullines. These and hundreds of other gifts, mostly books, testified to a life lived with integrity, enthusiasm, and an unquenchable thirst for knowledge.[28]

Conclusion

Eddie Lovett was rare as a father, citizen, and book collector. He was literate and learned, if not lettered or formally educated. He certainly had opportunity enough, late in life, to garner the occasional honorary doctorate and to talk with large audiences about his life, his interests, and his achievements. But he was not fond of long-distance travel. And such occasions were sure to seriously intrude on his regimen of reading and writing about twelve hours each day. These are, after all, solitary pursuits, and he never lost the desire to engage in them. And thus Eddie Lovett continued to enlighten every dark corner of his mind. He sought to recruit his children as fellow soldiers in the effort to fight ignorance. So he accumulated his books, taught his children, and shared with his neighbors, and demonstrated over and over every day his faith in the power of the printed word. As he eloquently observed, "I conceded my ignorance a long time ago, and have tried to overcome it. And you want to know something? Reading a book is still the only way to do that."[29]

NOTES

The authors acknowledge with gratitude the resourceful service of Gingy Cuthbertson of the Warren Branch Library in Warren, Arkansas, and the wise counsel of Edward S. Lauterbach, Professor Emeritus of English, Purdue University.

1. *Oxford English Dictionary*, 2nd ed. (Oxford: Clarendon Press, 1989).
2. Vern E. Smith, "One Man's War on Ignorance," *Newsweek* 9 June 1975: 10.
3. William Thomas, "Man's Love for Books Not Destroyed by Fire," *Houston Chronicle* 18 August 1985: 5.
4. "Farmer-Librarian's Bumper Crop of Books," *Ebony* 29 December 1973: 86.
5. "Farmer-Librarian's," 88.
6. "Farmer-Librarian's," 86. Our study of Eddie Lovett cannot constitute an exercise in objectified biographical narrative. We make an effort at factual accuracy, but we have no interest in scholarly neutrality. We are attracted to our subject for his determination of mind, nobility of purpose, and generosity of spirit. We are unabashed admirers, and our desire to contribute to *Libraries to the People* springs from our desire to expand the numbers of those who admire and appreciate what Lovett accomplished. More specifically, in bringing Eddie Lovett to the attention of those who read the literature of professional librarianship, we hope that his ideals can become engrained more deeply in the consciousness of library workers.

It bears mention that some of the scholarly monographs in library history draw from the biblical vocabulary suggestive of the missionary zeal with which Lovett pursued his library dream. Lovett was familiar with biblical terminology, and had he known about these books he may well have approved of the connection they drew between libraries and outreach. See, for example, Dee Garrison, *Apostles of Culture: The Public Librarian and American Society, 1876–1920* (New York: Free Press. 1979); Gary E. Kraske, *Missionaries of the Book: The American Library Profession and the Origins of United States Cultural Diplomacy* (Westport, CT: Greenwood, 1985); and John V. Richardson, *The Gospel of Scholarship: Pierce Butler and a Critique of American Librarianship* (Metuchen, NJ: Scarecrow, 1992).

We are aware of the fact that biographers can offer numerous perspectives on how they view their subjects, how they treat delicate or controversial topics, and how they ultimately interpret—with the reader in mind—the range of material from which life-writing is constructed. Authors and subjects often experience revisions in judgment, changes in personality and recall abilities, and will undergo multiple large or small psychological variations as they mature. Numerous cultural and other external factors also influence one's interpretive framework. Among the possible approaches a biographer might take to interpret the life of another, we prefer the biographer as a center of reference. This is to acknowledge, with Catherine Drinker Bowen, that only the Deity could write with pure objectivity; see Catherine Drinker Bowen, *Biography: The Craft and the Calling* (Boston: Little, Brown, 1969) 92. The biographer finds ground to stand on and makes clear the parameters and perspectives inherent in the choices made. The reader may conclude that such a stand is acceptable, partly acceptable, or unacceptable, or may even suspend judgment. Ultimately, the reader will likely take a position on the continuum of possibilities offered by the biographer.

The role of the biographer becomes, then, to make his or her stance clear and we believe that with Eddie Lovett, we have clarified our frame of reference. See Wilson Snipes, "The Biographer as a Center of Reference," *Biography* 5 (1982): 215–25; Richard H. Blum, "Psychological Processes in Preparing Contemporary Biography," *Biography* 4 (1981): 193–211; Burton Raffel, "Emotional History: An Exploratory Essay," *Biography* 7 (1984): 352–62; and Eva Schepler, "The Biographer's Transference: A Chapter in Psychobiographical Epistemology," *Biography* 13 (1990): 111–29.

7. Richard E. Meyer, "Riddle of Sophocles: A Tale of Learning and Wisdom," *Los Angeles Times* 3 July 1988: 17.
8. Charles Kuralt, *On the Road with Charles Kuralt* (New York: G. P. Putnam's Sons, 1985) 254.
9. The previous six paragraphs are based on Meyer, "Riddle of Sophocles" 17–18.
10. "Letters to the Editor," *Eagle Democrat* 17 Feb. 1999: 7.
11. "Letters to the Editor," *Eagle Democrat* 3 Mar. 1993: 8.
12. "Letters to the Editor," *Eagle Democrat* 20 Jan. 1993: 8.
13. "Letters to the Editor," *Eagle Democrat* 4 Aug. 1999: 8.
14. "Letters to the Editor," *Eagle Democrat* 26 May 1999: 8.
15. "Letters to the Editor," *Eagle Democrat* 18 June 1997: 10.
16. "Letters to the Editor," *Eagle Democrat* 22 May 1991: 14.
17. "Letters to the Editor," *Eagle Democrat* 19 Dec. 1990: 5.
18. "Letters to the Editor," *Eagle Democrat* 1 Mar. 2000: 12.

19. "Letters to the Editor," *Eagle Democrat* 17 Feb. 1999: 7.
20. "Letters to the Editor," *Eagle Democrat* 17 Mar. 1999: 10.
21. "Letters to the Editor," *Eagle Democrat* 4 Sept. 1996: 8.
22. Meyer, "Riddle of Sophocles," 1, 17.
23. See "Farmer-Librarian's" and Meyer, "Riddle of Sophocles."
24. Edwin L. Kolen, "Mr. Eddie Lovett, a Polyhistor, Philologus, Grandfather, and Friend," unpublished manuscript. Enima "Nikki" Kolen shares Edwin's affection for the vision and accomplishments of her father. She reports that the library remains intact with its future under consideration by the family. Nikki Kolen, e-mail to Emily Branson, 1 May 2001.
25. Thomas, "Man's Love for Books," 5; and Meyer, "Riddle of Sophocles," 17.
26. "Letters to the Editor," *Eagle Democrat* 15 Sept. 1993: 14.
27. "Letters to the Editor," *Eagle Democrat* 5 Feb. 1996: 10.
28. "Letters to the Editor," *Eagle Democrat* 21 Jan. 1998: 10.
29. "Farmer-Librarian's," 86.

Contributors

Emily J. Branson serves as Bibliographic Assistant in the Humanities, Social Science & Education Library at Purdue University. She earned a bachelor of arts in English at Berea College. Her research interests include Appalachian history and culture as well as 19th Century English Literature. She won the 1994 Citizen's Award presented by the Indiana Library Federation for her "support for the promotion of Indiana libraries."

Robert S. Freeman, Associate Professor of Library Science and Bibliographer for Foreign Languages and Literatures at Purdue University, received a master of arts in Germanic languages and literatures from the University of North Carolina at Chapel Hill and a master's degree in library and information science from the University of Illinois at Urbana-Champaign. He has written on John Carter Brown for the *American National Biography* (Oxford UP) and on the Tübingen University Library for the *International Dictionary of Library Histories* (Fitzroy Dearborn).

John W. Fritch is Assistant Professor of Library Science and Reference and Instruction Librarian in the Hicks Undergraduate Library at Purdue University. He holds a master of library science from Indiana University. His recent publications include articles on ascribing cognitive authority to Internet information in *The Journal of the American Society for Information Science and Technology* and on reference services in *Library Trends*.

Gerald S. Greenberg, Reference and Bibliographic Instruction Librarian and Collection Development Officer for Physical Education and Sports at the Education, Human Ecology, Psychology & Social Work Library, Ohio State University, holds a master of arts in teaching from Fordham University and a master of library science from Kent State University. He is the author of *Tabloid Journalism: An Annotated Bibliography of English-Language Sources* (Westport, CT: Greenwood, 1996).

David M. Hovde, Associate Professor of Library Science at Purdue University, holds a master of arts in anthropology from Wichita State University and a master of library science from Louisiana State University. He has authored works in North American archaeology, ethnohistory, American history, semiotics, and library science.

Plummer Alston "Al" Jones, Jr., Associate Professor of Library Services at East Carolina University, received a Ph.D. in information and library science from the University of North Carolina at Chapel Hill. In 1993 he received the Phyllis Dain Library History Dissertation Award. His recent publications include *Libraries, Immigrants, and the American Experience* (Westport, CT: Greenwood, 1999).

Florence M. Jumonville, Head of Louisiana and Special Collections, Earl K. Long Library, the University of New Orleans, holds a master of arts in history and archival management from the University of New Orleans, a master's degree in library science from Louisiana State University, and a Ph.D. in education from the University of New Orleans. She is the author of many articles and several books including *Louisiana History: An Annotated Bibliography* (Westport, CT: Greenwood, 2002).

Cheryl Knott Malone, Associate Professor at the University of Arizona School of Information Resources and Library Science, holds master's degrees in library science and history from the University of Arizona and a Ph.D. in library and information science from the University of Texas at Austin. Her biographical entry on Dorothy Louise Burnette Porter Wesley will appear in Volume Five of *Notable American Women* (Harvard UP, forthcoming 2004).

Kathleen de la Peña McCook, Coordinator of Community Outreach in the College of Arts and Sciences and professor in the School of Library and Information Science at the University of South Florida, holds a master of arts in English from Marquette University, a master of arts in library science from the University of Chicago, and a Ph.D. in library and information studies from the University of Wisconsin at Madison. Her recent publications include *A Place at the Table: Participating in Community Building* (Chicago: ALA Editions, 2000).

Lotsee Patterson, Professor of Library and Information Science at the University of Oklahoma, holds a master of library science degree and a Ph.D. in Educational Technology from the University of Oklahoma. She has served on boards and councils of several national associations, including the American Indian Library Association, and has co-chaired the Native American Pre-Conference, White House Conference on Libraries and Information Services. In 1994 she received the American Library Association's Equality Award for outstanding contributions promoting equality in the library profession.

Toni Samek, Associate Professor in the School of Library and Information Studies at the University of Alberta, received a master's degree in library and information studies from Dalhousie University and a Ph.D. in library and information studies from the University of Wisconsin at Madison. She is a member of the Canadian Library Association Advisory Committee on Intellectual Freedom. Her publications include *Intellectual Freedom and Social Responsibility in American Librarianship, 1967–1974* (Jefferson, NC: McFarland, 2001).

Barry W. Seaver, a librarian at the Durham Public Library in Durham, N.C., holds a master of arts in history from the University of Connecticut, Storrs, a master of science in library science from Columbia University, and a Ph.D. in library and information science from the University of North Carolina at Chapel Hill. He is the editor of *Civic Duty: The Quarterly Newsletter of the North Carolina Civic Education Consortium*. His biography of Rebecca Browning Rankin is forthcoming from McFarland.

Larry E. Sullivan, Chief Librarian at the John Jay College of Criminal Justice and professor of criminal justice in the Graduate School and University Center, City University of New York, is also former Chief of the Rare Book and Special Collections Division of the Library of Congress. He holds a Ph.D. in history from Johns Hopkins University and is the author of *The Prison Reform Movement: Forlorn Hope* (Boston: Twayne, 1990). His exhibition, *Inside Editions: A Literature of Punishment*, featuring examples of American convict literature, was shown at the Grolier Club in New York.

John Mark Tucker, Humanities, Social Science, & Education Librarian and Professor of Library Science at Purdue University, holds master of library science and educational science degrees from George Peabody College for Teachers of Vanderbilt University, and a Ph.D. in library and information science from the University of Illinois. His recent publications include *Untold Stories: Civil Rights, Libraries, and Black Librarianship* (Champaign: Graduate School of Library and Information Science, University of Illinois at Urbana-Champaign, 1998).

Brenda Vogel, Coordinator of Library Services, Maryland Correctional Education Libraries, Maryland State Department of Education, holds a master of library science from Simmons College and a master of arts in history from Boston College. Named *Library Journal*'s Librarian of the Year for 1989, her publications include *Down for the Count: A Prison Library Handbook* (Lanham, MD: Scarecrow Press, 1995).

Paula Watson, Director of Electronic Information Services at the University of Illinois at Urbana-Champaign and Associate Professor of Library Administration, holds a master of arts in English from Columbia University and a master of science in library science from Syracuse University. She has published two previous articles on women and the public library movement and is currently working on an ALA Library Technology Report on the acquisition and management of electronic journals.

Index